FOUR COUR ~~~~~~ **LIN**

Publish

IRELAND, 1870-1914
Coercion and Conciliation

Donnchadh Ó Corráin & Tomás O'Riordan, editors

354pp. Illustrated. Paperback. £17.50

The publisher will be obliged if the Editor sends a copy
of the review, when it appears, to the address below.

About the Editors

Donnchadh Ó Corráin is emeritus professor of medieval history at
University College Cork. He has published widely on early medieval Irish
institutions, culture, law, literature, historical sources, and the Viking wars.
Tomás O'Riordan works as a researcher and part-time lecturer in
University College Cork.

For additional details about the book and publisher, or to arrange an interview
with the editors, contact: Anthony Tierney, Head of Marketing & Sales,
Four Courts Press, 7 Malpas Street, Dublin 8. Tel.: (00 353) 1 453 4668;
Fax.: (00 353) 1 453 4672. E-mail: anthony.tierney@fourcourtspress.ie

Also in this series:

Ireland, 1815–70: Emancipation, Famine and Religion

Ireland, 1870–1914

Ireland, 1870–1914

Coercion and Conciliation

Donnchadh Ó Corráin & Tomás O'Riordan

EDITORS

FOUR COURTS PRESS

Set in 10 on 13 point AGaramond for
FOUR COURTS PRESS LTD
7 Malpas Street, Dublin 8, Ireland
http://www.fourcourtspress.ie
and in North America by
FOUR COURTS PRESS
c/o ISBS, 920 N.E. 58th Avenue, Suite 300, Portland, OR 97213.

ISBN 978-1-84682-233-9

A catalogue record for this title
is available from the British Library.

Printed in England
by MPG Books, Bodmin, Cornwall.

Contents

List of illustrations and tables 9
Foreword *by Joseph Carey* 11
Introduction 13

1. Politics and administration, 1870–1914
Maura Cronin (with a contribution by Fidelma Maguire)

1. Home Rule: origins and early development, 17 **2.** The Home Government Association, 17–19 **3.** The Home Rule League, 19–20 **4.** Obstructionism, 20–1 **5.** Parnellism as politics, 21–3 **6.** Home Rule and Irish Unionism, 23–4 **7.** The fall of Parnell, 24–5 **8.** The Home Rule Bills of 1893 and 1912, 25–7 **9.** Varieties of Unionism, 27–9 **10.** A more assertive nationalism, 1870–1914, 29–30 **11.** Protestantism and Irishness, 30–1 **12.** The Suffrage Movement in Ireland, 1870–1914, 31–4 **13.** The first Sinn Féin Party, 34–6 **14.** The Irish Volunteers, 36–7

2. Society and economy, 1870–1914
Myrtle Hill & John Lynch (with a contribution by Fidelma Maguire)

1. Introduction, 38 **2.** Marriage and migration, 38–9 **3.** Land agitation and land reform, 39 **4.** Agricultural depression, 39–40 **5.** Rural distress and organisation, 40 **6.** The Land League, 40–1 **7.** The Land War, 1879–82, 41–5 **8.** The Congested Districts Board, 45–6 **9.** The Co-operative Movement, 46–7 **10.** Education, 47–9 **11.** Employment, 49–50 **12.** Industrialisation, 50–1 **13.** Improvements in health care, 51–2 **14.** Housing, 52–3 **15.** The coming of the railway, 53 **16.** The Labour Movement and the 1913 Lockout, 53–4 **17.** A conservative society, 54

3. Culture and religion, 1870–1914
Myrtle Hill (with a contribution by Donnchadh Ó Corráin)

1. Introduction, 55 **2.** Religious denominations in Ireland, 1870–1914, 55 **3.** The Church of Ireland, 55–7 **4.** The Roman Catholic Church, 57–8 **5.** The Presbyterian Church, 58 **6.** Protestantism and the problem of Home Rule, 58–60 **7.** Irish popular culture, 60–1 **8.** Cultural and religious politics, 61 **9.** Unionist culture, 61–2 **10.** Cultural nationalism, 62–4 **11.** Anglo-Irish literary revival, 64–5 **12.** Arts and Crafts Movement, 65–6 **13.** Conclusion, 66–7

4. Home Rule and the elections of 1885–6
Tomás O'Riordan

1. Introduction, 68 **2.** What was Home Rule? 68–9 **3.** Who were the voters? 69 **4.** How was the Irish Parliamentary Party organised? 70 **5.** Keeping Ireland quiet! 70

6. Joseph Chamberlain's plan for Ireland, 70–1 **7.** The fall of the Liberals, 72
8. 'Tory kindnesses', 72–3 **9.** 'Promises, promises …', 73–4 **10.** The 1885 general
election, 74–6 **11.** Gladstone's Home Rule Bill (1886), 77–9 **12.** How was Ireland to
be governed? 79–83 **13.** Defeat of the Home Rule Bill, 83–4 **14.** The Belfast riots of
1886, 84–5 **15.** Conclusion, 85–7

5. Home Rule and the elections of 1885–6: documents
Gillian M. Doherty & Tomás O'Riordan

1. Parnell in Cork, January 1885, 88–9 **2.** Gladstone's conversion to Home Rule, 89–90
3. Parnell in Wicklow, October 1885, 90–2 **4.** 'A Proposed Constitution for Ireland',
92–4 **5.** Parnell's election manifesto to the Irish electors in Britain, November 1885,
94–6 **6.** Opposition to Home Rule – the Irish Loyal and Patriotic Union, I–II, 96–9
7. Cardinal Cullen on Home Rule, 99–100 **8.** The case against Home Rule, 100–1
9. MP John Bright's opposition to Home Rule, 101–2 **10.** The Galway by-election of
1886, I–V, 102–6 **11.** Lord Randolph Churchill plays the 'Orange card', I–II, 106–7
12. Gladstone and Parnell on the Ulster question, 1886, I–II, 107–8 **13.** Gladstone
on the Home Rule Bill, April 1886, 108–12 **14.** Parnell on the Home Rule Bill,
June 1886, 112–15 **15.** The Government of Ireland (Home Rule) Bill, 1886, 115–17
16. Lord Salisbury on the Irish question, May 1886, 118–20
17. Gladstone's 1886 manifesto – 'Address to the electors of Midlothian', 120–2
18. Sectarian rioting in Belfast, 1886, 122–6

6. Early history of the Gaelic Athletic Association, 1884–91
Gillian M. Doherty

1. Michael Cusack and the promotion of Irish games, 127–8 **2.** The foundation of the
Gaelic Athletic Association (GAA), 128–9 **3.** Controversy with the Irish Amateur
Athletic Association (IAAA), 130 **4.** The expansion of the GAA, 130–1 **5.** The GAA's
first Annual General Meeting, 131–2 **6.** The lifting of the IAAA boycott rule, 132
7. The GAA and the IRB, 132–3 **8.** The Annual General Meeting of 1886, 133
9. The politicisation of the GAA, 133–4 **10.** The Executive and tensions within the
GAA, 134–5 **11.** Dr Croke and the search for compromise, 135–6
12. The Convention of 1887, 136–7 **13.** The IRB and the Central Executive of the
GAA, 137–9 **14.** The reconciliation, January 1888, 139–40

7. Early history of the Gaelic Athletic Association, 1884–91: documents
Gillian M. Doherty & Tomás O'Riordan

1. The games of hurley and hurling, I–III, 140–4 **2.** Origins of the Gaelic Athletic
Association, 1884, I–II, 144–6 **3.** First meeting of the GAA, November 1884, 146–8
4. Archbishop Croke and the GAA, November 1884, 148–50 **5.** The social impact of
the GAA, 150–1 **6.** Parnell and the GAA, December 1884, 151 **7.** Archbishop Croke

appeals for the abolition of the ban, 152 **8.** GAA game rules, 1885, 152–5
9. Opposition to the GAA, 156–7 **10.** GAA Central Committee meeting, July 1885,
157–8 **11.** GAA sporting events, 158 **12.** The GAA ban and the Executive, 158–9
13. GAA Convention of 1889, 159–60 **14.** Drink and the GAA: letter from
Archbishop Croke, 160–1 **15.** Pastoral letter of Archbishop Logue of Armagh, 161–3
16. Special Branch reports on the GAA, 1889–91, I–IV, 163–5 **17.** The Parnell split and
the GAA, I–IV, 165–7.

8. Dublin, 1913 – strike and Lockout
John Paul McCarthy & Tomás O'Riordan

1. Introduction, 168 **2.** A tenement city, 168–70 **3.** Human conditions in the city,
170–2 **4.** Employment in Dublin, 172–3 **5.** James Larkin and the rise of the
ITGWU, 173–5 **6.** 'A most formidable foe' – William Martin Murphy, 176 **7.** The
'Titanic struggle' begins, 176–8 **8.** The strike intensifies, 178–80 **9.** The Askwith
Inquiry, 180–1 **10.** 'Save the kiddies': deepening hostilities, 181–3 **11.** The 'fiery cross'
campaign and the breaking of the strike, 183–5 **12.** Connolly and the aftermath of the
Lockout, 185–7 **13.** Patrick Pearse, 187 **14.** The Lockout remembered, 187–9
15. Outcomes, 189–90

9. Dublin, 1913 – strike and Lockout: documents
Gillian M. Doherty & Tomás O'Riordan

1. Impressions of a Dublin Medical Officer, 191–5 **2.** The state of the poor, 195–8
3. The problem of the Dublin slums: a Catholic view, 198–202
4. Workers' resentment towards employers, 203 **5.** Larkin addresses the workers, I–II,
203–4 **6.** On the eve of the Lockout, 204–6 **7.** An 'orgy of anarchy', 206–10
8. Report of the Dublin Disturbances Commission, 1914, 210–15 **9.** Larkin vows
to fight, 215–16 **10.** Larkin's speech to the Askwith Inquiry, October 1913, 216–19
11. George Russell condemns the employers, 219–22 **12.** 'Save the Dublin kiddies'
campaign, I–III, 222–8 **13.** James Connolly urges strikers to stand their ground,
I–II, 228–32 **14.** In defence of the employers, 232–4 **15.** Workers' defence at
the Askwith Inquiry, October 1913, 234–6 **16.** James Connolly on the origins of
the Lockout, 236–8 **17.** Mr Murphy's 'New Year's Eve speech', 238–41 **18.** After
the Lockout, 241–4

10. Key concepts
*Margaret Fitzpatrick, Eoin Hartnett, John Paul McCarthy, Fidelma Maguire, Donnchadh
Ó Corráin & Tomás O'Riordan*

1. Anglicisation and de-Anglicisation, 245–8 **2.** Democracy, 248–51 **3.** Feminism,
251–5 **4.** Home Rule, 255–9 **5.** Irish Ireland, 260–3 **6.** Militarism/separatism, 263–9
7. Political agitation, 269–71 **8.** Socialism, 271–7 **9.** Suffragette, 277–80 **10.** The
Anglo-Irish, 280–83

11. Key personalities

Margaret Fitzpatrick, Eoin Hartnett, Fidelma Maguire, Donnchadh Ó Corráin & Tomás O'Riordan

1. Edward Carson, 284–7 **2.** James Connolly, 287–9 **3.** Michael Davitt, 290–4
4. Douglas Hyde, 295–9 **5.** James Larkin, 299–302 **6.** Charles Stewart Parnell, 302–7
7. John Redmond, 307–10 **8.** Hanna Sheehy-Skeffington, 310–13 **9.** Isabella Tod,
313–16 **10.** William Butler Yeats, 316–19

Index 320

Illustrations and tables

ILLUSTRATIONS
appear betwen pages 160 and 161

1 Photograph of Parnell *c.*1880 by his nephew, Henry Thomson

2 Members of the Irish Parliamentary Party. *Illustrated London News*, 10 April 1886

3 Cartoon: 'The political graveyard.' *Weekly News*, 12 November 1885

4 Cartoon: 'Lord Randolph Churchill ...' *Weekly News*, 27 February 1886

5 'Land League Cruelty.' Facsimile of a propagandist poster, of uncertain date and provenance

6 Crowd at the Ulster Convention at Balmoral, Belfast, 17 June 1892

7 Facsimile of a copy of Ulster's Solemn League and Covenant, signed by Carson, 28 September 1912

8 Postcard issued to commemorate the signing of the Solemn League and Covenant, 28 September 1912

9 Second reading of the Home Rule Bill in the Commons, 10 May, 1886. *Weekly News*, 15 May 1886

10 John Devoy photographed in prison clothes, Mountjoy Gaol, 1866

11 Cartoon: 'Drive him under the surface.' Supplement, *Weekly Freeman*, 6 October 1883

12 Arthur James Balfour, Chief Secretary of Ireland, 1895–1900, photographed *c.*1892

13 Herbert H. Asquith, Liberal Prime Minister of Great Britain, 1908–16

14 Photograph of Michael Davitt *c.*1886

15 John Redmond and members of the Irish Volunteer Force, September 1914

16 Cartoon: 'Second Thoughts.' *Punch*, 8 October 1913.

17 Anti-suffrage demonstration in Strabane, Co. Tyrone, *c.*1910

18 The first nine women to be awarded degrees from the Royal University of Ireland, Dublin, 1884

19 Michael Cusack photographed *c.*1880s

20 Douglas Hyde photographed at the Gap of Dunloe, Co. Kerry, September 1914

21 Facsimile of a page from *An Claidheamh Soluis*, official organ of the Gaelic League

22 Photograph of the National Library of Ireland and Leinster House *c.*1890

23 The great poet and dramatist William Butler Yeats *c.*1923

24 View of Victoria Channel and the *SS Titanic* in dry dock at Queen's Island, Belfast, 1911

25 Tenement building in Fade Street, Dublin *c.*1890s

26 Two barefoot young children from the tenements *c.*1910

27 Interior of a tenement flat, Dublin *c.*1913

28 New National Executive of the Irish Trades Union Congress and Labour Party, 1914
29 The controversial business magnate William Martin Murphy *c*.1910

TABLES

1 Extract from reports on the GAA, 1890–1 by the RIC (Northern Division)   163
2 Board of Trade wage figures, November 1913   173

Foreword

These books are the fruits of the great enterprise of the MultiText Project at University College Cork. Many scholars have collaborated in the work and have given freely of their time, knowledge and skills. I am happy to fund this enterprise because the more I know the modern world of business the more I realise that an understanding of the past is essential for the welfare of society – political, economic and cultural. I have found strength, support and inspiration in the history of Ireland and in my understanding of the cultural achievements of the Irish people. My engagement with Irish history and culture makes me happy to share this book with the people of Ireland and with all others who are interested in our story.

There are as many views of history as there are historians. My interest in this period stems from the political, social, and economic transformation of Ireland that mark the years from 1870 to 1914. The first Liberal administration of W.E. Gladstone (1868–74) began with his declaration that his mission was to pacify Ireland. Measures were introduced dealing with Ireland's religious, educational and land grievances. However, a deep depression led to evictions of tenants and violent reactions.

Soon the Home Rule movement, led by the second great Irish leader of the century, Charles Stewart Parnell, placed Ireland at, or near, the top of the British political agenda. An Irish Protestant landowner, Parnell believed, optimistically, that once Ireland was given back its parliament it could solve its own problems. In 1885 Parnell's Home Rule Party won all but eighteen seats, and held the balance of power in parliament between the Liberals and the Conservatives. Gladstone was convinced that the only way to achieve peace and stability in Ireland was to grant Home Rule, but the measure met the combined opposition of the Conservatives and of some of his own Liberal Party. Ulster Protestants, fearing they would be swamped in a Home Rule Ireland, organised themselves in implacable opposition, leading to their close association with the Conservatives from 1886. One immediate outcome was the rejection of Gladstone's second Home Rule Bill in 1893 by the House of Lords where the Conservatives had an unassailable majority. This resulted in two major and mutually exclusive developments: a gradual intensification of an Irish nationalism that identified itself with Catholicism and Gaelic culture; and the emergence in Ulster of a combative Unionism dedicated to preserving its separate regional and religious identity – discord and distrust that were to dominate Irish history for a century to come.

While attempts at a political solution to Ireland's problems foundered, the land problem was resolved, though not to everyone's satisfaction, by a series of revolutionary land acts, brought in by both the Liberals and the Conservatives, that transferred the bulk of the land of Ireland from the landlords to their tenants. These measures essentially wiped out, politically and economically, an aristocracy that had dominated most aspects of Irish life since the end of the seventeenth century. Ireland became a land of deeply conservative peasant proprietors.

At the very end of the period, a bitter and protracted struggle between Irish capitalists and the growing trade union movement signalled the arrival of socialism and contemporary concepts of workers' rights. Unusually gifted leaders, especially James Connolly and Jim Larkin, heavily influenced by experience abroad, set out the agenda that was to dominate Irish labour relations in the twentieth century.

There is nothing provincial about this history of land, possession, identity and the rights of individuals and classes. The poet, Patrick Kavanagh, famously had Homer say: 'I made the Iliad from such a local row. Gods make their own importance'. What Michael Davitt called 'the fall of feudalism' in Ireland happened in different ways in most European countries in the nineteenth century, and gave rise to serious conflict in Spain and Italy in the twentieth. As in Ireland, nationalism, in its many forms, stalked Europe of the nineteenth and twentieth centuries, leading to violent conflict, the fall of empires, the rise of nation-states. And Ireland experienced, though relatively peaceably, the conflict between capitalism and labour and the clash of mutually hostile ideologies that racked much of Europe.

It is essential that people (and especially the young) should know the history of their own country and see it in the wider context of world history. They must learn the dangers and the futility of violence; they must appreciate the absolute necessity of understanding, toleration and co-operation between classes, countries and religions. All this they can learn from history, as some Renaissance thinkers believed, but this is no easy task. Consider the words of George Bernard Shaw: 'How incapable must Man be of learning from experience'. But try we must, and try hard for, as the philosopher George Santayana wrote: 'Those who cannot remember the past are condemned to repeat it'.

JOSEPH CAREY
Chairman of the MultiText Project.

Introduction

This work offers a fresh approach to Irish history, 1870–1914. In place of a general narrative, it focuses on three major aspects: the foundation of the Gaelic Athletic Association (GAA) and the promotion of 'Irish Ireland'; the pursuit of Home Rule and the elections of 1885–6; and the struggle between labour and capital that culminated in the Lockout of 25,000 Dublin workers in 1913. All three events, in varying ways, changed the face of late nineteenth- and early twentieth-century Ireland. To get depth, we have narrowed the focus. However, three short survey essays at the beginning – on politics and administration, society and economy, and culture and religion – place these themes in their broader context. Two chapters are devoted to each major theme: the first is an analytical historical essay; the second is a broad selection of original historical documents, each with an introduction, an exact citation of source, and a concise presentation of its paraphrasable content. Lastly, there are short essays on historical concepts important in the period and brief biographies of major figures (each with a select bibliography). This book is designed to meet the full requirements of the Department of Education's Leaving Certificate syllabus, but it goes far beyond that, especially in its rich original documentation. It will answer to the needs of university students, the general reader, and all those interested in Irish history.

Readers will soon see that topics are touched on by the different authors in varying contexts, and there appears to be repetition and, on occasion, contradiction. This is deliberate. We preserve the integrity of our authors' essays and this will show, we hope, that professional historians may arrive honestly at disparate interpretations of historical evidence. Such genuine differences of opinion are vital to the discipline of history, and can bring about original and valuable insights that deepen and enrich historical understanding by asking new questions, prompting new arguments and starting new lines of inquiry. This is part of the historian's experience, and it should be part of the student's education to know that things are so. Here there are manifold points of view: those of various modern historians, from quite different backgrounds and diverse in attitudes and interpretations, and those of the actors themselves, equally different in background, class and convictions, expressed in a broad and generous selection of contemporary sources bearing on the great issues of the day. Readers must form their own opinions.

This is the second book in a series on Irish history that is dynamically linked to a dedicated internet site that extends its range and greatly supplements it, the MultiText Project (http://www. multitext.ie), established by Donnchadh Ó Corráin in 2000 and now managed by Tomás O'Riordan. The website has over one million words of modern Irish history and over 3,500 graphics – photographs, maps, cartoons and drawings – and serves the needs of those interested in Irish history worldwide. Available on the website is a full text of this work (and of several other works in preparation), updates, additional historical materials, an archive of relevant graphics (far more than the samples in this book), and an extensive bibliography of Irish history and Irish studies, compiled by Donnchadh Ó Corráin, that will shortly be half-a-million words in size. MultiText's sister project CELT (http://celt.ucc.ie) (Corpus of Electronic Texts) is the largest full-text scholarly data base of Irish history and literature on the internet – a digital library of twelve million words of historical sources, original texts and translations and bibliography. All texts on both sites are fully browsable and searchable, and may be freely downloaded by the readers of this book.

To help readers to find what they need quickly and easily, this book may be searched in three ways: by using the analytical table of contents, the detailed index, and the search utility on the MultiText website. References in the index are to chapter number and section number (e.g., 5.14 refers to chapter 5, section 14), except where otherwise specified (e.g., table and figure numbers). We have tried to keep the spelling and punctuation of original documents. However, minor changes have sometimes been made to make them more readable, but these do not alter the sense.

We are indebted to many people and to many institutions, and we record with pleasure their contributions, their help, their co-operation and their patience. First we thank our authors who, in the middle of busy academic lives where duties multiply, have given generously of their scholarship and their time and who have had to wait so long to see their work in print. Readers will observe a noteworthy north-south collaboration in this book, and this is something we are very glad about. Dr Gillian M. Doherty, project manager of MultiText (2000–2), brought dedication and professionalism to the undertaking and gave it a solid scholarly foundation from the start. To Tiarnán Ó Corráin we owe the architecture of the web site, the software that lies behind its user friendly interface (much praised by its users), and the day-to-day maintenance of the site itself. On the teaching side, we have had generous support. We thank John Dredge of the Second Level Support Service (SLSS) as well as the History Teachers' Association of Ireland (HTAI) for valuable feedback and help in publicising the project. Fidelma Maguire, former regional development officer with the History In-Service Team (HIST), read the whole work in draft and made important criticisms and suggestions. Dr Jacinta Prunty (NUI Maynooth) kindly allowed us to reproduce photographs and maps from her important publications on Dublin's former slums. We are also grateful to Gerard O'Sullivan and Dr Pat Callan (both formerly of HIST) for comment and publicity. We thank present and former staff of the CELT Project, especially Beatrix Färber, Emer Purcell, Dr Benjamin Hazard, and Dr Julianne Nyhan, for their willing co-operation.

We are most grateful to the libraries, repositories, and organisations and their supportive staff, who readily shared their valuable resources with us, especially historical documents and images: Kilmainham Gaol, the National Library of Ireland, the National Archives, the National Gallery of Ireland, the National Museum of Ireland, the Royal Irish Academy (RIA), the Royal Society of Antiquaries of Ireland (RSAI), Raidió Teilifís Éireann (RTÉ), the Public Record Office of Northern Ireland, the National Portrait

Gallery in London, the Ulster Museum, Cork City and County Libraries and the Boole Library at University College Cork.

Nowadays, projects of this kind have to be funded outside the ordinary University budget. We are grateful to Professor Gerry Wrixon, for a seed-capital grant from the President's Fund that made it possible to begin. We are even more indebted to Mr Joseph Carey, chairman of MultiText, whose financial support and constant encouragement has alone made this project and this publication possible. His practical patriotism and public-spirited generosity is a model for all who are concerned about culture and the arts in Ireland.

Lastly, we thank our publishers, Four Courts Press and the late Michael Adams (1937–2009), who were willing to publish a new type of historical text linked to the internet and suffer in patience an old type of academic tardiness.

DONNCHADH Ó CORRÁIN AND TOMÁS O'RIORDAN

CHAPTER I

Politics and administration, 1870–1914

1. Home Rule: origins and early development

1.1. Before the Great Famine, popular political tendencies in Ireland had swung between two contrary objectives: the repeal of the Act of Union – that is, the establishment of limited self-government for Ireland – and the maintenance of the Union. Some legal, administrative and political reforms enacted in Britain were swiftly introduced in Ireland. The catastrophe of the Great Famine and the collapse of O'Connell's Repeal Movement in the late 1840s changed the course of Irish politics. The more extreme nationalists, notably the Irish Republican Brotherhood (the Fenians), sought a republic completely separate from Britain. The moderate political movements of the 1850s and 1860s largely abandoned the objective of self-government in favour of reform. One important moderate reformist nationalist was Archbishop (later Cardinal) Paul Cullen (1803–78). Though anti-English and anti-Protestant, he was a pragmatist who saw that vital reforms, especially in education, could be won in the Westminster parliament. He therefore supported Union up to a point as the most likely means of speeding up reform, already well advanced by the late 1860s.

1.2. The fresh demand for self-government in the 1870s, called Home Rule, did not come from moderate nationalist Catholic community but from Irish Protestants. The reason for this change is clear enough: Irish Protestants distrusted the reforming tendencies of successive United Kingdom governments. The reforms since the late 1820s had, in their view, threatened to undermine the Union and the political and religious safeguards enjoyed by Irish Protestants. A series of Acts, beginning with the Emancipation Act in 1829, brought reform in local government, parliamentary representation, education and land ownership. The Disestablishment Act of 1869 broke the legal connection between the Church of Ireland and the State and reduced the influence of both the Protestant ascendancy and the Church of Ireland.

2. The Home Government Association

2.1. One response to reform – 'too far, too fast' – was the formation in 1870 by a small group of Irish Protestants of a new political movement, the Home Government Association. Its first public meeting was held at the Rotunda, Dublin, on 1 September that year. The principal persons involved were George F. Shaw, a prominent fellow of Trinity College, Dublin; Major Lawrence E. Knox, editor and proprietor of the *Irish Times* (founded in 1859); E.R. King-Harman, member of a leading landlord family; and Isaac Butt, former Professor of Political Economy in Trinity College and a prominent barrister and politician. These Protestant leaders feared that the values, structures and heritage consolidated by the Union were being endangered by a weak-kneed United Kingdom parliament. They aimed to preserve this political heritage by establishing a federal system for the United Kingdom, with an Irish parliament in Dublin dealing with national affairs. Butt explained his strategy thus:

> to make an assault all along the whole line of English misgovernment, and to bring forward every grievance of Ireland, and to press the English House of Commons for their redress ... I believed, and believe still, that if once we got liberal-minded Englishmen fairly to consider how they would redress the grievance of Irish misgovernment, they would come in the end to the conclusion that they had but one way of giving us good government, and that was by allowing us to govern ourselves.

2.2. The Home Government Association did not, however, want a return to the pre–1800 Protestant ascendancy. Its leaders saw that the tide of reform could not be turned back and that Irish Protestants must accommodate themselves to changing ideas and situations. Indeed, they saw in Home Rule the chance to reconcile Irish Protestantism with reform, and ensure the continued role of Protestants in Irish political leadership. Some of its leaders had a real sympathy for those in the separatist republican Fenian movement. Among its sixty early members were Protestants and Catholics, landlords and tenants, Conservatives, Liberals and Fenians.

2.3. Isaac Butt most clearly represented these complex and sometimes contradictory motivations among the leaders of the Association. In 1843, he had opposed Daniel O'Connell in a major debate in Dublin Corporation on the issue of Repeal of the Union. O'Connell was impressed by young Butt and he acknowledged Butt's patriotism when he spoke to him after the debate: 'Isaac, you are young, and I am old. I will fail in winning back the parliament, but you will do it, when I shall have passed away'. Thomas McNevin described the young Conservatives, Isaac Butt and Samuel Ferguson, as 'Orange Young Ireland', in a letter to William Smith O'Brien. From 1852 to 1868, Butt had sat in parliament as Conservative MP for Youghal which, despite progressive extensions of the franchise, remained one of the safest strongholds of Protestantism and Conservatism. Why did Butt become a leading light in this new drive for 'Home Government'? He certainly shared the unease felt by Irish Protestants at government reform in Ireland from the late 1860s on. As a barrister, he was involved in the defence of Fenian prisoners in the late 1860s and had come to believe that changes in the political position of Ireland were essential. He considered the Fenians to be patriots, deeply concerned with their country's welfare, but thoroughly misguided in their methods. Political reform might help stem the rising tide of militant separatism which had encouraged young (and not so young) men to join the Fenians.

2.4. Fenian sympathisers began to give the Home Government Association guarded support and behind-the-scenes agreements between the two groups were made at election time. In February 1872, two supporters of Home Rule, Captain John Philip Nolan in Galway and Rowland Ponsonby Blennerhasset in Kerry, comprehensively beat their Conservative and Liberal candidates in by-elections. On 8 January 1873, Butt founded the Home Rule Confederation of Great Britain to garner the support of Irish people in Britain for Home Rule candidates. It was soon infiltrated by members of the IRB. In May of that year, Gladstone gave his first speech in the House of Commons on the demand for home government. He visited Ireland, 17 October–12 November 1877, and was presented with the Freedom of the City of Dublin (7 November). In 1873, the Home Government Association and disappointed Catholic bishops began to move closer together; the Catholic hierarchy's hostility to the largely Protestant make-up of the Association gave way to the belief that each could be of use to the other politically. On 18–21 November 1873, a conference between the two sides (originally called by Dr William Keane (1805–75), the Catholic Bishop of Cloyne) was held in the Rotunda in Dublin and from it emerged a new body to replace the old Home Government Association. This new organisation was the Home Rule League, a far larger body than its predecessor, and one with much more political clout.

3. The Home Rule League

3.1. Pragmatism gave this new body its strength. Although its main objective was limited self-government for Ireland through the re-establishment of a parliament in Dublin, its leaders realised that a more practical programme was needed to gain the widest possible popular support. Thus, much emphasis was put on the demand for a Catholic University to get the support of the Catholic bishops, who had been campaigning for this for over thirty years, and win the wealthy Catholic middle classes who had benefited politically from the reforms and who saw university education as a means of advancing their children. The Home Rule League also courted the farmers by campaigning for land reform. It kept links open with the Fenians by continuing to support the movement for amnesty (or pardon) of Fenian prisoners. In the February 1874 general election the Home Rule League won 59 seats (including two in Ulster), Conservatives won 33 and Liberals 10. Liberal Prime Minister, William Ewart Gladstone (1809–98) lost the election and was succeeded by Benjamin Disraeli (1804–81), an imperialist with little interest in Irish affairs. The Conservative Government remained in power until 1880. The Home Rule MPs agreed to constitute themselves as 'separate and distinct party in the House of Commons, united on the principle of obtaining self-government for Ireland.' On 2 July 1874, Butt's Home Rule motion was defeated in the House of Commons by 458 votes to 61.

3.2. Butt's remarkable political imagination and intuitive judgement enabled him to identify Home Rule as a national objective. A majority of Irish people responded with clear enthusiasm to the idea of Home Rule and were to promote it as a solution to the Irish question for close on half a century. However, there were other pressing concerns. Isaac Butt, though politically astute, lacked the drive, organisation and ruthlessness nec-

essary to give the strong lead needed to turn a catch-all movement into an effective political machine. His mounting debts meant that he was frequently away from Westminster
working as a barrister to pay his creditors. Many of the Home Rule MPs were also absent
from Westminster even when important issues were being debated. The lack of an organised branch system around the country meant the Butt lacked widespread support in
Ireland. Depending on social status, the average supporter was interested in better
employment, land reform, or a Catholic University. Besides, there were tensions between
the constituent groups – tensions that threatened to wreck the fragile unity of the movement. The Catholic Church, for instance, still distrusted the Protestant element in the
leadership. Urban working-class supporters of Home Rule had little time for the farming element that appeared to be more interested in the practical issue of land reform.
Above all, there were tensions between the Fenians on the one hand, and the Catholic
Church and moderate Home Rulers on the other.

4. Obstructionism

4.1. Leadership was the other main problem. Butt was challenged by prominent and up-
and-coming members of the movement. Chief among these were the obstructionists led
initially by Joseph Gillis Biggar (1828–90), a Fenian and member of the Supreme
Council of the IRB, and later by Charles Stewart Parnell (1846–91), MP for Meath, 1875–
80. Butt's approach was too tame and unrealistic for Parnell's liking:

> I gladly agree with Mr Butt that it is very possible, and very probable, that he would
> be able to persuade a fair-minded Englishman in the direction that he has indicated;
> but I still do not think that the House of Commons is mainly composed of fair-
> minded Englishmen. If we had to deal with men who were capable of listening to
> fair arguments there would be every hope of success for the policy of Mr Butt as car-
> ried out in past sessions; but we are dealing with political parties who really consider
> the interests of their political organisations as paramount, beyond every other con-
> sideration.

4.2. Obstructionism involved holding up parliamentary business by making very long
speeches about minor issues, a technique that, as one historian put it, would hasten the
advent of Home Rule by goading the London parliament into 'wishing that the Irish had
a parliament of their own'. On 22 April 1875, Biggar made a three-and-a-half-hour
speech in the House of Commons on the coercion bill. Although obstructionism was
considered a most ungentlemanly technique, it certainly succeeded in forcing the British
public to take notice of Irish affairs and of the Home Rule Association's demands. It is
said of Biggar that no MP with such unimpressive qualifications ever occupied more of
the House's time. It has been argued, too, that Biggar's obstructionist activity made constitutional politics more acceptable to many physical-force nationalists in Ireland.

4.3. In June 1876, another Home Rule motion by Butt was debated in the House of Commons but defeated by 291 votes to 61. The Obstructionists had their eyes on the leadership. On its own, this challenge might not have been serious, but it was coupled with internal tensions and weaknesses in the movement. In 1877, the IRB Supreme Council forbade Fenian involvement in the Home Rule movement. Biggar and John O'Connor Power were expelled when they refused to obey the order. However, many ordinary IRB members, particularly in Connacht and Munster, continued their organisational involvement with the Home Rule movement. By the end of the 1870s, the Home Rule movement was about to shake off the old leadership and become a powerful popular movement with a new charismatic figure at its head. On 9 January 1879, Archbishop MacHale of Tuam wrote to the editor of the *Freeman's Journal* calling for unity among Irish Home Rule MPs.

5. Parnellism as politics

5.1. Butt died on 5 May 1879. William Shaw, a wealthy Protestant banker from Cork, was elected chairman of the party. He proved to be an undistinguished and short-term leader. The general election in March 1880 was a triumph for the rising star, Charles Stewart Parnell, an Irish Protestant landlord, seasoned obstructionist, advanced nationalist and President of the Land League. He contested and won three seats including Cork, which he chose to represent for the rest of his career. On 26 April 1880, Parnell, an instinctive political genius, was elected leader, defeating Shaw by 23 votes to 18. This led to a new stage in the development of the Home Rule Party. Parnell was willing to use new methods unacceptable to his predecessor. He had also been elected President of the Home Rule Confederation of Great Britain on 28 August 1877 in place of Butt. He declared in 1880 that he would not be content 'until we have destroyed the last link which keeps Ireland bound to England.' He turned a moderate and constitutional Home Rule movement into an aggressive, obstructive and relentless movement that dominated parliamentary proceedings throughout the 1880s.

5.2. In reality, Parnell's leadership style was authoritarian. He saw himself as the ultimate authority in the party, he was frequently in conflict with local party activists and, despite his democratic style, his social attitude was elitist. Some historians argue that even his participation in Home Rule politics, frequently ascribed to an anti-Englishness inherited from his American mother and sharpened by his own bad experiences in an English public school and at Cambridge, was really due to his belief that his own landlord class should claim again its rightful place in Irish political and social leadership.

5.3. Parnell's undoubted social elitism was matched by his political shrewdness. He seized the political opportunity to make a most unlikely alliance for an Irish Protestant landlord, that is, with the land agitation movement that emerged in the West of Ireland in late 1879, an agitation that would spread rapidly through much of Ireland in the following two years. When Michael Davitt (1846–1906) organised the Irish Land League in 1879, Parnell, realising its strong political potential, became its leader and he succeeded in weaving together the twin causes of land reform and Home Rule. He also kept the support of hard-line separatist nationalists in the Irish Republican Brotherhood (Fenians) who had little time either for Home Rule or land reform. While Parnell did not necessarily agree with their aims, he took care not to alienate them by condemning their aims or their methods. In one of his first speeches in parliament in 1876, he defended the Fenian 'Manchester Martyrs' and declared: 'I do not believe, and never shall believe, that any murder was committed at Manchester'. There was widespread agrarian violence during the Land War of 1879–81 and many at Westminster feared there would be revolution in Ireland. Parnell was jailed in Kilmainham in 1881 for his vociferous public attack on Gladstone's Land Act. It soon became obvious that his imprisonment had actually resulted in an escalation of crime and disorder. So a compromise was reached. Under the terms of the 'Kilmainham Treaty', the government vowed to improve the 1881 Land Act by extending it to leaseholders and providing remission of rent arrears. Parnell in turn promised to use his influence to end agitation in Ireland. He distanced himself from the Fenians after the brutal murders of the newly appointed Chief Secretary, Lord Frederick Cavendish (1836–82), (married to Gladstone's niece Lucy) and the Permanent Under Secretary, Thomas Henry Burke (1829–1882), in the Phoenix Park, Dublin on 6 May 1882. The much-condemned action was carried out by members of the Irish National Invincibles, a splinter group of the IRB, formed in 1881 to attack high-ranking government officials. Seventeen Invincibles were arrested in January 1883, five of whom were executed. As a result the influence of the Fenians waned and they became a spent force for over twenty years. Parnell's poor health after his period in jail and his financial difficulties meant that he played a less active role in politics between 1882 and 1885.

5.4. The Irish National League was founded in October 1882. It put Home Rule before land reform. It aims were also to be pursued by parliamentary action rather than mass agitation and MPs were paid from the League's funds. Within three years the League has over 1,200 branches nationwide. Parnell was becoming an extremely popular and influential figure. At the foundation meeting of the Gaelic Athletic Association (GAA) in November 1884 he was invited to become a patron with Dr Croke, Archbishop of Cashel, and Michael Davitt.

5.5. Parnell's succeeded in building a highly centralised and strictly disciplined party. It was bound by a pledge that made the individual parliamentary representative subject to the combined will of the party and its leader. In parliament, the party members diligently attended, spoke eloquently, sat together, and voted as a bloc. Their unity and effectiveness were formidable, and this was noted with surprise by other politicians. The movement was democratic: its policies reflected the wishes of the wider population. Parnell courted the public in his speeches throughout the country. He used down-to-earth language, tailored his words to appeal to differing interests, and he made sure to meet personally with representatives of different groups – for example, farmers, trade Unionists and clergy – to hear their grievances and listen to their opinions.

5.6. Parnell's other beneficial alliance was with the Catholic clergy. Although neither trusted the other, a pragmatic understanding could prove useful. Parnell used the local Catholic clergy to spread the Home Rule organisation, particularly in the rural areas, and often to chair its meetings. This put the stamp of respectability on his politics. For their part, the Catholic clergy and hierarchy needed the support of an astute political leader who could push their demands in Westminster. In the mid–1880s an arrangement to their mutual benefit was reached between Parnell and the Irish Catholic bishops: the bishops agreed to back Home Rule as long as Parnell pushed in parliament for the establishment of a Catholic University as a counterbalance to the non-denominational Queen's Colleges (in existence since the middle of the century) to which the bishops objected strenuously.

6. Home Rule and Irish Unionism

6.1. The Home Rule movement in Ireland had gained new momentum under Parnell. This was helped by the changing of constituency boundaries and voting requirements in 1884–5 that greatly increased the Irish electorate. The Irish Parliamentary Party won eighty-six seats in the 1885 general election. Supporters of Home Rule were now in control of nearly every constituency outside of Trinity College, Dublin and north-east Ulster, where non-Home Rule candidates were returned. This shows that, long before Ireland was officialy partitioned, there was a clear division between the counties of north-east Ulster and the rest of the country. Parnell was willing to deal with Liberals or Conservatives as long as they were prepared to help advance the Irish cause. Irish Unionists were fearful about any tampering with the Act of Union, and the effectiveness of the Home Rule movement only confirmed their anxieties. In 1886, their worst fears were realised when the first Home Rule Bill came before parliament.

6.2. By the mid–1880s, Home Rule was supported by a broad popular movement in Ireland, and by influential members of parliament at Westminster – the Irish Home Rule representatives, the Liberal Prime Minister, Gladstone and a large section of the Liberal Party. Gladstone eventually concluded that conceding Home Rule was the only way to 'Irish contentment'. For twenty-six years Home Rule Bills (in 1886, 1893 and 1912) threatened the Union. This was a sustained challenge, popular and parliamentary, and supporters of the Union now began to describe themselves as 'Unionists'.

6.3. The first Home Rule Bill was introduced by Gladstone on 8 April 1886. The bill proposed an Irish legislature of two 'orders'. The first order was to have 103 members, comprising of 75 members elected for a ten-year term on a restricted franchise, and 28 peers. The second order would have 204 members, elected for a five-year term on the existing franchise. This legislature would deal with all Irish affairs except the Crown, defence, war and peace, trade and navigation, lighthouses, weights and measures, coinage, the post office and colonial affairs. Parnell thought the bill inadequate but believed it could be a stepping stone to future advancement. The bill aroused enormous hostility in Britain. It was defeated in the House of Commons on 8 June 1886 by 343 to 311. Ninety-three members of Gladstone's party voted against him. He resigned after the 1886 general election when the Conservatives and Liberal Unionists between them won a clear majority. In 1885–6 too, there emerged a strong united Unionist party to replace the Liberals and Conservatives in Ireland as the voice of the Irish Protestant community. The policy advanced by Arthur Balfour, Chief Secretary (1887–91) and later Prime Minister (1902–5), was one of 'killing Home Rule by kindness', that is, through a mixture of firmness and reform. This would remain the cornerstone of Conservative policy in government.

7. The fall of Parnell

7.1. The new Conservative government's opposition to Home Rule left Parnell with little room to manoeuvre. There was a public outcry in Britain when *The Times* wrongly linked him to the Phoenix Park murders. However, it was Parnell's private life that brought about his downfall. He had a long-standing affair with Katharine O'Shea (1847–1921), the wife of Captain William Henry O'Shea (1840–1905). He was deeply in love and they had a family. The affair was not completely secret, but neither was it common knowledge. It might have remained so had not Katharine O'Shea's aunt died, leaving her a considerable legacy from which her husband was excluded. Only at this point did Captain O'Shea (possibly realising that he would get nothing from continuing to turn a blind eye to the affair) make the matter public. O'Shea now sued for a divorce, on the grounds of his wife's adultery with Parnell. The matter was now public knowledge, a great scandal and a political time-bomb.

7.2. Even after the defeat of the 1886 Bill, Gladstone still hoped to achieve Home Rule with the support of Parnell's MPs. This now seemed impossible, and Liberal leader, fearful of losing votes in the next election, pressed Parnell to resign saying that his 'continuance at the present moment in the leadership [of the Irish Party] would be productive of consequences disastrous in the highest degree to the cause of Ireland'. The Catholic Church and the majority of the Irish Parliamentary Party believed that if Parnell was to remain on as leader of the party, then it might damage any chance of Home Rule. When Parnell refused to resign the party and its supporters throughout Ireland split into two bitterly hostile groups: those who wished Parnell to remain leader (at least for the time being), and those who condemned him for betraying the Party, the country, and the cause of Home Rule. Dr Croke, Archbishop of Cashel criticised those who still continued to support Parnell. Writing to Archbishop William J. Walsh (1841–1921) of Dublin he said:

> I have flung him [Parnell] away from me. His bust which for some time had held a
> prominent place in my hall I kicked out yesterday. As for the 'party' generally, I go with

you entirely in thinking that they make small or no account of Bishops and priests now as independent agents, and only value them as money gatherers and useful auxiliaries in the agitation … without us, they would simply be nowhere and nobodies.

7.3. On 1 December 1890, seventy-three members attended a meeting in Committee Room 15 of the House of Commons. Parnell refused to make any concessions. He did offer to resign if Gladstone gave assurances about a forthcoming Home Rule bill, but the Liberal leader was unwilling to give any. On 6 December, Justin McCarthy led 44 members out of the same room, leaving Parnell with 27 supporters. His candidates were roundly beaten in subsequent by-elections in North Kilkenny and North Sligo. Parnell's affair with a married woman was most often cited as the cause of public disillusionment, but Parnell's refusal to resign as leader was just as important. He was seen to be putting his personal emotions and ambitions before the ultimate objective of winning Home Rule.

7.4. Parnell died prematurely on 6 October 1891. His immediate legacy was one of romantic legend and bitter political discord. An aura of tragic romance soon came to surround his memory. He was portrayed by his supporters and by those disillusioned by political infighting as a hero betrayed. The anniversary of his death was known as Ivy Day, when solemn and emotive commemorative ceremonies took place. The profound sense of tragedy later entered Irish literature, most notably in the works of William Butler Yeats (1865–1939) and James Joyce (1882–1941). The legend of the betrayed 'Chief' simplified the complex realities of the time, and added Parnell's name to a long list of perceived nationalist martyrs.

8. The Home Rule Bills of 1893 and 1912

8.1. After Parnell's fall, the Home Rule campaign continued, though divisions inside and outside parliament did the movement no good. Nevertheless, Gladstone introduced a second Home Rule Bill in January 1893 that differed only slightly from the 1886 bill. The proposed legislature for Ireland would consist of a Council of 48 members, elected for an eight-year term on a restricted franchise, and an Assembly of 103 members, elected for five years on the existing franchise. Disagreements were to be resolved by joint majority vote. The bill was strongly resisted in the House of Commons, and finally rejected by the Conservative-dominated House of Lords in September 1893. Gladstone resigned and retired the following year. The Liberal leader had proposed a campaign to reduce the power of the House of Lords, but it came to nothing. Long and troublesome parliamentary manoeuvring had ended in defeat and the Party itself was seriously divided on the issue of Home Rule. The Conservatives returned to power in 1895 and remained in office until 1905. Home Rule was now firmly off the agenda.

8.2. The Irish Party was fragmented and ineffectual for much of the 1890s. The party only reunited through the gentlemanly diplomacy of John Redmond (1856–1918) in

January 1900. His father William (*d.* 1880) had been MP for Wexford. He himself became MP for New Ross in 1881. Redmond was a fine speaker, a skilled negotiator and was respected by leading British politicians. He became one of Parnell's most loyal colleagues and he stood by him during the O'Shea divorce scandal. After Parnell's death he moved away from agrarian radicalism and he also worked alongside Unionists in the Recess Committee of 1895, organised by Sir Horace Plunkett (1854–1932), which led to the establishment of the Department of Agriculture (1899). Most Parnellites boycotted the body as they saw it as another attempt to 'kill Home Rule with kindness'.

8.3. Home Rule was often ruinous to the parties and individuals who took it up. This is clear in the case of Devolution proposal of 1904 and Irish Council Bill in 1907. These two well-intentioned proposals attempted to reconcile Unionist and Home Rule demands by establishing a new Irish assembly which would control certain government departments, such as agriculture and education. They offered Home Rulers some degree of autonomy and would help calm Unionist fears since this autonomy would be far less than Home Rule. These measures, precisely because they were compromises, pleased nobody. Parliament was faced, as it had long been, with the task of solving the seemingly insoluble Irish problem, namely, meeting demands for independence and maintaining the Union at the same time. The Liberals who returned to government in 1906 with a large majority knew that any Home Rule bill would not get through the Tory-dominated House of Lords. So they concentrated on dealing with social reforms such as the old age pension and unemployment and sick benefits. In 1908, the Chief Secretary, Augustine Birrell (1850–1933), gave the Catholic bishops the university they had long demanded when he established the National University of Ireland (Irish Universities Act). A Land Act introduced in 1909 made more funds available to continue the Wyndham land purchase programme of 1903.

8.4. Redmond's opportunity finally came during the 1909 budget crisis. The Chancellor of the Exchequer, David Lloyd George (1863–1945), sought to increase income tax and death duties as well as taxes on tobacco and alcohol to help pay for social reforms and for British re-armament. The budget was thrown out by the House of Lords. The Liberal Prime Minister, Herbert Asquith (1852–1928), resolved to go to the people and called a general election. The Liberals won 272 seats, Conservatives 252, and Redmondites 73. Asquith needed Redmond's votes to stay in power. The Parliament Act of 1911 finally reduced the veto of the House of Lords to a delaying power. Any bill that passed the Commons in three successive sessions would henceforth become law, even if rejected in the House of Lords. This meant that Home Rule for Ireland was now a real possibility.

8.5. Two years before the outbreak of the Great War threw all Europe into disarray, another attempt was made to solve the Irish question. The third Home Rule Bill was introduced by Asquith in April 1912. The Bill provided for an Irish parliament consisting of two houses: a Senate of 40 members, to be nominated by the Lord Lieutenant (but thereafter elected for five years) and a House of Commons of 164 members, also elected for a five-year term. Ireland would also send 42 representatives to Westminster.

A Liberal member of parliament, T.C. Agar-Robartes proposed on 2 May that counties Antrim, Armagh, Derry and Down be excluded from Home Rule. However, the suggestion got little support from Liberals or Conservatives. The Bill passed in the House of Commons, despite opposition from Ulster Unionists, led by Edward Carson (1854–1935), and the Conservatives. Although it was overwhelmingly rejected by the House of Lords, the Bill finally passed into law due to the provisions of the Parliament Act. Home Rule was enacted and later signed into law by King George V on 18 September 1914. Irish Unionists were aghast; Home Rulers were euphoric. John Redmond and John Dillon represented the Irish Party at the Buckingham Palace Conference in July 1914 when Unionists were prepared to settle for the exclusion from Home Rule of the six north-eastern counties. Redmond, however, was strongly against any form of partition. But Britain declared war on Germany on 4 August 1914, and the implementation of the Home Rule Act was suspended until peace returned. Unionists were assured that the Act would not be enforced until the position of Ulster had been resolved.

9. Varieties of Unionism

9.1. Outside Ulster, Unionists were a minority and they could not campaign as effectively against Home Rule as they did in north-east Ulster. In fact, there was a widening gulf between Unionists in Ulster and those in the rest of Ireland. From 1885 the Ulster Unionists, formed a united and threatening front determined to maintain the Union at all costs. In June 1892, they staged a major demonstration in Belfast, the Ulster Unionist Convention. This allowed all classes to voice their opposition to Home Rule. Following this Convention, a network of Ulster Unionist Clubs was formed to keep up the pressure. In 1905, in response to the Devolution crisis, the Ulster Unionist Council was formed to unify and centralise their efforts. The very titles of these organisations show how Ulster-based they were.

9.2. A vital feature of Ulster Unionism during this period was the way in which social and economic divisions were bridged by the common commitment to the Union. Ulster Unionism crossed the class divide: it included people of all backgrounds – landlords, substantial farmers, businessmen, agricultural labourers and urban manual workers. Only in Ulster did this happen. In the other provinces Unionist farmers and workers had always been in a minority, and separated from their social superiors. Here most Unionists were upper and middle class. As a well connected elite (among them were the Marquis of Lansdowne (1845–1927) and the Earl of Midleton), southern Unionists mounted a remarkable propaganda campaign and made good use of their connections, in parliament and throughout Britain, to argue the case eloquently against Home Rule. However, numbers were against them and many began to lose heart.

9.3. Gladstone's third Home Rule Bill in 1912 saw the most determined action of the Ulster Unionists. The traditional organising and speech-making took place, but there was also violent rioting in Belfast and workers were even expelled from the shipyards. There was a new and disturbing militarism. An Ulster Volunteer Force (UVF) was set up to help resist Home Rule. Arms were imported, volunteer companies drilled regularly, and ambulance corps were organised by women. Some threatened to withhold taxes should Home Rule become law. Much of this activity was of dubious legality. That a community priding itself on its loyalty should treat the law so casually, shows just how disillusioned Ulster Unionists had become with government that had, they believed, betrayed them. Their loyalty was now conditional: they remained loyal so long as the government supported the Union.

9.4. The conditional nature of their loyalty became very clear at a great public event staged in 1912 to demonstrate Unionist opposition to Home Rule, that is, the signing (in blood by some) of the Solemn League and Covenant. There was a deliberate allusion to God's Old Testament covenant with the Jews and to the seventeenth-century Scottish Covenanters. This document was signed by Unionists from all over the country, but most especially by those in Ulster (there were 471,414 signatories in all). Ulster Unionists, beginning with their leaders, Edward Carson and James Craig, lined up in public and put their names to a Covenant pledging to resist Home Rule. The Covenant was signed by men, and the Declaration, which was signed by women (as many Unionists were opposed to female suffrage).

> *Ulster's Solemn League and Covenant (signed by 237,368 men)*
>
> BEING CONVINCED in our consciences that Home Rule would be disastrous to the material well-being of Ulster as well as of the whole of Ireland, subversive of our civil and religious freedom, destructive of our citizenship and perilous to the unity of the Empire, we, whose names are underwritten, men of Ulster, loyal subjects of his Gracious Majesty King George V, humbly relying on the God whom our fathers in days of stress and trial confidently trusted, do hereby pledge ourselves in solemn Covenant throughout this our time of threatened calamity to stand by one another in defending for ourselves and our children our cherished position of equal citizenship in the United Kingdom and in using all means which may be found necessary to defeat the present conspiracy to set up a Home Rule parliament in Ireland. And in the event of such a parliament being forced upon us we further solemnly and mutually pledge ourselves to refuse to recognise its authority. In sure confidence that God will defend the right we here to subscribe our names. And further, we individually declare that we have not already signed this Covenant.
>
> The above was signed by me at
>
> 'Ulster Day', Saturday, 28th September, 1912.
>
> GOD SAVE THE KING

The Declaration (signed by 234,046 women)

We, whose names are underwritten, women of Ulster, and loyal British subjects of our gracious King, being firmly persuaded that Home Rule would be disastrous to our Country, desire to associate ourselves with the men of Ulster in their uncompromising opposition to the Home Rule Bill now before parliament, whereby it is proposed to drive Ulster out of her cherished place in the Constitution of the United Kingdom, and to place her under the domination and control of a parliament in Ireland. Praying that from this calamity God will save Ireland, we here to subscribe our name:

9.5. The event was well organised and the signing was orderly. In this way the Ulster Unionists demonstrated discipline and determination. It also emphasised the religious crusading spirit that had always been part of Unionism. It their own eyes, their campaign was on a plane higher than mere politics. They saw themselves as defenders, of not only the Union and the constitution, but also of the integrity of the entire British Empire.

9.6. The outbreak of the Great War in August 1914 turned minds to European matters and Unionists rallied with fervour to the war effort.

10. A more assertive nationalism, 1870–1914

10.1. As the Home Rule movement was becoming more organised under Parnell's leadership, fundamental questions were asked about what it meant to be Irish. Was limited independence enough for those who believed Ireland capable of self-government? Was more needed to prove Ireland's distinctiveness from England? Varying answers to the questions came from different sections of Irish society. During the nineteenth century many Catholics believed that to be truly Irish one must be Catholic. Irish Unionists felt no less Irish for being Unionists and mostly Protestant. By the 1880s, new voices were heard, mostly those of an increasingly well-educated lower-middle class, men and women whose interest in cultural and sporting pursuits was made possible by rising pay, shorter working hours. These well-educated young people found their way to advancement blocked by the stagnant social and economic structures of their day – young clerks and shop assistants, caught in moderately paid but dead-end jobs; national teachers forced to toe the line by conservative and often domineering parish priests; and, above all, a new type emerging in the late nineteenth century, the junior civil servant who often spent time in London and thus became more conscious of an Irish identity. This was the social group that provided much of the personnel of the 'new nationalism' of the late nineteenth century.

10.2. Such people supported new organisations such as the Gaelic Athletic Association, founded 1884, to develop Gaelic sports; the Gaelic League, founded 1893, to foster the use of the Irish language; and Sinn Féin, founded 1905, which stressed economic self-reliance and political self-sufficiency. These new organisations, each in its own way,

believed that Irishness depended on cultural and economic distinctiveness from England.
They were not the first to hold such a view. Forty years earlier, Thomas Davis and Young
Ireland had promoted similar ideas, stressing the importance of self-reliance, praising the
traditional pastimes of ordinary people and urging the preservation of the Irish language.
But Davis' nationalism was balanced by two things: he was a university-educated and
open-minded Protestant, and his definition of Irishness was broad and included all Irish
people regardless of origins, religion or culture. His vision is best expressed in his lines:

> What matter that at different shrines
> We pray unto one God –
> What matter that at different times
> Your fathers won this sod –
> In fortune and in name we're bound
> By stronger links than steel;
> And neither can be safe nor sound
> But in the other's weal.

10.3. The Irishness propounded by the late nineteenth-century movements was narrower
than that of Davis and tended to be exclusive. The purpose of these movements'
Irishness was to shape (and, in part, to invent) a national identity based on language and
culture, in some ways a perilous undertaking. The emphasis was on all things Gaelic –
hence the titles 'Gaelic Athletic Association' and 'Gaelic League'. If national identity was
essentially Gaelic, where did that leave the Anglo-Irish and the anglicised parts of the
population? What of the English-speaking majority? What of Irish literature in English?
If one did not play Gaelic games, dance Irish dances, sing Irish songs and speak Irish,
was one really Irish? If the answer to these questions was 'no', then obviously the emergent sense of Irishness was exclusive, and excluded the majority.

11. Protestantism and Irishness

11.1. Many Protestants in Ireland believed that Irishness was not based exclusively on any
one religion or any one culture, and that they had as much right to be considered Irish
as any player of Gaelic games or Irish language revivalist. They stressed, instead, the
common sense of Irishness based on a shared history and past cultural achievements.
They also tried to identify Irishness in the simple, unvarnished life of rural Ireland, an
Ireland that they knew and sometimes wrote of, but from which many of them were separated by a wide cultural and social gulf. Lady Gregory, for instance, though she knew,
loved and wrote about the country people around her husband's estate at Coole, Co.
Galway, really belonged to different worlds, those of the intelligentsia and the landlord
class. When John Millington Synge (1871–1909), who had attended lectures on modern
languages and Celtic at the University of Paris and who knew the West of Ireland inti-
mately, wrote his controversial plays, *The playboy of the western world* and *In the shadow*

of the glen, he was meticulous in conveying the language and attitudes of the people, though of course in literary form. Some of these Protestant writers found themselves at odds with people who objected to their realist pictures of Irish life. Dublin audiences, for instance, were outraged at parts of the *Playboy*, seeing it (wrongly) as an attempt to ridicule Irish life. Realism did not appeal when many were trying to glorify and romanticise Irish culture and the values they thought it had.

11.2. Some writers of Protestant Ireland, however, were drawn to the romanticisation of Ireland's Gaelic culture. In these early years, the great poet William Butler Yeats, who later cast a much more critical eye on Irish society, set great store by Ireland's mythological past, and by its legendary heroes. In exquisite lyric poetry, he celebrated the glories of Oisín and Meadhbh, Fergus and Oscar. He celebrated, too, what he saw as the tragic heroism and idealism of latter-day Fenian leaders, contrasting their noble qualities with the hard-nosed and grasping materialism of his own day.

11.3. The 1898 centenary celebration of the 1798 Rebellion was one event that helped to reinterpret history and to establish the myth of heroic national tragedy beyond the confines of literary society, and indeed among the wider population. The original rebellion, driven by a complex mixture of sectarian hatreds, imported French revolutionary republican ideals and local power-struggles, was now portrayed as simple patriotic heroism in the face of unbearable oppression. Patriotic celebrations took place widely, particularly in those places (especially in Wexford, Mayo and Antrim-Down) where the major actions in the rebellion had occurred. Monuments were erected to honour the rebels; old songs were re-worked and fresh ones written to honour those who took part; and new periodicals, like the *Shan Van Vocht* (published in Belfast), exhorted the people of 1898 to honour the memory and imitate the virtue of their forebears a century earlier. The many local and regional committees established to organise the celebrations were drawn from a wide spectrum of Irish society – trade unionists, Home Rulers, local politicians, Catholic clergy and, very importantly, underground republican activists and sympathisers who continued the Fenian/IRB tradition.

11.4. These latter-day republicans – a very small minority – were disillusioned by what they saw as the futility of the Home Rule movement, in existence since 1870, but no nearer to achieving its goal. They also felt that constitutional politics was both pointless and spineless. Some saw the limited objective of Home Rule as scarcely worth the effort, and in their quest for a separate republican Ireland they glorified military action as the only honourable and courageous way.

12. The Suffrage Movement in Ireland, 1870–1914

12.1. Until the 1860s, a woman in the United Kingdom had few rights. Women were classified politically with 'lunatics and criminals' and were not allowed vote in parliamentary elections or hold any public office. A single woman could own property in her own right but her property passed to her husband on marriage. Even her wages were considered his, and he alone had control over their children. A husband could also divorce his wife more easily than a wife could divorce her husband.

12.2. The first Irish women's suffrage association was the Dublin Women's Suffrage Association, founded in 1876. It later became the Irish Women's Suffrage and Local Government Association (IWSLGA). The organisation was founded by two Quakers (a religion that had never differentiated between the rights of men and women): Thomas Haslam (1825–1917) and his wife Anna Haslam (1829–1922), two pioneering feminist activists. The IWSLGA was a peaceable association but had close links with the more militant suffrage organisations when the agitation was at its height in 1910–12.

12.3. About the same time a campaign to get better education for women began. A leader of the movement was the Quaker Anne Jellicoe, born in Laois in 1823. In 1861, she set up a Dublin branch of the British-based Society for Promoting the Employment of Women to help working-class women train for jobs. In 1866, she established Alexandra College to train governesses, and Alexandra School in 1873 to give girls a good secondary education. Pressure from Jellicoe and from the Scots-born suffragist, Isabella Tod (1836–96), among others, led the government to include girls' education in the Intermediate Education Act (1878). Women's access to higher education was very limited. To remedy this, girls' colleges were set up to give women a university education. On 22 October 1884, nine women received degrees from the Royal University of Ireland. They were the first women to graduate in Ireland. In 1904, Trinity College, Dublin admitted women to its degrees and in 1908, when the National University and Queen's University of Belfast were set up, women entered on equal terms with men.

12.4. Better education gave women the resources to become politically active. When the Land League was banned, the Ladies' Land League continued its work. It was founded in New York on 24 October 1880 by the poet and nationalist Frances [Fanny] Parnell (sister of Charles Stewart Parnell). Anna Parnell (1852–1911), Charles' younger sister, was a also a leading force in the Ladies' Land League after it was publicly launched in Ireland in January 1881. With over 300 branches nationwide, it organised resistance to evictions and gave financial help to evicted tenants. The Catholic Archbishop of Dublin, Edward Cardinal McCabe (1816–85), condemned the League for taking women out of their 'proper place' in the home. Several women were arrested and sent to jail for their League activities.

12.5. In 1896, women were allowed, for the first time, to become Poor Law Guardians. In 1898, women were given the vote in local government elections. In 1899, 85 women were elected Poor Law Guardians and 35 were elected to district councils. These successes further roused women's political awareness.

12.6. During Queen Victoria's last visit to Ireland in 1900 (3–26 April), a group of women led by the nationalist, Maud Gonne (1866–1953), and the Dublin businesswoman, Jennie Wyse Power (1858–1941), organised a vigorous protest. They followed this up by forming Inghinidhe na hÉireann ('Daughters of Ireland'), a nationalist organisation for women. They ran 'buy Irish' campaigns, held free classes for children in Irish, history and music, organised *céilís* and put on plays. The organisation was republican in outlook but by 1914 it had faded away and was replaced by Cumann na mBan ('Women's League').

12.7. Johanna Mary [Hanna] Sheehy-Skeffington (1877–1946) and Margaret Cousins (1878–1954) formed the Irish Women's Franchise League (1908) and demanded 'suffrage first before all else!' The Franchise League held public meetings and demonstrations, lobbied Irish Parliamentary Party MPs, and heckled political leaders, such as MPs John Dillon and John Redmond, who were determined that women should not be given the vote. Dillon stated that 'women's suffrage will, I believe, be the ruin of our western civilisation. It will destroy the home, challenging the headship of man, laid down by God. It may come in your time – I hope not in mine.'

12.8. The twenty years after the second Home Rule Bill (1895) witnessed the rise of militant movements in England and Ireland. In 1903 Emmeline Pankhurst and her daughters established the Women's Social and Political Union in Manchester. The concept of militant action soon spread to Ireland. Thirty-five Irish suffragettes were imprisoned for their actions between 1912 and 1914, and several went on hunger strike. When the Liberal Prime Minister, Herbert H. Asquith (1852–1928), visited Dublin in 1912, two English suffragettes threw a blunt hatchet at his open carriage. Asquith along with Unionist leaders such as Sir Edward Carson and Andrew Bonar Law had little sympathy for their cause. The militant tactics adopted by some activists, while they shocked many observers, failed to win any major concessions.

12.9. Anna Haslam was also a co-founder of the Women's Liberal Unionist Association, but she worked side by side with nationalist and Catholic suffragists in the early twentieth century. In 1911, the Irish Women's Suffrage and Local Government Association and smaller local suffrage societies were absorbed into Louie Bennett's (1870–1956) and Helen Chenevix's (1890–1963) Irish Women's Suffrage Federation. As secretary of the Irish Women Workers' Union, Bennett believed that a strong trade union movement was essential for a thriving Labour Party. This Union was set up as a sister organisation to the Irish Transport and General Workers Union (ITGWU). Delia Larkin (1878–1949) was its first general secretary. One of the most notable Presidents of the Women's Suffrage Federation was the scholar and historian Mary Hayden (1862–1942). When the National University of Ireland was founded (1908), Hayden was the only woman on its Senate (1909–24). She was also a Gaelic scholar closely associated with the Gaelic League and was Professor of Modern Irish History at University College Dublin (1911–38). The distinguished writer George Russell (Æ) (1867–1935) was one of the Federation's vice-presidents.

12.10. The Home Rule crisis of 1912–14 did much damage to the women's suffrage movement. While some women continued to see the fight for the vote as the primary objective, others felt that winning Home Rule or preserving the Union, depending on one's political outlook, was ultimately more important. As a result, the movement split and lost much of its force and energy. The outbreak of the First World War changed everything. As the armies recruited ever-increasing numbers of men, women took jobs outside the home and soon women's work was seen as vital if the war was to be won. Others remained dedicated pacifists, while some devoted themselves to the struggle for Irish independence.

12.11. Cumann na mBan ('Women's League') was founded on 5 April 1914 as an auxiliary to the Irish Volunteers. Membership of the contemporary Irish Citizen Army organised by the Dublin trade unions was open to both sexes. James Connolly had long supported the extension of the franchise to women. However, the Irish Volunteers kept Cumann na mBan in a subordinate role. They were to be nurses, cooks, messengers, and fundraisers. There was no question of their taking part in any fighting 'except in the last extremity'.

12.12. Under the Representation of the People Act, 1918, women over the age of thirty got the vote, despite opposition from the Irish Party and Unionists. Among the first women to exercise the franchise was Anna Haslam at the age of eighty-nine. The Irish Free State constitution of 1922 went further and granted the right to vote to all men and women over the age of twenty-one.

13. The first Sinn Féin party

13.1. Arthur Griffith (1871–1922) is one of the makers of modern Ireland and its most significant nationalist thinker. He provided the inspiration, the ideas, and the leadership of Sinn Féin ('We Ourselves'), a nationalist movement that developed between 1905 and 1908, and came ultimately to shape modern Irish nationalism. Griffith, a patriot and at heart a republican, was politically subtle and culturally sensitive, but he could also be stubborn and narrow-minded. He was a fine writer and journalist. His movement attracted supporters from diverse backgrounds: nationalists, radicals, feminists, artists and writers searching for a new politics, the Dungannon Clubs (an advanced nationalist group founded by Bulmer Hobson (1883–1969) in 1905), the National Council (formed by Griffith and Maud Gonne in 1903 to protest against Edward VII's visit to Dublin), Inghinidhe na hÉireann, Fenians and Home Rulers. It superseded Cumann na nGaedheal, founded by Griffith in 1900. Sinn Féin was the first Irish political party to admit women as full members. The title was suggested to Griffith by Mary Lambert Butler (Máire de Buitléir), a cousin of Sir Edward Carson. Butler said that 'the people of Ireland are a free people and no law made without their authority or consent is, or ever can be, binding on their conscience'.

13.2. The first president of the party was John Sweetman; Griffith and Hobson were vice-presidents. Other prominent members were W.T. Cosgrave, Seán MacDiarmada,

Countess Markievicz, and Seán T. O'Kelly. Sinn Féin's concept of Irish independence was that of Dual Monarchy, that Ireland and Britain should have the same monarch, a concept proposed by Griffith in his *Resurrection of Hungary: a parallel for Ireland* (1904). He hoped to win over Unionists by keeping the King. This idea was based on the Hungarian solution within the Austro-Hungarian Empire. The Hungarian deputies withdrew from the Imperial parliament in Vienna, and established their own parliament in Budapest which the Emperor subsequently recognised in 1867. Griffith saw the Hungarian solution as being similar to Grattan's parliament (1782–1800).

13.3. The movement's newspaper, *Sinn Féin*, was founded and edited by Griffith from 1906 until its suppression in 1914. Here he promoted Sinn Féin's economic policy. This was based largely on the thinking of the German economist Friedrich List (1789–1846), the founding father of economic nationalism and author of *The national system of political economy* (1841). List believed that nationalist energies should be pumped into economic pursuits. Vigorous industry, he argued, was a 'tonic for the national spirit'. Griffith promoted the economic benefits of protective tariffs against English imports. In the words of F.S.L. Lyons, for Griffith 'a protective tariff was as much a factor in emergent nationalism as a country's language, literature or history'. He stressed that 'our declared object was to make England take one hand from Ireland's throat and the other out of Ireland's pocket'. He wanted to develop indigenous industry behind a protectionist barrier:

> … the establishment of protection for Irish industry and commerce by combined action of the County Councils and Local Boards; development of … mineral resources; creation of a national civil service; national control and management of transport and of waste lands; reform of education; non-consumption as far as possible of articles requiring duty to the British Exchequer; non-recognition of the British parliament.

13.4. Initially, these policies had little political impact. The party fought its first by-election on 21 February 1908 when Charles J. Dolan (who had resigned his membership of the Irish Parliamentary Party) contested the seat for Sinn Féin in the North Leitrim. He was defeated by the nationalist, Francis Meehan, by 3,103 votes to 1,157. However, Sinn Féin became a focal point for fringe movements, and Griffith's writings had an important influence on political thinking.

13.5. Some of the more radical members of Sinn Féin accused Griffith of diluting the party's nationalism to make it more acceptable to Unionists and Home Rulers. The fortunes of the Irish Party were revived in 1912 when Asquith introduced the third Home Rule Bill and Sinn Féin declined. The revival of the Irish Republican Brotherhood (IRB) made some of Griffith's young followers impatient with his pacifism. They set up a rival newspaper, *Irish Freedom* (1910), which took many of Griffith's readers and left him on the verge of bankruptcy.

13.6. The suspension of the Home Rule Act until the end of the First World War disappointed many nationalists. There was some revival of interest in Sinn Féin and many nationalists began to describe themselves as 'Sinn Féiners' and the more radical members of the Irish Volunteers called themselves 'Sinn Féin Volunteers'. Griffith still published *Sinn Féin* on an occasional basis. Over the next few years he continued to preach his ideas to a seemingly indifferent world.

14. The Irish Volunteers

14.1. The Irish Volunteer Force (IVF) was founded on 25 November 1913. It following the publication of a call to arms by Eoin MacNeill in *An Claidheamh Soluis* (1 November 1913), the official newspaper of the Gaelic League. In his article, entitled 'The North Began', MacNeill proposed that southern nationalists should form a volunteer movement along the lines of the Ulster Volunteer Force. MacNeill was then approached by Bulmer Hobson of the IRB who organised a public meeting at the Rotunda in Dublin where the new force was established. MacNeill insisted that the purpose of the Irish Volunteers was to defend Home Rule.

14.2. Branches were set up throughout the country and the initial response was strongest in the North. It attracted followers of Sinn Féin and the Gaelic League. It also attracted the IRB who had their own views about the future of the new force. This IRB involvement made John Redmond, the Home Ruler leader, hesitant to support it. Funds were collected through John Devoy (1842–1928) and Clan na Gael in the United States and by Sir Roger Casement (1864–1916) and Alice Stopford Green (1847–1929) in England. In July 1914, Darrell Figgis and Robert Erskine Childers arranged to buy guns in Germany. About 1,500 rifles and 45,000 rounds of ammunition were shipped from Hamburg to Howth, Co. Dublin on board Childers' yacht *Asgard* on 26 July 1914. The event became known as the 'Howth gun-running'. The rifles were quickly distributed to waiting Irish Volunteers who managed to escape with them before the Dublin Metropolitan Police, supported by troops of the King's Own Scottish Borderers arrived to intercept them. Troops returning to barracks opened fire on a hostile crowd in Bachelor's Walk in the city, killing 4 people and injuring over 30.

14.3. There were now two armed volunteer armies in the country and it seemed that Ireland was heading for civil war. The Ulster Volunteer Force had made clear that it would resist Home Rule by all means, and had the support of the Conservatives and their leader, Andrew Bonar Law (1858–1923). Redmond was concerned lest the actions of the Volunteers should prevent the passage of the third Home Rule Bill. To prevent a split the movement, in June 1914 provision was made for 25 nominees of the Irish Parliamentary Party to represent its interests in the Provisional Committee of the Volunteers. When the First World War broke out in August 1914, the government rejected Redmond's offer that Irish Volunteers could act as a defence force for Ireland.

The gesture of Irish nationalist goodwill was calculated to impress British public opinion. The Home Rule Act finally received the Royal Assent on 18 September, despite the walk-out of the entire Conservative opposition. Its operation was suspended until after the war, and the problem of Ulster still had to be revisited.

14.4. There were now 180,000 Irish Volunteers. On 20 September 1914, in an impromptu speech at Woodenbridge, Co. Wicklow, Redmond urged Volunteers to support Britain in the war against Germany 'for the freedom of small nations'. His call was answered by a majority of the Volunteers, who became known as National Volunteers. Many were attracted by the adventure and excitement of war and by the pay. Some argue that Redmond was under great pressure from the Volunteers to make his declaration at Woodenbridge and that, in any case, he could not have prevented most of them from signing up for the war. Most Volunteers flocked to the war effort as enthusiastically as the Ulster Volunteers.

14.5. This left some 12,000 'Irish Volunteers', firmly opposed to involvement in the war. In August 1914 the supreme council of the revitalised IRB decided that a nationwide rebellion should take place before the war ended. The First World War, according to R.F. Foster,

> Should be seen as one of the most decisive events in modern Irish history. Politically speaking, it temporarily defused the Ulster situation; it put Home Rule on ice; it altered the conditions of military crisis in Ireland at a stroke; and it created the rationale for an IRB rebellion.

When the Irish Volunteers were reorganised in October 1914, the three important posts were in the hands of the IRB: Patrick Pearse was director of military organisation; Thomas MacDonagh director of training; and Joseph Plunkett director of military operations. In December 1916 the IRB military council decided upon Easter Sunday, 23 April 1916 as the date for the rising. This Rising and its aftermath changed Irish politics beyond recognition and the Home Rule Act was no longer relevant or acceptable to nationalists.

MAURA CRONIN (WITH A CONTRIBUTION BY FIDELMA MAGUIRE)

CHAPTER 2

Society and economy, 1870–1914

1. Introduction

1.1. The period 1870–1914 was critical in the development of modern Ireland. Social and economic change, already at work and greatly accelerated by the Great Famine, moved rapidly in these years. Some believe that, as a result, late nineteenth-century Ireland became one of the most politically modernised societies in Europe. A new political awareness among the common people was reflected in demands for change at all levels of society. In these years, Belfast became one of the great industrial cities of the British Empire and eastern Ulster formed the heartland of Ireland. Improved communications – in the form of railways, telegraph and better postal services – drew the under-developed West into wider national developments.

2. Marriage and migration

2.1. Other changes were less positive. In these years mass migration became a central feature of Irish society. There were also changes in social practices relating to inheritance, marriage, religious observance and hospitality. This produced a society seen by some as unjust and closed. Some argue that the Irish experience of industrialisation, even in Belfast, was not matched by comparable 'modernisation' in the usual sense. For example, instead of increasing secularisation, usually thought typically 'modern', the power and social influence of the various churches actually increased. One may say that Ireland underwent an incomplete social revolution: many aspects of its social and economic life changed but it remained fundamentally a traditional society. Later and fewer marriages were a marked characteristic of Irish society. For example, in 1901, over half of all women aged between 25 and 34 remained unmarried, a significantly higher proportion than in England and Wales.

2.2. The system of inheritance continued: one child inherited and for the others this often meant emigration. In some families, if the cash brought in by dowry was sufficient, it was used to train other children for a profession. This also involved migration to larger towns and cities. Migration was made easier by improvements in transport and communication, and it became a normal part of life for most Irish families. In the 1870s the rate of migration varied from a high of 16.9 per 1,000 in 1873 to a low of 7.1 per 1,000 in 1876. This increased dramatically in the 1880s as a result of the downturn in agriculture: emigration averaged 16.1 per 1,000 per annum compared to 11.3 for the period 1870–80.

2.3. While emigration was a common in Europe – in Germany, Italy, Norway, Sweden, Poland, Russia and elsewhere – only Ireland had a smaller population in 1900 than in

1800. In certain periods, women emigrants significantly outnumbered men. Over 14,390 women left Ireland between 1901 and 1911, the majority young and single. This reflected the limited opportunities for marriage or employment at home. As a result of this huge outflow Ireland became a country where the very young and the very old were over-represented in the population. Some argue that the continuing emigration of young people enabled Ireland to change in some ways but keep its conservative social structure.

3. Land agitation and land reform

3.1. The Great Famine greatly reduced Ireland's population. It also changed its social make-up. By 1870, starvation and migration had dramatically reduced the numbers of the labourers and cottiers, the largest class in pre-Famine Irish society. 'Strong farmers' were establishing themselves as the dominant social and political class. Their habits and views increasingly became those of society as a whole. One major consequence of this was the agitation for land reform that re-surfaced in this period. Gladstone's Landlord and Tenant (Ireland) Act, 1870, was the first (though unsuccessful) attempt to use legislation to resolve long-standing hostility between those who owned land and those who occupied and worked it.

3.2. Tenants' demands for land reform, particularly their demand for the 3 Fs (fair rent, fixity of tenure, and freedom to sell one's interest in a holding), had been met, in part, despite great opposition in parliament and the assertion by one MP that 'tenant right was landlord wrong'. The Ulster custom was given legal force where it already existed: any tenant evicted for reasons other than non-payment of rent was to be compensated by the evicting landlord. The 'Bright Clauses' in the Act provided for loans of two-thirds of the purchase price to tenants who wished to buy their holdings. Only 877 tenants bought on these terms.

4. Agricultural depression

4.1. The long depression from the mid-1870s to the late 1890s changed the economy. Demand for Irish beef, butter and other products went into a long decline and, in consequence, the incomes of farmers fell. Cheap imports of South American beef, Australian and New Zealand lamb and American grain competed with local produce due to better shipping and new developments in refrigeration. Prices fell sharply and the incomes of farmers fell with them.

4.2. To make matters worse, there was cold wet weather in Ireland for the three successive years from 1877. The growing season of 1879 was the coldest and wettest on record. Grain did not ripen, the potato crop failed in many areas, and hay could not be saved. The total value of all crops in Ireland, estimated at £36.5 million (approximately €2.9 billion at 2009 values) in 1876, fell to £22.7 million (approx. €1.8 billion) in 1879, a drop of almost 38 per cent. Irish labourers failed to find the usual seasonal work on English farms (English farmers, too, were suffering). Competition from new artificial fertilisers greatly weakened the demand for kelp, an important industry on the western seaboard and even the market for eggs and poultry, an important source of income for farmers' wives, failed. Many farmers had to use their savings or credit in 1879 to pay their rent. Poorer farmers without savings or credit were in danger of eviction. Many local shop-keepers, who had given credit, could do so no longer. Evictions increased dramatically from 463 in 1877 to 1,238 in 1879, 2,110 in 1880 and 3,415 in 1881. Meanwhile, poor farm-ers and labourers faced starvation with the near failure of the potato crop. Famine was averted by charity. The Mansion House Committee in Dublin raised £181,665 (approx. €15.6 million at 2009 values) from far and wide – Australia, Europe, Asia, America and Africa – for half-a-million foodless paupers. Charles Stewart Parnell raised £60,000 (approx. €5 million) for famine relief on his 1880 visit to the USA.

5. Rural distress and organisation

5.1. When Michael Davitt visited Mayo in April 1879 he found the county in turmoil. James Daly, editor of the *Connacht Telegraph*, had organised a public meeting in Irishtown, on 20 April, to protest against imminent evictions. It was attended by 10,000 people and there was remarkable solidarity among different classes. It was remarkable, too, in its results – a reduction in rent was granted to many tenants by their landlords. Tenants, their leaders, and politicians such as Parnell and John Devoy of Clan na Gael took note. A further meeting was organised for Westport on 8 June 1879 and, though it was condemned by the Archbishop of Tuam, Parnell agreed to speak. Davitt spoke first, Parnell last. Parnell's powerful speech became a rallying cry for tenants throughout the country and his words were widely reported and often quoted throughout the subse-quent land agitation, known as the Land War. He declared:

> A fair rent is a rent that the tenant can reasonably pay according to the times, but in bad times a tenant cannot be expected to pay as much as he did in good times, three or four years ago. Now what must we do to induce the landlord to see the position? You must show the landlord that you intend to keep a firm grip of your homesteads and lands. You must not allow yourselves to be dispossessed as you were dispossessed in 1847.

6. The Land League

6.1. Michael Davitt set out aims, rules, and principles for a new important organisation, the National Land League of Mayo, which he set up in August 1879. Other counties fol-lowed suit. Two months later, at a meeting in Dublin, Davitt founded the Irish National Land League. Its immediate aims were to reduce rents and prevent evictions. It ulti-mately aimed to end landlordism and to make tenants the owners of the land they farmed. Branches were set up throughout the country and had the widespread support, not only of farmers but also of labourers and shopkeepers. However, there were fewer branches in Ulster where the Ulster Custom gave tenants more protection. The League's popular slogan 'the land of Ireland for the people of Ireland' seemed to promise land to all and few questioned its implicit contradictions. Parnell was elected President, Michael Davitt Secretary, and Joseph Biggar Treasurer. John Dillon, J.J. Louden, Matthew Harris, James Daly were also very active in the League. Fenians played a leading role in this quasi-revolutionary organisation over which Parnell had little control. The financial backing of the American-based Clan na Gael and its leader, John Devoy, was crucial to the success of the League. It is estimated that Irish-Americans contributed over £250,000 (approximately €21.5 million at 2009 values) between 1879 and 1882. This short-lived, though very influential, organisation was first suppressed in 1881 and then replaced in 1882.

7. The Land War, 1879–82

7.1. The harvest of 1880 was good: the threat of famine receded. However, evictions rose as food prices and farmer's incomes continued to fall. Many tenants had exhausted their credit, could not pay rent and faced eviction. The traditional response to evictions had been direct action by tenants. Some joined secret agrarian organisations. Their methods included violence, intimidation, houghing of cattle, burning of hay and grain, the destruction of property and sometimes even murder. The Land League set its face against these groups and urged tenants to achieve their aims by public action, peaceful means and moral persuasion. The Land League held great demonstrations to protest against evictions and brought moral force to bear on the community so that no tenant took the land from which another had been evicted. The aim was to ensure that no landlord could find replacement tenants after an eviction. 'Land grabbers' were fiercely denounced. Parnell, himself a landlord, gave the lead in a speech in Ennis, Co. Clare in 1880 in which he urged people to respond by putting an evicting landlord into a 'moral Coventry,' by isolating him from his kind as if he were a leper of old'.

7.2. Within a week of the Ennis speech moral force was used against Captain Boycott. During a long campaign servants and labourers refused to work for him, shopkeepers refused to serve him and even his post was not delivered. His crops were harvested by volunteer labourers from Ulster sent by the Orange Order who were guarded at great expense by police and soldiers. Finally Captain Boycott's nerve broke and he emigrated. He had given a new word to the English language.

7.3. Besides moral persuasion tenants resorted to the traditional remedies not approved of by the Land League. Violence and intimidation increased as evictions increased. Agrarian outrages rose: 236 in 1877; 301 in 1878; 863 in 1879; 2,585 in 1880 and 4,439 in 1881.

7.4. Prime Minister Gladstone and the Chief Secretary, William E. Forster (1818–86) agreed that reform of Irish land law was necessary and they determined to bring it about. However, the government could not be seen to give into violence, intimidation and boycotting. It thought it necessary to restore order to Ireland first. Forster introduced his Protection of Person and Property Bill early in 1881 which was fiercely obstructed by Parnell and his party – one sitting lasted 41 hours. The rules of debate were changed to give the Speaker the power to close the debate, and the Bill became law. This coercion act gave the authorities power to intern those suspected of encouraging unlawful activities, and leading Land League activists were jailed without trial.

7.5. The way was now clear for Gladstone's second attempt to reform land law in Ireland and he introduced his second Land Act to the House of Commons in April 1881. This Act sought to provide security for tenants by giving them legal rights based on the 3 Fs – Fair Rent, Fixity of Tenure and Freedom of Sale. This Act allowed the fixing of judicial rents for fifteen years by Land Courts and was a radical solution to the land question since it effectively removed the landlords' right to fix the rent payable for land they owned.

7.6. These important concessions satisfied the more wealthy tenant farmers, anxious for lower fixed judicial rents. They no longer needed the support of the Land League and the grand alliance of strong farmer, smallholders, cottiers and labourers was being undermined by the successful Land Act. The Act offered little to the poorest tenants and smallholders of the west of Ireland where the agitation had begun. Those in arrears of rent were excluded from the Land Courts. Leaseholders, too, were unhappy at their exclusion. Parnell and his followers had played a clever political game by supporting the Bill in parliament for the sake of some followers while pointing out its weaknesses and trying to amend it for the sake of others. Parnell's speeches attacking Gladstone landed him and several followers in Kilmainham Jail as suspects. He wrote to Katharine O'Shea from prison: 'Politically it is a fortunate thing for me that I have been arrested, as the movement is breaking up fast'.

7.7. Parnell had warned the government that Captain Moonlight (that is, agrarian terrorism) would take his place if he were arrested. Meanwhile, the Ladies' Land League led by Anna Parnell took over the remnants of the movement while the suspects were in prison. They gave help to those evicted, built Land League cabins for them, and organised resistance to evictions. Agrarian violence grew as evictions of those in arrears increased while the leaders, particularly Davitt, whose brilliance as organiser was sorely missed, were in prison The 'No Rent Manifesto' issued by the imprisoned leaders, 14 October 1882, was condemned by the clergy and the press and had little effect beyond impoverishing Parnell himself whose tenants followed his instructions and did not pay him rent. It gave Forster an 'excellent excuse', as he said, and he issued a proclamation, 20 October 1882, suppressing the Land League as 'an unlawful and criminal association'.

7.8. Strong farmers, meanwhile, were getting rent reductions of around 20 per cent in the Land Courts and some few hundred of them were buying out their holdings with 75 per cent loans at 5 per cent over 35 years, the terms offered by the 1881 Act.

7.9. Parnell was anxious to get out of jail for personal, health and political reasons. Both he and Gladstone were appalled at the growing violence. After negotiations between Captain William O'Shea for Parnell and Joseph Chamberlain for Gladstone a gentleman's agreement, known as the Kilmainham Treaty, was arranged. Gladstone agreed to amend the 1881 Land Act to include leaseholders, to give grants to tenants to pay their arrears so that they, too, could get judicial rents fixed by the Land Courts, to release the leaders and to end coercion. Parnell promised to try to end violence and to calm the country and to cooperate with Gladstone and the Liberal Party in bringing in reforms. Parnell and the other suspects were released from jail, on 2 May 1882, and Davitt, on ticket of leave, on 4 May 1882.

7.10. Davitt, Dillon, Fenians and other activists disliked the Kilmainham Treaty but kept quiet about their objections. Chief Secretary Forster resigned in protest but Gladstone replaced him with his beloved godson Lord Frederick Cavendish. On the day they were to take office – 6 May 1882 – Cavendish and Under Secretary Thomas H. Burke were brutally murdered in the Phoenix Park, by the Invincibles, a small, extremist group. Parnell was shattered, feared the ruin of all he had worked for and even considered retiring from politics. The murders were greeted with horror and outrage in Britain. Gladstone brought in a new Coercion Act. Parnell now withdrew his promise to cooperate with the Liberal Party.

7.11. However, all was not lost. The Arrears of Rent (Ireland) Act, 1882, provided grants which allowed 100,000 poor tenants to pay their arrears and bring claims to the Land Courts for rent reductions which were generally granted. As a result there were fewer evictions, and consequently fewer agrarian outrages. The Labourers' (Ireland) Act, 1883, enabled local authorities to borrow money on security of rates to build dwellings for agricultural labourers, and was much resented by the ratepayers.

7.12. Land reform was also a concern of the caretaker Conservative government of 1885 and Lord Ashbourne, the Irish Lord Chancellor, introduced effective land purchase measures. The Purchase of Land (Ireland) Act ['Ashbourne Act'], 1885 (which Ashbourne drafted almost single-handedly), made £5 million (approx. €425 million at 2009 values) available to provide 100 per cent loans at 4 per cent interest over 49 years. A very successful Act, it allowed 25,000 tenants to buy their holdings. In 1889 Arthur James Balfour (1848–1930) provided another £5 million (approx. €425 million) to extend its operation and land purchase became an enlightened and key policy of Conservative governments thereafter. He went on to introduce the Purchase of Land (Ireland) Act ['Balfour Act'] in 1891. The Act also established the Congested Districts Board. Balfour wanted it to be a 'heroic measure' to solve the land question. It provided £33 million (approx. €3 billion) for 100 per cent loans to be paid back over 49 years. However, the mechanism for buying land stock that went up and down on the market, was unpopular with landlords and tenants alike. Nonetheless, it was the most successful land purchase act to date and it enabled 47,000 tenants to buy, though these results disappointed Balfour.

7.13. Balfour had to contend with the Plan of Campaign, launched by John Dillon, Timothy Harrington and William O'Brien in the pages of *United Ireland*, 23 October 1886. According to that Plan, the demands of tenants for further rent reductions should be achieved by collective action on each estate. Tenants were to offer the landlord a rent they could afford and if he refused they were to put it into an estate fund to support evicted tenants. Farms were to be left empty in the case of eviction and land grabbers were to be boycotted. The Plan was in force on 116 estates by the end of 1886. Parnell opposed the Plan and Balfour was determined to crush it.

7.14. In 1887 Balfour, true to his word, amended the 1881 Land Act. The 1887 Land Law (Ireland) Act gave the land courts the power to fix rents of leaseholders, to reconsider rents every three years, and to adjust them in line with shifts in agricultural prices. Most rents were reduced further, on average by 15 per cent. This legislation gave Irish tenants substantial protection and put them in a far stronger position than their English or Scottish equivalents.

7.15. Balfour encouraged landlords to band together to oppose the Plan of Campaign. He also introduced the Perpetual Crimes Act (or 'Coercion Act'), 1887, which gave power to declare certain organisations illegal, to proclaim that certain districts were disturbed and to introduce special courts that sat without a jury in 'proclaimed' districts. On 60 of the 116 estates landlords gave into tenants; on 24 estates terms were agreed after agitation; on 15 estates tenants went back on the landlord's terms; and on 18 estates no settlement was reached by the end of the century; and in these cases many of the evicted tenants did not return to their holdings until 1907. The Plan of Campaign was extremely costly and certain ventures such as the building of New Tipperary for the evicted tenants of Tipperary town were expensive failures.

7.16. Balfour was succeeded as Chief Secretary by his brother Gerald in 1895. In 1899, Gerald Balfour was responsible for setting up Department of Agriculture and Technical Instruction. Horace Plunkett was put in charge and he attempted to improve Irish farming. Agricultural instructors brought new knowledge and techniques to country people and though some innovations were adopted speedily, such as spraying potatoes with copper sulphate to prevent blight, change was mostly gradual and slow.

7.17. William O'Brien started the United Irish League in 1898 to agitate for the division of large farms or ranches as he termed them among smallholders. He also demanded a new land purchase bill. Soon he had over 100,000 followers. The government did not want another land war.

7.18. George Wyndham was appointed Chief Secretary in 1900. Like his first cousins, the Balfour brothers, he too was interested in reform. When Captain John Shawe-Taylor (a cousin of Lady Gregory) wrote to the *Irish Times* on 2 September 1902 proposing a land conference to plan a new land bill, Wyndham responded positively. The conference was held in Dublin in December 1902. The unanimous report formed the basis of Wyndham's Land Act, which passed into law in 1903. Landlords were encouraged to sell their whole estates and were offered a 12 per cent bonus if they did so. Tenants got 100 per cent loans at an interest rate of 3.25 per cent over 68 years and the tenant's annual repayment was less than the previous fixed rent. The legal costs of transfer were met out of public funds. The success of Wyndham's Land Act was immediate. By 1909 as many as 270,000 tenants had bought and a further 46,000 were buying and by 1920 nine million acres of Irish land had changed hands. Within a decade landlordism was virtually a thing of the past. An extraordinary transformation had taken place in the ownership of the land, peaceably for the most part. Thus the demand for land reform was ended, but not, as the British government had hoped, the demand for Home Rule.

8. The Congested Districts Board

8.1. Arthur Balfour, Chief Secretary for Ireland, driven by his conviction that state paternalism was necessary to remedy the special problems of isolation, poverty, and unemployment that beset the West of Ireland, established the Congested Districts Board in his Land Act of 1891. Under the Act parts of Cork, Kerry, Galway, Mayo, Roscommon, Leitrim and Galway came under the Board's area of jurisdiction. By 1901, it was responsible for an area of nearly 3.7 million acres inhabited by half a million people. Later another 3 million acres were added.

8.2. The Board was staffed with sympathetic and well-informed persons and it was given financial independence. Its purpose was to develop the West of Ireland, to relieve poverty by paying for public works, such as the construction of piers at small ports on the west coast to help fishing, building roads and bridges, and sponsoring local factories to give employment and reduce emigration. It surveyed and identified the problems.

8.3. From 1909 the Board had a large annual budget of £250,000 (approx. €30 million at current values). It improved the economy by giving credit and by subsidising new industries and agricultural products. It purchased land for tenants and re-distributed it in economic holdings. In fact, it bought over 2,000,000 acres of land from which it created or improved 60,000 farms. It spent a total of £2 million (approx. €203 million) on improvements to land, farm buildings, drainage, roads, and fences. It also built over 3,000 houses for smaller farmers and renovated over 6,000 more. It encouraged a wide range of cottage industries – bee-keeping, spinning, knitting, crochet, lace-work, carpentry, kelp-gathering – and taught invaluable skills, for example, in domestic economy, poultry and egg production, and horse-breeding. Among the successful industries encouraged by the Board were Foxford Woollen Mills and Killybegs Carpets. It employed agricultural instructors to advise farmers. It vigorously promoted the fishing industry: it built piers, gave capital grants to fishermen for boats and tackle and introduced marketing strategies. The sales of fish more than trebled between 1891 and 1913. And by 1912, the board had assets of £530,000 (approx. €45 million at 2009 values). Michael Davitt, who ironically described the Board as 'enlightened state socialism', wrote:

> though opinions differ as to the amount of good done by this body there can be no doubt that much benefit has been conferred by its labours upon the several districts comprised within its area.

8.4. The nationalist Frank Hugh O'Donnell (1848–1916) sharply criticised the Board in 1908 for giving money to the Catholic clergy to establish industrial schools where poor young workers were exploited and badly paid. He felt that capital loaned to real businesses would be more effective than advancing money to parish councils run by priests that were not properly supervised.

8.5. The Board, however, brought immense benefits. It is the ancestor of all modern regional development agencies, a highly advanced arm of government of a kind not seen elsewhere in the United Kingdom for many decades to come.

9. The Co-operative Movement

9.1. Improvements in transport were critical to the success of another great experiment in Irish economic development, the Co-operative Movement. The country's first co-operative society was the Ralahine Agricultural and Manufacturing Co-operative Association established by John Scott Vandaleur in Co. Clare (1831). This early venture failed when Vandaleur lost his estate through gambling. A fresh start was made in the late 1880s through the strenuous and tireless efforts of Sir Horace Plunkett (1854–1932), helped by Revd Thomas Finlay (1848–1940) and George W. Russell (known as Æ) (1867–1935). They sought to put Irish farmers in charge of their own destinies by attempting to improve methods and distribution. They looked to the co-operative movement of Denmark for inspiration as prosperous Danish farmers supplied much of the butter and bacon products in the British market. The first co-operative creamery was opened in Dromcollogher, Co. Limerick, in 1889. The growth of the organisation was impressive. By the end of 1891 there were 17 creameries, increasing to 33 co-operative creameries and 13 co-operative agricultural societies by 1894 when Plunkett formed the Irish Agricultural Organisation Society (IAOS) in Dublin. The Doneraile Agricultural Bank was established in Co. Cork in the following year. Another organisation, the Irish Co-operative Agricultural Agency Society Ltd (ICAAS), was founded in Dublin on 15 January 1897 to source quality supplies for co-operative societies, particularly seeds and fertilisers. It was renamed the Irish Agricultural Wholesale Society Ltd (IAWS) in December 1897. The co-operative spread its ideas through its weekly journal the *Irish Homestead* (1895), which was edited by George Russell.

9.2. By 1900, there were 171 large creameries, 65 auxiliary facilities, 106 agricultural societies and 76 credit societies. The movement claimed a membership of over 46,000 and an annual turnover of nearly £800,000 (approx. €92 million at current values). By 1915, there were 344 co-operative creameries and 219 agricultural societies. Raising sufficient capital proved to be an initial problem for the movement. Many feared financial reliance on merchants and dealers and the banks generally sought adequate guarantees for finance. Some financial support was provided by the Department of Agriculture and Technical Instruction for new pasteurising plants. The Carnegie Trust made the Society an annual grant of £500 (for five years) from 1899 and additional grants were provided by county councils throughout the country. However, during the First World War state funds from the Development Commission and Congested Districts Board were temporarily withdrawn. The creameries did much to improve standards of dairy husbandry and milk quality. Creamery co-operatives became some of the largest firms in the country. In the meat sector, livestock marts throughout the country became very successful, although meat processing co-operatives did not enjoy great success.

10. Education

10.1. Education prepared those children who did not inherit the land for other employments or for migration. Ireland was far ahead of Britain in education because of the national system of education, introduced in 1831 under Chief Secretary Edward G. Stanley. He was a keen advocate of non-denominational education. By 1900 there were 8,684 national schools in Ireland. Though there was some regional variation, overall levels of illiteracy (a standard measure of the development of any society) fell rapidly, from 53 per cent in 1841 to 18 per cent in 1891. Most of those unable to read and write were older people. Irish children had the benefits of a standardised syllabus and the attentions of inspectors whose task was to ensure that a good standard of education was kept throughout the country.

10.2. The Intermediate Education (Ireland) Act, 1878, funded secondary education on a payment-by-results basis and made it more widely available. Payments of between £3 and £10 were made to schools for students who passed the Intermediate Examinations. The government grant for the national schools increased from £125,000 (approx. £14 million at 2009 values) to £1.14 million (approx. £131 million) in 1900. Further finance was provided under the National Teachers' Residences (Ireland) Act, 1875, whereby funding was provided for the construction of schools with residences attached. This funding allowed for the great advance in the provision of education generally, particularly for girls. Students could sit any number of subjects but they had to include two of the following: Latin, Greek, English, mathematics and modern languages. The marks allocated to subjects varied. Latin, Greek, English and mathematics were worth 1,200 marks; German and French 700, Celtic (Irish) 600. Valuable exhibitions (scholarships) were awarded on a candidate's aggregate marks. Girls' schools competed on an equal basis, and the curriculum in girls' schools changed dramatically as a result. Because school funding and exhibitions depended directly on the marks of the candidates in the Intermediate Examination girls did the high-value subjects (Latin, Greek, English, and mathematics), despite objections from many that such studies were damaging to girls, and unladylike.

10.3. The Irish Education Act, 1892, abolished fees in national schools and made school attendance compulsory for children between the ages of six and fourteen. However, it applied only to towns and made allowances for children to help with farming and fishing. By 1900, over 770,000 children were enrolled although less than two-thirds attended regularly.

10.4. Because most schools were under effective or actual clerical control, they tended to reinforce the influence of the clergy and harden religious divisions. In 1862, 53 per cent of Irish schools were inter-denominational. By 1900, this number had fallen to 35 per cent. Nonetheless, the schools themselves were to create a major social revolution and generated a vast number of new 'lower-middle class' professional jobs. By 1874, the Catholic schools alone employed 2,640 college-trained and 5,000 other teachers. A further 800 teachers worked in Church of Ireland schools. By 1901 there were 20,478 teachers in Ireland, 60 per cent of whom were female, earning about 80 per cent of the corresponding male wage. In 1883, teacher training college were opened for men at St Patrick's College Drumcondra, Dublin and for women at Our Lady of Mercy College, Blackrock, Co. Dublin.

10.5. A dark chapter in Irish education began with the Industrial Schools Act of 1868 that established industrial schools for 'neglected, orphaned and abandoned children'. There was a building boom in the provision of premises for these schools: by 1875, there were 50 industrial schools, by 1898 there were 71. By 1884, according to a parliamentary statement, there were 5,199 Roman Catholic children in these schools (one in every 761 of the Roman Catholic population), and 850 Protestant children (one in every 1,365 of the Protestant population), and there were applications for more. The schools for Catholics were paid for by the government and run by Catholic clergy, Christian Brothers and various orders of brothers and nuns. From the beginning, there were serious complaints (by Frank Hugh O'Donnell MP, Sir Rowland Blennerhassett and others) about these schools, the treatment of the children, filth, inadequate diet and the absence of education or training. There were also serious complaints about the sweated labour of young girls in convent lace-making establishments, run for profit by the convents but heavily funded by the Congested Districts Board.

10.6. The Royal University of Ireland was founded in accordance with the University Education (Ireland) Act, 1879, as an examining and degree awarding university. It allowed females to finally take university degrees on the same basis as males. In fact, many religious schools (for example, Dominican College, Eccles St, Dublin; Alexandra College, Dublin; Loreto College, St Stephen's Green, Dublin; Methodist College,

Belfast; High School for Girls, Derry; Rutland School, Mountjoy Square, Dublin; Dominican College, Sion Hill, Dublin; St Angela's College, Cork; St Louis', Monaghan, Presentation College, Cork; Christian Brothers' College, Cork; Rochelle College, Cork) prepared students for the examinations (including degree examinations) of the Royal University. Catholic girls' schools were slower than Protestant girls' school in doing so but, despite the opposition of senior Catholic leaders, the more progressive religious orders gradually began to enter their female students for the university examinations.

10.7. Progress was, nevertheless, slow and most universities remained male bastions. In 1901, over 1,350 men and 400 women passed the Royal University examinations. In response to the demands of Catholic bishops, the Irish Universities Act, 1908, established two new universities, the National University of Ireland (comprising the existing Queen's Colleges of Cork and Galway together with University College Dublin) and the Queen's University of Belfast. The non-denominational National University was not allowed to have chairs of theology or sacred scripture. In practice, it was Catholic-controlled. Lack of demand from industry meant that technical education was largely underdeveloped. The Royal College of Science (1845) had only about 50 students in 1900. The Samuelson Commission on Technical Education (1884) recognised the need for change and in 1899 the Department of Agriculture and Technical Instruction (DATI) was established to assist county councils with grants, specialist advice, standards and examinations. It also helped to develop a science curriculum. Although lack of finance and trained staff proved to be problems, by 1903 most Irish counties had a technical schools offering subjects like science, building construction, drawing, crafts, commerce, domestic economy, and needlework.

11. Employment

11.1. 'Modernisation' itself created growing employment for the sons and daughters of farmers. Local government, the police force and the civil service provided ever-increasing employment. The well-educated could gain access to these jobs through competitive examinations and selection. The role of the civil servant in many aspects of life became increasingly important as government expanded in the later nineteenth century. The Post Office, a large organisation, spread across Ireland, changing the whole structure of rural life. Local government also expanded and carried out a wide range of functions including poor relief and other welfare activities.

11.2. Overall, between 1881 and 1901, there was a 17 per cent increase in the number of persons employed in government in Ireland. By 1901, there were 34,281 government employees in total, one for every 104 inhabitants of Ireland (excluding the armed forces). This compared to one for every 127 for the United Kingdom as a whole, and one for every 128 for England and Wales.

11.3. Ireland's police force, controlled from and reporting to Dublin Castle, also increased in size and expanded its functions as the nineteenth century went on. Unlike

their English counterparts, Irish policemen took the census, compiled agricultural statistics, undertook surveys, reported contagious diseases, and acted as the eyes and ears of
the Dublin government in every town and rural area. Policemen in other parts of the
United Kingdom were under county or borough control and had much more limited
functions than their Irish equivalents.

11.4. The Post Office was regarded as the pioneer of women's employment, offering positions as telegraph operators or counter hands to intelligent, educated working-class girls.
The country's first civil service typist took up her post in the Department of Agriculture
and Technical Instruction in 1901. Guinness' Brewery held its first examinations for four
lady clerkships in June 1906. By 1914, almost 8,000 women were employed as clerks, the
fastest-growing area of female employment in the twentieth century. For those middle-
class girls, benefiting from the academic curriculum offered by increasing numbers of
colleges and convent schools, the Universities Act of 1879 offered further opportunities
for access to the professions. However, progress was very slow. For example, despite
women's very important role in nursing, only 33 qualified female medical doctors and 68
female medical students are recorded in the census of 1911.

12. Industrialisation

12.1. Urbanisation and industrialisation are important elements in 'modernisation'.
These tended to be limited and regional in late nineteenth-century Ireland. These developments were heavily concentrated in eastern Ulster. Belfast was one of the fastest growing urban industrial centres in the United Kingdom during these years. Its population
increased from about 174,000 to almost 387,000 by 1911 (122 per cent growth). In the
1870s and 1880s the number of houses quadrupled as streets of terraced 'kitchen-and-
parlour' houses were built to accommodate the workers from the mills, factories, and
shipyards. In 1870, the shipyard of Harland and Wolff built a floating dry-dock and
launched five vessels with a total tonnage of 15,571. In 1913, the city's yards completed sixteen vessels with a combined tonnage of 147,489, and the 48,158-ton giant *Britannic* was
about to be launched. The city attracted migrants from other areas of Ireland and from
the rest of the United Kingdom. Throughout this period up to a quarter of Belfast's population was born outside the counties of Antrim and Down, and the proportion of out-
siders in the active labour force was considerably higher. Belfast was a thriving industrial
boom-town at the centre of a heavily industrialised region.

12.2. Why was the Irish experience so localised? If industry could fuel massive growth in
Belfast or Derry, why not in Dublin or Cork? In fact, there is nothing unusual, in many
ways, about the Irish experience. No country underwent industrialisation evenly or universally. Rather, it occurred in those areas that enjoyed the advantages of effective communications or a good supply of raw materials. In Ireland's case the north-east was
geographically close to northern English and Scottish coalfields. It also had a strong local

tradition of domestic craft industries that formed the basis of industrial development. In contrast, southern cities tended to be commercial and transport hubs rather than manufacturing centres, and did not develop extensive industrial activity. The most-often quoted example of failed industrialisation in this era is Dublin, which certainly performed poorly compared to Belfast, and as a result suffered some of the worst social conditions in nineteenth-century Britain.

12.3. However, the contrast has often been overstated. Dublin had some very successful industries, such as the brewing giant Guinness and the biscuit-maker Jacobs, but neither of these could provide the volume of employment that shipbuilding or linen did in Belfast. Moreover, it must be recognised that Dublin was very much a capital city and, like London and Edinburgh, the white-collar employment sector was far more significant than in Belfast. So too was casual unskilled employment and domestic service. Much of the difference between Dublin and Belfast in the later nineteenth century had to do with different economic functions and employment patterns: capital cities seldom become industrial centres.

12.4. These economic differences go a long way to explain the emergence of working-class Unionism within the industrial towns and cities of Ulster in the wake of the first Home Rule Bill (1886). For workers in the linen and shipbuilding industries of the north-east, the policy of economic development protected by tariff barriers, put forward by Irish nationalists, was nonsense. Few of the ships built in Belfast were for Irish owners and only a small proportion of the linen and finished goods produced in Ulster was sold on the domestic market. The establishment of tariff barriers to protect fledgling industries in the south of Ireland would, Unionists argued, deprive the successful manufactures in the north of the export markets on which they depended. This economic argument was perhaps the strongest and most coherent Unionist objection to Home Rule and one that nationalists failed to answer.

13. Improvements in health care

13.1. In the later nineteenth century, Irish society generally experienced improving living standards and there emerged a prosperous middle class in both rural and urban areas. Family size remained large – over a third of married women in 1911 (36 per cent) had seven children or more. Some aspects of health care improved. Under the Medical Poor Relief (Ireland) Act of 1851 a system of local dispensaries had been established. This gave Ireland a system of medical care not matched in England until the National Insurance Act of 1911, if not the introduction of the Welfare State in the 1940s.

13.2. But even in the early decades of the twentieth century, childbirth was life-threatening for many mothers. Geographical location and social class were major determining factors in mortality. Irish infant mortality rates as a whole were fairly low by European standards, but babies born in urban areas were almost twice as vulnerable as those born in the country: the urban infant mortality rate was 150 per 1,000 live births, rural mortality was 74. A baby born into the family of a labourer was seventeen times more likely to die within a year than the child of a professional.

13.3. However, pre-natal and infant care was a major concern in most Western European countries in this period, and Ireland was no exception. A growing body of health visitors and voluntary workers visited the poor to offer advice and practical help. From 1908 the Women's National Health Association operated mother and baby clubs in Dublin and Belfast. Babies were weighed, doctors were on hand to provide medical advice, and nurses visited homes to ensure that their advice on feeding and hygiene was acted on. The provision of free or cheap pasteurised milk was probably the most effective part of the work of this Association: infant mortality dropped where this was introduced.

13.4. Among young adults, male and female, the greatest danger to health in late nineteenth-century Ireland was tuberculosis (TB). Death rates from 'the white plague' rose rapidly among the 15–25 age groups (more than 11,500 deaths a year) at a time when deaths from other diseases were in decline. There was considerable local variation. The highest death rates were in areas of high population density, such as Belfast where conditions in the linen mills made workers particularly liable to infection. At the beginning of the twentieth century only two sanitoria – Crooksling in Co. Wicklow and Heatherside in Co. Cork – had been built by local authorities. Sufferers, therefore, had little option but to go to the fever hospital, and many were unlikely to ever return. In this context, the Women's National Health Association launched an intensive educational campaign, involving travelling exhibitions that brought both entertainment and enlightenment to rural areas. Between 1905 and 1918, better economic and social conditions, improving standards of domestic hygiene, and public recognition of the dangers of infection combined to reduce the annual number of deaths from TB by about a quarter.

14. Housing

14.1. Health was obviously affected by standards of housing, and experience in this area varied greatly. It was noted in 1911 that nearly every family in Belfast had its own house. There was a range of styles and rents available for different groups of workers. Further advances were made when the Housing of the Working Class (Ireland) Act, 1908, gave local authorities the power to build houses and to establish funds to support home construction. Belfast, like most cities, had its share of slums and health problems. Nonetheless, it contrasted strongly with Dublin where the great Georgian terraces, formerly the luxurious and comfortable homes of the gentry, were now divided into filthy cramped accommodations for over 21,000 families. An enquiry in 1914 reported that 28,000 Dubliners were living in houses considered 'unfit for human habitation'. Largely as a result of the unsettled nature of early twentieth-century political life, poor conditions prevailed until well into the 1940s. Indeed, in some cases they got worse. Housing conditions in rural areas varied considerably, but by the early years of the twentieth century it was reported that around 70 per cent of the rural population lived in houses classed by officials as 'good farmhouses' or better.

15. The coming of the railway

15.1. One of the most important developments in Ireland, and one that affected the lives of everyone, was the building of a railway system. In 1872, there were already 2,000 miles of track. By 1914, there were 3,400 miles of track and the rural community was now effectively linked into the transport system. It has been claimed that the railway was a negative influence on Ireland, economically and socially: it made emigration easier and opened the Irish market to cheap imported goods that quickly destroyed Irish local industries, which were unable to compete in scale and cost.

15.2. Certain groups in Ireland benefited greatly from the coming of the railway. If small local industries were put out of business by cheaper rail-assisted imports, the Irish consumer benefited from cheaper prices and improved choice and this stimulated the retail sector. Some historians claim that these developments benefited English or Scottish producers and damaged Irish firms, but this ignores the fact that some Belfast and Dublin companies were very successful in using the railways to increase their customer base. The prime example of this is the Dublin brewer Guinness. Its successful domination of the Irish beer market was based on effective communications and transport throughout the whole island of Ireland.

15.3. The railways greatly accelerated the commercialisation of Irish agriculture by opening up new markets to Irish producers and allowing perishable goods to be moved quickly and safely. By the end of the nineteenth century insulated railway vans enabled the shipment of fish from the western seaboard to markets in Dublin and even in Britain. Eggs, traditionally too fragile to transport over long distances, became a major Irish export. This trade raised the incomes of Irish farmers and fowl numbers greatly increased in the later nineteenth century. Railways were very much a life-changing experience for the Irish in the last decades of the nineteenth century, giving the rural population access to cheap consumer goods and improved markets on the one hand, while destroying local industries and traditional life styles on the other.

16. The Labour Movement and the 1913 Lockout

16.1. This period closes with one of the few examples of class conflict that might be said to challenge our interpretation of change in pre-First World War Ireland. The period between 1909 and 1913 was one of acute hardship for the unskilled workers of Dublin. They, with their families, formed perhaps a third of the city's population and were a rich recruiting ground for the newly established Irish Transport and General Workers Union (ITGWU) under the leadership of James Larkin (1874–1947).

16.2. In 1911, Larkin called on the employers to enter into discussions, but William Martin Murphy (1844–1919), the leader of the Employers' Federation which represented nearly 400 employers in the city, rejected this. The employers were determined to resist any attempt to unionise unskilled labour and effectively declared war on Larkin and his Union. Crisis was reached in August 1913 when the employers issued a united demand that their workers sign a written undertaking not to join the ITGWU or any other union. The employers sacked the workers who refused their demand. Larkin retaliated by calling out the workers in Murphy's Dublin United Tramways Company and 700 of the company's 1,700 employees walked off the job. This action resulted in mounting industrial conflict characterised by bitterness and violence on both sides.

16.3. In early September, the Employers' Federation decided to lockout their workers in order to break their resistance. By the end of the month, 25,000 workers were said to be affected. Although the employers' actions were widely condemned, they refused to consider negotiation or compromise with the Union. Finally, under mounting public and government pressure, the Employers' Federation agreed to negotiations organised through the British Trades Union Congress (TUC) in December 1913. However, these broke down on 20 December 1913 without a resolution. By early 1914, financial and food aid from Britain, America and Europe were slowly drying up, there was no sign of a compromise from Murphy's members, and the clergy were urging workers to return. The strikers' determination began to crumble. Any hope of continued resistance collapsed in February 1914 when the TUC announced it was winding up its relief fund. By the end of the month, the dispute which came to be known as the 'Lockout', was over and the employers claimed victory.

17. A conservative society

17.1. The process of modernisation is a highly complex one but certainly the shifts in Irish society do not seem to fit the typical 'modernisation' pattern. Ireland was changing at a dramatic pace though, and the social and economic order that had emerged by 1914 was more easily recognised as 'modern' than that of 1870. These developments can be seen as largely positive in many ways. However, as with all social and economic change, there were costs that certain groups in Irish society had to pay in order that others might benefit. One has to ask whether the costs of change were greater than the benefits. Certainly Ireland emerged as a stable and socially conservative country that did not suffer excessive upheaval during its period of change. The country achieved this only through high levels of emigration. The removal of potentially discontented elements within Irish society allowed it to develop in a way that was stable but not innovative. In fact, emigration ensured that modernised Ireland was deeply conservative.

MYRTLE HILL, JOHN LYNCH (WITH A CONTRIBUTION BY FIDELMA MAGUIRE)

CHAPTER 3

Culture and religion, 1870–1914

1. Introduction

1.1. Major changes in institutional religion had already taken place at the beginning of this period. For most congregations this was a time of consolidation. Pastoral, spiritual and missionary activity reflected the dynamic nature of Irish religious life. Churches were deeply involved in influencing and directing the social and moral lives of their flocks. They also provided leadership in the political arena, supporting or challenging proposals for constitutional change. While there were many rich and distinct areas of secular cultural activity, religion also had a major impact on leisure time and intellectual activities. At the end of the period, as political movements helped shape developing nationalist and unionist ideas, cultural life in Ireland became sharply divided along religious lines.

2. Religious denominations in Ireland, 1870–1914

2.1. While telling us little about the practice of faith, census statistics allow us to outline the religious make-up of Ireland's population in the post-Famine era. A little over three-quarters (76.9 per cent) of the Irish population belonged to the Catholic Church, 12.34 per cent were Anglican, and 9.2 per cent were Presbyterian. The most important of the minority religions were Methodists at 8 per cent, and 'others' – Baptists, Brethren, Quakers, etc. – together amounted to less than 1 per cent. By the beginning of the First World War there had been a slight decrease in the number of Catholics (73.86 per cent), and slight increases in Anglicans (13.13 per cent) and Presbyterians (10.04 per cent). There were also important changes in other congregation sizes: Methodists by 1914 made up 1.42 per cent of the population, and others accounted for 1.55 per cent.

2.2. However, the most important aspect of the religious make-up of Ireland remained the concentration of Protestants in the North-East. Although their majority in the nine counties of Ulster as a whole was minimal (they were, in fact, in a minority in Donegal, Cavan, Monaghan and Fermanagh), they were particularly strong in Antrim and Down. The decline of southern Protestantism was well under way even before the First World War. The geographical trends in religion affected, and were affected by, wider trends in the political, social and cultural arenas.

3. The Church of Ireland

3.1. Since the Reformation, the Church of Ireland had been the official state church although its members made up only one-eighth of the population. Both Catholics and

Presbyterians resented this privileged position. Following the Fenian insurrection of 1867, Gladstone made Disestablishment part of his programme for pacifying Ireland. Census returns and a series of parliamentary inquiries confirmed the image of an establishment whose wealth and political power contrasted sharply with its minority position. Despite strong objections by the Queen, the opposition parties and the Church of Ireland itself, Gladstone's Irish Church Act became law on 26 July 1869.

3.2. In the period immediately following this separation of Church and State, the Church of Ireland began administrative and financial reconstruction, and a reassessment of its place in Irish society. Not surprisingly, the hierarchy, clergy and laity of the Anglican Church in Ireland implemented their new regime with what has been described as 'cautious conservatism'. Financial concerns were uppermost in the minds of the first General Convention, which met at the beginning of 1870, and were the concern of the new Representative Church Body (RCB), an unknown and untested organisation. However, a majority of the clergy agreed to commute the annuities to which they were entitled to lump sums. These funds were then placed with the RCB, which was, in turn, responsible for the payment of clerical salaries. A Sustentation Fund was established to meet the long-term needs of the Church, and by 1906 it had raised £6,500,000 (approx. €750 million at 2009 values). A mixture of generosity and sound investment reflected the willingness of the Anglicans to accept responsibility for their religious institutions. This ensured the Church of Ireland's financial security.

3.3. New administrative arrangements included the election of bishops by diocesan synods and voting arrangements that gave the laity a strong say in church matters. Within a decade of its legal separation from the state, the Church of Ireland stood independent and stronger. Subsequent change was slow, more a matter of consolidation than reform. Attempts were made to standardise clerical salaries and the number of curates in smaller parishes was reduced. Although there was some rebuilding and renovation of church buildings, the major work in this area took place in Belfast, which was rapidly outgrowing the old parish structure. By 1914, the city had a total of 34 parishes, with 37 churches.

3.4. In both rural and urban congregations, Bible and Sunday school classes were supplemented by organisations such as Friendly Societies, Bands of Hope, ladies organisations, the Young Men's Christian Association (YMCA) and Young Women's Christian Association (YWCA). A Social Services committee was established in 1899, and in 1911 the General Synod united with the Presbyterian General Assembly to deal with issues such as temperance and industrial schools.

3.5. The *Ne temere* decree promulgated by Pope Pius X in 1907 (and which came into effect in April, 1908) insisted that an inter-faith marriage had to be celebrated by a Catholic priest if it was to be valid under Catholic canon law. The children of a mixed marriage should also be baptised as Catholics and educated in Catholic schools. The Catholic partner also undertook to encourage their spouse to follow the true faith. This ensured that Protestant–Catholic relations continued to be tense in this area.

3.6. Foreign missions were also important, and the Church of Ireland was able to claim in 1914 that 266 of its members had answered the call to service abroad. By the end of this period, the Church of Ireland had demonstrated its renewed spiritual strength but, like the other Protestant denominations, a major focus for its energies, from the 1880s onward, was the new and more dangerous threat posed by Home Rule.

4. The Roman Catholic Church

4.1. Disestablishment affected all religious institutions in Ireland and while Catholics rejoiced in the ending of Church of Ireland privilege, the loss of the government grant to Maynooth seminary was a less satisfactory consequence. Members of the Catholic hierarchy were also disappointed in their hope of a redistribution of original church lands that had become the property of the Established Church in the course of the Reformation. This was, in the main though, a period of continued growth and consolidation for the Irish Catholic Church. Held in high regard by the majority of its community, its income from the voluntary contributions of its members and its place in society were secure. Religious life in towns, and increasingly in villages and rural areas, was centred on the chapel. Individuals and families depended on the Church for the celebration of the rites of passage – baptism, marriage and death. Sunday mass and a range of sodalities, societies and devotions provided a wide range of opportunities for the cultivation and expression of religious faith and strengthened the links between priest and people.

4.2. The Catholic Church was an important social, cultural and political institution and its views and its values, expressed by a united hierarchy, informed all levels of Catholic experience. The influence of the numerous religious orders was particularly strong. The number of nuns, for example, which had already greatly increased during the earlier nineteenth century, more than doubled in this period, from 3,700 in 1870 to 8,000 by 1900. Held in high regard by the people generally, the clergy were in a strong position to influence the younger generation through their work in schools. Nuns and brothers played an important role in teaching Catholic social and moral values. Their emphasis on the traditional place of women in family life and on sexual modesty, if not repression, ensured that those who stepped beyond the boundaries of a rigid moral code were condemned by the whole community.

4.3. In the world of politics the influence of the hierarchy ebbed and flowed, but the informal alliance between the Catholic bishops and Parnell's Irish Parliamentary Party strengthened both. Archbishop Walsh's support for the Plan of Campaign was strong enough to withstand papal objections, and the Church's influence on political life would continue even after the political, Episcopal and popular condemnation of Parnell when the scandal of his relationship with Mrs Katharine O'Shea became a public issue.

4.4. During the cultural revival of the 1880s, Archbishop Croke recognised the potential for popular national games to replace the apathy, drunkenness and less acceptable activities of the ordinary people. The Church thus aligned itself with the emerging nationalist movement, helping to shape its religious and spiritual thinking.

5. The Presbyterian Church

5.1. Disestablishment also affected the Presbyterian Church. Many were glad to see the end of Anglican privilege, though they were resentful that the name 'Church of Ireland' was retained, and keenly aware of the overwhelming presence of its members in official positions in law and local government. But others saw the separation of church and state as a threat to Protestantism in general, left even more vulnerable in a country with a large Catholic majority. There was also a financial consideration: the *regium donum* ('king's gift or bounty'), an annual payment made by the government to the Presbyterian Church, was discontinued. This meant a complete reorganisation of the Church's income and resources. As with their Anglican counterparts, the Presbyterian clergy received compensation (amounting to £750,000 (approx. €61 million at 2009 values)), and they, too, in the interest of the Church, gave an overwhelming endorsement to the ending of their annual payments in return for a lump sum.

5.2. Internal disputes within Irish Presbyterianism in this period reflected wider changes in religious, social and political life. In public worship, for example, particularly after the 1859 Revival, the singing of hymns and the use of instrumental music were becoming popular. The General Assembly, the Church's ruling body, was bitterly divided on these issues and many ministers and congregations continued to reject their use.

5.3. A range of missions, stretching from the west of Ireland to colonial and continental outposts, had been in operation for some considerable time. The General Assembly's role in founding the World Presbyterian Alliance in 1873 further demonstrated their commitment to looking beyond their own provincial situation. In the same year, the formation of the Zenana Mission encouraged young middle-class women to travel as missionary teachers, nurses, or doctors first to India, and then China, thus opening a new chapter in Irish Presbyterian missionary history.

6. Protestantism and the problem of Home Rule

6.1. Politically, though supportive of reform on land issues, disillusionment with the Liberal Party following Gladstone's conversion to Home Rule impacted strongly on the Presbyterian community. A small number of Gladstone's supporters remained committed to an older tradition of Protestant nationalism. But the Irish Protestant Home Rule

Association, divided between north and south, and composed of a minority of prosperous, forward-looking individuals, was both ineffective and unrepresentative of wider Protestant opinion. Indeed, for most Presbyterian clergy and laity, anti-Catholic and anti-Home Rule arguments were no departure from traditional Presbyterian liberalism. The first Home Rule Bill (1886) was thought to be giving in to forces which were not in the least liberal – namely the Irish Parliamentary Party and agrarian campaigners, extremists who would threaten Protestant freedoms. The Church of Ireland Synod and the Presbyterian General Assembly were totally united, and clergymen of both traditions preached opposition to the measure from their pulpits.

6.2. The response of Irish Methodism, which had opposed in turn Catholic Emancipation, national education, the Repeal Campaign, the Maynooth grant, and the Disestablishment of the Church of Ireland, was predictable. Irish Methodism was strengthened by the union of Wesleyan Methodists with its main body in 1878 and the vast majority of societies and churches were based in Ulster. Irish Methodists, like most evangelicals, remained convinced that the Roman Catholic religion was the primary cause of all Irish problems.

6.3. There was, therefore, much that united the major Protestant denominations in late nineteenth- and early twentieth-century Ireland. All were concerned with social problems such as poverty, and immoral behaviour, particularly that connected with alcohol. Support of foreign missionary work was central to churches and meeting halls, and the World Missionary Conference held in Edinburgh in 1910 provided a significant stimulus. All were involved in church extension movements in Belfast, and support for popular gospel missions, such as that led by the Americans, Dwight Lyman Moody (1837–99) and David Sankey (1840–1908) in 1874, was demonstrated by the presence of clergy of all denominations on crowded platforms.

6.4. Although the Disestablishment of the Church of Ireland marked a major shift in church–state relations, the political uncertainties of the following decades clearly demonstrated that many Ulster Protestant men and women still looked to their clergy for leadership in times of crisis. Through a wide range of organisations and services, charities, soirées, fêtes, fairs and excursions, or choral festivals, such as that held by the Church of Ireland in 1866, the churches reached deep into their local communities. Central to all the major rituals of the life cycle, and marking the passing of the seasons with harvest or watch-night services, they represented a central aspect of a rich and vibrant culture, even for those who rarely entered their doors. Church-centred meetings could be occasions of sociability and entertainment, and provided an opportunity for the sexes to mix. In addition to the Catholic agencies already mentioned, Pioneer Societies, temperance associations, Friendly Societies, the YMCA and YWCA, Girls' and Boys' Brigade were all popular. By the 1890s, Gospel Hall and Salvation Army bands had also become part of this lively religious heritage.

7. Irish popular culture

7.1. Drink, 'the national curse of Ireland', was under sustained attack from religious quarters, but the reported reduction in alcohol consumption was also part of a wider reform of manners and the development of a busy working life. Also important were legislative measures aimed at lessening the opportunities for excessive drinking. The Sale of Intoxicating Liquors (Ireland) Act of July 1902 reduced the number of pub licences and introduced 10.30 p.m. closing. A bill banning Sunday opening was passed in November 1906.

7.2. Traditional activities did not disappear in the late Victorian period, but took on a different form. Entertainment, sports and recreations were more tightly organised and disciplined, moved indoors, and provided sources of revenue for their promoters. Since hours of work had become more rigidly fixed, so too leisure time was largely confined to weekends, and recreations were organised accordingly. Thus, spectator sports, such as boxing or horse racing, were commercially arranged for the recreation of the masses. Commercialisation was also obvious in trends such as the change of public houses from the old transport-based coaching houses to social centres. Entertainers and spectators alike moved in from the village green, to circuses, such as Batty's in Belfast, which had seating for over 1,000. Music hall and theatres such as Dublin's Gaiety Theatre (founded 1871) were also popular. There were touring song-and-dance acts, visiting companies and light opera performed by local amateurs. Of course, the transition was by no means complete and in urban areas in particular, street entertainment would continue – hurdy-gurdy men, horse-drawn carousels, Punch and Judy shows, performing dogs, bears and monkeys, ballad singers, fire-eaters, jugglers and the like. Many clubs and organisations were formed during the final decades of the nineteenth century to meet the demand for activities that combined instruction and relaxation for adults; photographic societies were a particularly popular example.

7.3. Changes in transport were important and cheap excursion tickets encouraged weekend trips to the zoo, the seaside or the countryside. Tramways, running in Belfast, Dublin and Cork by 1872, and electrified in the early twentieth century, greatly facilitated local travel while cycling clubs demonstrated the popularity of a machine which could quickly transport young couples to a romantic day in the country. Although cost at first confined this activity to the middle classes, bicycles were becoming more accessible to the general public by the end of the period. Wealth was particularly visible when the motor car arrived, and the Royal Irish Automobile Club was formed in 1901 to cater for this new phenomenon. Touring motor enthusiasts flocked to Ireland's empty roads. The arrival of the charabanc (a large bus, typically used for sightseeing) from 1905 also catered for what was to become an important industry.

7.4. The wealthy, of course, ventured further afield. When not travelling abroad, much of the leisure time of the social elite revolved around sports such as yachting, racing and hunting. Irishwomen excelled at golf, and won the British Open Championship in 1899, 1900, 1902 and 1903. Bridge, tennis, garden parties, balls and selective rounds of social visits, provided young women with time on their hands with opportunities to show off the latest fashions and enabled both sexes to keep in touch with events. Young middle-class women were given the opportunity to widen their intellectual horizons with the passage of the 1879 Universities (Ireland) Act, which established the Royal University of Ireland as an examining body, and which opened its degrees and scholarships to women. By the end of the century 25 per cent of the Royal University candidates were women. Further progress was made in 1908 when the Royal University was dissolved and replaced by the National University and Queen's University in Belfast. The central effect of these Acts was, of course, to further dismantle Anglican and indeed Protestant privilege.

7.5. The spread of 'improving' and instructional societies, which had begun in the mid-nineteenth century, together with the church-based educational activities, continued to popularise an expanding range of reading materials. Apart from books on religion and instruction, the removal of taxes on newspapers by 1861 brought an increase in the local and national news available to the reading public. The publication of cheap editions of quality books made the classics widely available, while the Public Libraries (Ireland) Act of 1894 prompted the first stirrings of a universal free library service. Writers such as Somerville & Ross and George Moore described and commented on different aspects of the contemporary Irish life. Moore's *A drama in muslin* (1886), *The lake* (1905) and his realistic short stories are of particular literary significance. Many aspects of Ireland's diverse cultural heritage were, however, to be overshadowed by the emergence and promotion of cultures more distinctively linked to nationalist traditions.

8. Cultural and religious politics

8.1. The capacity for conflict between the religious cultures in Ireland had already been well demonstrated in preceding decades, and sectarian violence was to become a recurring feature of life in Belfast and in some Ulster country towns in the late nineteenth century. Open-air sermons, Orange parades, election platforms, funeral processions, the great Protestant Protest meetings in the city's Botanical Gardens, Catholic festivals (such as the feast day of the Assumption) and celebrations of historical events brought the tensions of the countryside into towns and cities. All contributed to riots at one time or another. In parades and processions people flaunted their effigies, slogans, party tunes, banners and rituals. To a remarkable extent, clubs and processions became a way of life and parades marked out what was perceived as ethnic and religious territory. In the final decades of the nineteenth century, however, political events greatly deepened and intensified the link between culture and identity.

9. Unionist culture

9.1. Long rejected, or ignored, by social historians, Unionist cultural identity was inextricably bound up with the wider British and Imperial world to which most Irish

Protestants gave their political and emotional allegiance. Links to this broader culture were particularly evident on the occasions of royal anniversaries or visits, such as Queen Victoria's Jubilee celebrations in 1897, and her three-week visit in the Spring of 1900 when demonstrations of enthusiastic flag-waving loyalists were deemed particularly important in offsetting nationalist hostility. The industrialisation of the north-east, which set it apart from much of the rest of Ireland, also strengthened its links with the towns and cities of Britain. It has been argued, however, that popular Unionism pre-dated, and indeed helped generate popular imperialism.

9.2. The Liberal Party's support for Home Rule caused a major crisis of identity for many Unionists. Societies and loyal associations were formed to oppose it. The Orange Order, with its parades, sashes, and banners, was the most potent and visible expression of Unionism. Satirical half-penny postcards lampooning the claims of nationalism, lapel badges, the constant display of the Union flag and mass public demonstrations reflected the emotion and anger of a people whose heritage seemed to be under threat from both the British and the Irish. In this context the promotion of Empire became a matter of critical importance in influencing English opinion. Empire Day, 25 May 1895 (Queen Victoria's birthday), for example, was mainly promoted by organised Unionism and by the Protestant churches and youth associations. The Boer War (1899–1902) was also significant in rousing popular enthusiasm for the Empire. The sensationalist images of the popular press struck a chord among a people whose patriotism was also reflected in the many memorials erected to those who had sacrificed their lives. Ulster Day in 1912 generated particular emotion as thousands of men and women gathered around their churches and public buildings to sign, often in blood, the Solemn League and Covenant.

9.3. Despite appearances, Ulster Protestant culture was not monolithic. The individualist and austere heritage of Scots Presbyterianism was evident throughout the north-east counties, particularly in Antrim and Down, where names and local dialects reflected a link that was both ancient and ongoing. Nonetheless, denominational and traditional differences were buried when Protestantism as a whole was believed to be under threat. The local church or meeting house provided a focal point in which political aspirations were accepted as an important aspect of a broader religious, social and cultural identity.

10. Cultural nationalism

10.1. The creation of an Irish identity that was Catholic and nationalist was not the result of a unified campaign, but of several different strands operating together. Now that the rhetoric of the politicians was growing stale and cliched and the major social and economic grievances largely under control, the time was ripe for a fresh approach to the problem of Ireland's identity. In the twenty years before the 1916 Easter Rising, a refreshingly romantic and idealistic nationalism attracted the youth of Ireland, stimulating intellectual activity and directing attention to the wealth of Irish culture and traditions, which were in danger of being swamped by the influence of her dominant neighbour. Irish language, literature, history and sport were revived (or re-invented) with enthusiasm in the quest for an 'Irish Ireland'.

10.2. The Gaelic cultural revival owed much to the work of scholars and antiquarians – George Petrie (1790–1866), John O'Donovan (1806–1861), Eugene O'Curry (1794–1862), Bishop William Reeves (1815–92), the outstanding philologist Whitley Stokes (1830–1909), William Maunsell Hennessy (1828/9–89), and others – who studied the antiquities of Ireland and published its literature. The work of some of these had been popularised in the 1840s by Thomas Davis (1814–45). Standish James O'Grady (1846–1928) is another link in the chain. His two-volume *History of Ireland* (1878–80) has versions of the early mythological and heroic tales and inspired a new generation of writers and poets with the vividness of its literature.

10.3. There were important developments on the Continent that had serious implications for cultural nationalism at home. The great Johann Caspar Zeuss (1806–56) published his monumental *Grammatica Celtica* in Leipzig in 1853, a revolutionary work that put the grammar of Irish and related languages on a firm scientific footing. Irish was now shown to be as important in linguistics as Greek, Latin, and Sanskrit. In 1870 *Revue Celtique* was founded in Paris by Henri Gaidoz (1842–1932), director of the École des Hautes Études. This was the first great scholarly journal to be wholly devoted to Celtic studies, that is, the literature and philology of the Celtic languages. In 1896 Kuno Meyer and Ludwig Christian Stern founded another great journal in Germany, *Zeitschrift für celtische Philologie*: it carried the writings of the greatest Celtic scholars, and still flourishes. Irish was now studied in major continental universities and among the many leading continental scholars were Ernst Windisch (1844–1918) in Berlin; Heinrich Zimmer (1851–1910) in Greifswald; Kuno Meyer (1858–1919) in Liverpool and Berlin; Henri d'Arbois de Jubainville (1827–1910) and Joseph Vendryes (1875–1960) in Paris; Count Constantino Nigra (1828–1907), the distinguished Italian diplomat; Graziadio Ascoli (1829–1907) in Milan; Holger Pedersen (1867–1953) in Copenhagen; and the greatest of them all, Rudolf Thurneysen (1857–1940) in Freiburg and Bonn. This scholarly revolution had two effects: Irish was given a new international status as a language of culture, and the remarkable, original, and extensive medieval literature of Irish was edited and translated, much of it for the first time, into English, German, French and Italian.

10.4. There had been important cultural clubs and societies in late nineteenth-century Ireland, but it was only with the formation of the Gaelic League or Connradh na Gaeilge (July 1893) that a popular cultural transformation became clearly evident. The decline of the Irish language – only 18 per cent of the population is recorded as Irish-speaking in 1881 – was of particular concern to those wishing to de-anglicise Ireland. The Society for the Preservation of the Irish Language had been founded in 1876 (and it had less influential predecessors), but the Gaelic League would prove most influential of these movements. It was founded by the great scholar and historian Eoin MacNeill (1867–1945). The gifted Douglas Hyde (1860–1949) and Eugene O'Growney (1863–99) were among its leaders. It widened and strengthened the Irish consciousness of the lower and middle classes, and gave Irish a respect and status that it had lacked. Building on foundations laid by Young Ireland during the 1840s, the League aimed to give the nation 'a soul'. Although it never succeeded in making Irish the everyday language of a majority of people, it was an important nationwide cultural movement that had 600 registered branches by 1908. Travelling teachers of Irish (*timirí Gaeilge*) taught Irish all over the country in halls in towns and villages to enthusiastic classes, and the League set up Coláiste na Mumhan in Balligeary, Co. Cork (1904) to train teachers of Irish.

10.5. As a result of its activities Irish was being taught in 3,000 schools by 1909, compared with only 100 a decade earlier. In 1908, through its efforts, Irish was made a necessary qualification for admission to the new National University of Ireland. Apart from language classes and summer schools, members of the League organised Irish music, dancing, singing, literary competitions and festivals (*feiseanna*), the most important being the vastly influential Oireachtas, an annual national literary and cultural festival. It had an extremely active publishing programme: it had a weekly newspaper, *An Claidheamh Soluis*, and it created and published a modern literature in Irish. It provided the textbooks and grammars needed for the teaching of Irish and made a wide range of older literature in Irish available to a growing and enthusiastic readership. These activities were to influence a whole generation and inspired a new type of nationalist politics.

10.6. The Gaelic Athletic Association (GAA), formed in 1884, focused on replacing English games such as soccer, cricket and rugby with Gaelic football, hurling and handball. It further discouraged 'foreign' sports by barring from membership members of the British military establishment. The GAA was strongly supported by the Catholic clergy and by Irish nationalists of all shades and, as a result, was extremely popular in rural Ireland where sporting competition at county level enlivened local life.

11. Anglo-Irish literary revival

11.1. While the GAA stirred feelings of national pride and the Gaelic League concerned itself with reviving Irish and Irish culture, a small tightly knit group of Anglo-Irish writers also turned to the Gaelic past. Inspired by Irish myths and heroic tales, they set about creating a literature, that 'would move men's minds and imaginations anew'. Writers such as William Butler Yeats (1865–1939), John Millington Synge (1871–1909), and Lady Augusta Gregory (1852–1932), had been prompted by the political and social changes of the times to review their situation and to search for an identity in the new Ireland that was coming into being. They found such an identity in Irish literature and legends, the ancient sagas (many made available in the original and in striking English translation by Standish Hayes O'Grady (1832–1915) in his *Silva Gadelica*, published in London in 1892 and in the works of a new and brilliant generation of Celtic scholars, at home and abroad), and in folklore, which was now beginning to attract serious attention, in Ireland as in other countries. Their writings lifted Dublin from its provincial obscurity to become a lively new literary centre with a theatre that attracted European critical acclaim.

11.2. Yeats founded the Irish Literary Society in London in 1891, the National Literary Society a year later, and, in 1898, the Irish Literary Theatre. With Lady Gregory and Edward Martyn (1859–1923), Yeats' intention was 'to build up a Celtic and Irish school of dramatic literature'. Performances were first held in the Ancient Conference Rooms in Dublin. Yeats' *The Countess Cathleen* attracted large audiences and, ominously, sharp criticism as a 'slanderous caricature'. An important step forward came with the involvement of the brothers, Frank (1871–1931) and William Fay (1872–1947), who had been putting on plays in Irish and English in a small hall in Dublin. Yeats offered them *Cathleen Ni Houlihan*, and they joined forces to form the Irish National Theatre Society in 1903. The building, which would become the Abbey, was acquired in 1904. Although early works were acceptable to nationalist opinion, Yeats was soon indignant at attempts to make art subservient to the wider national cause.

11.3. The outrage which greeted the Abbey's production of Synge's plays is well known and reflects the extent to which the romantic 'Irish Ireland' movement had taken hold. Contemporary nationalist feeling demanded an idealised and pious peasantry and rejected any taint of coarse realism. Synge's interpretation of rural Catholic Ireland in *Riders to the sea* (played in the Abbey in 1904) incensed nationalist feeling. More serious, however, was his portrayal of the peasantry of the West in *The playboy of the western world* (1907). The writer's imaginative realism was regarded as a crude defamation of the Irish character. Sensitivity to national pride, particularly where morality was concerned, ensured that Synge, acknowledged as the 'genius of the Irish theatre', provoked the anger of the puritans of the Gaelic revival.

11.4. With the exception of Lady Gregory, the role of women in this cultural revival has often been ignored, but they were very much at the heart of the movement. They were, for example, active in the Gaelic League, teaching Irish language and dance, and in the productions of the Abbey Theatre and the Ulster Literary Theatre (1902). Ellen Duncan, curator of Hugh Lane's Art Gallery, was secretary of the Dublin United Arts Club. Sarah H. Purser (1848–1943), like Lady Gregory, frequently played hostess to local and visiting intellectuals at Dublin literary gatherings. Women fulfilled a range of important functions in the world of higher culture, whether as patrons, contributors or participants.

12. Arts and Crafts Movement

12.1. Another important dimension of the new national culture was the Arts and Crafts movement. The Arts and Crafts Society of Ireland was founded in 1894 to foster artistic industries and, from 1896, it held regular exhibitions of clothes and other items of Irish manufacture. It was important in reviving the economy. It was not overtly political, and even the ladies of the Vice-Regal Lodge were able to participate in these activities. The wives of the Lord Lieutenants – Lady Cadogan, Lady Dudley, Lady Londonderry and Lady Aberdeen – all encouraged local arts and crafts. Lady Aberdeen was particularly active as President of the Irish Industries' Association.

12.2. Standards were greatly improved by the work of the outstanding and remarkably successful Dun Emer Guild, founded in 1902 by Susan Mary Yeats (1866–1949), her sister Elizabeth Corbet Yeats (1868–1940), and their friend, the artist and designer, Evelyn Gleeson (1855–1944). The Guild was an important centre of Irish embroidery, printing and bookbinding. Though the partnership between the Yeats sisters and Gleeson was brief, Dun Emer trained young women in many artistic skills, supplied churches with vestments and banners, and contributed to the annual exhibitions. The Guild of Irish Art Workers, founded in 1910, focused on jewellery, enamel and metalwork. The intricate metalwork of Mia Cranwell (1880–1972) and the ecclesiastical decorative work of Sister Concepta Lynch (1874–1939) were particularly notable. The artist Sarah Purser (1848–1943), a prolific portrait painter, established *An Túr Gloine* ('the Tower of Glass') in 1903, an important studio from which came superb designs and works in stained glass, including those of Michael Healy (1873–1941) and Wilhelmina Geddes (1887–1955) and the magnificent east window in Eton College Chapel is among many outstanding works of Evie Hone (1894–1955). The glass, fittings, banners and furnishings of Loughrea Cathedral demonstrate the high standards that Irish-produced work had reached. Many of the leading contemporary literary and artistic figures were captured in the work of the portrait painter, John Butler Yeats (1839–1922), while his son, Jack Butler Yeats (1871–1957), focused on the people of the West of Ireland, in highly acclaimed works such as *At the feis* (1912) and *The man from Aranmore* (1905).

13. Conclusion

13.1. The cultural national revival was the result of a combination of circumstances and influences. The movement was a reaction against the rise of the slums and the factories, which came with industrialisation – a recoil from machines, commerce and modernity to the 'world we had lost', a romantic world of myth and legend. This rejection of modern civilisation by poets and thinkers was a worldwide phenomenon, one which saw the commercialism of the modern age as an evil threat to individualism and to the aesthetic life. For the majority, evil in Ireland, however, was most often linked with England, and the battle of the nationalists was almost always against English morals, influence, religion, and rule. As the period drew to a close, collective nationalist and unionist cultural and religious identities were moving along ever-diverging paths.

13.2. The trend towards violence between these distinctive nationalist and unionist identities in the immediate pre-war period should be seen in the context of a broader European militarism. Demands made by suffragettes and unionised workers, by nationalists and Unionists, by political radicals and revolutionaries, challenged the social and political *status quo* in Ireland as elsewhere. Noisy and often violent demonstrations and counter-demonstrations contributed to the conviction that, in more ways than one, an era was coming to an end.

MYRTLE HILL (WITH A CONTRIBUTION BY DONNCHADH Ó CORRÁIN)

CHAPTER 4

Home Rule and the elections of 1885–6

1. Introduction

1.1. William Ewart Gladstone (1809–98), became Prime Minister of Great Britain in 1868. His first administration lasted until 1874. He stated that his 'mission was to pacify Ireland'. The fear of Fenian (IRB) violence, especially in England, and the growing awareness of the strength of nationalist feeling drove Gladstone to tackle the 'Irish question'. He had a sincere desire to bring peace to Ireland. Among his first measures was the Disestablishment of the Church of Ireland in order to break the formal link between the state and a minority church. His Irish University Bill (1873) failed by a small margin in the House of Commons: it was attacked as too godless by one side and too favourable to Roman Catholics by the other. The Landlord and Tenant (Ireland) Act, 1870, gave greater security to some tenants, and those who left their holdings could claim compensation for improvements they had made. However, the Act was unsatisfactory in practice, and agitation for land reform steadily grew. Gladstone had considered Irish local government reform as early as 1882 in order to relieve 'Great Britain from the enormous weight of the government of Ireland unaided by the people'. By 1886, when he became prime minister for a third time, the demand for Home Rule was so well organised, the Home Rule party so disciplined, and the Irish public so supportive of the party that Gladstone concluded that the only solution was to give Ireland its own legislative body (the word 'parliament' was deliberately avoided).

2. What was Home Rule?

2.1. Home Rulers demanded an elected legislature and an executive in Dublin to deal with the internal affairs of Ireland within the British Empire. In 1870, Isaac Butt, a Protestant lawyer, formed the Home Government Association to achieve this objective. The term 'Home Rule' was first used by Revd Joseph A. Galbraith, a Fellow of Trinity College, Dublin and a member of the Association. It was, however, Butt who founded and led the Home Rule movement. In 1873, the Home Rule League replaced the Home Government Association. The obstructionist Charles Stewart Parnell and his supporters vied for authority and influence with Butt. Parnell was elected President of the Home Rule Confederation of Great Britain (where the IRB was influential) but in Ireland Butt remained leader until his death. Parnell, however, won the leadership battle within a year of Butt's death – after the general election of 1880.

2.2. The nationalist organisation, the Irish National League (INL), was formed in October 1882 as a replacement for the Land League, which had been suppressed. Local branches of the League represented local nationalist opinion, especially in the strict selection of parliamentary candidates. The Nationalist Party, or Irish Parliamentary Party, grew into a strong, centralised, tightly structured organisation – the first modern political party in the true sense. By-election results in the early 1880s showed increased support for the Irish Parliamentary Party. By the end of 1883, Home Rule candidates were successful in Monaghan, Tipperary, Mallow, Wexford, Waterford, and Sligo. There was much-needed Catholic Church support, too, particularly after Parnell condemned interdenominational education. By 1886, there were 1,200 National League branches spread across the country. The Catholic clergy played a big role in the local branches. Protestants were alarmed. They saw Catholic Church involvement as evidence of the political power which Catholic priests might have in a Home Rule parliament. The land question was no longer at the centre of the political arena.

3. Who were the voters?

3.1. The Representation of the People Act, 1884 (also known as the Third Reform Act) gave the vote in parliamentary elections to all male householders who owned or rented property (that is, men who owned or rented even a single room). As a result, the Irish electorate rose from 224,018 to 737,965. Before 1884, only 4.4 per cent of Irish people had the vote. In England, nearly 9.7 per cent of the population had the vote. Now roughly 16 per cent of the population had the vote in both countries. Indeed, Ireland was slightly over-represented. The Act gave Ireland 25 extra parliamentary seats. This created a much-enlarged Catholic electorate that included not just the wealthier classes but also cottiers and agricultural labourers. Many poor farmers were strong supporters of Parnell. The reforms favoured the Home Rulers who gained at least ten extra seats. Home Rule became a momentous issue in the years 1885–6 when both the Tories and Liberals courted the Home Rule party. The Redistribution of Seats Act, 1885 had abolished the preference given to the boroughs in the past where only 2 per cent of the population elected 15 per cent of the MPs. Tory and Protestant influence was virtually ended in the southern counties outside of Trinity College, Dublin. Catholic voters vastly outnumbered the Protestant minority in Ireland outside Ulster. Irish representation in parliament was not reduced, even though the population had fallen.

3.2. Electoral reform had consequences for Home Rule in Great Britain as well. An Irish population, variously estimated between 750,000 and 2,000,000, was spread across Britain, and some constituencies had large numbers of Irish voters. Before the electoral changes the Irish immigrant influence on British elections was not seen as significant. After 1885, the situation changed to the advantage of the Irish Parliamentary Party. Parnell believed that this increased Irish vote could be used to pressurise Liberals into responding to Ireland's needs.

4. How was the Irish Parliamentary Party organised?

4.1. T.M. Healy helped draft a tight Parliamentary Pledge for the Irish Party which was first used at the Dungarvan Convention, August 1884:

> I, [...], pledge myself that in the event of my election to parliament, I will sit, act and vote with the Irish Parliamentary Party; and if at a meeting of the party, convened upon due notice, specially to consider the question, it be determined by a resolution, supported by a majority of the Irish Parliamentary Party, that I have not fulfilled the above pledge, I hereby undertake forthwith to resign my seat.

4.2. The local organisation of the Party, the National League, was very effective. Few of the former controlling members of the Land League were on its executive. It organised county conventions to control the candidates who ran on the Home Rule platform. Local branches also had a wider social mix than their Land League predecessors. Nevertheless, the Home Rule Party after 1880 was a predominantly middle-class organisation with a tendency towards the lower rather than the upper end. The growth of the National League was slow until the 1885 general election. Following the electoral reforms of 1884–5, the number of branches expanded threefold and reached 1,200 by 1886. Parnell managed the near-impossible task of satisfying almost everyone by giving no clues about what specific reforms he had in mind. Neither did he state what he meant by Home Rule, but he kept citing Grattan's parliament as the limit of the demand possible under the British Constitution.

5. Keeping Ireland quiet!

5.1. As 1884 ended, Ireland was high on the British political agenda. The Prevention of Crime Act was due to expire in July 1885. A Coercion Act gave the Lord Lieutenant emergency powers to quell unrest and put down disturbances. There were 52 such acts between 1800 and 1882. Such measures allowed extra police to be drafted into troubled districts. *Habeas corpus* (a writ requiring the production in court of a detained person) was suspended in 1871 and again in 1881. The Protection of Person and Property Act of March 1881 temporarily re-introduced detention without trial for up to three months. The Prevention of Crime Act, in force for three years from 1882, permitted trial for specific offences by a panel of three judges and created the legal offence of intimidation. Because of social unrest the matter of coercion was a serious issue in Irish affairs between November 1885 and June 1886.

6. Joseph Chamberlain's plan for Ireland

6.1. Joseph Chamberlain (1836–1914), the ambitious radical Liberal MP for Birmingham and President of the Board of Trade in the Liberal government hoped to make his name and political reputation as the man to bring about 'the settlement of the Irish difficulty'.

Chamberlain disliked Home Rule as defined by Isaac Butt: for him it was too close to independence. He stated that 'if nationalism means separation, I, for one am prepared to resist it'. Instead, he developed a scheme for the reform of Irish local government that included a Central Board (also called the 'Irish Board') to deal with central concerns such as education, communications, and land. In 1885, local government in Ireland remained in the hands of unelected grand juries, though increasing responsibilities had, over the years been granted to partly elected Poor Law Boards established after 1838. Under Chamberlain's scheme democratic county councils would elect the Central Board for Ireland. As part of any deal, the government would also soften its crime legislation. Parnell saw the scheme as a limited and temporary measure until an Irish parliament was restored. Chamberlain saw it as a more lasting alternative to full Home Rule. Cardinal Henry Manning (1808–92), Archbishop of Westminster, gave Chamberlain the impression that the Catholic hierarchy supported the Board. Captain William O'Shea, in turn, told Chamberlain that Parnell was satisfied with the scheme as an answer to the demand for Home Rule.

6.2. In fact, Parnell had told O'Shea that the Central Board scheme was acceptable only as a step to Home Rule. When Chamberlain was finally informed of this, he blamed Parnell for deceiving him and took a personal dislike to him. In any event, Chamberlain failed to win over his fellow ministers (although Gladstone supported it) and on 9 May 1885, the Central Board proposal was thrown out by the cabinet. Henry du Pré Labouchère (1831–1912), journalist and Liberal MP (Northampton), remarked that Chamberlain was 'just as amazed at anyone not accepting his inspired plan as Moses would have been had an Israelite suggested an amendment in the Ten Commandments'. He resigned his ministry. Parnell did not worry himself too much about alienating Chamberlain but he made a fatal error in doing so. Shortly after, Gladstone indicated to a select few colleagues that 'the field is open for the consideration of future measures [for Irish autonomy]' and that he was prepared to go 'rather farther' than the scheme outlined by Chamberlain. In September 1885, speaking at Warrington, Chamberlain claimed that Home Rule would fundamentally undermine the integrity of the United Kingdom:

> This new programme of Mr Parnell's involves a greater extension than anything we have hitherto known or understood by Home Rule; the powers he claims for his support in parliament are altogether beyond anything which exists in the case of the State Legislatures of the American Union, which has hitherto been the type and model of Irish demands, and if this claim were conceded we might as well for ever abandon all hope of maintaining a United Kingdom. We should establish within 30 miles of our shores a new foreign country animated from the outset with unfriendly intentions towards ourselves. Such a policy as that, I firmly believe, would be disastrous and ruinous to Ireland herself. It would be dangerous to the security of this country, and under these circumstances I hold that we are bound to take every step in our power to avert so great a calamity.

7. The fall of the Liberals

7.1. Tory leaders were alarmed with the government. They felt that Gladstone was incompetent, especially in foreign and imperial policy. News of the death of General Charles Gordon (1833–85) at Khartoum, in Sudan, in February 1885 confirmed Tory fears. Having resigned from office in 1880 due to ill health, Gordon agreed to a government request to help evacuate Egyptian forces from Sudan in 1884. They were threatened by an army of the rebellious 'Mahdi', Muhammad Ahmed (1844–85). The British public reacted to his death by acclaiming 'Gordon of Khartoum' as a martyred warrior-saint and by blaming the government, particularly Gladstone, for failing to relieve the siege in time. Critics inverted his GOM nickname (for 'Grand Old Man') to MOG ('Murderer of Gordon'). Nor were Tories content with his conduct of Irish affairs. Most leading Tories accepted the need for land purchase, supported denominational education and many were prepared to set up local government. Irish MPs had been effective critics of Gladstone's government, they attended the House of Commons regularly, and their co-operation with the Tories brought satisfying results.

7.2. The government renewed coercion and, on 9 June 1885, a combination of Tories and Irish, assisted by Liberal absentees, defeated the government on a budget amendment. Gladstone resigned. The Liberal leader claimed later that he had decided in favour of Home Rule but was waiting to see what the Conservatives would do. Parnell, however, did not know this. Normally, a general election would follow the fall of the government. This, however, could not take place because the work of drawing up the new constituencies, demanded by the Reform Act of 1884, was not finished. Lord Salisbury (1830–1903), the Tory leader, now formed a caretaker government with the support of the Irish Parliamentary Party. The Tory government made serious concessions to Ireland to get the support of Home Rule MPs with an eye to the elections due in 1886.

8. 'Tory kindnesses'

8.1. Lord Carnarvon (1831–90) was appointed Lord Lieutenant in June 1885. He had been responsible for the introduction of federal self-government in Canada in 1867 and was known to be in favour of some form of self-government in Ireland. He pursued a policy of conciliation and the Home Rulers thought the Tory party as a whole might be open to the idea of a Dublin legislature. While in Ireland, Carnarvon made friendly gestures to Catholics. In late summer he toured the west to learn at first hand about conditions there. On 1 August 1885, he held a secret interview with Parnell, who later claimed that Home Rule had been discussed. The Prime Minister, Lord Salisbury, had refused to meet Parnell. The Coercion Act was not renewed.

8.2. The Conservative Lord Chancellor of Ireland, Lord Ashbourne (1837–1913), sponsored a Land Act in 1885 that provided £5 million (approx. €430 million at 2009 values) for tenants who wished to buy out their holdings. Tenants could borrow the full purchase price of their farms. Repayments were made over 49 years (at 4 per cent interest) and they were generally less than the old rents. The Act was hugely successful and 25,367 tenants bought out their farms. Lord Ashbourne himself had large estates in Co. Meath and he was one of the first landowners to sell under the Act. It marked a major step in the destruction of the Irish landlord class; the staunchest allies of the Tories. It seemed that Tories were now abandoning them, indeed helping to destroy them. They had outlived their usefulness and they were now cast aside. The Ballot Act 1872 had destroyed the landlords' political influence over their tenants. The tenants, would-be petty landowners to a man, were the coming political force in the land, and the Tories were keen to win them over.

8.3. The Educational Endowments (Ireland) Act, 1885, set up a commission to draw up schemes for the management of endowments. It benefited Catholic education in Ireland to the tune of £140,000 (approx. €12 million at 2009 values).

8.4. As hope of a political settlement rose, so too did the flow of funds from the United States. The National League had collected £11,686 (approx. €1 million) in 1884–5, but contributions rose to over £47,000 (approx. €4 million) during 1885–6. From a modest base up to the end of 1884 (371 branches in April 1883) the League expanded to 818 in July 1885, possibly reaching 1,261 by the end of the year.

8.5. However, the Irish Party was unaware that Carnarvon did not have the support of his party. Any self-government proposal for Ireland that was supported by the Tories stood a much greater chance of getting through the House of Lords than any Liberal measure since the Tories dominated the House of Lords. The Liberals frequently proclaimed their affection for Ireland but they were reluctant to apply very radical solutions to the problem of landlord-tenant relations. Because of this failure, Home Rulers distrusted the Liberals and hoped for more from the Tories than they were ever likely to get. Gladstone's contacts with Parnell, however, were not an isolated event. Other Liberals kept in touch with various Irish politicians. It was clear that the Liberals, like the Tories, were prepared to agree to a significant granting of local control over Ireland's affairs. How much control and what kind of measures remained very unclear.

9. 'Promises, promises ...'

9.1. Between June and November 1885, Parnell tried hard to persuade either the Tories or the Liberals to commit themselves openly to Home Rule. Both parties needed the support of Home Rulers in the Commons and hoped to benefit from Parnell's influence with Irish voters in Britain. But the Home Rule cause was generally unpopular in Britain and neither party was willing to give Parnell what he wanted. Neither Gladstone nor Salisbury would talk directly with him, although their followers did. Chamberlain talked vaguely about his Central Board scheme though Parnell and the Liberals had already rejected it. Lord Carnarvon and the highly unpredictable Lord Randolph Churchill (1849–95) also spoke vaguely of concessions to Ireland and Salisbury declared that the Tories' 'first principle was to extend to Ireland as far as they could all the institutions of this country'.

9.2. Gladstone's calculations had to take account of the growing bond between the Tories and Parnell. He feared that Parnell, when courted by both parties, might inflate his demands. On 1 November 1885, he received Parnell's 'Proposed Constitution for Ireland' and later in the month, while staying at Dalmeny House for the Midlothian election campaign, Gladstone drafted an Irish Home Rule Bill. It closely followed Parnell's paper and was based on colonial, chiefly Canadian, models. Gladstone, however, was adamant that he would not be part of any 'counterbidding of any sort against Lord Randolph Churchill'. The Tory courtship raised the question whether the party might concede something in the nature of Home Rule. This would probably help ease the measure through the House of Lords. When it later became clear that this would not happen, Gladstone pondered whether the Tories could have 'made one of those Party sacrifices which seem now to have gone out of fashion, but which in other days – the days of Sir Robert Peel and the Duke of Wellington – were deemed the highest honour'.

10. The 1885 general election

10.1. Lord Salisbury's keynote speech at Newport on 7 October 1885 was read by some Liberals as not entirely 'closing the door' on an Irish settlement. Parnell believed that the Tories were prepared to deal and on 21 November 1885, he issued a 'Manifesto to the Irish in Great Britain' calling on them to vote for Tory candidates. On 15 December, Gladstone approached Arthur J. Balfour (1848–1930), the Tory President of the Local Government Board (and Salisbury's nephew), urging a cabinet response to the issue of Irish government. He believed it was of crucial importance in light of the recent victories of the Parnellites and the risk of violence in Ireland if the demand for Home Rule was resisted. He followed this with a letter on 20 December promising that, if the Tories were willing to settle the 'whole question of the future government of Ireland', his party would give their full support. Balfour greeted Gladstone's move with some scepticism.

10.2. The general election took place between 24 November and 19 December 1885. Three-hundred-and-thirty-three Liberals, 251 Tories and 86 Home Rulers were elected. It has been estimated that Parnell's manifesto in which he opposed the Liberals as the 'party of coercion' cost them between 25 and 40 seats. This offended many in the Liberal Party. Parnell and the Home Rulers now held the 'balance of power' in the House of Commons: the Irish Party could now support either the Liberals or the Tories, depending on the attitude of each to Home Rule.

10.3. The 1885 election left the province of Ulster divided, between 17 nationalist Home Rulers (largely Catholic, representing the west and south of the province) and 16 anti-Home Rule Tories (largely Protestant, representing the more prosperous eastern part of the province). Gladstone's biographer John Morley recorded that:

... the whole of the Liberal candidates in Ulster fell down as dead men. Orangemen and Catholics, the men who cried damnation to King William and the men who cried 'To Hell with the Pope', joined hands ... it is true the paradox did not last, and that the Pope and King William were speedily back on their old terms again.

10.4. The obliteration of southern Irish Tories in the election meant that opposition to Home Rule in Ireland now lay in the hands of the Tory Ulster MPs and their supporters in Britain. The Irish Loyal and Patriotic Union was established in Dublin in May 1885 to co-ordinate resistance to Home Rule. It distributed propaganda against Home Rule throughout the country but it failed to attract popular support. It fared poorly in the 1885 election: with 52 candidates, it took just one seat (Trinity College, Dublin). Home Rulers won every other seat in Munster, Leinster and Connacht. However, the solid base of support in the north-east allowed the formation of the Ulster Loyalist Anti-Repeal Committee on 8 January 1886 which would later evolve into the central core of the Ulster Unionist Party. The Anti-Repeal Committee was supported by businessmen, landowners, and Protestant clergy and was dedicated to fighting Home Rule. It had the backing of the editor of the *Belfast Newsletter*, who was the Committee treasurer. By the spring of 1886, over 20 local associations had formed into what now became the Ulster Loyalist Anti-Repeal Union.

10.5. On 17 December 1885, Gladstone spoke about Home Rule to Lord Hartington (older brother of Lord Frederick Cavendish who had been assassinated in the Phoenix Park by the Invincibles, 6 May 1882). Hartington thought the Irish people temperamentally unfit for self-government. On that very day, through the intervention of Gladstone's son, Herbert, the *Leeds Mercury* and London *Standard* revealed that his father had been so impressed by the success of the Parnellites in taking 86 of the 103 seats in Ireland that he was now convinced that Home Rule by orderly secession was possible. He also declared that if his father was elected Prime Minister he would introduce Home Rule legislation. This was one of the most momentous changes in policy in British politics in the nineteenth century – 'the mighty heave in the body politic'. By flying the 'Hawarden Kite', as it was called (named after Gladstone's home, Hawarden Castle, Flintshire), Herbert Gladstone hoped to break the Home Rule/Tory alliance and help his father to become Prime Minister. There is no evidence that the Liberal leader was aware of his son's intention, but few of Gladstone's political opponents gave him the benefit of the doubt. Gladstone had been converted to Home Rule, but was reluctant to adopt it as policy since he felt that his party was not yet ready to embrace it. Indeed, a serious split in his party was likely. Gladstone hoped for an agreed bipartisan solution to the problem and believed that the Tories should adopt it since it would be easier for them to get it through the House of Lords. The search for a solution to the Irish question was a sufficient 'supreme moment' for Gladstone to suspend his plans for retirement. An outraged Queen Victoria appealed on 20 December 1885 to 'to all moderate, loyal, and really patriotic men to come together and save the Empire and the throne from Gladstone's reckless hands'.

10.6. Gladstone's tactics gave the Tories every chance to take the initiative. They failed to do so. Salisbury believed the Liberal leader was playing games with him and hence he turned his back on Home Rule. In the Queen's Speech in 21 January, Salisbury stated that the 'unity and integrity of Empire' must take precedence over Irish demands for Home Rule. If necessary, 'Ireland must be kept, like India, at all hazards, by persuasion, if possible; if not, by force'. Five days later he announced his intention to re-introduce coercion to suppress the National League. This prompted the Home Rulers to combine with the Liberals to defeat the caretaker government. The Irish issue came to the test on the question of agrarian reform, specifically the 'three acres and a cow' amendment to the Queen's Speech on 28 January 1886 – the vote on which would determine whether or not Gladstone would form a Home Rule government. Liberals and Irish Nationalists votes in support totalled 332. Against were 234 Tories and 18 Whigs, elected as Liberals, with 76 Liberals absent or abstaining. The historian, Roy Jenkins, saw this division as the 'the beginning of the volvulus which knotted British politics for the next thirty years'. Gladstone took office for the third time on 1 February 1886. The historian E.J. Feuchtwanger concluded that:

> It was a remarkable achievement, demanding consummate skill and tactical dexterity, that Gladstone managed to form a government, outmanoeuvring his recalcitrant and self-seeking colleagues yet keeping his hands free to take whatever course he wished.

10.7. Lord Hartington refused to take office; Joseph Chamberlain and George O. Trevelyan (1838–1928), Minister for Scotland, both resigned over Home Rule. Gladstone was only too aware of the consequences for his party if he proceeded with Home Rule. He wrote to the former Foreign Secretary, Lord Granville:

> Hartington writes to me a letter indicating … his determination 'to maintain the legislative union', that is to proclaim a policy (so I understand the phrase) of absolute resistance without examination to the demand made by Ireland through five-sixths of her members. This is to play the Tory game with a vengeance. They are now most rashly, not to say more, working the Irish question to split the Liberal party. It seems to me that if a gratuitous declaration of this kind is made, it must produce an explosion; and that in a week's time Hartington will have to consider whether he will lead the Liberal Party himself, or leave it in chaos. He will make my position impossible.

10.8. John Bright (1811–89), the Liberal elder statesman, was a long-standing advocate of church and land reform in Ireland but he attacked Gladstone's proposals arguing that 'the Irish parliament would be constantly struggling to burst the bars of the statutory cage in which it is sought to confine it'. He stated that he could not support Home Rule simply because Gladstone was party leader, among other things, he had to consider the 'the views and feelings of the Protestant and loyal portion of the people'.

11. Gladstone's Home Rule Bill

11.1. The entire Home Rule project was extremely complex and Gladstone had to formulate a bill that would give Ireland a meaningful measure of self-government while at the same time preserving the sovereignty of the Westminster parliament. He had to devise financial arrangements that would allow Irish trade and industry to develop without damaging British interests. He needed to reconcile Unionists and Protestants with Catholics and nationalists. He believed that it was essential to solve the land problem once and for all by buying out the landlords. However, he devoted far too little time to considering how Ulster's Unionists and Protestants might react to Home Rule. The same could be said of Parnell and his followers, many of whom were in daily contact with the self-same Protestants and Unionists.

11.2. Lord Randolph Churchill who had been Secretary for India in Salisbury's 1885 government had flirted with Parnell's nationalists and pursued conciliation in Ireland. However, once Gladstone's intentions became clear, Churchill decided that 'the Orange card would be the one to play'. Much of the Tories' campaign against the first Home Rule Bill centred on the evils likely to be inflicted on Protestants and Unionists, especially in Ulster by vengeful, savage and sub-human Catholics and nationalists. It is unlikely that many Tories actually believed their own propaganda. However, they were quite prepared to use it to undermine the Liberals. Unfortunately, very many ordinary Unionists and Protestants, in Britain as well as in Ireland, believed it and it served to poison the political atmosphere on both islands for generations. Sir Charles Russell lampooned Churchill as:

> Stiff in opinion, often in the wrong,
> Everything by starts and nothing long,
> But in the course of one revolving moon,
> Was green and orange, statesman and buffoon.

11.3. The Ulster Loyalist Anti-Repeal Union arranged a series of monster meetings, appealing to the hardline militancy of popular Protestantism. The wealthy landowner and popular MP for Cavan, Colonel Edward J. Saunderson (1837–1906), was a central figure in organising Ulster Unionists to resist Home Rule. He was a member of the Orange Order and was made Deputy Grand Master in 1884. Saunderson helped to arrange for Churchill's appearance at a rally in Belfast in February 1886. Churchill sought to harvest Ulster opposition to Home Rule and damage the new Liberal government. Shortly before that he had written rather caustically of the 'foul Ulster Tories who have always ruined our party'. On 22 February 1886, Churchill landed at Larne and travelled by rail to Belfast. That evening he spoke at a large demonstration of Unionists in the Ulster Hall. 'The Hall was crowded to excess', the *Belfast Newsletter* reported. Churchill urged loyalists to organise and prepare so that Home Rule might not come upon them 'as a thief in the night'. He promised those present that if the dark hour came when they had to defend themselves 'there will not be wanting to you those of position and influence in England who are willing to cast their lot with you – whatever it may be – and who will share your fortunes and your fate'. He declared that 'Ulster will fight and Ulster will be right.' A cartoon in the *Weekly News* (27 February) depicted Churchill leading the devil to stir up bigotry and sectarian hatred in Ulster. While Saunderson later rejected a possible 'rising in arms' against any Dublin legislature, he said Ulster would never acknowledge its legitimacy.

11.4. Some Ulster loyalists took Churchill at his word and began to arm themselves. Most Ulster Liberals deserted Gladstone. The partners at Harland & Wolff made emergency arrangements to move the yard to Seacombe on the Mersey. William Pirrie (1847–1924), senior partner and later chairman of the firm was outspoken in his attack on Home Rule and publicly threatened to move the business to the Clyde, saying publicly 'most certainly this would be done'. It is not known whether he had any hand in the expulsion of Catholic workers, but he did nothing to prevent it or to discourage riots by Protestant workers that summer.

11.5. The Orange lodges, which had been disbanded in the 1830s, were re-established when the Home Rule Bill was introduced. The sectarian Orange Order (founded in 1795) had been in decline for many years. It began to revive around 1880 in response to the activities of the Land League in Ulster and organised a force of harvesters for Captain Charles Boycott when he was ostracised by the League in Co. Mayo (1880). The Order had three principal aims: to protect Protestants from Catholics, to support the Protestant religion and to uphold the Protestant constitution of the United Kingdom with its Protestant monarch. The Order was spread throughout Ulster and had some branches in the south. Orange halls were important meeting places and annual marches were arranged to commemorate the ending of the Siege of Derry (1689) and Protestant victory at the Battle of the Boyne (1690). Indeed, the origins of the Ulster Unionist Party lie in a meeting of seven members of parliament, who were also members of the Order in London, in January 1886. In April 1886, 20,000 Orangemen resolved: 'we shall not acknowledge that government [Dublin legislature]; we will refuse to pay taxes imposed by it and we will resist to the uttermost all attempts to enforce such payments'. Protestant Unionists were not going to be dismissed easily.

11.6. Gladstone worked quickly and secretly drafting his measure for Irish self-government. Most of his cabinet colleagues were kept in the dark. He informed Sir William Harcourt, Chancellor of the Exchequer, of his intentions only on 7 March. The wider issue was first brought up at cabinet, by Chamberlain, on 13 March. A complete draft was discussed by cabinet on 26 March, when Chamberlain and Trevelyan walked out in protest. In his resignation speech in the House of Commons on 8 April, Trevelyan said that that he could not accept the proposed Land Bill under which Irish landlords were to be expensively bought out. The Irish Parliamentary Party, he explained, could not be trusted with the responsibility for law and order. He feared that the powers of the police and judiciary would ultimately be undermined in a 'degenerate Ireland'. Chamberlain saw the proposal to restore an Irish legislature as 'tantamount to a proposal for separation. It would set up a temporary and unstable form of government, which would be a source of perpetual irritation and agitation until the full demands of the Nationalist party were conceded.' He resigned the same day stating his concern for 'the honour and influence and integrity of the Empire' as his reason. So Gladstone's desire for Home Rule lost him some valuable supporters. This group of dissident Liberals now formed into a group known as the Liberal Unionists.

11.7. Although Gladstone was not in favour of negotiations over terms with the Irish, he met Parnell for talks in early April, a few days before the launch of the measure. Parnell fought for a reduction in the Irish contribution to imperial expenditure, and conceded control of customs and excise to Westminster. On 7 April 1886, Parnell informed his party colleagues of the measure's contents. The following day, the Bill was first introduced into the Commons.

12. How was Ireland to be governed?

12.1. The much feared Home Rule Bill was, in reality, fairly tame. It was, however, more radical than the Home Rule Bills which followed it, as the Irish legislature had more powers. There was to be an Irish legislative body with two orders. The first order with 103 peers, comprising the existing 28 representative peers who, under the terms of the Act of Union, already sat in the House of Lords, and an additional 75 members who had to possess capital of £4,000 (approx. €345,000 at 2009 values) or property worth £200 (approx. €17,250) a year. They were elected on a restricted franchise (electors with property worth £25 (approx. €2,200) per annum) for a period of ten years; half were to retire every fifth year. The second order with 204 representatives (or 206 if graduates of the Royal University were to elect two MPs) was to be elected by the ordinary voters. It comprised the present 103 Irish MPs, plus 101 new representatives. The two orders would sit together, but each order had a right of veto over legislation introduced by the other. The Irish legislature therefore had 307 members. Controversially, there was to be no Irish representation at Westminster. This raised the important question of 'taxation without representation'. The first order had no right of veto; it could however delay legislation for up to three years. By voting with the second order the first order could see legislation enacted.

12.2. The Irish legislature would be responsible for a wide range of domestic Irish concerns but the Crown would retain control over matters of war and peace; foreign and colonial affairs; currency; the powers and prerogatives of the Crown; the lighthouses; titles and honours; trade and navigation; weights and measures; copyrights and patents and other areas. The Irish legislature could not change the rights of any corporation established by royal charter except with the permission of the Queen in Council. The questions of the Post Office, the decennial census, and quarantine regulations were left open for the moment. The Irish legislature would also have an executive responsible to it. This was a step further than 'Grattan's parliament' to which the Dublin Castle administration was not responsible. The Lord Lieutenant (who could now be a Catholic), as the Queen's representative, was responsible for appointing ministers and summoning or dissolving the legislature. He was not compelled to choose ministers from the majority party, or even from the legislature. Parnell feared British government interference in the Irish legislature and argued that there should be no Lord Lieutenant or 'offices in Ireland under the Crown connected with the domestic affairs of the country'. Judges were to be appointed on the advice of the government and they could only be removed on a joint address of the two orders.

12.3. Under the terms of the Bill, the Irish government was to be made responsible for domestic tax charges (but not Irish customs and excise which were imposed and collected by Westminster) and she was to pay fixed contributions to the Consolidated Fund of the United Kingdom. Under the Act of Union Ireland paid two-seventeenths as an annual contribution to the British Exchequer. Ireland would now be asked to provide one-fifteenth of the revenue needed to run the empire. Some like Parnell thought this was too much. Gladstone calculated that Ireland would raise some £8.35 million (approx. €715 million at 2009 values) from customs and excise and other sources. Ireland would contribute £1.46 million (approx. €125 million) as its annual share of the National Debt (calculated to be some £48 million (approx. €4.1 billion)) and £1 million (approx. €86 million) to fund the Dublin Metropolitan Police (DMP) and Royal Irish Constabulary (RIC). Ireland would take control of the DMP after two years but the RIC would remain under imperial control for the foreseeable future. However, local authorities in Ireland might be allowed to set up their own forces in time. A further £1.66 million (approx. €142 million) was to be provided for the maintenance of the British army and navy, and £110,000 (approx. €9.5 million) per annum to cover Civil Service expenditure in Ireland. Gladstone hoped by these measures to reduce the cost to the British Exchequer, while leaving the Dublin administration an annual surplus of some £400,000 (approx. €34.5 million). The existing system of policing in Ireland he thought 'a waste of treasure and enormous expense, not with good results, but unhappy'.

12.4. No special provisions were made for Ulster but there were strong safeguards to prevent any form of religious discrimination. These were designed to dispel Protestant fears of any form of 'Rome Rule'. The Irish legislature could not endow any church, interfere with religious practices, or impose any religious tests for candidates for public office. Children would also be prohibited from receiving religious instruction at school. Despite such safeguards, the religious and economic position of Irish Protestants (and the special case of Ulster) featured prominently in subsequent Parliamentary debates.

12.5. Gladstone introduced his Government of Ireland (Home Rule) Bill on 8 April 1886 and it was debated until 7 June 1886. There was a parallel debate on the land purchase measure from 16 April to 3 May. In what is regarded as one of his greatest speeches to parliament, Gladstone outlined the reasons why Ireland should be allowed conduct her own affairs. He referred to Grattan's parliament, 1782–1800, the legislative Union of England and Ireland (1801), and the various acts which were subsequently introduced to address Irish grievances. The policy of coercion had failed miserably. The Home Rule Bill sought to reconcile Irish autonomy with the continuance of the United Kingdom. Gladstone concluded his lengthy speech by saying: 'it is sometimes requisite not only that good laws should be passed, but that they should be passed by the proper persons … We stand face to face with Irish nationality which vents itself in the demand for local autonomy.'

12.6. The question of devolution was examined in depth, particularly its consequences for Irish Unionists and how it might weaken the unity of the British Isles. The implications of the Bill for English party politics, the imperial relationship with India and the possible threat to the security of private property were also subject to scrutiny. The Tories opposed the Bill on predictable racial, religious, economic and imperialist grounds. Ireland was the oldest colony, and Dublin was considered the Empire's second city. Chamberlain and his radical followers within the Liberal Party feared that it would be the first step in the destruction of the empire. He noted that Ireland would have no say in military, naval or imperial affairs and asked: 'Where in all this is the integrity of the Empire?' He believed that total separation would be preferable to the half-way house that was Home Rule: 'I would prefer that Ireland would go free altogether from any claim on the part of this country, provided also that we might be free from the enormous responsibility a sham Union would certainly entail'.

12.7. George J. Goschen, MP for Edinburgh believed that the measure would set a dangerous precedent and mean 'that every subject race, that India, that Europe would know that we were no longer able to cope with resistance, if resistance were offered'.

12.8. Parnell welcomed it as 'the first cup of cold water that has been offered to our nation since the recall of Lord Fitzwilliam' and he stressed that while the measure enjoyed the support of the American Democrats and Republicans, it contained 'great faults and blots'. Unionists were naturally sceptical when Parnell declared that 'we look on the provision of the Bill as a final settlement of this question, and I believe that the Irish people have accepted it as such a settlement'. The Nationalist MP, Timothy M. Healy (1855–1931) sought to reassure Unionists, saying:

> I want to live at peace with my fellow countrymen; I want to give them all the guarantees that we can give … if I thought there would continue … those horrid religious animosities, I would rather see my country perish forever from the face of the earth.

12.9. Despite the safeguards in the Bill, many Protestant Unionists believed that they would be discriminated against and feared that their economic interests and private property could be threatened. Lord Hartington, speaking for the Whigs in the Liberal Party, believed that the Roman Catholic clergy would have great influence in Dublin parliament:

The parliament which would be restored would not be a Protestant but would be a Roman Catholic parliament. The Established Church has been swept away; and instead of a Roman Catholic priesthood, which at the time of the Union was without political influence at all, we have a Roman Catholic clergy wielding a large political influence.

12.10. Hartington thought Home Rule would be the minimum demand from Irish nationalists. He would only advocate a gradual extension of local self-government. He strongly objected to giving in to pressure and threats of violence from the Parnellites. Ireland under Home Rule, it was claimed, would be the haunt of 'Captain Moonlight' (that is, agrarian terrorism) and the activities of the National League. A number of Irish, particularly Ulster Unionist leaders suggested that armed resistance could be expected if the Bill succeeded. William Johnston, MP for south Belfast, stated that 'the dictates of that Irish parliament would be resisted by the people of Ulster at the point of the bayonet'. An outspoken Orangeman, he had been a central figure in the formation of a separate Irish Unionist parliamentary party in January 1886. He made several calls to arms in various parts of Ulster in April and May 1886. Other Unionists were less threatening but just as determined that Ireland should not be reduced to the status of a rural backwater – and they had reason. Unionists saw no sense in leaving the richest Empire in the world. The industries of the north-east of Ulster, shipbuilding in particular, relied heavily on the British market. The North Down MP, Colonel Thomas Waring, said on 8 April that 'Irish loyalists were now part of one of the greatest Empires of the world … and were utterly determined that they should not be changed into colonials'. He believed that if Home Rule were granted, it would open the floodgates and complete Irish independence would be almost inevitable. Waring was supported in his comments by Robert T. O'Neill, MP for Mid-Antrim, who argued that:

> it was hopeless to suppose that a measure, even of a sweeping character such as that suggested by the Prime Minister, were passed in its integrity, the people of Ireland could stand still under the circumstances, for it would be regarded by certain classes in Ireland as nothing more than an instalment towards an end, which meant the Repeal of the Union.

12.11. Those in support of the measure included James Bryce (1838–1922), MP for South Aberdeen. He was a loyal middle-of-the-road Liberal and a friend of Gladstone's. Although the measure was more radical than he would have wished, Bryce believed that the force of Irish nationalism had to be reckoned with. He stated that Home Rule had worked in places like Iceland, Poland and Finland, why not in Ireland? Charles Arthur Russell (1832–1900) had been appointed attorney-general in Gladstone's government of 1886. His speeches on Home Rule in the House of Commons were probably his best parliamentary performances. Russell echoed Bryce's comments; Ireland could not be compared with Wales or Scotland, and local government measures would not suffice. He viewed 'the so-called loyal minority' not as an aid but a hindrance to the Union, since he saw their loyalty as being strongly based on their self-interest. The threats of violence were not to be taken seriously since 'no words are too strong for those who fan the flames of religious rancour, and who divide, while they plunder, the farmers of Ulster'.

12.12. In mid-April, the first major joint rally of the anti-Home-Rulers took place at the Opera House. Salisbury, Hartington and Goschen joined in criticising Gladstone and Parnell. The queen wrote to congratulate Goschen on the successful meeting and urged him to 'organise as many such meetings, large and small, all over England and Scotland as you can'. With renewed vigour, Goschen set about organising the Liberal Unionists. He made speeches in several key cities and even attended meetings organised by the Irish Loyal and Patritic Union.

13. Defeat of the Home Rule Bill

13.1. By mid-May, however, it was clear that the Home Rule Bill was in trouble. The *Pall Mall Gazette* reported on military preparations by Unionists in Ulster involving tens of thousands of men. At Westminster the Land Purchase Bill was abandoned on 29 May and formally withdrawn on 11 June. Parnell and his supporters had nothing to gain by making any further demands. In one of the final speeches of the debate, Parnell warned the House:

> If you reject this Bill … you will have to resort to coercion … it will be inevitable … there is no half-way house between the concession of legislative autonomy in Ireland and the disfranchisement of the country and her government as a crown Colony.

13.2. Gladstone reminded that House that:

> Any rejection of the conciliatory policy, might have an effect that none of us could wish in strengthening that party of disorder, which is behind the back of the Irish representatives, which skulks in America, which skulks in Ireland, which … will lose ground in proportion as our policy is carried out … Have Hon. Gentlemen considered that they are coming into conflict with a nation? Can anything stop a nation's demands? … Ireland stands at your bar expectant, hopeful, almost suppliant … we hail the demand of Ireland for what I call a blessed oblivion of the past …

13.3. The prime minister concluded his speech early on the morning of 8 June by saying:

> This, if I understand it, is one of those golden moments of our history; one of those opportunities which may come and may go, but which rarely return, or, if they return, return at long intervals, and under circumstances which no man can forecast.

13.4. On 8 June 1886, the first Home Rule Bill was defeated by 341 votes to 311. Significantly, 93 Liberals voted with the Tories. Gladstone was convinced that his policy was morally and politically sound and he resolved to go to the people on the matter. Parliament was quickly dissolved, and the country went to the polls in early July. It is possible, though of course not certain, that if Parnell had supported the Liberals in the 1885 election, enough Liberal MPs might have been elected to offset the 93 who voted against the Home Rule Bill. A bitterly disappointed Parnell was later to comment 'we cannot persuade the English people. They will only do what we force them to do.' Chamberlain and his party followers, the Liberal Unionists, generally voted with the Tories and finally joined them.

13.5. The general election that took place from 1 to 27 July 1886 was fought on the single issue of Home Rule. Gladstone's hopes were dashed – the Liberals won just 191 seats, the Home Rulers won 85, but the Tories and Liberal Unionists took 393. Although there was some support in Scotland and Wales for Home Rule, the majority of English voters were clearly opposed to it. It was a major reversal of the election results of 1885 and the split in the Liberals paved the way for a period of Conservative dominance in British politics. On 20 July, the cabinet decided to resign without meeting in parliament to be voted out. Gladstone left office on 30 July. With his majority alliance, Lord Salisbury formed a government, which remained in power until 1892.

14. The Belfast riots of 1886

14.1. Serious riots were already taking place in Belfast as Home Rule was being debated in the House of Commons. At noon on 4 June 1886, shipwrights marched out of Queen's Island to Alexandra Dock. The day before a Protestant navvy had been expelled by Catholics who taunted him, saying that after Home Rule that 'none of the Orange sort would get leave to work or earn a loaf of bread in Belfast'. The yard men attacked with such ferocity that ten Catholic navvies had to be taken to hospital and another, 18-year-old James Curran, drowned in full view of the mob while trying to escape across the river Lagan. On 8 June, when the Home Rule Bill was defeated, Catholics in the Falls area of Belfast set their chimneys on fire in protest. Protestants lit bonfires in celebration across the city. On the following day hundreds of Protestant rioters attacked members of the Royal Irish Constabulary (RIC) who were trying to prevent the looting of a liquor store on the Shankill Road. The police officers were forced to retreat to Bower's Hill barracks. The rioters pursued them, using paving stones and bricks as missiles. Seven civilians were killed when officers opened fire on the crowd. At 10 p.m. that night the Highland Light Infantry intervened to restore order. Hundreds of police reinforcements were also drafted into the city. Reverend Hugh Hanna, commonly called 'the Roaring Red Hanna', preaching at St Enoch's in Belfast on June 13 1886, denounced the government saying:

> It was right that the loyalty of the land should celebrate as it did that God has given us … But that celebration has cost us dear. It incurred the wrath of a government that has been traitorous to its trusts … The armed servants of that government are sent to suppress rejoicing loyalty by the sanguinary slaughter of a people resolved to resist a wicked policy.

Intermittent rioting continued for several months until mid-September when torrential rain fell for three days and 'took the heart out of the fighting'. About 50 people had been killed, hundreds were injured and much damage was done to property. Protestants were appalled at the prospect of being governed by a Dublin legislature and this was reflected in the high casualties, which exceeded those of all previous riots combined. Other clashes followed in Ballymena, Derry and Portadown, although on a smaller scale. One might well ask, what could have happened had the Home Rule Bill actually been carried in 1886? It is likely that the response from Nationalist and Unionists communities would have been both swift and severe. The MP for Sheffield Eccleshall, Sir Ellis Ashmead-Bartlett MP was not alone among politicians (and others) when he said the Home Rule Bill might contain the 'seeds of civil war'.

15. Conclusion

15.1. Many of those who favoured Home Rule dismissed some of its details as unworkable. The land purchase measure attracted even sharper criticism, especially among Liberals and nationalists. Introduced by Gladstone on 16 April, it was taken no further. Self-government was previously seen as extensive local government with perhaps some central body with limited legislative powers. After 1886, it meant a Dublin assembly, with or without regional sub-authorities, legislating on virtually all Irish affairs. The 1886 Home Rule Bill had an immense impact on British political life. Down to 1914 and after, the Irish problem was dominated by that Bill. By the winter of 1886, most of the Liberal Party had gone back to their old position – local government in the short term as a step towards future legislative autonomy. It is clear that many nationalists did not fully understand what exactly Home Rule would involve – indeed, they were largely unprepared for it. Parnell recognised the merits of Gladstone's measure but contributed little to the debate about the making of the Bill. It is clear that Gladstone was driven by a strong sense of a moral mission and by the fear of the consequences for Westminster of a strong group of disaffected Irish representatives. He had a sense of history, and was conscious of previous injustices done to Ireland.

15.2. Despite the defects of the Government of Ireland Bill of 1886, it was to provide the template for subsequent Home Rule Bills. It was by far the most radical of all the Home Rule Bills and its powers were in reality greater than those of Grattan's parliament. The removal of Irish MPs from Westminster would have put Ireland on the same footing as, for example, Canada. Once established, it is hard to see how (without the use of military force) total separation could have been prevented.

15.3. But Gladstone's Home Rule project was expected to bear too many political burdens – the solution to all of Ireland's problems. He made several misjudgements in the handling of Home Rule affair. He kept the British public and his fellow MPs in the dark as to his intentions. When Gladstone finally declared his support for Home Rule, he laid himself open to the charge of changing his principles. Salisbury and the Tories felt duped and they were having none of it. Randolph Churchill described Gladstone as 'an old man in a hurry', and other MPs argued that he introduced the proposal too early in the new parliament instead of preparing the ground. Although he offered to withdraw, reconstruct and reintroduce the Home Rule Bill in the autumn if it passed its second reading, he should have admitted that the country required more time to consider the matter when the Bill faltered. The British public made it clear that it was not yet ready for such an experiment. The 1886 election results showed that the majority of the English electorate was opposed to Home Rule although there was support in Scotland and Wales. No serious effort was made to reconcile the Irish national aspiration with Ulster Unionism, something that soon became glaringly evident. The Bill made no mention of Ulster's Protestant majority. Until 1885 the representation of Ulster had divided on political lines between Liberals and Conservatives. However, the advent of Home Rule nationalism in 1885–6 helped to strengthen organised Unionism and led to the formation of many loyalist protest bodies. The Irish Uninionist Party was to replace the Liberal and Conservative Parties in Ireland. The Home Rule Bill was not an acceptable solution to Unionists. The divisions between unionism and nationalism had a geographical dimension which foreshadowed partion, and some MPs went so far as to suggest it. Gladstone's detractors saw it as an unrealistic objective, doomed to failure from the outset and not worth the political convulsions it caused.

15.4. The historian William C. Lubenow acknowledges the important point that the British party system was able to accommodate the great challenge of Irish nationalism; indeed, 'the party system revolutionised the Home Rule issue by domesticating it, by making it a creature of parliamentary politics, and by so containing it for thirty years'.

15.5. His Home Rule Bill of 1886 failed, but Gladstone's commitment to Home Rule remained strong. In trying to implement his Irish policy, he risked his political career on a point of principle rather than political expediency and pitched himself against very powerful opponents in the British establishment. The Liberal Party's commitment to Home Rule forged a 'union of hearts' with Parnell and his successors that lasted until the First World War. Gladstone went on to become Prime Minister for the fourth time in 1892 (then in his 80s) and introduced his second Home Rule Bill in February 1893. It was roundly defeated in the House of Lords in September of that year by 419 to 41. However, when Gladstone retired in 1894 the Liberals became much more lukewarm towards Home Rule. He did not live to see a Home Rule measure passed, but as his old nemesis, Benjamin Disraeli, once declared: 'Change is inevitable, change is constant.'

15.6. Parnell's influence was at its height in 1886. His political reputation was enhanced rather than diminished by the whole episode. However, subsequent events meant that he would never again enjoy such a commanding position in British politics. The defeat of Home Rule shifted interest to the land question and new leaders, such as John Dillon (1851–1927) and William O'Brien (1852–1928), came to the fore. After 1885–6, neither

Liberals nor Tories could be seen to be openly courting Parnell or bending to Irish nationalist demands. The new Conservative government was committed to reform and 'killing Home Rule with kindness'. It was hoped that such a policy would help undermine Parnellism in Ireland. Chief Secretary Balfour wasted little time in outlining his Irish policy: 'I shall be as relentless as Cromwell in enforcing obedience to the law, but at the same time, I shall be as radical as any reformer in redressing grievances ...' Indeed, the historian Lewis Perry Curtis characterised Conservative policy towards Ireland in subsequent years as one of both 'coercion and conciliation'. Balfour was determined that the 'rebels' who continued to agitate for Home Rule would not ultimately succeed.

TOMÁS O'RIORDAN

CHAPTER 5

Home Rule and the elections of 1885–6: documents

1. Parnell in Cork, 21 January 1885

1.1. *Introduction.* During the general election campaign of 1885, Parnell emphasised that his party's goal was Home Rule and gave some indications of what kind of arrangement he would be prepared to accept. Having spent much of the period 1882–5 building the Irish Parliamentary Party into a formidable political machine, Parnell now returned fully to active politics. He supported Gladstone's first Government of Ireland Bill (Home Rule Bill) when it was introduced to the House in April 1886. A phrase from Parnell's speech in Cork is inscribed on his monument in Dublin. SOURCE: *Cork Examiner*, 22 January 1885.

> **1.2.** … At the election in 1880 I laid certain principles before you and you accepted them (*applause, and cries of 'we do'*). I said and I pledged myself, that I should form one of an independent Irish party to act in opposition to every English government which refused to concede the just rights of Ireland (*applause*). And the longer time which is gone by since then, the more I am convinced that that is the true policy to pursue so far as parliamentary policy is concerned, and that it will be impossible for either or both of the English parties to contend for any long time against a determine band of Irishmen acting honestly upon these principles, and backed by the Irish people (*cheers*) …

> **1.3.** We shall also endeavour to secure for the labourer some recognition and some right in the land of his country (*applause*). We don't care whether it be the prejudices of the farmer or of the landlord that stands in his way (*hear, hear*). We consider that whatever class tries to obstruct the labourer in the possession of those fair and just rights to which he is entitled, that class should be putdown, and coerced if you will, into doing justice to the labourer …

> **1.4.** I come back – and every Irish politician must be forcibly driven back – to the consideration of the great question of National Self-Government for Ireland (*cheers*). I do not know how this great question will be eventually settled. I do not know whether England will be wise in time and concede to constitutional arguments and methods the restitution of that which was stolen from us towards the close of the last century (*cheers*). It is given to none of us to forecast the future, and just as it is impossible for us to say in what way or by what means the National question may be settled, in what way full justice may be done to Ireland, so it is impossible for us to say to what extent that justice should be done. We cannot ask for less than restitution of Grattan's parliament (*renewed cheering*) … We cannot under the British constitution ask for more than the restitution of Grattan's parliament. But no man

has the right to fix the boundary to the march of a nation (*great cheers*). No man has a right to say to his country: 'Thus far shalt thou go, and no further', and we have never attempted to fix the *ne plus ultra* to the progress of Ireland's nationhood, and we never shall (*cheers*).

1.5. But gentlemen, while we leave those things to time, circumstances, and the future, we must each one of us resolve in our own hearts that we shall at all times do everything which within us lies to obtain for Ireland the fullest measure of her rights (*applause*). In this way we shall avoid difficulties and contentions amongst each other. In this way we shall not give up anything which the future may put in favour of our country, and while we struggle today for that which may seem possible for us with our combination, we must struggle for it with the proud consciousness, and that we shall not do anything to hinder or prevent better men who may come after us from gaining better things than those for which we now contend (*prolonged applause*).

2. Gladstone's conversion to Home Rule

2.1. *Introduction.* Gladstone soon became a convert to Home Rule, if not a very committed one. His conversion to Home Rule was disclosed prematurely (the 'Hawarden Kite') by his son Herbert (16 December 1885). The announcement was published in the London *Standard* and *Leeds Mercury*. Gladstone was forced to make his intentions public and any hope of a bipartisan measure with the Tories was lost. Parnell then entered into an alliance with the Liberals, bringing an end to Salisbury's caretaker administration. In March 1885 Lord Hartington thought that Gladstone was 'in a fool's paradise about everything'. He refused office in Gladstone's government of 1886. He voted against the Home Rule Bill and went on to lead the distinct Liberal Unionists group in parliament. Gladstone writes to Hartington in an attempt to reassure him that his intentions are honourable. He has decided on nothing and does not wish to get into counter-bidding of any sort with Parnell. He states that any measure would have a better chance of success with Tory support (since they controlled the House of Lords) but that no commitments should be rushed into. SOURCE: Letter to Lord Hartington, 17 December 1885, quoted in J. Morley, *The life of William Ewart Gladstone* (2 vols, London, 1930), ii, p. 377.

2.2. The whole stream of public excitement is now turned upon me, and I am pestered with incessant telegrams which there is no defence against but either suicide or Parnell's method of self-concealment. The truth is I have more or less of opinions and ideas, but no intentions or negotiations. In these ideas and opinions there is I think little that I have not conveyed in public declarations: in principle, nothing. I will try to lay them before you.

2.3. I consider that Ireland has now spoken; and that an effort ought to be made by the government without delay to meet her demands for the management of an Irish legislative body of Irish as distinct from Imperial affairs.

2.4. Only a government can do it and a Tory government can do it more easily and safely than any other. There is first a postulate – that the state of Ireland shall be such as to warrant it. The conditions of an admissible plan I think are:

1. Union of the empire and due supremacy of parliament.

2. Protection for the minority – a difficult matter, on which I have talked much with [Lord John Poyntz] Spencer, certain points however remaining to be considered.

3. Fair allocation of imperial charges.

4. A statutory basis seems to me better and safer than the revival of Grattan's parliament, but I wish to hear more upon this; as the minds of men are still in so crude a state on the whole subject.

5. Neither as opinions nor as intentions have I to any one alive promulgated these ideas as decided on by me.

6. As to intentions, I am determined to have none at present – to leave space to the government – I should wish to encourage them if I properly could – above all, on no account to say or do anything which would enable the Nationalists to establish rival biddings between us.

2.5. If this storm of rumours continues to rage, it may be necessary for me to write some new letter to my constituents, but I am desirous to do nothing, simply leaving the field open for the government, until time makes it necessary to decide …

2.6. With regard to the letter I sent you, my opinion is that there is a Parnell party and a separation or civil war party, and that the question which is to have the upper hand will have to be decided in a limited time.

2.7. My earnest recommendation to everybody is not to commit himself. Upon this rule, under whatever pressure, I shall act as long as I can. There shall be no private negotiation carried on by me but the time may come when I shall be obliged to speak publicly. Meantime I hope you will keep in free and full communication with old colleagues. Pray put questions if this letter seems ambiguous.

[P.S.] Pray remember I am at all times ready for personal communications here should you think it desirable.

3. Parnell in Wicklow, October 1885

3.1. *Introduction.* The general election of 1885 was a huge success for Parnell. The Home Rule Party won every seat outside east Ulster and the University of Dublin. In the run-up to the election, Parnell addressed the public in his native Co. Wicklow. He sought to both launch the Irish campaign and to unify the party behind the 'single plank' platform of 'legislative independence'. Parnell describes the negative consequences of Ireland's Union with England. He calls for the protection of the Irish manufacturing industry in order to allow it to survive. England in the past protected her own industries at Ireland's expense. Why must Ireland be treated differently to other British colonies? He demands full legislative independence for Ireland and real powers to manage domestic affairs. While not giving any guarantees to Britain, Parnell states that self-government was the only way for her to earn the confidence and respect of the Irish people. SOURCE: *Freeman's Journal*, 6 October 1885.

3.2. ... I am of the opinion – an opinion that I had expressed before now – that it would be wise to protect certain Irish industries, at all events, for a time ... Possibly protection continued for two or three years, would give us that start which we have lost, owing to the nefarious legislative action of England in times past. I can think also that Ireland could never be a manufacturing nation of such importance as to compete to any great extent with England ...

3.3. I will proceed a little further, and I will deal with the claim that has been put forward, that some guarantee should be given that the granting of legislative powers to Ireland should not lead to the separation of Ireland from England. This claim is one which at first sight may seem a fair one, it may appear preposterous, and it undoubtedly would be preposterous, to ask England to concede to us an engine which we announced an intention to use to bring about separation of the two countries, and which we accepted silently with the intention of so using it; but there is a great difference between having such an intention, or announcing such an intention, and giving counter guarantees against such an intention. It is not possible for human intelligence to forecast the future in these matters, but we can point to this – we can point to the fact that under 85 years of parliamentary connection with England, Ireland has become intensely disloyal and intensely disaffected; notwithstanding the Whig policy of so-called conciliation, alternative conciliation and coercion, and ameliorative measures, that disaffection has hardened, deepened and intensified from day to day.

3.4. Am I not, then entitled to assume that one of the roots of this disaffection – this feeling of disloyalty – is the assumption by England of the management of our affairs? It is admitted that the present system cannot go on, and what are you going to put in its place? My advice to English statesmen considering this question would be this – trust the Irish people altogether, or trust them not at all. Give with a full and open hand, give our people the power to legislate upon all domestic concerns, and you may depend upon one thing, that the desire for separation – the means of winning separation at least – will not be increased or intensified ... that whatever chance the English rulers may have of drawing to themselves the affection of the Irish people lies in destroying the abominable system of legislative union between the two countries by conceding fully and freely to Ireland the right to manage her own affairs.

3.5. It is impossible for us to give guarantees, but we can point to the past; we can show that the record of English rule is a constant series of steps from bad to worse – that the condition of English power is more insecure and more unstable at the present moment than it has ever been. We can point to the example of other countries, of Austria and Hungary, to the fact that Hungary having been conceded self-government became one of the strongest factors in the Austrian empire. We can show the powers that have been freely conceded to the colonies, to the greater colonies, including this very power to protect their own industries against and at the expense of those of England. We can show that disaffection has disappeared in all the greater English colonies: that while the Irishman who goes to the United States of America carries with him a burning hatred of English rule – that while that burning hatred constantly lives in his heart, never leaves him, and is bequeathed to his children. The Irishman coming from the same village, and from the same parish, and from the same townland, equally maltreated, cast out on the road by the relentless landlord, who goes to one of the colonies of Canada or one of the colonies of Australia, and finds there another and a different system of English rule to that which he has been accustomed to at home, becomes to a great extent a loyal citizen and a strength and a prop to the community amongst whom his lot has been cast, that he forgets the little memories of his experience of England at home, and that he no longer continues to look upon the name of England as a symbol of oppression, and the badge of the misfortunes of his country …

3.6. It is the duty of English statesmen at the present day to inquire and examine into these facts for themselves with their eyes open, and to cease the impossible task, which they admit to be impossible, of going forward in the continued misgovernment of Ireland, and persisting in the government of our people by a people outside herself who know not her real wants. And if these lessons be learned, I am convinced that English statesman who is great enough and who is powerful to carry out these teachings, to enforce them on the of his countrymen, to give to Ireland full legislative liberty, full power to manage her own domestic concerns, will be regarded in the future by his countrymen as one who has removed the greatest peril to the English Empire – a peril, I firmly believe, which, if not removed, will find some day – perhaps not in our time – some year, perhaps not for many years to come – but will certainly find, sooner or later, and it may be sooner than later, an opportunity of severing itself – to the destruction of that British empire for the misfortunes, the oppressions, and the misgovernment of our country.

4. 'A Proposed Constitution for Ireland'

4.1. *Introduction.* A document entitled 'A Proposed Constitution for Ireland' was delivered to Gladstone by the well-connected Katharine O'Shea (her uncle Lord Hatherley (1801–81) had been Lord Chancellor (1868–72), and her brother Sir Henry

Evelyn Wood (1838–1919) was a leading Liberal) on 30 October 1885. Parnell hoped to elicit a response from Gladstone before deciding to support either the Liberals or the Conservatives. Gladstone revealed nothing of his intentions other that stating that 'the important subject to which it relates could best be considered by the government of the day'. Parnell's plan called for an Irish legislature with complete control over domestic affairs. The Irish chamber would have the power to levy taxes (including tariffs), control of the courts and justice, and all administration. Ireland would pay a fixed annual charge as part of its contribution to the British Exchequer. The office of Lord Lieutentant was to be abolished. However, the question of Irish representation at Westminster was left open for the time being. A fortnight later, during the Midlothian election campaign, Gladstone closely followed Parnell's plan when drafting his Irish Home Rule Bill. SOURCE: Katharine O'Shea, *Charles Stewart Parnell: his love story and political life* (2 vols, London, 1914), ii, pp 18–20.

4.2. An elected Chamber with power to make enactments regarding all the domestic concerns of Ireland, but without power to interfere in any Imperial matter.

4.3. The Chamber to consist of three hundred members. Two-hundred-and-six of the number to be elected under the present suffrage, by the present Irish constituencies, with special arrangements for securing to the Protestant minority a representation proportionate to their numbers; the remaining ninety-four members to be named …

4.4. The Chamber shall have power to enact laws and make regulations regarding all the domestic and internal affairs of Ireland, including her sea fisheries.

4.5. The Chamber shall also have power to raise a revenue for any purpose over which it has jurisdiction, by direct taxation upon property, by customs duties and by licences.

4.6. The Chamber shall have power to create departments for the transaction of all business connected with the affairs over which it has jurisdiction, and to appoint and dismiss chief and subordinate officials for such departments, to fix the term of their office, and to fix and pay their salaries; and to maintain a police force for the preservation of order and the enforcement of the law.

4.7. This power will include the constitution of Courts of Justice and the appointment and payment of all judges, magistrates, and other officials of such Courts, provided that the appointment of judges and magistrates shall in each case be subject to the assent of the Crown.

4.8. No enactment of the Chamber shall have the force of law until it shall have received the assent of the Crown. …

4.9. The right of the Imperial parliament to legislate regarding the domestic concerns and internal affairs of Ireland will also be held in suspense, only to be exercised for weighty and urgent cause.

4.10. The abolition of the office of Lord Lieutenant of Ireland and all other offices in Ireland under the Crown connected with the domestic affairs of that country.

4.11. The representation of Ireland in the Imperial parliament might be retained or might be given up. If it be retained the Speaker might have power to decide what questions the Irish members might take part in as Imperial questions, if this limitation were thought desirable.

4.12. Such naval and military force as the Crown thought requisite from time to time would be maintained in Ireland out of the contribution of one million pounds (approx. €86 million at 2009 values) per annum to the Imperial Treasury; any excess in the cost of these forces over such sum being provided for out of the Imperial revenue (i.e. by Great Britain).

5. Parnell's election manifesto to the Irish electors in Britain, November 1885

5.1. *Introduction.* In theory, at least, the Irish vote in Britain had a decisive role in the 1885 general election, influencing the result some believed of 25 to 40 British constituencies. Many informed politicians thought that the Irish vote had a considerable value. Much depended on the result of the election. When balloting ended on 9 December 1885, the Liberals had won 335 seats, Conservatives 249 and Home Rulers 86. Attempts by the Irish Loyal and Patriotic Union to undermine the Home Rule movement in Ireland failed. Home Rulers won 85 of 103 constituencies, including 17 – a majority of one – in Ulster. T.P. O'Connor's victory in Liverpool brought the total number of Home Rule seats to 86. The effect of the Irish vote on British constituencies is not clear. Liberals were defeated in more than a half-dozen places by the Irish vote. At the end of the balloting no party had an outright majority. Tory and Irish numbers equalled the Liberal. Gladstone had remained silent on Home Rule, and Parnell believed (mistakenly) that the Conservatives were moving toward Home Rule. The election manifesto reproduced here, was released on Saturday, 21 November 1885. It was a directive to Irish electors to vote against all but a handful of Liberal and Radical candidates. Parnell condemns the Liberal Party for its false promises, its repressive laws, its interference in religion and schools, its attempts to crush the power of anti-radical members in parliament and its general bad government. The Executive of the Irish National League would draw up a list of election candidates whom they believed acceptable. He alienated many Liberals (including Chamberlain) and the Liberal Party became bitterly divided on Home Rule. SOURCE: Charles Stewart Parnell, *Manifesto to the Irish electors in Britain*, 21 November 1885 (Home Rule pamphlets, National Library of Ireland).

> **5.2.** ... To Ireland, more than any other country, it [the previous Liberal government] bound itself by most solemn pledges, and these were most flagrantly violated. It denounced coercion, and it practiced a system of coercion more brutal

than that of any previous Administration, Liberal or Tory. Under this system juries were packed with a shamelessness unprecedented even in a Liberal Administration, and innocents were hung or sent to the living death of penal servitude. Twelve hundred men were imprisoned without trial. Ladies were convicted under obsolete Acts directed against the degraded of their sex; and for a period every utterance of the popular press and of popular meetings was completely suppressed as if Ireland were Poland, and the administration of England, a Russian autocracy. The representatives of Liberalism in Ireland were men like Mr Forster and Lord [John Poyntz] Spencer, who have left more hateful memories in Ireland than any statesmen of the century.

5.3. The last declaration of Mr Gladstone was that he intended to renew the very worst clauses of the Coercion Act of 1882; and if our long-delayed triumph had not turned the Liberal government from office, Lord Spencer would at this hour be in Dublin Castle, coercion would be triumphant in Ireland, and the landlords, instead of making the reasonable abatements demanded by the depression of agriculture, and conceded by every landlord in England and Scotland, would be evicting wholesale, with the encouragement of Lord Spencer and the backing of police, soldiery, coercion magistrates, and filled jails.

5.4. The Liberals began by menacing the Established Church, and under the name of free schools made an insidious attempt to crush the religious education of the country, to establish a system of State tyranny and intolerance, and to fetter the right of conscience, which is as sacred in the selection of school as in the free selection of one's church. The cry of Disestablishment has been dropped; the cry of free schools has been explained away; and the two last cries left to the Liberal party are the so-called Reform of Procedure and a demand to be independent of the Irish Party. Reform of procedure means a new gag, and the application to all enemies of Radicalism in the House of Commons of the despotic methods and the mean machinery of the Birmingham caucus [the Chamberlains and their followers].

5.5. The specious demand for a majority against the Irish party is an appeal for power to crush all anti-Radical members in parliament first, and then to propose to Ireland some scheme doomed to failure because of its unsuitability to the wants of the Irish people, and finally to force down a halting measure of self-government upon Irish people by the same method of wholesale imprisonment by which durability was sought for the impracticable Land Act of 1881. Under such circumstances we feel bound to advise our countrymen to place no confidence in the Liberal or Radical party, and so far as in them lies to prevent the government of the empire falling into the hands of a party so perfidious, treacherous and incompetent.

5.6. In no case ought an Irish Nationalist to give a vote in our opinion to a member of that Liberal or Radical party, except in some few cases in which courageous fealty to the Irish cause in the last parliament has given a guarantee that the candidate will not belong to the servile, and cowardly, and unprincipled herd that would break every pledge and violate every principle in obedience to the call of the whip and the mandate of the caucus.

5.7. The Executive of the Irish National League will communicate the names of the candidates whom they think would be excepted from the terms of this manifesto. In every other instance we earnestly advise our countrymen to vote against the men who coerced Ireland, deluged Egypt with blood, menaced religious liberty in the school, freedom of speech in parliament, and promised to the country generally a repetition of the crimes and follies of the last Liberal Administration.

(signed) T.P. O'Connor

President of the Irish National League of Great Britain

Justin McCarthy	Thomas Sexton	James O'Kelly
T.M. Healy	J.E. Redmond	J.G. Biggar

6. Opposition to Home Rule – the Irish Loyal and Patriotic Union (ILPU)

6.1. *Introduction.* The Irish Loyal and Patriotic Union (ILPU) was founded in Dublin (1 May 1885) to resist Home Rule. It reflected the views of an influential southern Unionists like Lord Castletown (1849–1937) and Lord Longford (1819–87), rather than more militant Ulster Unionists. Operating from its offices in Dublin, it printed thousands of propaganda leaflets and pamphlets to alert people to 'Parnellite tactics'. It was replaced by the Irish Unionist Alliance in 1891. The ILPU published a news sheet, *Notes from Ireland*, as well as its annual series of pamphlets. They provide a rich source of material for the study of Irish Unionism and of the Anglo-Irish community in Ireland. As the ILPU hoped to win seats outside of Ulster, it is not surprising to see its focus (Document I) on economic rather than religious issues. In contrast, the Ulster Loyalist Anti-Repeal Union founded in Belfast on 8 January as a rival to the ILPU, referred to the defence of the Protestant religion. It played on fears of Catholicism and the danger of a hostile power controlling Belfast Lough and threatening the Clyde. A special effort was made in Scotland where meetings were organised and thousands of pamphlets distributed.

I

SOURCE: Pamphlet, 'Ought I join the Loyal and Patritotic Union?' Published by the Irish Loyal and Patriotic Union (London 1885).

6.2. For prospective members:

1. Ought I join the Loyal and Patriotic Union?

Yes – Because it is the only organization that is steadily working by public meeting and through the Press, to inform the English public as to the dangers of Home Rule, and the decision rests with the English and Scottish electors.

2. But what harm would Home Rule do me?

It would paralyse trade, it would drive the gentry, who, with the traders, are the largest employers of labour, from the country. It would lower wages and it would leave Ireland the poorest instead of being a part of being the richest country in the world.

3. How do I know all this?

Because all who have anything to lose are opposed to Home Rule. The country gentlemen, the merchants, the Professional men are all against it. See the declarations of the Chambers of Commerce, the resolutions of Grand Juries. The Commercial men in Dublin and Belfast have joined the Irish Loyal and Patriotic Union notwithstanding the terrible danger that they run by doing so, but they know that Home Rule means ruin to them, and if all the employers of labour what is to become of the unhappy labourer?

4. How should I be worse off as a member of a poor country than as a member of a rich one?

Because without capital there can be no great works or manufactures carried on, and Ireland having little of her own is mainly dependent on loans of English capital. At present we get money at 3 per cent from the Imperial government for all important works, such as harbours, fisheries, tramways, drainage, public buildings of all sorts, labourers' cottages … but if we had Home Rule, Ireland being a poor country would have to borrow money at so high a rate of interest that none of these works could be carried out. The taxes would all be doubled at once.

5. What matter does it make whether one more or less joins the Irish Loyal and Patriotic Union?

It matters much, because –
1.   Union is strength. It is only by banding together that we can show the vast number of Irishmen who are opposed to Home Rule.
2.   Because it is not fair to leave it to a few to fight our battle for us.
3.   Because the work the Union is doing costs a lot of money, and every shilling is of importance.

6. But my income is small and has become smaller of late. I cannot afford to subscribe.

Can you then to afford to lose what's left of income, as you probably will do if Home Rule is carried, and Home Rule will be carried unless we all unite in one great, well sustained effort to avert it. Then join the Union. Do not content yourself with signing protests and talking, but ACT. Encourage the hearts and strengthen the hands of those who are in the front of the battle; and then if we stand together like one man, we shall yet see this wretched League which has brought the country to such a state of misery put down, and Ireland once more truly free, prosperous, and happy.

II

6.3. *Introduction.* This ILPU pamphlet focuses on the potential damage to the Irish economy if Home Rule was to become a reality. Persecution of Protestants would probably be unlikely, although church property might be confiscated. The main fear for businessmen, is taxation and the protection of Irish industry by the imposition of tariffs. Such measures rather than hurting England could bring about the ruination of Ireland. The author argues that an end to agitation in the countryside and hard work would be far more beneficial to fledgling Irish industries. SOURCE: The Irish Loyal and Patriotic Union, *The real dangers of Home Rule* (Dublin, 1886), pp 2–13.

6.4. But the more important question is the effect which Home Rule (that is, supposing Home Rule to mean the power of making laws, and, in particular, of imposing taxes) would have upon the interests of the minority. As I have said, persecution, in the old sense of the word, may be dismissed as, to say the least, highly improbable. But is there no way of affecting Protestants, or the interests of Protestants injuriously, except by direct and open persecution? It is tacitly admitted that the Roman Catholics of Dublin would not be unlikely to put in a claim for at least one of the Dublin Cathedrals, both of which have been restored by the outlay of immense sums of money by Protestants. There is, in print, in a recently published history of the Roman Catholic Diocese of Kildare a hint, by no means obscure, of the coming time, when the Cathedral of Kildare – which has been partially restored with money contributed by Protestants – shall be restored to its 'rightful owners'. These are but trifles – straws, perhaps; but the old proverb has not yet lost its force. The more serious question, however, is the question of taxation …

6.5. One of the objects which the Parnellite party set before them for accomplishment, when they shall have been installed in College-Green, and in a 'purified' Dublin Castle, is the 'fostering of Irish industries'. What that means is not left a matter of doubt; what the men engaged in the various Irish industries understand by it is not a matter of doubt. At a meeting some time ago of what was then called the Irish Protection Association, but is now called the Irish Industrial League, and which was attended by about a score of people, most of those present representing different branches of industry, the necessity for protection, all around, was insisted on. 'Burn everything from England, except her coal', was the motto of the meeting. Now, if I were an Englishman I should not object to that. Mr [Joseph] Chamberlain never made a greater mistake in his life than when he expressed an 'apprehension' that an Irish parliament would seek, by protection, to exclude English manufacturers. He showed a lamentable want of appreciation of the true character and objects of Free Trade. By any such policy as that suggested Ireland could only injure herself. The apostles of Free Trade in England made a great mistake in showing any anxiety, and even in entertaining any desire, that other nations should become converts to the principle of Free Trade. People are always sceptical when professions of disinterested philanthropy are made.

6.6. The essential principle of Free Trade is that it benefits the nation which adopts it, whether other nations adopt it or not. If commercial treaties are beneficial, if the principle underlying them is a true principle, then the principle of Free Trade is utterly wrong. The two things are diametrically opposed to each other. Yet England has had her commercial treaties since she formally adopted Free Trade. And therefore, Mr Chamberlain may be excused for thinking that the adoption of a system of protective duties in Ireland would injure England. If it would injure England, there would be some reason for anticipation that it would benefit Ireland. But the loss would be Ireland's, not England's. Nothing will so effectually kill any industry as the 'fostering' of it by protective duties. In any case, it is the people who thus tax the necessaries, the conveniences, or the comforts of life, who suffer, not those who produce the articles which minister to these objects.

6.7. It is, therefore, Irishmen who have most reason to fear the establishment of an Irish parliament, if that Irish parliament would be likely to take to the 'fostering' of Irish industries. There are many Irish industries which are capable of development; but a forced growth, a hothouse development of any industry, will never bring that industry to a healthy condition. The most effective way of fostering Irish industries is to get rid of the unhealthy agitation which has prevailed in the country for the last half-dozen years: to instil into the minds of the people of all classes that the true secret of industrial progress is hard work …

7. Cardinal Cullen on Home Rule

7.1. *Introduction.* Paul Cardinal Cullen (1803–1878), Archbishop of Dublin, did not approve of the Home Rule movement or its leadership. For him it was too Protestant and too Fenian. He was soon described as a 'west Briton' and a 'Castle bishop'. Cullen was shaken by the ending of the Temporal Power of the Papacy in 1870, when the Italian Army entered Rome. He felt that such revolutionary movements lacked moral probity. Such an attempt in Ireland would, he believed, lead to bloodshed and instability. Cullen's views were used as propaganda by the Irish Loyal and Patriotic Union in 1886. Though his attitude to Home Rule later softened, he remained deeply suspicious of nationally based political parties. SOURCE: *The Tablet*, 27 March 1886.

7.2. My first duty is to approach all questions from my own standpoint, that is, as a bishop, and to examine into and see what the effect of any great political change would be on religion and the Church's interests ... I must admit, then, that I do not like this new movement for what is called Home Rule, for of this I am convinced that the first future attack on the liberty of the Church and on the interest of religion will come from a native parliament if we ever have one ... I am convinced, that the moving spring in this new agitation in Ireland is identical with that in Italy, that is the spirit of the revolution so loudly and so authoritatively condemned by the Holy See; but for this power and this spirit the movement in Ireland would have no strength. We all know what the Revolution has done in Rome and in France. It first drove the Pope from the Eternal City ... In Paris what have we seen? – an archbishop shot down in the streets and priests murdered in that city ... France was once as Catholic as Ireland, but the Revolution undermined her faith. Should an Irish parliament, whose strength, I believe, will come from revolutionary sources, pass laws that are subversive of justice, morality, or religion, it will be the duty of the bishops to speak out to warn their flocks and to condemn such acts ... With this conviction in my mind, I for one can never advocate this revolutionary movement, as I believe it to be, for Home Rule.

8. The case against Home Rule

8.1. *Introduction.* The British professor of law, Albert Venn Dicey (1835–1922), author of the treatise *Lectures introductory to the study of the law of the constitution*, played a leading part in political controversy. Between 1886 and 1913 he wrote four books opposing Home Rule in Ireland. Originally a Liberal and sympathiser with Irish nationalism, the extremism of the 1880s when Fenians conducted assassinations and bombings in Britain, alienated him from the Irish cause. In this document, he questions whether Home Rule would really offer the independence sought by nationalists. SOURCE: A.V. Dicey, *England's case against Home Rule* (London, 1886), pp 32–3, 54, 67–70.

> **8.2.** ... Home Rule does not mean National Independence. This proposition needs no elaboration. Any plan of Home Rule whatever implies that there are spheres of national life in which Ireland is not to act with the freedom of an independent state. Mr Parnell and his followers accept in principle Mr Gladstone's proposals, and therefore are willing to accept for Ireland restrictions on her political liberty absolutely inconsistent with the principle of nationality. Under the Gladstonian constitution her foreign policy is to be wholly regulated by a British parliament in which sit no Irish representatives; she is not to have the right either of raising an army or of endowing a Church; she is in fact to surrender any claim to the rights of a nation in consideration of receiving a certain number of state-rights. In all this there is nothing unreasonable and nothing blameworthy. One part of the United Kingdom is prepared to accept new terms of partnership. But this acceptance, though reasonable and fair enough, is quite inconsistent with any claim for national independence. A nation is one thing, a state forming part of a federation is quite

another. To ask for the position of a dependent colony like Victoria, or of a province such as Ontario, is to renounce the demand to be a nation …

8.3. … the advocates of Home Rule (honestly enough, no doubt) confuse the matter … by a strange kind of intellectual shuffle. When they wish to minimise the sacrifice to England of establishing a parliament in Ireland, they bring Home Rule down nearly to the proportions of local self-government; when they wish to maximise – if the word may be allowed – the blessing to Ireland of a separate legislature, they all but identify Home Rule with National Independence. Yet you have no more right to expect from any form of state-rights the new life which sometimes is roused among a people by the spirit and the responsibilities of becoming a nation, than you have to suppose municipal councils will satisfy the feelings which demand an Irish parliament.

8.4. … The vast majority of the United Kingdom, including a million or more of the inhabitants of Ireland, have expressed their will to maintain the Union. Popular government means government in accordance with the will of the majority, and therefore according to all the principles of popular government the majority of the United Kingdom have a right to maintain the Union. Their wish is decisive, and ought to terminate the whole agitation in favour of Home Rule …

9. MP John Bright's opposition to Home Rule

9.1. *Introduction.* John Bright (1811–89), was the son of a Quaker textile manufacturer and by 1886, he was the elder statesman of British politics. A dedicated pacifist, he was generally sympathetic to Ireland. He was a long-standing advocate of church, land and local government reform in Ireland. In fact, he introduced significant amendments to Gladstone's Irish Church Act, 1870 and his Landlord and Tenant Act, 1870 (the 'Bright Clauses'). However, Bright did not support Gladstone's Home Rule Bill and he viewed Home Rule MPs as a 'Rebel Party'. He thought the Bill disregarded the 'loyal and Protestant' people of Ulster, and this he could not tolerate. SOURCE: R.J.A. Walling (ed.), *The diaries of John Bright* (London, 1930).

20 March 1886

9.2. Downing Street – Long interview for 2 hours with Mr Gladstone at his request … He explained much of his policy as to a Dublin parliament and as to Land Purchase. I objected to the Land policy as unnecessary … As to a Dublin parliament, I argued that he was making a surrender all along the line. A Dublin parliament would work with constant friction, and would press against any barrier he might create to keep up the unity of the Three Kingdoms.

9.3. What of a volunteer force, and what of import duties and protection as against British goods? He would not object, but any armed force must be under officers appointed by the Crown; and he did not think duties as against England would be imposed.

9.4. Mr Gladstone is in favour of excluding all Irish representation from the Imperial parliament. Thinks Irish members in Dublin and at Westminster not possible. Irish members think they could not supply representatives for both Houses.

9.5. I told him I thought to get rid of the Irishmen from Westminster, such as we have known them for 5 or 6 years past, would do something to make his propositions less offensive and distasteful in Great Britain, though it tends to more complete separation …

9.6. I thought he placed far too much confidence in the leaders of the Rebel Party [Parnell's Home Rule Party]. I could place none in them, and the general feeling was and is that any terms made with them would not be kept, and that, through them, I could not hope for reconciliation with discontented and disloyal Ireland.

10. The Galway by-election of 1886

10.1 *Introduction.* In 1881, Irish Party MPs became aware of Parnell's involvement with Katharine O'Shea, the wife of Captain William O'Shea. Parnell's secretary, Timothy Michael Healy, resigned on his return to London. In February 1886, when Parnell proposed O'Shea for a vacant parliamentary seat in Galway (without taking the Party pledge), Healy and other MPs went to Galway to support the local candidate Joseph Lynch. The vacancy arose from Thomas Power O'Connor's double election in Liverpool and Galway (he chose the former constituency). O'Shea had failed to win a seat as a Liberal in the election of 1885 and had neither voted nor sat with the Irish Party at Westminster. In the words of Randolph Churchill, he had become 'repugnant politically and from every point of view to the Irish Party'. Biggar had declared that he and other members of the party were 'mere machines' to be directed in any way Parnell saw fit. Healy and Biggar arrived in Galway on 7 February to speak in support of Lynch. The revolt in Galway shocked many in the party and the situation demanded a quick response. The editor of the *Freeman's Journal* wrote on 9 February 1886:

> … the issue is not between Captain O'Shea and Mr Lynch but whether at the very moment of the crisis, when the question of Home Rule hangs in the balance, when Mr Parnell almost holds it in the hollow of his hands, Galway will strike a blow at his prestige and authority.

10.2. Parnell arrived in Galway on 9 February accompanied by leading party members, Thomas Sexton, J.J. O'Kelly, J. Deasy and his private secretary, Henry Campbell. He had the support of Edmund Dwyer Gray (owner of the *Freeman's Journal*) as well as important clergy. The pressure on Healy mounted and he received many telegrams from colleagues advising him to back down. On 9 February, after a private meeting between

Parnell and the party members, it was announced publicly that O'Shea was to get the Party nomination. Healy admitted defeat saying: 'I retire from this contest and Captain O'Shea becomes, I suppose, the member for Galway, it is a bitter cup for you. God knows, to me it is a cup of poison, but even so. Let it be taken for the sake of the unity of the party we love.' While resistance had collapsed in Parnell's presence, many of the party faithful were deeply offended by O'Shea's candidature. Parnell argued that a rejection of O'Shea would be a blow to his own power and would make Home Rule more difficult to achieve. Although Lynch's name had remained on the ballot paper, O'Shea won by a big majority, on 10 February 1886. John Dillon believed that restraint and silence were vital if the party leader thought that the moment was ripe for Home Rule. Farmers and labourers, he stated, would have to make sacrifices. On the same day, the Church hierarchy endorsed the Parnellite position and Home Rule, 'it alone can satisfy the wants, the wishes, as well as the legitimate aspirations of the Irish people' (Archbishop Walsh to Gladstone, 17 February, published in *Freeman's Journal*, 22 Feb. 1886).

I

10.3. *Introduction.* T.M. Healy had earlier written to the *Freeman's Journal* (5 February 1886) questioning O'Shea's motives for standing in the Galway by-election. How, he asked, could O'Shea stand as a Nationalist when he had never supported the Irish Party in the past. Two days later, speaking in Eyre Square, Healy reminded the crowd that he had asked if 'Captain O'Shea intended to take the pledge of the Irish Party to sit, act, and vote with the party in the House of Commons. I could get no information … Let me say if Captain O'Shea poses here as the representative or choice of the Irish Party, I am here to say that the Irish Party was never consulted.' SOURCE: *Freeman's Journal*, 5 February 1886.

10.4. Of course it may be that he [Captain O'Shea] intends to hold himself out as a Nationalist but in that case the atmosphere of defeat must have forced his conversion with hot-house rapidity. It is not two months since he presented himself to an English constituency as a Liberal – armed in his enterprise with letters of marque from Mr Gladstone, Mr Chamberlain, and Lord Richard Grosvenor [Liberal Chief Whip]. For six years he sat in parliament on the government side of the House, and on nearly every critical occasion he either voted against the Irish Party, or else kept prudently away from embarrassing divisions. If now that he has failed to secure a seat on any other conditions, Captain O'Shea announces himself as a Nationalist, prepared to take the pledge of the Irish Party, the deathbed character of his repentance would be so apparent that his sincerity would at once be questioned …

II–IV

10.5. *Introduction.* Telegrams played an important part in the final outcome of the Galway crisis. Healy received many, some were in his support, but most called on him to back Parnell. The contents of three of the telegrams are reproduced below. SOURCE: Timothy M. Healy, *Letters and leaders of my day* (2 vols, London, 1928), i, pp 242, 244–5.

Telegram sent by Parnell to Lynch, 7 February 1886.

10.6. I am informed that you are being urged to contest Galway in opposition to Captain O'Shea. Before you decide, it is my duty to inform you that I leave for Galway tonight to support O'Shea's candidature, and that the responsibility resting upon you or anybody else who attempts to weaken my power and influence at present juncture will be grave.

Telegram sent by Gray to Healy, 8 February 1886.

10.7. My information tonight convinces me of the vital importance of carrying out Parnell's policy and of the ruinous effect of defeating him. I entreat you to reconsider your action before it is too late, and to subordinate your personal feelings to those of Parnell and to try and induce Lynch to retire.

Matthew Harris, MP who had been T.P. O'Connor's main helper in Galway in 1880, sent a message to Healy, 9 February 1886.

10.8. If you give way to Parnell now and make provision for liberty by giving the selection of members in future to a committee elected by the Party you will accomplish a great work. Compromise on this basis, as public feeling here is strongly against disunion. Lynch is my friend, and an honest Nationalist. I ask him to do, what in like case, I would do myself. Do not be led astray by excitement of the people. Their course is right but inexpedient at present.

V

10.9. *Introduction.* At 12 o'clock on 11 February 1886, Parnell, accompanied by Revd Peter Dooly, PP; Revd John Carolan, PP; Revd Eugene Sheehy, CC; Mr J.J. O'Kelly, MP; and Mr Campbell, MP; left the Railway Hotel, and drove out to Castlegar to address the electorate there. After spending a short time in the house of the Parish Priest, Rev. John Carolan, he addressed the villagers. In his speech Parnell outlines the reasons why he chose Captain O'Shea to stand for Galway city. SOURCE: *Irish Times*, 11 February 1886.

10.10. People of Castlegar, I am obliged to you for having assembled in such numbers and on such short notice. I am glad to be able to announce to you that the dispute in reference to the representation of Galway has been settled by the self-sacrifice of Mr Lynch and his friends, who have retired in favour of the candidate, Captain O'Shea, recommended by me to the constituency. I shall take this opportunity of telling you that if I had known that Mr Lynch was coming forward for the representation I should have accepted him, for I believe that he is an honest man and a gentleman, in every way suited to represent with honesty and ability the people of Galway.

10.11. But in the duty which has devolved on me as leader of the Irish party and of the nation, to advise the people of Galway with regard to the selection of a candidate, it became necessary for me ten days ago to inquire as to whether there was any local candidate in existence who desired to offer himself to the constituency, and I was informed by Mr T.P. O'Connor that the only local candidate, Mr Lynch, would not offer himself; that he had declined; and that, not under any circumstances could he be induced to offer himself for the representation.

10.12. It therefore became necessary for me to look for some outside person unconnected with Galway – for the best candidate I could find. I therefore took it on myself to recommend Captain O'Shea, but, owing to some misunderstanding, Mr Lynch was induced to put himself in opposition to Mr O'Shea. A crisis of some gravity, difficulty and danger then arose, but, as I have told you, that crisis has happily terminated by the patriotic withdrawal of Mr Lynch.

10.13. I wish now to say a few words in favour of Mr O'Shea and of his action in the last parliament, and of his willingness to work with us. I say that you may go to the poll and record your votes in his favour. Although Mr Lynch has withdrawn it will yet be necessary for you to go to the poll and record your votes for Captain O'Shea. Mr Lynch's name is on the ballot paper, and it is possible that the Tories and Orangemen of Galway will go and vote for Lynch, and endeavour to return him if the people do not come forward in sufficient numbers to return Captain O'Shea. It will, however, not be Mr Lynch's fault should they do so, for he has done everything that an honourable man could do by withdrawing from the contest. It will therefore be your duty to go tomorrow to the poll and put a cross opposite the name of Mr O'Shea.

10.14. Now, with regard to Mr O'Shea's candidature. He represented the County of Clare without my recommendation – in fact he was not at the time my candidate; but notwithstanding this fact, immediately after his return in 1880 he came up to Dublin and attended a meeting of the Irish Parliamentary Party, held in the City Hall, when the famous division took place on the question whether Mr William Shaw or I should be leader of the party, and at that crisis in the history of Ireland, he cast his vote in my favour. My election on that occasion was carried by a majority of two votes, and it is right for me to remember now the service then rendered by O'Shea to me and in the cause of Ireland. If he and one other had voted against me then I should have been deprived of the leadership of the party, and many of the great things that have since been done would not have been accomplished. There are men in the Parliamentary Party who did not vote for me on that occasion, and if that be so shy should not I remember that vote he then gave in my favour.

10.15. I have one fault to find with Mr O'Shea's public action. I repeatedly told him that I should not recommend his election unless that fault were amended, and I declined to support him for Galway until he had given me a promise that his conduct in future should not be open to that charge. The only fault I found with him during the last parliament was that he consistently refused to sit on the same side of the House with us in opposition. But he has now given me this promise, and I guarantee to you that he has given me this promise, that in future he will sit with us as the Irish Party. Therefore the last possible objection that could be raised against him has disappeared.

11. Lord Randolph Churchill plays the 'Orange card'

11.1. *Introduction.* Lord Randolph Churchill (1849–1895) was secretary to his father, John Winston Spencer-Churchill, 7th Duke of Marlborough (1822–83), who served as Lord Lieutenant of Ireland, 1876–80. Randolph Churchill was first elected MP for Woodstock in 1874. Though he supported a policy of conciliation in Ireland, he opposed Home Rule. It was, he believed, a fight to defend the British Empire. His words 'Ulster will fight, and Ulster will be right' became a powerful rallying call to Unionists. After the fall of Gladstone's government and the defeat of the Home Rule Bill, Churchill became Chancellor of the Exchequer and leader of the House of Commons (July 1886). Gerald Fitzgibbon (1837–1909) was a judge and prominent freemason, he had served with Churchill on the Royal Commission appointed in 1878 to inquire into the condition and management of the endowed schools of Ireland. SOURCE: Quoted in W.S. Churchill, *Lord Randolph Churchill* (2 vols, London, 1906), ii, pp 59, 62, 65.

I

Churchill to Gerald Fitzgibbon, 16 February 1886

11.2. I decided some time ago, that if the G.O.M. ['Grand Old Man', or, according to Disraeli, 'God's Only Mistake', that is, Gladstone] went for Home Rule, the Orange card would be the one to play. Please God may it turn out the ace of trumps and not the two …

11.3. It may be that this dark cloud which is now impending over Ireland, will pass away without breaking. If it does. I believe you and your descendants will be safe for a long time to come. Her Majesty's government hesitates. Like Macbeth before the murder of Duncan, Mr Gladstone asks for time. Before he plunged the knife into the heart of the British Empire he reflects, he hesitates … The Loyalists of Ulster should wait and watch – organise and prepare. Diligence and vigilance ought to be your watchword; so that the blow, if it does come, may not come upon you as a thief in the night and may not find you unready and taken by surprise …

11.4. No portentous change such as the Repeal of the Union, no change so gigantic, could be accomplished by the mere passing of a law … I do not hesitate to tell you most truly that in that dark hour there will not be wanting to you those of position and influence in England who would be willing to cast in their lot with you and who, whatever the result, will share your fortunes and your fate.

II

Speech in the Ulster Hall, Belfast, 22 February 1886

11.5. If political parties and political leaders, not only parliamentary but local, should be so utterly lost to every feeling and dictate of honour and courage as to hand over coldly, and for the sake of purchasing a short and illusory parliamentary tranquility, the lives and liberties of the Loyalists of Ireland to their hereditary and most bitter foes, make no doubt on this point – Ulster will not be a consenting party; Ulster at the proper moment will resort to the supreme arbitrament of force; Ulster will fight, Ulster will be right; Ulster will emerge from the struggle victorious, because all that Ulster represents to us Britons will command the sympathy and support of an enormous section of our British community …

12. Gladstone and Parnell on the Ulster Question, 1886

12.1. *Introduction.* The day before the Home Rule Bill was defeated Gladstone stated in the House of Commons that the entire island of Ireland could not be held to ransom by a Protestant minority. Parnell also dismissed as unworkable the idea of separate legislature for Ulster arguing that over 400,000 Protestants lived outside the province. Was their welfare any less important? SOURCE: W.E. Gladstone and Charles Stewart Parnell on the Government of Ireland Bill, 7 June 1886, *Hansard*, 3rd ser., vol. 304, cols. 1036–85 & 1179–80 (extracts).

I

[Gladstone]

12.2. … I will deviate from my path for a moment to say a word upon the state of opinion in that wealthy, intelligent and energetic portion of the Irish community which predominates in a certain portion of Ulster. Our duty is to adhere to a sound general principle, and give the utmost consideration we can to the opinion of that energetic minority. The first thing of all, I should say, is that if … violent measures have been threatened in certain emergencies, I think the best compliment I can pay to those who have threatened us is to take no notice whatever of the threats, but to treat them as momentary ebullitions … I cannot conceal the conviction that the voice of Ireland, as a whole, is at this moment clearly and constitutionally spoken.

I cannot say it is otherwise when five-sixths of its lawfully chosen representatives are of one mind in this matter. Certainly, sir, I cannot allow it to be said that a Protestant minority in Ulster, or elsewhere, is to rule the question at large for Ireland. I am aware of no constitutional doctrine tolerable on which such a conclusion could be adopted or justified. But I think that the Protestant minority should have its wishes considered to the utmost practical extent in any form that they may assume ...

II

[Parnell]

12.3. ... But the Right Hon. Member for West Birmingham [Mr Joseph Chamberlain] has claimed for Ulster a separate Legislature for that Province of Ulster. Well, Sir, you would not protect the loyal minority of Ireland even supposing that you gave a separate Legislature to the Protestants of Ulster, because there are outside the Province of Ulster over 400,000 Protestants who would still be without any protection ... but you would not even protect the Protestants of Ulster because the Protestants, according to the last Census, were in the proportion of 52 to 48 Catholics ... Well, being driven away from the fiction of Protestant Ulster and the great majority of Protestants which until recently was alleged to exist in Ulster, the opponents of this Bill have been compelled to seek refuge in the north-east corner of Ulster, consisting of three counties ... Seven-twelfths of the Protestants of Ireland live outside these three counties ... in the north-east corner of Ulster, and the other five-twelfths of the Protestants of Ireland inside those counties. So that, whichever way you put it, you must give the idea of protecting the Protestants either as a body or as a majority by the establishment of a separate legislature, either in Ulster or in any portion of Ulster. No, Sir, we cannot give up a single Irishman.

13. Gladstone on the Home Rule Bill, 8 April 1886

13.1. *Introduction.* Gladstone introduced the first Home Rule Bill on 4 April 1886, in one of his finest speeches that lasted nearly four hours. It was partly historical and partly an explanation of his proposals. Since the Act of Union in 1800 all efforts to govern Ireland through the parliament at Westminster had failed, and special laws for the suppression of poltical and agrarian crime had been enforced. Discontent and disloyalty remained. In Gladstone's opinion, the only way of meeting such challenges effectively was to entrust Irishmen with the conduct of Irish legislation and administration, in so far as it did not conflict with British or Imperial interests. An Irish legislature, with an Irish executive responsible to it, would, Gladstone thought, be able to solve the problem of combining local autonomy with the supreme authority of Westminster. It was the first time that a concrete proposal for Home Rule had been authoritatively presented to the

British parliament. Gladstone commended the bill to the House saying: 'Do not let us disguise ourselves. We stand face to face with what is termed Irish nationality. Irish nationality vents itself in the demand for local autonomy or separate and complete self-government in Irish not in Imperial affairs. Is this an evil in itself?' SOURCE: William Ewart Gladstone, edited by Arthur Tilney Bassett, *Gladstone's speeches: descriptive index and bibliography* (London, 1916), pp 601–44; *Hansard* 3 (Commons), 3rd series, vol. 304, 1036–81, 8 April 1886.

13.2. … Law is discredited in Ireland, and discredited in Ireland upon this ground especially – that it comes to the people of that country with a foreign accent, and in a foreign garb. These Coercion Bills of ours, of course for it has become a matter of course – I am speaking of the facts and not of the merits – these Coercion Bills are stiffly resisted by the Members who represent Ireland in parliament. The English mind, by cases of this kind and by the tone of the press towards them, is estranged from the Irish people and the Irish mind is estranged from the people of England and Scotland … If coercion is to be the basis for legislation, we must no longer be seeking, as we are always laudably seeking, to whittle it down almost to nothing at the very first moment we begin, but we must, like men, adopt it, hold by it, sternly enforce it, till its end has been completely attained – with what results to peace, good will and freedom I do not now stop to inquire. Our ineffectual and spurious coercion is morally worn out …

13.3. … The case of Ireland, though she is represented here not less fully than England and Scotland, is not the same as that of England and Scotland. England, by her own strength, and by her vast majority in this House, makes her own laws just as independently as if she were not combined with two other countries. Scotland – a small country, smaller than Ireland, but a country endowed with a spirit so masculine that never in the long course of history, excepting for two brief periods, each of a few years, was the superior strength of England such as to enable her to put down the national freedom beyond the border – Scotland, wisely recognised by England, has been allowed and encouraged in this house to make her own laws as freely and as effectually as if she had a representation six times as strong. The consequence is that the mainspring of law in England is felt by the people to be English; the mainspring of law in Scotland is felt by the people to be Scotch; but the mainspring of law in Ireland is not felt by the people to be Irish.

13.4. … Something must be done, something is imperatively demanded from us to restore to Ireland the first conditions of civil life – the free course of law, the liberty of every individual in the exercise of every legal right, the confidence of the people in the law, apart from which no country can be called, in the full sense of the word, a civilised country … [The government must decide] how to reconcile Imperial unity with diversity of legislation. Mr Grattan not only held these purposes to be reconcilable, but he did not scruple to go the length of saying this 'I demand the continued severance of the parliaments with a view to the continued and everlasting unity of the Empire.'

13.5. Was that a flight of rhetoric, an audacious paradox? No, it was the statement of a problem which other countries have solved; and under circumstances much more difficult than ours. ...

13.6. ... The unity of the Empire must not be placed in jeopardy; the safety and welfare of the whole – if there is an unfortunate conflict, which I do not believe – the welfare and security of the whole must be preferred to the security and advantage of the part. The political equality of the three countries must be maintained. They stand by statute on a footing of absolute equality, and that footing ought not to be altered or brought into question. There should be what I will at present term an equitable distribution of Imperial burdens ...

13.7. ... Sir, I cannot allow it to be said that a Protestant minority in Ulster, or elsewhere, is to rule the question at large for Ireland. I am aware of no constitutional doctrine tolerable on which such a conclusion could be adopted or justified. But I think that the Protestant minority should have its wishes considered to the utmost practicable extent in any form which they can assume.

13.8. Various schemes, short of refusing the demand of Ireland at large, have been proposed on behalf of Ulster. One scheme is, that Ulster itself, or, perhaps with more appearance of reason, a portion of Ulster, should be excluded from the operation of the bill we are about to introduce. Another scheme is, that certain rights with regard to certain subjects – such, for example, as education and some other subjects – should be reserved and should be placed, to a certain extent, under the control of Provincial Councils ... there is no one of them which has appeared to us to be so completely justified, either upon its merits or by the weight of opinion supporting and recommending it, as to warrant our including it in the Bill and proposing it to parliament upon our responsibility. What we think is that such suggestions deserve careful and unprejudiced consideration ...

13.9. I have spoken now of the essential conditions of a good plan: for Ireland, and I add only this – that, in order to be a good plan, it must be a plan promising to be a real settlement of Ireland ... The great settlement of 1782 was not a real settlement ... [because of] the mistaken policy of England listening to the pernicious voice and claims of ascendancy. It is impossible, however, not to say this word for the Protestant parliament of Ireland. Founded as it was upon narrow suffrage, exclusive in religion, crowded with pensioners and place-holders, holding every advantage, it yet had in it the spark, at least, and the spirit of true patriotism. It emancipated the Roman Catholics of Ireland when the Roman Catholics of England were not yet emancipated.

13.10. ... There cannot be a domestic Legislature in Ireland, dealing with Irish affairs; and Irish and Representatives sitting in parliament at Westminster to take part in English and Scotch affairs ... Is it practicable for Irish Representatives to come here for the settlement, not of English or Scotch, but of Imperial concerns. No. There may be conflicts of interest. It would be extremely difficult to decide on which matters Irish representatives were entitled to vote. Irish representation would have to be reduced and this would be opposed. It would be difficult for Ireland to run a domestic parliament and participate effectively in Westminster.

13.11. ... The passing of many good laws is not enough in cases where the strong permanent instincts of the people, their distinctive marks of character, the situation and history of the country require not only that these laws should be good, but that they should proceed from a congenial and native source, and besides being good laws should be their own laws ...

13.12. The principle that I am laying down I am not laying down exceptionally for Ireland. It is the very principle upon which, within my recollection, to the immense advantage of the country, we have not only altered, but revolutionised our method of governing the Colonies ... the colonies said 'We do not want your good laws; we want our own'.

13.13. We admitted the reasonableness of that principle, and it is now coming home to us from across the seas. We have to consider whether it is applicable to the case of Ireland. Do not let us disguise this from ourselves ...

13.14. We have no right to say that Ireland, through her constitutionally-chosen Representatives, will accept the plan I offer. Whether it will be so I do not know – I have no title to assume it; but if Ireland does not cheerfully accept it, it is impossible for us to attempt to force upon her what is intended to be a boon; can we possibly press England and Scotland to accord to Ireland what she does not heartily welcome and embrace. There are difficulties; but I rely upon the patriotism and sagacity of this House; I rely on the effects of free and full discussion; and I rely more than all upon the just and generous sentiments of the two British nations.

13.15. Looking forward, I ask the House to assist us in the work which we have undertaken, and to believe that no trivial motive can have driven us to it – to assist us in this work which, we believe, will restore parliament to its dignity and legislation to its free and unimpeded course. I ask you to stay that waste of public treasure which is involved in the present system of government and legislation in Ireland, and which is not a waste only, but which demoralises while it exhausts. The concession of local self-government is not the way to sap or impair, but the way to strengthen and consolidate unity ...

13.16. The best and surest foundation we can find to build upon is the foundation afforded by the affections, the convictions, and the will of the nation; and it is thus, by the decree of the Almighty, that we may be enabled to secure at once the social peace, the fame, the power, and the permanence of the Empire.

14. Parnell on the Home Rule Bill, June 1886

14.1. *Introduction.* The 1885 general election was a huge success for Parnell. His party won every seat outside east Ulster and Trinity College, Dublin. Gladstone, convinced by Parnell's success, supported the Home Rule movement for the rest of his career. The first Home Rule Bill of 1886 met with fierce opposition from the Conservatives who saw it as a betrayal of Empire and of the loyalist and Protestant elements of Ireland. Gladstone subsequently lost office in the general election of 1886, the first in Britain to be fought on the Home Rule question. This marked a turning point in British relations with Ireland: for the first time a major political party had committed itself to granting at least a measure of self-government to Ireland. Here is Parnell's speech made in the House of Commons on 7 June 1886, during the second reading of the Home Rule Bill. SOURCE: *The Times* (London), 8 June 1886 (extracts).

14.2. If, Mr Speaker, I intervene in the contest of giants which has been proceeding for so many days in this House in reference to this great question, it is not because I suppose that that intervention is specially suitable to the moment; and I certainly should not, under ordinary circumstances, have felt any self-confidence whatever in following so able and eloquent a member of this House as the Right Honourable gentleman, the member for the Eastern division of Edinburgh [Mr Goschen]. But 'Thrice is he armed who hath his quarrel just.'

14.3. … and even a man so inferior from every point of view to the Right Honourable gentleman as I am, may hope upon this occasion not to be so much behind him as usual. The Right Honourable gentleman has sought – I think, very unfairly – to cast a lurid light upon the situation by an allusion to those unhappy outrages which have occurred in Kerry. I join the Right Honourable gentleman in expressing my contempt for these cowardly and disgraceful practices. I join him in that respect to the fullest extent.

14.4. Nor do I say that because for months evictions have been more numerous in Kerry than in all the rest of Munster taken together – neither do I say that that constitutes any excuse for these outrages, although it may supply us with a reason for them; but when I denounce outrages I denounce them in all parts of Ireland, whether they occur in Ulster or in Kerry. But certainly I do condemn these outrages in Kerry; and the Right Honourable gentleman says very rightly that they must be put a stop to. Well, so say we all; but the Right Honourable gentleman would try to put a stop to them by resorting to the old bad method of coercion, which he and his friends have been using for the last eighty-six years, while we say with the prime minister: 'Try the effect of self-government'

14.5. … and if Kerry men then resort to outrages they will very soon find that the rest of Ireland will put a stop to them …

14.6. With reference to the argument that has been used against us, that I am precluded from accepting this solution as a final solution because I have claimed the restitution of Grattan's parliament, I would beg to say that I consider there are practical advantages connected with the proposed statutory body, limited and subordinate to this Imperial parliament as it undoubtedly will be, which will render it much more useful and advantageous to the Irish people than was Grattan's parliament, and that the statutory body which the Right Honourable gentleman [Gladstone] proposes to constitute is much more likely to be a final settlement than Grattan's parliament.

14.7. We feel, therefore, that under this Bill this Imperial parliament will have the ultimate supremacy and the ultimate sovereignty. I think the most useful part of the Bill is that in which the Prime Minister throws the responsibility upon the new Legislature of maintaining that order in Ireland without which no state and no society can exist. I understand the supremacy of the Imperial parliament to be this – that they can interfere in the event of the powers which are conferred by this Bill being abused under certain circumstances …

14.8. I believe this is by far the best mode in which we can hope to settle this question. You will have real power of force in your hands, and you ought to have it; and if abuses are committed and injustice be perpetrated you will always be able to use that force to put a stop to them. You will have the power and the supremacy of parliament untouched and unimpaired, just as though this Bill had never been brought forward. We fully recognize this to be the effect of the Bill. I now repeat what I have already said on the first reading of the measure that we look upon the provisions of the Bill as a final settlement of this question, and that I believe that the Irish people have accepted it as such a settlement …

14.9. I will now leave this question of the supremacy of the Imperial parliament, and I will turn to one that was strongly dwelt upon by the Right Honourable gentleman the member for East Edinburgh [Mr Goschen]. I mean the influence which he fears the Irish priesthood will seek to exercise upon the future education of the Irish people. I may say at once that I am quite sure that the Right Honourable gentleman's apprehensions upon this subject are genuine, so far as they go, and that at the same time he has no desire to fan the flame of religious discord. On the whole, I think that the Right Honourable gentleman has spoken very fairly in reference to this part of the question; and I will not say that, perhaps as a Protestant, had I not had, as I have had, abundant experience of Ireland, I might not have been inclined to share his fears myself …

14.10. I can, however, assure the Right Honourable gentleman that we Irishmen shall be able to settle this question of Irish education very well among ourselves … You may depend upon it that in an Irish Legislature Ulster, with such representatives as she now has in the Imperial parliament, would be able to successfully resist the realization of any idea which the Roman Catholic hierarchy might entertain with regard to obtaining an undue control of Irish education. But I repeat that we shall be able to settle this question and others very satisfactorily to all the parties concerned among ourselves.

14.11. I observe that reticence has been exercised with regard to the financial question, of which such a point was made upon the first reading of the bill … The speech of the Right Honourable gentleman … argued on that occasion that Ulster was wealthier than either of the three other provinces, and that consequently the burden of taxation would chiefly fall upon her, and that without Ulster, therefore, it would be impossible to carry on the government of Ireland. The Right Honourable gentleman did not press the financial question very far today; but it would not be improper, perhaps, if we were to direct a little more of our attention to it. For instance, the great wealth of Ulster has been taken up as the war cry of the Loyal and Patriotic Union … The fair measure of their relative wealth is their assessment to the Income Tax under all the different schedules, and also the value of the rateable property in Ireland; and these tests show conclusively that, so far from Ulster being the wealthiest of the four provinces – and the Right Honourable gentleman does not deny it now – Ulster comes third in point of relative wealth per head of the population. She comes after Leinster and Munster, and she is only superior to impoverished Connaught.

14.12. I come next to the question of the protection of the minority. I have incidentally dwelt on this point in respect to the matter of education; but I should like, with the permission of the House, to say a few words more about it, because it is one on which great attention has been bestowed. One would think from what we hear that the Protestants of Ireland were going to be handed over to the tender mercies of a set of thugs and bandits. The honourable and gallant member for North Armagh [Major Saunderson] cheers that. I only wish that I was as safe in the North of Ireland when I go there as the honourable and gallant member would be in the South. What do honourable gentlemen mean by the protection of the loyal minority? In the first place, I ask them what they mean by the loyal minority …

14.13. You must give up the idea of protecting the Protestants either as a body or as a majority by the establishment of a separate legislature either in Ulster or in any portion of Ulster. No, sir, we can not give up a single Irishman. We want the energy, the patriotism, the talents, and the work of every Irishman to insure that this great experiment shall be a successful one. We want, sir, all creeds and all classes in Ireland. We can not consent to look upon a single Irishman as not belonging to us.

14.14. Now, sir, what does it all come to? It comes to two alternatives when everything has been said and everything has been done. One alternative is the coercion which Lord Salisbury put before the country, and the other is the alternative offered by the Prime Minister, carrying with it the lasting settlement of a treaty of peace …

14.15. I am convinced there are a sufficient number of wise and just members in this House to cause it to disregard appeals made to passion and to pocket, and to choose the better way of the prime minister – the way of founding peace and good will among nations; and when the numbers in the division lobby come to be told, it will also be told, for the admiration of all future generations, that England and her parliament, in this nineteenth century, was wise enough, brave enough, and generous enough to close the strife of centuries, and to give peace, prosperity, and happiness to suffering Ireland.

15. The Government of Ireland (Home Rule) Bill of 1886

15.1. *Introduction.* The *Bill to amend the provision for the future government of Ireland, 1886,* also known as the Government of Ireland Bill or the first Home Rule Bill (1886), marked the first of Gladstone's attempts to secure a separate legislature for Ireland. Ireland would no longer be represented at Westminster, and would pay a share of taxation, raised by her own Legislature, proportionate to her financial capacity. The powers of the Irish Legislature would be limited by the express provisions of the Act creating it, and would not extend to any matter not exclusively Irish. There would be, for instance, no right to a protective tariff, or to customs duties upon British goods at the Irish ports. The army and the navy would be unaffected. There would still be a Lord Lieutenant, responsible to the British Ministry, with control over the forces of the Crown in Ireland. Parnell recognised that the Bill had faults but also recognised that it could be a 'final settlement' to the Home Rule question. SOURCE: Sidney Charles Buxton. *Mr Gladstone's Irish Bills: what they are and the arguments for them* (London, 1886).

15.2. *Edited extract, Government of Ireland (Home Rule) Bill, 1886:*

Part I. Legislative Authority

1. – On and after the appointed day, there shall be established in Ireland a Legislature consisting of Her Majesty the Queen and an Irish Legislative Body.

Powers

2. – With the exceptions and subject to the restrictions in this Act mentioned, it shall be lawful for Her Majesty the Queen, by and with the advice of the Irish Legislative Body, to make laws for the peace, order, and good government of Ireland, and by any such law to alter and repeal any law in Ireland.

Limitations

3. – The Legislature of Ireland shall not make laws relating to the following matters or any of them:

(1) The status or dignity of the Crown, or the succession to the Crown or a Regency.

(2) The making of peace or war.

(3) The army, navy, militia, volunteers, or other military or naval forces; or the defence of the realm.

(4) Treaties and other relations with foreign States, or the relations between the various parts of Her Majesty's dominions.

(5) Dignities or titles of honour.

(6) Prize or booty of war.

(7) Offences against the law of nations, or offences committed in violation of any treaty made or hereafter to be made between Her Majesty and any foreign State; or offences committed on the high seas.

(8) Treason, alienage, or naturalistion.

(9) Trade, navigation, or quarantine.

(10) The postal and telegraph service, except as hereafter in this Act mentioned with respect to the transmission of letters and telegrams in Ireland.

(11) Beacons, lighthouses, or sea marks.

(12) The coinage, the value of foreign money, legal tender, or weights and measures; or

(13) Copyright, patent rights, or other exclusive rights to the use or profits of any works or inventions.

Any law made in contravention of this section shall be void.

Further Limitations

4. – The Irish Legislature shall not make any law:

(1) Respecting the establishment or endowment of religion, or prohibiting the free exercise thereof; or

(2) Imposing any disability or conferring any privilege on account of religious belief; or

(3) Abrogating or derogating from the right to establish or maintain any place of denominational education, or any denominational institution or charity; or

(4) Prejudicially affecting the right of any child to attend a school receiving public money, without attending the religious instruction at that school; or

(5) Impairing, without either the leave of Her Majesty in Council first obtained, on an address presented by the Legislative Body of Ireland, or the consent of the corporation interested, the rights, property, or privileges of any existing corporation, incorporated by Royal Charter or local or general Act of Parliament; or

(6) Imposing or relating to duties of Customs and duties of Excise, as defined by this Act, or either of such duties, or affecting any Act relating to such duties, or either of them; or

(7) Affecting this Act except in so far as it is declared to be alterable by the Irish legislature.

Queen's Perogative

5. – Her Majesty the Queen shall have the same prerogatives with respect to summoning, proroguing, and dissolving the Irish Legislative Body as Her Majesty has with respect to summoning, proroguing, and dissolving the Imperial parliament.

6. – The Irish Legislative Body, whenever summoned, may have continuance for five years and no longer, to be reckoned from the day on which any such Legislative Body is appointed to meet.

Executive Authority

Lord Lieutenant's powers

7. – (1) The Executive Government of Ireland shall continue vested in Her Majesty, and shall be carried on by the Lord-Lieutenant on behalf of Her Majesty, with the aid of such officers and such Council as to Her Majesty may from time to time seem fit.

(2) Subject to any instructions which may from time to time be given by Her Majesty, the Lord-Lieutenant shall give or withhold the assent of Her Majesty to bills passed by the Irish Legislative Body, and shall exercise the prerogatives of Her Majesty in respect of the summoning, proroguing, and dissolving of the Irish Legislative Body, and any prerogatives the exercise of which may be delegated to him by Her Majesty. ...

16. Lord Salisbury on the Irish question, 15 May 1886

16.1. *Introduction.* Lord Salisbury addressed the National Union of Conservative Associations on 16 May 1886. While he had some positive things to say about Ireland, his comments about the Irish people (and their supposed propensity to violence and popery) reflect the racial prejudices of the time. He stated that while he would not 'offer opposition in principle to the idea of that local government being extended of Ireland, if only you are careful first that it is not a step to something very different, and secondly, that the interests of minorities are protected.' Salisbury was determined to defend the integrity of the Empire. He argued that some 'races' (such as the Irish) were not fit to rule themselves. What Ireland needed, he believed, was twenty years of resolute and consistent government. His rather contemptuous 'out of sight, out of mind' attitude to the Irish was further reflected in his statement that emigration to Canada might cost less than the £150 million (approx. €13 billion at 2009 values) allocated for land purchase in Ireland. SOURCE: *The Times* (London), 17 May 1886 (extracts).

> **16.2.** … There are two or three words upon which the whole burden of this controversy rests, and your chance of persuading the English people to resist the fallacies poured upon them rests upon your being able to make them understand these words rightly. Now, the first word I would take is what Mr Parnell said the other night, that Ireland is a 'nation'. Well, if a nation only means a certain number of individuals collected between certain latitudes and longitudes, I admit in that sense Ireland is a nation. But if there is anything further necessary – if to make a nation you require a past united history, traditions in which you all can join, achievements of which you all are proud, interests which you share in common, and sympathies which belong to all – then emphatically Ireland is not a nation (*great cheers*); Ireland is two nations (*hear, hear*) … Because Ireland is not a nation, for it contains two deeply divided and bitterly antagonistic nations. Well, then, another word which has done a great deal of duty in this controversy is the word 'confidence' (*cheers and laughter*) … Confidence depends upon the people in whom you are to confide (*cheers*). You would not confide free representative institutions to the Hottentots, for instance. Nor, going higher up the scale, would you confide them to the Oriental nations whom you are governing in India – although finer specimens of human character you will hardly find than some of those who belong to these nations (*hear, hear*), but who are simply not suited to the particular kind of confidence of which I am speaking. Well, I doubt whether you could confide representative institutions to the Russians with any great security. You have done it to the Greeks, but I do not know whether the result has been absolutely what you wish (*cheers*). And when you come to narrow it down you will find that this which is called self-government, but which is really government by the majority, works admirably well when it is confided to people who are of Teutonic race, but that it does not work so well when people of other races are called upon to join in it (*cheers*).

16.3. And, again, the confidence you repose in people will depend something upon the habits they have acquired. Well, the habits the Irish have acquired are very bad (*laughter*). They have become habituated to the use of knives and slugs, which is wholly inconsistent with the placing of unlimited confidence in them (*cheers*) ... I am not one who would say a word in disparagement of the Roman Catholic religion. (*Hear, hear*). I believe that it has been a great messenger of Christianity and civilization to great multitudes of our fellow creatures (*cheers*). But it has this peculiarity – that it has, more than any other religion, a wonderful system of organized discipline, applied, of course, in the first instance to its spiritual objects ... In Ireland, owing to the character of the people and the history of the country, the Roman Catholics have been singularly exposed to the temptation of thus misusing an organization meant for high spiritual ends. And it is impossible in contemplating the future of Ireland, in contemplating the fate of your Loyalist friends, who are in the main Protestants – it is impossible to ignore the fact that your confidence is seriously diminished because this tremendous, this grievously misused weapon is in the, hands of their opponents (*hear, hear*). But covering all these considerations there is one ground why for this purpose I would never advise my countrymen to place confidence in the inhabitants of Ireland, and that is because they are a deeply divided people. Confidence where it carries with it the grant of representative institutions is only fitly bestowed upon a homogeneous people. It is only a people who in the main are agreed – who upon the deep questions that concern a community ... who have sympathy with each other, and have common interests, and look back on common traditions and are proud of common memories – it is only people who have these conditions of united action who can be with any prospect of prosperity and success, entrusted with the tremendous powers which have been granted in the past, and – let us thank God for it – granted safely and with great and prosperous results to the British people (*loud cheers*). Therefore repel with indignation and contempt any one who asks you, because we have confided in the British people, and we find no harm from our confidence, that therefore we should confide in a people who differ from them in every respect, who differ from them in race, who differ from them in religion, and who differ from them above all in this – that they are deeply divided among themselves (*cheers*).

16.4. Well, there is one other word which has done yeoman service in this controversy, and that is the word 'coercion' ... Now, just consider for a moment what this Irish coercion is (*A voice* – 'Maintaining the law') ... Many people have been discontented with the institutions under which they lived. Sometimes they have agitated, sometimes they have rebelled, sometimes they have fought; and a portion of the Irish people – I must be careful to notice that portion which we principally see in parliament – has been content with these weapons. But there is another very powerful section of Irish people who employ a totally different sort of weapon. They murder agents, they mutilate cattle, they prevent honest men from earning their livelihoods, they shoot people in the legs who presume to pay their lawful debts, and by these actions and threats of these actions they punish all who give any support to or have any dealings with the supporters of the existing polity, and by that means they reduce a large mass of the people of Ireland over a large space of the country to what is nothing less than an intolerable servitude, and they do all this in the name of freedom, on behalf of which so many crimes have been committed. Now, when you hear the word coercion, of course you imagine there is some great tyranny in question, and you think of the dragonnades of Louis XIV or the guillotine of Robespierre; but coercion means nothing else than forcing people to abstain from this peculiar mode of propagating their political opinions. Have what opinions you please, we say; maintain those opinions as well as you can; send what representatives you please to parliament; preach your opinions in the public places if you will – but what you must not do is to shoot your agent or vivisect his cows because he does not agree with you (*laughter and cheers*).

17. Gladstone's 1886 manifesto – 'Address to the electors of Midlothian'

17.1. *Introduction.* The first Home Rule Bill was defeated on 8 June 1886 after its second reading by 341 votes to 311. Gladstone decided to go to the public on the question and a general election followed in July. An outstanding speaker (who rarely ever used notes), he was a formidable political opponent in any constituency. On 12 June 1886 Gladstone addressed the electors of Midlothian. His speech was clearly aimed at a national audience. He tried to temper criticism of the Bill by stating that it was only the principle of Home Rule that was to be judged. His appeal pointed to the pragmatic benefits of Irish self-government: it would help strengthen the Empire; the measure would also help reduce wastage in treasury spending; Ireland would now be able to prosper economically; it would help redeem Britain's honour on the world stage while freeing up parliament to deal with other issues of the day. SOURCE: *The Times* (London), 14 June 1886 (extracts).

> **17.2.** Gentlemen, in consequence of the defeat of the Bill for the Better Government of Ireland, the Ministers have advised and Her Majesty has been pleased to sanction a dissolution of parliament for the decision by the nation of the gravest and likewise the simplest issue which has been submitted to it for half a century.

> **17.3.** It is only a sense of the gravity of this issue which induces me at a period of life when nature cries aloud for repose, after sitting in 13 parliaments, to seek a seat in a 14th, and with this view to solicit for the fifth time the honour of your confidence.

> **17.4.** At the last election I endeavoured in my address and speeches to impress upon you that a great crisis had arrived in the affairs of Ireland ...

17.5. Two clear, positive, intelligible plans are before the world. There is the plan of the government and there is the plan of Lord Salisbury. Our plan is that Ireland should, under well-considered conditions, transact her own affairs. His plan is to ask parliament for new repressive laws, and to enforce them resolutely for 20 years, at the end of which time he assures us that Ireland will be fitted to accept any gifts in the way of local government or the repeal of coercion laws that you may wish to give her.

17.6. I leave this daring project to speak for itself in its unadorned simplicity and I turn to the proposed policy of the government.

17.7. Our opponents, gentlemen, whether Tories or Seceders, have assumed the name of Unionists, I deny their title to it. In intention, indeed, we are all Unionists alike, but the Union which they refuse to modify is in its present shape a paper union, obtained by force and fraud, and never sanctioned or accepted by the Irish nation …

17.8. Enfranchised Ireland, gentlemen, asks through her lawful representatives for a revival of her domestic Legislature, not on the face of it an innovating, but a restorative proposal.

17.9. She urges with truth that a centralisation of the parliament has been a division of the peoples, but she recognises the fact that the Union, lawlessly as it was obtained, cannot and ought not to be repealed. She is content to receive her Legislature in a form divested of prerogatives which might have impaired Imperial interests and better adapted than the settlement of 1782 to secure her the regular control of her own affairs.

17.10. She has not repelled, but has welcomed, stipulations for the protection of the minority. To such provisions we have given, and shall give, careful heed. But I trust that Scotland will condemn the attempts so singularly made to import into this controversy the venomous element of religious bigotry. Let us take warning from the deplorable riots at Belfast and some other places in the North.

17.11. Among the benefits, gentlemen, which I anticipate from your acceptance of our policy are these:

The consolidation of the unity of the Empire and a great addition to its strength; the stoppage of a heavy, constant and demoralising waste of public treasure; the abatement and greater extinction of ignoble feuds in Ireland, and that development of her resources which experience shows to be the natural consequence of free and orderly government; the redemption of the honour of Great Britain from a stigma fastened upon her from time immemorial in respect to Ireland by the judgement of the whole civilised world and lastly, the restoration to parliament of its dignity and efficiency and the regular progress of the business of the country.

17.12. Well, gentlemen, the first question now put to you is – How shall Ireland be governed? There is another question behind it and involved in it – How are England and Scotland to be governed? You know how, for the last six years especially, the affairs of England and Scotland have been impeded and your Imperial parliament discredited and disabled. All this happened while Nationalists were but a small minority of Irish members, without support from so much as a handful of members not Irish. Now they approach 90 and are entitled to say, 'We speak the voice of the Irish nation.' It is impossible to deal with this subject by half measures. They are strong in their numbers, strong in the British support which has brought 313 members to vote for their country and strongest of all in the sense of being right. But, gentlemen, we have done our part. The rest remains with you, the electors of the country. May you be enabled to see through and to cast away all delusions, to refuse the evil and to choose the good.

I have the honour to be, gentlemen, your most faithful and grateful servant,

W.E. Gladstone, 10 Downing Street, June 12th 1886

18. Sectarian rioting in Belfast, 1886

18.1. *Introduction.* The rapid growth of the city of Belfast during the nineteenth century meant that the boundaries between Catholic and Protestant working-class neighbourhoods were continuously shifting. In June 1886, when the first Home Rule Bill was defeated, Protestants lit bonfires in celebration. From 4 to 10 June there was serious rioting in the city, mainly by Protestant mobs against the Royal Irish Constabulary (RIC). Members of the RIC were detested by Belfast loyalists as southern Catholics, though nearly all the officers were Protestant. Hundreds of police reinforcements had to be brought into the city. Rioting continued intermittently until mid-September when wet weather finally drove the rioters indoors. It was was the worst episode of prolonged violence in nineteenth-century Ireland. About 50 people were killed, 371 police officers injured, 190 Catholics were expelled from the shipyards, 31 public houses had been looted, and the damage to property was substantial. Riots also took place in Derry, Lurgan, Fintona, Ballymena, Portadown and Monaghan. The report of the government inquiry into the riots exceeded 600 pages and put much of the blame on the fighting talk of politicians earlier in the year.

18.2. The extract below is taken from that report. It details the events of June 1886 which sparked the rioting. A Protestant labourer was intimidated by Catholic navvies on 3 June, at the new Alexandra Graving Dock in Belfast. He was assaulted and warned that neither he nor any other Protestant would be able to work in Belfast if the Home Rule Bill was passed. The worker reported the incident to the police, who subsequently investigated. News reached the largely Protestant workforce of Harland and Wolff on the following day. At midday at least one hundred Protestant shipwrights gathered at the

Queen's Island and marched down to the mudflats to seek their revenge. Using the tools of their trade as weapons, the shipwrights drove some of the Catholic workers into the River Lagan. Some of the Catholics were stoned from both sides of the quays. One boy named Curran drowned as a result. Police were later drafted in to prevent riots between Protestants returning to their homes on the Shankill and Crumlin Roads, and Catholics who lived in their path. The behaviour of the Protestant mob was described as 'murderous and dastardly'. Catholics held a massive demonstration at the drowned boy's funeral. Starting in Ballymacarrett, an estimated seven thousand men, women, and children walked in procession through the city. Although the police succeeded in separating the two sides, the funeral demonstration further heightened tensions. SOURCE: *Origin of the Riots in Belfast, 1886: The Report of the Commission of Inquiry respecting the Origin and Circumstances of the Riots in Belfast in June-September, 1886*, British Parliamentary Papers, vol. VI, pp 8–14.

18.3. … On Thursday, 3rd June in the north-east of the town of Belfast, and on the eastern side of the River Lagan, there is being constructed by Messrs. McCrea and McFarland a new graving dock, known as the 'Alexandra', and on the 3rd June, 1886, there were at this work about 100 or 150 labourers, a number of them being Protestants but the majority Roman Catholics. All had hitherto worked together in perfect harmony; and, according to a witness, George Smith, they continue to do so. Near to, and outside this graving dock, several of the harbour men were employed, these being both Protestant and Roman Catholics. Some few hundred yards from the entrance to the Alexandra Dock there is the well-known Queen's Island Shipbuilding Yard, of the firm Harland & Wolff Co. The employees at this yard numbered about 3,000 of whom only about 200 were Roman Catholics, the remainder being Protestants, and a large proportion of the latter are generally believed to belong to or actively support the Orange institution.

18.4. A man named Robert Blakeley, a Protestant, started work at the Alexandra Dock on Monday, 31st May, and having completed some job, his then 'gaffer' John Reid, sent him on Thursday, 3rd June, to work under his former 'gaffer', George Smith, a Protestant. It appears that during this day, whilst Blakeley was at work making a drain, with a squad of men consisting of three brothers, Roman Catholics, named Murphy, and several others, the father of these Murphys joined the squad, and he at once picked a quarrel with the man Blakeley, used violent language, and struck him twice on the thigh with a shovel, but did him no injury; one of the sons also attacked Blakeley, and the father made use of these words, which subsequently became notable, namely, that 'neither he (Blakeley) nor any of his sort should get leave to work here or earn a loaf there or any other place'. Blakeley complained to the 'gaffer', George Smith who told him that if he not agree, the best thing he could do was to leave. Blakeley then left the works and being questioned by some of the harbour men as he came out, he told them why he was leaving. He at once went to the police barracks near hand, at Ballymacarrett, and told the police what had happened, but he states that the constables 'were more jibing him than anything else', until he met Sergeant Morton, who told him to come down the next day at eleven o'clock. This he did, and then Sergeant Morton and Constable Nesbitt accompanied him to the Alexandra Dock to obtain the name and address of the elder Murphy, but the timekeeper told them that both father and sons had left the works. ...

18.5. On Friday, 4th June, in the highly excited state of political feeling, this 'Blakeley and Murphy' incident was certain to be discussed by the other Protestants working at the Alexandra Dock, and also by the harbour men to whom Blakeley had mentioned it, and as the phrase made use of by Murphy passed from mouth to mouth, it probably gathered that sinister interpretation which it so readily admits of; whether this was so or not, it is certain that the ship carpenters, rivetters, or others – anti-Home Rulers employed at the Queen's Island yard – heard of it, and some of these appear to have wickedly resolved that for the supposed outrage upon on one of their political party, they would have their full measure of revenge on the Home Rulers engaged at the Alexandra Dock.

18.6. Between 11 and 12 o'clock on Friday, 4th June, a rumour reached the dock labourers that the Island men would attack them during the dinner hour. At this time the Island men usually leave their yard by the gate convenient to the Alexandra Dock, and at 1.15 p.m., an organised body of 100 or more of the Queen's Island men were seen entering the Dock armed with sticks and other weapons and shouting for 'Home Ruler'; these rioters were also accompanied by several hundreds of onlookers and sympathisers. This hostile force struck terror and dismay into the dock labourers, many of whom are said to have been old and others, quite young lads. The Roman Catholic Home Rulers fled, making no resistance; a number of them sought to escape by taking to the River Lagan and swimming, others by pushing out on a raft and on pieces of timber. Whilst thus struggling for their lives, their cowardly assailants are said to have stoned them in the water and to have beaten or maltreated any they could lay their hands on – one young lad named Curran being drowned not withstanding the efforts of two men to save him – and it was currently reported that seven or nine men were so severely injured as to require hospital treatment.

18.7. Telegrams reporting that this serious riot was going on reached the Town Inspector at 2 o'clock; he instantly wired to each district head-quarter Constabulary barrack, ordering all available police to be sent to the Queen's Island, and in his magisterial capacity he sent a requisition to the officer commanding the troops asking for two companies of soldiers to be held in readiness. In a brief space of time a large force of constabulary reached the Alexandra Dock, but they found that the rioters had left and had resumed work in the Queen's Island Yard. Inquiries were set on foot, and a search, which was ultimately successful, was made to recover the body of the young lad Curran. The force of constabulary assembled during the afternoon is estimated at 200 foot-police. Great fears were entertained that this dastardly outrage on the Roman Catholic Home Rulers would lead to further disturbances in the evening, especially during the homeward journey of the Queen's Island employees. It is necessary to explain that the Queen's Island artisans and skilled workmen mostly live in the north-west central district of the town, occupying modern and superior dwelling houses on the Shankill Road, Old Lodge Road, Crumlin Road, or localities convenient thereto. They cease to work daily at 6 p.m., except on Saturday, when they leave off at 1 o'clock; and their route homewards, after crossing the river by the Queen's Bridge, is through North Street and Petershill, a central district thickly populated by Roman Catholics.

18.8. On this evening the town Inspector, Mr Carr, adopted special measures in these localities to prevent any collision between the Roman Catholic Home Rulers and the Queen's Island men returning home. And it was well that he did so, for there was a very hostile demonstration at Petershill against the Island men as they passed, and irritating cries were used to them by the Roman Catholic Home Rule population, but it is proved that on this occasion the body of the Queen's Island men appeared to be conscious of their disgrace, and bore an ashamed and downcast look, and were extremely quiet; in fact On the following day, Saturday, 5th June, an Inquest was held on the body of the young lad Curran, and the resident magistrates, Colonel Forbes and Mr McCarthy, held an inquiry into the incidents of the two previous days. The Queen's Island employees left their yard, proceeding homewards at 1 o'clock, and special police precautions were taken, very similar to those adopted on the preceding evening, to guard against any collision … in two or three places some slight rioting did take place but the police were always able to get between the parties and put a stop to it …

18.9. We may feel assured that the hundreds of Queen's Island men who had been present in the attack on the Roman Catholic Home Rule labourers would be likely to exaggerate the sinister character of the 'Blakeley and Murphy' incident, in order to extenuate their own murderous and dastardly conduct, and the large bulk of the Protestant artisan community would undoubtedly lend a ready ear to this version, harmonising as it did with their political prejudices at the time. On the other hand, each one of the Alexandra Dock Roman Catholic Home Rulers must have told to his sympathetic and enraged hearers the heart-stirring tale of savagery and manslaughter witnessed during his dinner hour on Friday, while the effect of these sad recitals was heightened by the taking home of the deceased lad Curran and the holding of an Inquest on his body. Moreover, the events of the following day, to be presently related, indicate, if they do not prove, that a decision had by this time been come to by the Home Rule party, or by some considerable section of it, which was eminently calculated to prove fatal to the peace of the town – namely, a determination to make the funeral of the murdered lad, which was to take place on the following day (Sunday), the occasion for a great Roman Catholic Home Rule demonstration throughout the town of Belfast …

GILLIAN M. DOHERTY AND TOMÁS O'RIORDAN

CHAPTER 6

Early history of the Gaelic Athletic Association, 1884–91

1. Michael Cusack and the promotion of Irish games

1.1. During the last quarter of the nineteenth century efforts were being made across Europe to organise sports by drafting new rule codes for standardised games. Michael Cusack (1847–1906) helped to develop distinctively Irish games. From Carron, Co. Clare, he qualified as a national school-teacher, and later opened a successful Civil Service Academy in Dublin to prepare candidates for entry into the professions, police, and civil service. 'Cusack's Academy', as it came to be known, was very successful and made him a significant income. He was greatly interested in Gaelic culture, language and literature. An athlete in his youth, he was also interested in Irish games. He organised athletics in Dublin while he worked as a civil servant and there was a hurling club attached to his Academy. Indeed, students at the Academy were encouraged to get involved in all forms of physical exercise.

1.2. English games were better organised and were popular in urban areas in Ireland. By the 1880s, Cusack believed that Irish sports such as hurling, bowling and other games were in danger of dying out. Athletics in particular declined. Irish athletes were then under the control of the English Amateur Athletics Association. Rugby, seen as typically English, was becoming popular in Irish towns. Football, also popular in towns, was thought to be more like English soccer than any Irish form of football. 'Hurley', a version of hurling played in Dublin, was more like hockey than hurling. Cusack wanted to revive what he saw as Irish games and promote an Irish Ireland. He wrote in the *Freeman's Journal* in 1885 that he wished to 'nationalise and democratise sport in Ireland'. He persuaded some hurley players to join a Dublin Hurling Club which was established in December 1882. However, it had folded within a year. Cusack founded another more successful club in its place, the Metropolitan Hurling Club, in December 1883.

1.3. Cusack now considered founding a national organisation to preserve Irish games, and he published anonymous articles on the subject in nationalist newspapers. On 11 October 1884, the papers published his article 'A word about Irish athletics'. Here Cusack appealed to the Irish people to reject English sports and customs, which he described as 'imported and enforced'. He believed they would destroy Irish nationality. He condemned the holding of athletic meetings in Ireland under the rules of England's Athletic Association. That Association's rules did not allow competitors to take part in sporting events held by other organisations. He thought Irish people were abandoning their sports and activities, played in the open, in fields and at cross-roads. He felt that they

127

had been demoralised by the Great Famine of 1846–52, by poverty, by English laws and that they had gone 'back to their cabins'. He urged them to come out and play distinctively Irish games. These, he believed, would improve their physical condition and their morale, discourage Anglicisation, give them an interest in Irish culture and traditions and stimulate their pride in place and nation.

1.4. Within days, Maurice Davin wrote to the papers supporting Cusack's ideas and he declared that he was willing to help establish and run a new sporting organisation. Davin (1864–1927) had been a talented and successful international athlete. During the 1880s he and his brothers Patrick and Thomas held more than half the world records for running, hurdling, jumping and weight-throwing. His ideas about sport and his reputation as a moderate nationalist won him great respect in the countryside and among the urban Catholic middle class. At the end of October 1884, Cusack and Davin put a notice in the *Freeman's Journal, United Ireland,* and the *Irish Sportsman* announcing that a meeting was to be held in Thurles to discuss the future of sport in Ireland and the establishment of a society to promote national games such as hurling.

2. The foundation of the Gaelic Athletic Association

2.1. The first meeting of what became the Gaelic Athletic Association (GAA), was held on Saturday 1 November 1884, in the billiard-room of Miss Hayes' Commercial Hotel in Thurles, Co. Tipperary. Davin took the chair, and in his speech called for the drafting of rules for Irish games and the opening up of athletics to all Irishmen. Hurling and football were not mentioned at the meeting. Those present agreed to ask Archbishop Croke, Charles Stewart Parnell, leader of the Irish Parliamentary Party, and Michael Davitt, founder of the Land League, to become patrons of this new organisation for the 'preservation and cultivation of national pastimes'. All three accepted. Cusack gave a long speech at the meeting criticising the national press for ignoring Irish sports and suggested a national festival on the lines of the old Tailteann Games. The founders believed that there was a lot of money to be made from promotion of athletics, in consequence, the Association could easily fund itself. Cusack and Waterford journalist, John Wyse Power proposed and seconded Maurice Davin as president of the new Association. Cusack, Power and the Belfast journalist John McKay were then elected secretaries.

2.2. Cusack reported on the meeting for *United Ireland*, McKay for the *Leinster Leader,* and Wyse Power for the *Cork Examiner.* Other Irish reporters also made positive reports of the meeting. However, the English press coverage was less enthusiastic. The *Daily Telegraph* reported on 6 November 1884 that:

> Olympic Games for Ireland hardly seems a serious proposition, yet this is the objective of a new society just started by the Archbishop Croke, Mr Parnell, Mr Healy and others of the National Party in the sister Isle. We may be sure that agrarian offence is no qualification for a competitor.

2.3. Cusack's sharp reply appeared in the *United Ireland*:

> I presume you refer to the Gaelic Association for the Preservation and Cultivation of National Pastimes, which was established at Thurles on the 1st instant by about a dozen Irishmen, not a single one of whom has, as far as I am aware, ever aspired to the position of leader in the ranks of Irish nationalists. Whoever wrote it, it is as vile a production as had ever been evolved out of the wilful lie. Your representative will at all times be perfectly welcome at our meetings, but it may be necessary for him to be acquainted with the Irish language if he wants to report our war shouts on the hurling field.

2.4. A second meeting was held in the Victoria Hotel, Cork, on 27 December 1884. It passed a resolution that the governing body of the GAA was to consist of the officers already elected, the committee of the National League and two representatives from every athletic club in the country. The nationalist MP, William O'Brien, offered the GAA space in his newspaper, *United Ireland*, for weekly articles and notices.

2.5. Another important meeting was held at Hayes' Hotel on 17 January 1885. Here they discussed the drawing up of rules to regulate the various games. Davin was well versed in the development and codification of sport, and he played a central role in this process. It was decided to form a club (just one) in every parish in the country, and to ban (from January 1885) athletes who were members of any other sporting organisations from competing at GAA events. Those who played field games with other organisations were banned from March 1886.

2.6. One of the first organisations to object to the ban was the Dublin Harrier Club and it quickly set about organising a campaign in protest. They invited athletic and cycling clubs from all over the country to a meeting to oppose the ban. They declared that they 'would not be bossed, ignored, put aside, or dictated to by any organisation'. E.J. Macredy, of Trinity College, Dublin, proposed that athletes throughout Ireland should unite to 'quash the Gaelic Union', as he called the GAA He argued that it was more political than sporting, and it wanted to promote only hurling. Cusack denied all this in *United Ireland*. He argued that the GAA was not political and he condemned 'the pernicious influence of those who encourage nothing but what is foreign to the Irish people and at which they can be easily beaten'.

2.7. The GAA held its first official social function at the end of January 1885 in the Ancient Concert Rooms, Dublin, to commemorate the Scottish poet, Robert Burns. This sporting and literary festival was intended to bring Irish and Scottish 'Celts' together, and promote 'Celtic' sports and culture in their respective countries. Dublin Castle sent members of G Division (which investigated 'treasonable activities') to monitor the proceedings, and they reported that the GAA was 'a thinly masked Fenian conspiracy'.

3. Controversy with the Irish Amateur Athletic Association (IAAA)

3.1. GAA rules for hurling, football, athletics and weight-throwing were published in *United Ireland* in February 1885. The *Irish Sportsman*, in reply, published the rules of the Irish Amateur Athletic Association (IAAA), the older sporting organisation under the control of a British body. Davin publicly criticised the British Association's attempt to impose its rules in Ireland, and defended the GAA's decision. Davin's letter to the papers sparked more controversy. Mr Christian, spokesman for the IAAA, accused the GAA of 'putting through rules purporting to govern all athletic sports'. Cusack responded angrily. Davin now intervened and encouraged a sense of good will between all athletes. Cusack and other prominent leaders in the GAA attended the next meeting of the IAAA in early February 1885. There was a very heated debate between the rival organisations. The IAAA criticised the GAA for holding games on Sundays and violating the Lord's Day. Cusack retorted that rich people played games on the Sabbath and condemned poor people for doing the same. Rugby, soccer and cricket all barred Sunday play. Many workers who could not play other games during the week were able to play GAA games on Sundays after mass.

4. The expansion of the GAA

4.1. Far from damaging the GAA the controversy won the organisation sympathy and support because of its emphasis on national games and the perceived need to bring Irish athletics and other sports under national control. The number of affiliated athletic clubs grew rapidly, and athletics was the main concern of the GAA in its first year. New clubs sprang up all over the country and abroad to promote hurling and football. Many clubs were named after Irish nationalist heroes and martyrs. The games were to quickly become extremely popular and enjoy a widespread revival.

4.2. This popularity was made very clear by the welcome given Archbishop Croke, one of the most prominent and influential supporters of the GAA, on his return to Ireland from Rome in the beginning of May 1885. Workers in Kingsbridge station [now called Heuston] decorated the train taking Dr Croke back to Thurles with festive bunting and green flags, and enthusiastic crowds greeted the Archbishop's carriage all along the route.

4.3. Tension between the GAA and IAAA increased in June 1885 when Cusack brought a successful libel action against the Dunbar family, owners of the *Irish Sportsman*, an unofficial organ of the IAAA. It sharpened when the rival organisations held sports meetings in Tralee on the same day (17 June). The GAA meeting eclipsed the IAAA one: with 464 athletes, over 10,000 spectators, and four bands to add to the ceremony. The attendance at the IAAA meeting was very small. Controversy again followed this meeting. Edward Harrington, an MP and owner of a local newspaper, criticised the GAA's actions and was expelled from the National League days later. The GAA effectively broke its links with the National League after this episode, although members of the League continued to join and to support the GAA.

5. The GAA's first Annual General Meeting

5.1. The GAA held its first Annual General Meeting (AGM) on 31 October 1885 in Hayes' Hotel, Thurles. In the main address, Davin described the Association's achievements in its first year. Notably, 150 sporting meetings had been held throughout the country – athletics, hurling and football – all of which got great public support. The chairman read a letter from Michael Davitt appealing to them to establish a pan-Celtic festival, a subject he returned to frequently. The most important item for discussion was the ban on GAA athletes from playing other games. The day before the AGM, the *Freeman's Journal* published an article asking for reconciliation between the GAA and the IAAA, and urged both to abolish their exclusion rules and allow athletes to compete at all the meetings of both organisations. Croke appealed strongly for an end to the ban in a letter published in the *Freeman's Journal* two days later. John Purcell (an IAAA athlete) appealed in the same paper for an amicable settlement for the good of Irish athletics. Cusack said that Archbishop Croke's request would be submitted to the Executive Committee of the GAA, and, in the meantime, the ban would be removed. He wrote:

> The GAA prizes are now open to all. We shall see where the best athletes are. Our movement is a national one. He who is not a nationalist – I use the word advisedly – no matter what his religion or politics may be, need not come near us except for a prize. Our prizes are open to all honest men.

5.2. Controversy continued in 1886. A row developed between the Cork branches and the central Executive. Cork clubs protested at the outlawing of the Munster Football Association and the expulsion of its president, J. Murphy, from the GAA, where he had held office as Vice-President. A public meeting of protest was held in Cork. This was reported in the *Freeman's Journal*. Days later, Cusack attacked the *Freeman's Journal* for printing what he called a biased account of the event. At the same time, a resolution, reputedly from the North Tipperary GAA Club, repeated Cusack's criticisms, and accused the *Freeman's Journal* of cutting a speech Archbishop Croke had made in Dungarvan, Co. Waterford. It urged people not to support 'papers hostile to the National Pastimes'. Edmund Dwyer Gray, Nationalist MP and editor of the *Freeman's Journal*, rejected the accusations and insisted that he had always supported the GAA. Dr Croke, a personal friend of Gray's, also dismissed the allegations and criticised members of the GAA for fighting in this fashion in public (*Daily Express*, 8 March 1886).

5.3. Cusack wrote an angry letter to the Archbishop and claimed he would 'with God's help, face you and Gray', if necessary. The row intensified when Dr Croke again wrote to the *Freeman's Journal*, citing Cusack's words, and threatening to resign if he continued to bring the organisation into disrepute. Other officials in the GAA, shocked by the Archbishop's threat, condemned Cusack's letter in the *Cork Examiner*, 24 March 1886, and emphasised that it was not approved by the GAA. Davin, President of the GAA, called a special meeting in Thurles on 6 April to discuss the situation. Cusask, when asked for an explanation, admitted his behaviour was unacceptable, and stated that he had written to the Archbishop to express his deep regret. The meeting voted, 38 to 14, to accept Cusack's explanation and put the matter to rest.

6. The lifting of the IAAA boycott rule

6.1. In response to popular pressure, the IAAA lifted its boycott rule, and allowed its athletes to take part in competitions organised by other sporting bodies. A great meeting between the GAA and IAAA athletes was held in Queen's College Cork [now University College Cork] in April 1886. Another special general meeting was called for July 1886, at which officers of the GAA accused Cusack of seriously neglecting his administrative duties and claimed he was extremely difficult to work with. Cusack defended himself but was, nevertheless, forced to resign from the post of Secretary. Angry at being dismissed from the organisation that he had founded, and no longer given space in the *United Ireland*, Cusack started a rival weekly newspaper in January 1887, *The Celtic Times*, which was hostile to the current leadership. The GAA responded by setting up its own paper, *The Gael*.

6.2. In spite of internal conflicts, the GAA continued to grow in numbers and popularity. A great public event in November 1886 helped to boost its popularity even more. On the first of the month, six football matches between clubs from Wexford and Wicklow were played on the lawn of Parnell's family home and estate at Avondale, Co. Wicklow. Special trains were laid on from Dublin and Wexford for the event.

7. The GAA and the IRB

7.1. As the GAA grew, so too did the number of members who were sworn into the IRB (the Irish Republican Brotherhood, a secret militant organisation). W.F. Mandle who has written extensively on the history of the GAA argued that 'no organisation had done more for Irish nationalism than the GAA'. Similarly, Marcus de Burca, in his official history of the organisation, states 'that the GAA is national, and that the GAA is involved – has always been involved – in the mainstream of Irish nationalism'. The more militant political element in the Association was evident at a meeting in Thurles in September 1886. P.T. Hoctor, well known as a left-wing nationalist and a member of the IRB, was elected Vice-President. A motion was passed, with great enthusiasm, that John O'Leary, a Fenian leader in the failed rising of 1867, who had just returned from exile, be elected a patron of the GAA. Revolutionary nationalists took note of these events. They realised the potential of the GAA as a recruiting ground for new members and began to infiltrate the Association. A decision was also taken to help raise funds for a memorial to the Irish revolutionary, Charles Kickham.

7.2. The question of banning members of the GAA from playing soccer or rugby was also debated. A representative from a Limerick club pointed out that members of the GAA were not prohibited from playing cricket. The committee justified its decision because, it argued, the GAA did not cater for cricket, but it insisted on its right to make rules for games that did concern its members. The ban was adopted.

8. The Annual General Meeting of 1886

8.1. The Annual General Meeting of 1886 was held in Thurles on 15 November and it was an important one. Here political tensions between constitutional and militant nationalists came to a head. Eighty-four clubs were represented, evidence of the great success of the GAA countrywide only two years after its foundation. On the administrative side, the GAA wrote a constitution that still remains largely intact today. Athletics no longer had precedence over hurling and football. County Boards were established, and most importantly, a decision was taken to hold All-Ireland annual hurling and football championships.

8.2. The increasing politicisation of the GAA was clearly evident and deeply disruptive at this AGM. Davin, President, read a letter of thanks from John O'Leary (*Freeman's Journal*, 16 November 1886), newly elected patron of the GAA, that concluded with a quotation from Thomas Davis, 'our prophet and our guide', to the effect that physical strength would help nationalists prepare for battle: 'When we've skill our strength to wield, Let us take our own again.'

8.3. In spite of this widespread support for nationalism, members were divided. Some supported constitutional nationalism, namely, Parnell and the Irish Parliamentary Party; others supported radical, militant nationalism and the Fenians. An article concerning politics in the new constitution stated that 'the Gaelic Athletic Association shall not be used in any way to oppose any national movement which has the confidence and support of the leaders of the Irish people'. This statement was deliberately vague and could be interpreted in different ways. Parnellites could read it as meaning that the GAA would not interfere with the objectives and methods of the Irish Parliamentary Party. Fenians could interpret it as meaning that the GAA would not oppose any militant nationalists.

9. The politicisation of the GAA

9.1. Constitutional nationalism suffered a serious setback when the Conservative party won the mid-year elections in 1886 with a secure majority. Many tenants faced economic hardship, in places there were near-famine conditions because of two successive bad harvests. Many were unable to pay rent. Three Irish Parliamentary Party politicians, William

O'Brien, John Dillon and Tim Harrington, started a 'Plan of Campaign' to force land-lords to lower rents. Violence ensued in some areas between landlords, tenants and police. These conditions led to an increase in support for militant nationalists.

9.2. Dublin Castle took great interest in the Fenian infiltration of the GAA, as is evident from the detailed reports written by local policemen, government agents and informers within the GAA. The very names of clubs often represented the political opinions of the officials, if not always the members. The Parnells, the Davitts and the Smith O'Briens indicated supporters of the Irish Parliamentary Party; while the Ballina Stephenites, the Kickhams and others were Fenian supporters. In February 1887, the Executive decided to exclude members of the Royal Irish Constabulary (RIC) from the GAA, and from participating in sports or tournaments run by it 'in consequence of their action towards the people throughout the country … This resolution not to apply to the army or navy'.

9.3. Not everybody agreed. John Wyse Power, one of the founders, resigned his post as Assistant Secretary. Davin, who was not present at the meeting, objected strongly to ban-ning of members of the RIC. Two months later, Davin walked out of an Executive meet-ing in protest at the resolution which, he argued, the Executive did not have the power to make. In May of that year, Davin resigned as President of the GAA

10. The Executive and tensions within the GAA

10.1. At a meeting in May, the Executive suspended the Dublin Grocers' Assistants' Athletic Club because they held sports with a handicapper who was not certified by the GAA. The organisation insisted that clubs must only use an officially approved handi-capper to ensure that the sports were played according to the Association's rules. There were only a few qualified handicappers, however, and many clubs held their meetings without one, using local people instead. The Executive forbade a coming sports meeting organised by the Grocers' Assistants' Athletic Club, but the meeting went ahead as planned. The GAA issued a poster the night before the sports meeting that warned people not to participate, arguing that they would destroy the Association if they ignored official decisions:

> NATIONALISTS OF IRELAND! Down with dissension! Discountenance disunion! Support not the would-be wreckers of the GAA. Down with the men who would disgrace the Association that has for its patrons the tried true and illustrious Irishmen, Archbishop Croke, Charles Stewart Parnell, Michael Davitt and John O'Leary. Who are these men who try to prove that Ireland is not worthy of self-gov-ernment? The Grocers' Assistants' Sports Committee. Do not by your presence at their meeting commit an act of treason to Ireland. GOD SAVE IRELAND.

10.2. This seemed to be rather drastic step over a seemingly minor incident. It reflects the difficulties in creating an organisation under the control of a Central Executive, strains within the GAA and the attempts to hold the divided Association together. Tensions were high since Cusack's expulsion and Davin's resignation. After the meeting took place the GAA Central Committee responded with harsh measures. The Executive expelled the Grocers' Club from the GAA and suspended all athletes who participated in the meeting.

11. Dr Croke and the search for compromise

11.1. Dr Croke was displeased with the actions of the Executive and criticised it in a speech in Charleville, Co. Cork. Although he praised the successes of the GAA, the Archbishop advised the Executive to be wary of being dictatorial on issues. Controversy surrounded the Executive again in August 1887 when it suspended three Dublin clubs for not following official rules. The Freeman Athletic Club, suspended for planning to hold a sports meeting without an official handicapper, asked Dr Croke to intervene on their behalf. The Executive refused to discuss the matter with the Club or Archbishop Croke. He then suggested that Michael Davitt should act, with him, as an intermediary. The Executive, again, dismissed his offer. P.T. Hoctor, editor of *The Gael*, made it clear that the Executive did not want interference from patrons:

> We do not want one or all of the patrons as judges. We wish them to remain in their high and dignified position of honour, from which they should only descend to countenance, support, or protect us, but certainly not to judge or sentence us. We further can only recognise as judge in this, as in all other matters belonging to the Gaelic Athletic Association, the Central Executive of that body with, of course, the inevitable annual reference of all matters in dispute to the Convention as the final and supreme court of appeal.

11.2. Croke, Davitt and Parnell appealed to the Freeman Club to accept the GAA rules for the sake of unity, and to 'prevent a growing bitterness of dispute from becoming a cause' of disunion and possible disruption of a movement of which all Irishmen are proud'. The Club, comprising mainly employees of the *Freeman's Journal*, the unofficial paper of the Irish Parliamentary Party, refused to compromise. The conflict, in part, reflected tensions between the IRB-dominated Executive, including Hoctor, and constitutional nationalists, represented in the Dublin Club.

11.3. On 10 September the Freeman Club held their sports meeting as planned and without GAA sanction. The Central Executive suspended the Club, the athletes and the Dublin County Committee. The *Freeman's Journal* and other papers criticised the decision. In an interview in the *Freeman's Journal* in October, Davin explained that he had resigned because of his strong objections to the actions of the Executive in banning the RIC from the Association without holding a meeting of the General Committee. He argued that Article 15 in the GAA Constitution decreed that new rules could only be introduced, or existing rules changed, by the General Committee. He criticised the

Executive's refusal to allow Dr Croke and Davitt intervene in the dispute with the Freeman Athletic Club and accused its members of acting like dictators in an article in the *Freeman's Journal*, October 1887.

> As an illustration of how high feeling runs, I may mention I observed in two issues of the *The Gael* paragraphs and a letter amounting to threats of personal violence to members who seem to differ from the present Executive if they attend the meeting. I am convinced that the spirit of fair play among Irishmen generally would not for a moment condone conduct of that kind … Everyone should concentrate attention on the election of a proper Executive and the amendment of the Constitution.

11.4. In other words, Davin was calling on GAA members to oust the current Executive. Suspended clubs and athletes planned to attend the impending 1887 Convention and to demand that they be reinstated. Many GAA members blamed the Executive for ongoing controversies and were especially grieved about Davin's resignation. Others felt the rule excluding members of RIC from the GAA was 'looking for trouble' and criticised the 'introduction of politics into a purely athletic Association'. Many clergymen were concerned about the power of P.T. Hoctor, and another IRB man, P.N. Fitzgerald, who dominated the Executive, and were increasingly seen as extremist. Fitzgerald's agenda, 'to wipe out the British name and nation in Ireland', disturbed many GAA supporters who were solidly behind the constitutional movement. The Executive's treatment of Dr Croke also angered many supporters of the GAA.

11.5. Nevertheless, the Executive had many supporters in the GAA and among the public, especially from nationalists who wanted the 'Fenian section' to remain in power. Although they admitted that the Executive had made some bad decisions, these supporters argued that they were determined men with strong opinions but of the right political convictions. Thus, the main issue at the 1887 Convention was whether the 'Fenian section' or the parliamentarians should control the GAA.

12. The Convention of 1887

12.1. The Annual Convention of 1887, held in Thurles on 9 November, attracted large crowds of interested parties, and included two delegates from over 800 branches. Unfortunately, Maurice Davin did not attend, and his conciliatory manner might have eased tensions. The meeting was held in the courthouse because the gathering was too large to fit in Hayes' Hotel, where the first meetings of the GAA had been held. Trouble began when the Dublin clubs were refused admission. Opponents of the Executive, who filled the galleries, protested loudly.

12.2. There then followed trouble about the election of a chairman. Alderman Horgan of Cork and P.T. Hoctor proposed P.N. Fitzgerald, a prominent member of the IRB. Father Scanlan of Nenagh objected strongly to Fitzgerald and proposed instead Major

O'Kelly of one of the suspended clubs (Moycarkey). There were angry exchanges from the crowd. One delegate shouted 'Down with the National League'. Another shouted, 'Only men ready to die for their country should be at the head of the GAA'. An argument broke out between Scanlan, some priests that supported him, and others who supported Fitzgerald. Peace was restored only when Father Scanlan and his supporters were ejected from the courthouse, where they mingled with the Dublin delegates who had been prevented from entering, and held an opposition meeting behind Hayes' Hotel.

13. The IRB and the Central Executive of the GAA

13.1. The IRB got substantial control of the Central Executive of the GAA at this Convention. Fitzgerald was elected Chairman. He opened the meeting by stating that he regretted the fight that had just taken place, but he thanked God 'that there were men in Ireland who would not stand for clerical dictation'. Another IRB candidate, E.M. Bennett of Ennis, was elected President in preference to Maurice Davin, by 316 votes to 210. Opponents denounced the outcome and argued that Davin would have been elected if Scanlan and his supporters had not been ejected. Delegates approved of a vote of sympathy for William O'Brien who was in prison for his role in the Plan of Campaign.

13.2. In the meantime, delegates outside the courthouse passed their own resolutions. They also passed a voted of sympathy for William O'Brien, reaffirmed their support for Dr Croke as patron of the GAA, and for Maurice Davin as President, and finally, condemned the delegates in the courthouse. Father Scanlan warned that the Association was being taken over by Fenians who would destroy the National League. Later Dr Croke wrote to the papers to express his great disappointment and shock about the trouble in Thurles. He condemned 'sinister' elements in the Association, and threatened to resign as patron.

> Nothing, therefore, remains for me but to disassociate myself, as I now publicly do, from the branch of the Gaelic Athletic Association which exercised such a sinister influence on yesterday' proceedings.

13.3. The *Freeman's Journal*, which printed Archbishop Croke's letter in full on 11 November 1887, denounced those in the GAA who advocated armed revolution, arguing that a rising was doomed to fail, and would lead to terrible bloodshed:

> There has never yet been a revolution in Ireland every detail of which was not known to the government. If there be anything of the kind now on foot we are perfectly certain that the government knows all about it … They could put their hands upon every man connected with it whenever they thought fit … If they do not do so it is because … they would rather let the mischief ripen in order to utilise it for the purpose of destroying the Home Rule movement.

13.4. The paper also published a letter from the priests who had been turned out of the meeting. They denounced the outcome of the convention which, they argued, had been 'packed', that is, it had succeeded only because anyone who objected was thrown out. The new President, Mr Bennett, responded by emphasising that the GAA was non-political and was not against the clergy or the National League. This letter, in turn, provoked many angry replies, especially from clubs that objected to the Executive. Father Scanlan, whose father was a prominent Fenian and whose brothers had fought in the rising of 1867, denounced the way the Executive had handled the meeting in Thurles. He accused Bennett, Fitzgerald and John O'Leary of making slanderous speeches in Ennis against Parnell and the Irish Parliamentary Party. According to reports, the speakers claimed that the Party wanted 'the proud privilege of paying England's national debt, fighting England's battles and assisting her to spread the knowledge of Christianity by the aid of the bayonet and the bullet'.

13.5. Scanlan, and many others, appealed to Davin to resume the office of President of the GAA, which he agreed to attempt. A writer with the *Freeman's Journal* criticised the GAA's handling of the controversy, especially their mistreatment of Dr Croke and he urged the GAA to rethink its policies.

> When it comes to the point that a man like Dr Croke has publicly to disassociate himself from the Association which he fostered and practically created, then we say it is time for every man connected with the Association to pause and consider whether he is going.

13.6. Newspapers printed lists of clubs that objected to the new Executive and reported that these had formed a provisional Committee to replace the existing one. Supporters and opponents kept the debate alive in a spirited correspondence to the newspapers. Meanwhile, attempts were made to end the divisions in the GAA. On 22 November, Archbishop Croke invited Davitt and Davin to Thurles to discuss how to reorganise and reunite the Association. P.N. Fitzgerald, who was also in Thurles, met Davitt after his meeting with the Archbishop and they came up with plans for resolving the dispute. The Executive issued statements that the Thurles Convention had been legitimate, that it was not anti-clergy, and that any insults to clergymen were the rash remarks of individuals that did not reflect GAA policy or attitudes. Fitzgerald officially wrote to the Executive to appeal for reconciliation. In this letter, read before the Executive on 23 November, he also expressed the wish that Dr Croke be reunited with the Association.

> Whatever the future of the Association may be, I would respectfully ask His Grace, Archbishop Croke, to consult the other patrons and see if an amicable understanding could not be come to. It is not a time for division amongst any class of Irishman. The Gaelic Athletic Association should be open to all; an Irish nation should include all sections of Irishmen. To make independence easy, Ireland requires the aid of all her sons.

13.7. The Executive voted a motion to distance itself from any hostility to Dr Croke, to the clergy, and the National League. Croke responded generously, and in a letter to the *Freeman's Journal*, stated that he had no grievance with the Executive. He suggested that the GAA consider de-centralising power, that is, giving each county control of its own affairs, and setting up a Central Appeals Boards to deal with matters of common concern. Members of the Executive met Dr Croke in Thurles and agreed to discuss problems in another general Convention early in the New Year. Davin, Wyse Power and two others agreed to help organise the proposed Convention. So ended the great split.

13.8. The disputes in the GAA in 1887 did not destroy the Association. In fact, it continued to grow at an impressive rate. Michael Cusack later wrote rather boastfully that the 'Association swept the country like a prairie fire' and that 'in less than two years Ireland south of a line from Dundalk to Sligo was overwhelmingly Gaelic'. Dr Croke claimed that the membership was then over 50,000, only three years after its foundation. Over 400 clubs were affiliated to the GAA. W.F. Mandle argued that 'athletics played only a minor role' in the GAA by this time. Hurling and football matches were held all over the country in the summer and autumn of 1887 in preparation for the All-Ireland competition, although the final did not take place that year because of the ongoing controversy. The GAA stopped publishing its newspaper, *The Gael*, after the dispute was resolved, and Cusack's *Celtic Times* also ceased publication after 14 January 1888 (due to lack of funds, not peace overtures). In attempting to account for the early success of the GAA, Neal Garnham wrote that:

> The GAA was undoubtedly the beneficiary of the growth of the cult of games, but it was more important than that, it was peculiarly adapted to the conditions in which it existed. Gaelic games certainly projected for themselves an image that was precisely in tune with the aspirations and self-perceptions of many Irishmen … Gaelic games had a number of more practical advantages. Rugby or soccer was never an option for men whose only leisure time fell on Sundays. Cricket, or athletics … could not be enjoyed by those whose incomes were low or whose social standing made them unwelcome companions for those in control of these institutions … Gaelic games may have been politicised and imbued with a special national significance, but they were also accessible, great value for money, and extremely good fun. For many in Ireland they offered the only means of engaging in the late Victorian sporting revolution.

14. The reconciliation, January 1888

14.1. IRB dominance of the GAA Executive was ended at the Convention held in Thurles on 4 January 1888. Here, the 'Fenian section' was outnumbered, the IRB-dominated Executive ousted, a new Council appointed, and Davin unanimously re-elected President. Dr Croke submitted a letter to congratulate the Association for ending the dispute. He also urged the Executive to eliminate abuses such as heavy drinking at sports meetings and to ensure that players who had to travel to matches on Sundays and holidays attended mass. The committee agreed to send letters of thanks to Dr Croke, to Davin, and to others who had helped to end the dispute. Finally, a vote of sympathy was passed for the political prisoners.

14.2. Some changes were made in the playing rules of hurling and football: the referee was given greater control over members guilty of misconduct, he was to have a whistle, which he was to blow whenever the game had to be stopped, for any reason. The size of playing pitches was fixed at a minimum of 140 yards by 84, and a maximum of 196 yards by 140. The Convention decided, however, that the unfinished 1887 championships were to be played out under the old rules.

14.3. The final games of the championships, begun under the old administration, still remained to be played. At Birr, Co. Offaly, on Sunday, 1 April 1888, the first All-Ireland hurling final was played between the winners of the Galway and Tipperary county championships. The weather was perfect and special trains carried enthusiastic supporters from the adjoining counties. Tipperary won, their score being one goal and two points to nil.

14.4. It seemed as though the 'Fenian section' in the GAA had been rooted out and that the Association had emerged from its first great crisis, re-born and re-organised. But the Fenian movement had merely gone underground.

14.5. The link between the GAA and the nationalist movement was most apparent at the funeral of Parnell in 1891 when 2,000 men carried hurley sticks draped in black for the procession to Glasnevin Cemetery. The split in the Home Rule Party caused by Parnell and the divorce scandal was replicated in the GAA where splits occurred over political divisions. The GAA supported Parnell against those who felt he should retire from politics. Many other members, including sportsmen, Roman Catholic clergy and even some republicans, left the Association as a result. Indeed, the GAA was lucky to survive at all. One police report claimed that the number of clubs had fallen from over 1,000 in 1888 to 220 in 1891. In many counties there were no clubs. In an attempt to attract new members, the police ban was lifted in 1893, and the ban on foreign games in 1896. The centenary celebrations of the 1798 United Irishmen helped revive support for the organisation. Conscious of growing nationalist sentiment and its increasing membership, the GAA re-introduced the ban in 1901 for members of the police and extended it to include prison officers, army officers, military pensioners and merchant seamen serving in British registered-ships. This was followed in 1905 by a ban on those who watched foreign games. The organisation would continue to enjoy renewed success both as a sporting body and vehicle for the promotion of Irish nationalism. As Conor Cruise O'Brien wrote 'The GAA movement aroused the interest of large numbers of ordinary people throughout Ireland. One of the most successful and original mass-movements of its day, its importance has perhaps not even been fully recognised'.

GILLIAN M. DOHERTY

CHAPTER 7

Early history of the Gaelic Athletic Association, 1884–91: documents

1. The games of hurley and hurling

1.1. *Introduction.* By the middle of the nineteenth century hurling had almost died out in many parts of Ireland. The first extract relates to hurling in Co. Kerry in the year 1841. Mrs Anna Maria Hall (1800–71) was reared at Bannow, Co. Wexford. She collaborated with her husband Samuel Carter Hall (1800–89) on over 500 works. Their studies of Irish life such as *Tales of the Irish peasantry* (1840) tell much about society in pre-Famine Ireland. Their lively description of hurling below had a pen-and-ink illustration of a hurling scene.

1.2. Michael Cusack (1847–1907) was born in the Burren, Co. Clare and became a teacher in Blackrock College and Clongowes Wood. In 1877 he set up the Civil Service Academy, to prepare students for examinations into the British Civil Service. A talented athlete in his youth, he was passionate about Gaelic culture. He considered hurley (similar to hockey) to be inferior to hurling. He established the Dublin Hurling Club in 1882 but tensions soon arose between the hurley and hurling players. The Dublin Hurling Club was replaced by the more successful Metropolitan Hurling Club, in December 1883. It was one of the first clubs to be affiliated with the GAA after its foundation in 1884.

1.3. The third extract describes the game of hurley. Already in the 1880s moves were being made to bring the rules of hurley closer to those of English hockey. Edward Carson had played the game while he was a student at Trinity College, where the University Hurley Club had drawn up rules as early as 1870.

SOURCES: 1. 'The game of hurling', Mr & Mrs S.C. Hall, *Ireland, its scenery, character etc.* (London, 1841); 2. 'The Dublin Metropolitan Hurling Club', *Illustrated Sporting and Dramatic News*, 22 March, 1884; 3. 'Hurley and how to play it', in G.A. Hutchinson, *Outdoor games and recreation* (London, 1892).

I

1.4. The forms of the game are these: – The players, sometimes to the number of fifty or sixty, being chosen for each side, they are arranged (usually barefoot) in two opposing ranks, with their hurleys crossed, to await the tossing up of the ball, the wickets or goals being previously fixed at the extremities of the hurling-green, which, from the nature of the play, is required to be a level extensive plain. Then there are two picked men chosen to keep the goal on each side, over whom the opposing party places equally tried men as a counterpoise the duty of these goal-keepers being to arrest the ball in case of its near approach to that station, and return it back towards that of the opposite party, while those placed over them exert all their energies to drive it through the wicket. All preliminaries being adjusted, the leaders take their places in the centre. A person is chosen to throw up the ball, which is done as straight as possible, when the whole party, withdrawing their hurleys, stand with them elevated, to receive and strike it in its descent; now comes the crash of mimic war, hurleys rattle against hurleys – the ball is struck and re-struck, often for several minutes, without advancing much nearer to either goal; and when someone is lucky enough to get a clear 'puck' at it, it is sent flying over the field. It is now followed by the entire party at their utmost speed, the men grapple, wrestle, and toss each other with amazing agility, neither victor nor vanquished waiting to take breath, but following the course of the rolling and flying prize; the best runners watch each other, and keep almost shoulder to shoulder through the play, and the best wrestlers keep as close on them as possible, to arrest or impede their progress. The ball must not be taken from the ground by the hand; and the tact and skill shown in taking it on the point of the hurley, and running with it half the length of the field, and when too closely pressed, striking it towards the goal, is a matter of astonishment to those who are but slightly acquainted with the play.

II
THE DUBLIN METROPOLITAN HURLING CLUB

1.5. To the energetic exertions of Mr Cusack, of the Civil Service Academy, Dublin, we are indebted for the revival of hurling in Ireland. A club called the Dublin Metropolitan Hurling Club, consisting mostly of young men preparing for Civil Service appointments, has been started under his management. The club meets on Saturdays for practice, and some scratch matches have been played with an energy and skill which augurs well for the future excellence of this club. If we may judge by the constantly increasing number of spectators attending those matches, the game is likely to become even more popular than its kindred sport polo, or hurling on horseback. The rules of the game as played by this club, and adopted by county clubs started since, are few and simple, consisting of the following: –

1.6. The ball to be made of cork and thread covered with leather, the ground selected to be quite level, the size to be regulated by the number of players; two poles are placed about five yards apart in the centre of the end boundaries, and through which the ball must be driven to secure goal; if the ball should go beyond the end boundaries, but not through the poles, the goal-keeper is to drive it back opposite to where it passed the boundary. The hardest possible hitting, both right and left, is encouraged, to develop both sides of the body, except in a crush, when the timber is not to be 'lifted', as the ball is sure to be stolen from a 'swiper'. But in the open the ball is to be 'coaxed' and 'lifted' with the hurley – never with the hand – and when off the ground hit with the full strength of the player. Play begins by a lady on horseback galloping across the field and tossing the ball in the centre amongst the players – a custom which seems to have been followed in all matches of which we have any authentic record. In an historic match played between Kilkenny and Waterford some years ago, the parties being led by Lord Beresford and Sir Thomas May respectively, the leaders themselves galloped across the field in opposite directions after having dropped the ball in the centre.

III

HURLEY, AND HOW TO PLAY IT

1.7. In our chapter on hockey we allude to the fact that a modification of that fine old game is played in Ireland under the name of hurley. Between hockey and hurley, however, there are some strongly-marked differences, and as the Irish game, in the peculiar practice of carrying the ball on a stick, seems to be a distant imitation of lacrosse, a few words on its laws and principles will not prove uninteresting or useless.

1.8. Hockey is played with a stick having a curved head, but hurley is played with a 'hurl' or bat, made out of ash, well dried, so as to give a certain amount of springiness, and of a stated shape, with crescent curves and flat sides. This hurl, which has a blade two inches deep, is a very powerful implement, and with it some tremendous drives can be given. Like some hockey-sticks, it is occasionally hooped with wire; but the privilege of having it shod with iron has in the Union rules been done away with. Hurley, like hockey, has formed an association of its various clubs, and all the principal matches are now played under the code of the 'Irish Hurley Union'.

1.9. The players may number twenty-one a-side, and in village contests are chosen by the two captains in the ordinary way, the first choice being determined by 'handle or boss', instead of 'round or flat'. The goals are eight feet high and ten feet apart, and the goal-keepers have to hit off the ball from a spot twelve yards in front of them, called the twelve-yards line. No one is allowed to touch the ball until the goal-keeper's hurl has done so, and unless the ball is within the twelve-yards line the goal-keeper alone has the right to swipe.

1.10. These are the principal points of the game, and from them it will be seen that there is scope in it for good rattling play, and that the hits, owing to the massive nature of the hurl, must be very much longer and stronger than they are at hockey. At hockey, owing to the stick being curved and so thin, it requires very much more than ordinary dexterity to catch and keep the ball on it, but with the flat two inches of the hurl it is possible, by a sudden jerk, to hold the ball for a minute or so, during which a considerable run can be made; and this running is the best part of the game

– at least, to the spectators. It requires some adroitness to run with the ball on the crosse – it requires very much more to run with it on the hurl.

1.11. Hurley is, in fact, hockey with this special bat admitting of the carrying game. It is very popular all over Ireland, though of late years football has surpassed it in the schools and colleges. Amongst the townsfolk and villagers it, however, holds its own, and there are, as may well be imagined, few more exciting or lively sights than a genuine country hurley match ...

2. Origins of the Gaelic Athletic Association, 1884

2.1. *Introduction.* After founding the Dublin Metropolitan Hurling Club in December 1883, Michael Cusack considered founding a national organisation for the preservation of Irish games. He published anonymous articles about this in nationalist newspapers, *United Ireland* and the *Irishman*. On 11 October 1884, both papers published his article 'A word about Irish athletics'. Maurice Davin sent a letter of support which appeared in both papers a week later. Davin, from near Carrick-on-Suir, had been a successful international athlete in his youth. His ideas about sport and his moderate nationalism won great respect. Davin supported Cusack and agreed to help to organise a new sporting body. He recommended that it begin by compiling a handbook with rules for all Irish games. Cusack and Davin then drew up a circular on 27 October to invite interested people to attend a meeting to be held in Thurles on 1 November. This notice was published in the *Freeman's Journal, United Ireland* and the *Irish Sportsman.* SOURCES: 1. Michael Cusack, 'A word about Irish athletics', *Irishman*, 11 October 1884; 2. Maurice Davin, 'Irish athletics', *Irishman*, 18 October 1884.

I

CUSACK'S LETTER

2.2. No movement having for its object the social and political advancement of a nation from the tyranny of imported and enforced customs and manners can be regarded as perfect if it has not made adequate provision for the preservation and cultivation of the National pastimes of the people. Voluntary neglect of such pastimes is a sure sign of National decay and of approaching dissolution ...

2.3. The corrupting influences which, for several years, have been devastating the sporting grounds of our cities and towns are fast spreading to the rural population. Foreign and hostile laws and the pernicious influence of a hitherto dominant race drove the Irish people from the trysting places at the cross-roads and the hurling fields, back to their cabin where, but a few short years before, famine and fever had reigned supreme. In these wretched homes ... the Irish peasant too often wasted his evenings and his holidays, in smoking and card-playing.

2.4. A few years later a so-called revival of athletics was inaugurated in Ireland. The new movement did not originate with those who have ever had any sympathy with Ireland or the Irish people. Accordingly labourers, tradesmen, artists, and even policemen and soldiers were excluded from the few competitions which constituted the lame and halting programme of the promoters. Two years ago every man who did not make his living either wholly or partly by athletics was allowed to compete. But with this concession came a law which is as intolerable as its existence in Ireland is degrading. The law is, that all Athletic Meetings shall be under the rules of the Amateur Athletic Association of England, and that any person competing at any meeting not held under these rules should be ineligible to compete elsewhere. The management of nearly all the meetings held in Ireland since has been entrusted to persons hostile to all the dearest aspirations of the Irish people. Every effort has been made to make the meetings look as English as possible – foot-races, betting, and flagrant cheating being their most prominent features …

2.5. We tell the Irish people to take the management of their games into their own hands, to encourage and promote in every way every form of athletics which is peculiarly Irish, and to remove with one sweep everything foreign and iniquitous is the present system. The vast majority of the best athletes in Ireland are Nationalists. These gentlemen should take the matter in hands at once, and draft laws for the guidance of the promoters of meetings in Ireland next year. The people pay the expenses of the meetings, and the representatives of the people should have the controlling power. It is only by such an arrangement that pure Irish athletics will be revived, and that the incomparable strength and physique of our race will be preserved.

II

DAVIN'S RESPONSE

Deer Park, Carrick-on-Suir, Co. Tipperary.

October 13, 1884

2.6. Dear Sir – I am much pleased to see that you take an interest in Irish Athletics. It is time that a handbook was published with rules, &c., for all Irish games. The English Handbooks of Athletics are very good in their way, but they do not touch on many of the Irish games which, although much practised, are not included in the events on programmes of athletic sports. Weight-throwing and jumping appear to be going out of fashion in England; but such is not the case in Ireland, although those events are too often left out of programmes of what might be called leading meetings. I have some experience of those things, and see numbers of young men almost daily having some practice. It is strange that for one bystander who takes off his coat to run a foot race, forty strip to throw weights or try a jump of some kind.

Irish football is a great game, and worth going a very long way to see, when played on a fairly laid-out ground and under proper rules. Many old people say that hurling exceeded it as a trial of men. I would not care to see either game now, as the rules stand at present. I may say there are no rules, and, therefore, those games are often dangerous. I am anxious to see both games revived under regular rules. I cannot agree with you that Harrier Clubs are a disadvantage, as I believe they are a good means of bringing out long distance runners, and we want some more good men at this branch of sport … If a movement such as you advise is made purpose of reviving and encouraging Irish games and drafting rules, *&c.*, I will gladly lend a hand if I can be of any use.

Yours truly, Maurice Davin

3. First meeting of the Gaelic Athletic Association (GAA), November 1884

3.1. *Introduction.* This is a report of the first meeting of the Gaelic Athletic Association. On 1 November 1884, Michael Cusack published a letter in the *Irishman* (paper of the Irish Parliamentary Party) and *United Ireland*. He and Maurice Davin had invited various people to a meeting in Hayes' Hotel in Thurles to discuss the future of sport in Ireland, and to establish a society to promote national games. Several newspapers published reports of the meeting – the *Freeman's Journal*, the *Irish Sportsman* and an English paper, the *Daily Telegraph*. John McKay was a Belfast-born journalist with the *Cork Examiner*. His report, below, is one of the best accounts of this historic meeting. Something between seven to thirteen persons attended. Davin spoke first of the plan to start a new organisation for sport. He said that many Irish games were losing popularity and dying out in some cases in the countryside and appealed for a revival. Cusack criticised the national press for boycotting Irish sports and suggested a national athletic festival along the lines of the old Tailteann Games. He had some sixty letters from well-wishers who could not attend. The Secretary of the Caledonian Association, Morrison Millar, writing on behalf of Scotland, and Mr Kinnersley of Leeds, representing the Celts in Wales, offered enthusiastic support for the new Irish association. SOURCE: 'Gaelic Association for National Pastimes', *Cork Examiner*, 8 November 1884.

3.2. A meeting of athletes and friends of athletics was held on Saturday, at three o'clock, in Miss Hayes' Commercial Hotel, Thurles, for the purpose of forming an association for the preservation and cultivation of our national pastimes.

3.3. Mr Michael Cusack, of Dublin, and Mr Maurice Davin, Carrick-on-Suir, had the meeting convened by the following circular: –

'You are earnestly requested to attend a meeting, which will be held at Thurles on the 1st of November, to take steps for the formation of a Gaelic Association for the preservation and cultivation of our national pastimes, and for providing rational amusements for the Irish people during their leisure hours. The movement, which it is proposed to inaugurate, has been approved of by Mr Michael Davitt, Mr Justin McCarthy, MP, Mr W. O'Brien, MP, Mr T. Harrington, MP, and other eminent men, who are interested in the social elevation of our race.'

3.4. The meeting was but poorly attended, and several important athletic clubs in the south did not send a representative, but perhaps this was owing to the fact that the notice given was very short. Another meeting will be held in the course of a month or so, and it is to be hoped that all who take an interest in the revival of ancient Irish pastimes, carried out under strict and proper rules, will lend a hand in the good work which Mr Cusack and Mr Davin have originated. Amongst those present at the preliminary meeting on Saturday were: Mr Cusack, Mr Davin, Mr Bracken, Mr O'Ryan (Thurles), Mr Wise [Wyse] Power (Naas and Kildare Club), Mr Ryan, sol. (Callan); Mr John McKay (Cork Athletic Club), &c.

3.5. Mr Davin was called to the chair, and Mr Cusack read the circular convening the meeting. The Chairman then said that many of the good old Irish games had been allowed to die out in the country, which he and many others would like to see revived.

3.6. Mr Cusack then detailed the steps he had taken to get real Irish athletic events put in the programme of athletic meetings throughout the country, and how when he suggested to the promoters of the Caledonian Association games (which came off in Dublin on last Easter Monday) to introduce the high jump, the long jump, throwing, the hammer, slinging the 58lbs, and putting or throwing the 18lbs, that they at once consented to do so. The Caledonian Association expended £300 on their meeting, and it resulted in their having a balance of £200 on their hands at the close. He [Cusack] thought they should be able to have the Gaelic Association meeting in 1885, but Mr Michael Davitt thought it would be too soon – that it should be put off until 1888 – because it would require £1,000 to carry out such a meeting, and a general election was at present impending. Mr Davitt guaranteed that £500 of the £1,000 would be got from the Irish in America. Mr William O'Brien also promised his support, but cautioned him [Cusack] against the movement being political in any sense.

3.7. Mr Cusack went on to say that he did not send circulars to the members of parliament, so that, accordingly, he had no replies from them to read. Two clergymen – Father Keran, of Carton, County Clare, and Father Cantwell, of Thurles – wrote expressing their approval of the movement, and Mr Morrison Little, the Secretary of the Caledonian Association, also wrote in terms of warm approval. Mr C. Crowley, of Bandon; Mr George Listen, solicitor, Bruff; and Mr John Hargrave, Six-mile-bridge, County Clare, promised every assistance to the movement.

3.8. On the motion of Mr Cusack, seconded by Mr Power, Archbishop Croke, Mr Parnell, and Mr Davitt were appointed patrons of the new association; and on the motion of the same gentleman, the title of the new association was fixed as 'The Gaelic Association for the Preservation and Cultivation of National Pastimes'.

3.9. Mr Cusack then proposed that Mr Maurice Davin – an athlete who had distinguished himself so much both is Ireland and in England – should be the president of the association. Mr McKay (Cork) seconded the motion, and in doing so bore testimony to the appropriate selection of a president for the association. The name of Davin was one respected by all Irish athletes, and of that distinguished family in the arena of athletics, it was but meet that the Gaelic Association of Ireland should select the senior representative of it as their head. He (Mr McKay) had at first intended to oppose any business being done at that meeting on account of the small attendance; but he had changed his mind when he found what the nature of the propositions were. Who, he asked, could offer any opposition to their association being placed under the patronage of Archbishop Croke, Mr Parnell, and Mr Davitt, three names that went straight to the heart of every true son of the Green Isle (*applause*) – and as to their selection of Mr Maurice Davin as president, there was no meeting of athletes and friends of athletics that would not rejoice to have the opportunity of ratifying such a selection (*hear, hear!*). While he was now speaking, he wished to avail of the occasion to say that the club he represented looked with favour on any such movement as the present provided it was properly carried out; but he thought that the formation of the Gaelic Association should only form one step researching the goal they were all anxious to arrive at – namely, the formation of a general athletic association for Ireland – composed of representatives from all the leading clubs – to regulate the management of all meetings, to frame rules of their own for the government of such meetings, and put an end once and for ever to their being bound by the rules of the English Amateur Athletic Association (*hear, hear!*)

3.10. Mr M. Davin was then unanimously elected president of the association, while Mr Cusack, Mr Power, and Mr McKay were appointed honorary secretaries of the association. The meeting soon after terminated. Due notice will be given of the next meeting to be held in connection with the matter.

4. Archbishop Croke and the GAA, November 1884

4.1. *Introduction.* At the first meeting of the GAA, the committee nominated Dr Thomas William Croke (1824–1902), Archbishop of Cashel, as its first patron. He was educated at the Irish Colleges in Paris and Rome. An Irish nationalist and popular public figure, he was deeply involved in the Land League, the Gaelic League, and the Home Rule movement. Croke, then sixty years of age, was well known for his interest in national issues. A learned and widely-travelled man, he spent twenty years as curate, college President and parish priest in Cloyne before being appointed Bishop of Auckland, New Zealand (1870–5). He returned to Ireland in 1875 as Archbishop of Cashel (1875–

1902). The GAA's headquarters and its principal stadium were named after him. The following document is Croke's letter of acceptance, written the day after he was invited to be patron. It was published in several newspapers and helped to attract further support for the new organisation. Croke enthusiastically welcomed the movement which he hoped would put an end to 'youths and young men lolling by the roadside or sneaking about with their hands in their pockets, and with humps on them', a sight he claimed was a common and depressing one in the Irish countryside. SOURCE: 'The Gaelic Athletic Association', *Freeman's Journal*, 24 December 1884.

To: Mr Michael Cusack, Honorary Secretary of the Gaelic Athletic Association.

The Palace, Thurles,

18 December 1884.

4.2. My dear Sir – I beg to acknowledge the receipt of your communication inviting me to become a patron of the 'Gaelic Athletic Association', of which you are, it appears, the honourable secretary, I accede to your request with the utmost pleasure.

4.3. One of the most painful, let me assure you, and, at the same time, one of the most frequently recurring reflections that, as an Irishman, I am compelled to make in connection with the present aspect of things in this country, is derived from the ugly and irritating fact that we are daily importing from England not only her manufactured goods, which we cannot help doing, since she has practically strangled our own manufacturing appliances, but, together with her fashions, her accent, her vicious literature, her music, her dances, and her manifold mannerisms, her games also and her pastimes, to the utter discredit of our own grand national sports, and to the sore humiliation, as I believe, of every genuine son and daughter of the old land.

4.4. Ball-playing, hurling, football kicking, according to Irish rules, 'casting', leaping in various ways, wrestling, handy-grips, top-pegging, leap-frog, rounders, tip-in-the-hat, and all such favourite exercises and amusements amongst men and boys, may now be said to be not only dead and buried, but in several localities to be entirely forgotten and unknown. And what have we got in their stead? We have got such foreign and fantastic field sports as lawn-tennis, polo, croquet, cricket, and the like – very excellent, I believe, and health-giving exercises in their way, still not racy of the soil, but rather alien, on the contrary, to it, as are, indeed, for the most part the men and women who first imported and still continue to patronise them.

4.5. And, unfortunately, it is not our national sports alone that are held in dishonour, and dying out, but even our most suggestive national celebrations are being gradually effaced and extinguished, one after another, as well. Who hears now of snap-apple night, or bonfire night? They are all things of the past, too vulgar to be spoken of, except in ridicule, by the degenerate dandies of the day. No doubt, there is something rather pleasing to the eye in the 'get up' of a modern young man who, arrayed in light attire, with parti-coloured cap on and racket in hand, is making his way, with or without a companion, to the tennis ground. But, for my part, I should vastly prefer to behold, or think of, the youthful athletes whom I used to see in my early days at fair and pattern, bereft of shoes and coat, and thus prepared to play at hand-ball, to fly over any number of horses, to throw the 'sledge' or 'winding-stone', and to test each other's mettle and activity by the trying ordeal of 'three leaps', or a 'hop, step, and a jump'.

4.6. Indeed, if we continue travelling for the next score of years in the same direction that we have been going in for some time past, contemning the sports that were practised by our forefathers, effacing our national features as though we were ashamed of them, and putting on, with England's stuffs and broadcloths, her habits and such other effeminate follies as she may recommend, we had better at once, and publicly, abjure our nationality, clap hands for joy at sight of the Union Jack, and place 'England's bloody red' exultingly above 'the green'.

4.7. Deprecating, as I do, any such dire and disgraceful consummation, and seeing in your society of athletes something altogether opposed to it, I shall be happy to do all that I can, and authorise you now formally to place my name on the roll of your patrons.

4.8. In conclusion, I earnestly hope that our national journals will not disdain, in future, to give suitable notices of those Irish sports and pastimes which your society means to patronise and promote, and that the masters and pupils of our Irish colleges will not henceforth exclude from their athletic programmes such manly exercises as I have just referred to and commemorated.

I remain, my dear sir, your very faithful servant,

+ T.W. Croke,

Archbishop of Cashel.

4.9. Editor – Seeing that the movement so quietly and so unostentatiously inaugurated a few weeks ago has, in the face of the freezing neglect of the Press, been so successful as to meet the warmest approval of the leaders of the Irish people, we would advise every man who loves his country to fall into the Association immediately and give such practical assistance as will leave the Cusacks and Davins no longer what they have been – the powerless and grieving spectators of 'the rotting of a noble race'.

5. The social impact of the GAA

5.1. *Introduction.* Contemporaries testified and historians describe how that the GAA transformed social life in Ireland. Writing in 1907 for a collection of essays on the history and achievements of the GAA, Monsignor J.B. Dollard, then based in Ontario, described how the GAA revitalised the parish of Mooncoin, Co. Kilkenny, where he spent his youth. SOURCE: J.B. Dollard, *Gaelic Athletic Annual* (Dublin, 1907–8), pp 18–19.

5.2. I remember the great change that came over the country. Until then everything was lonely and stagnant, and the young men in their idle hours loitered in dull fashion by the street and fence corners. In a few months how different things became! The country was soon humming with interest and activity, the ambitions of the young men were aroused, every parish had its newly-formed hurling or football team, prepared to do or die for the honour of the little village.

5.3. The war of championships was on! We followed armies of Gaels many miles along the country roads to the field of combat, where as many as eight or ten teams, gaily clad in their coloured jerseys, struggled for supremacy before our dazzled eyes. To play on the first team was indeed the greatest honour a youth could hope for, and many of us looked forward to that day with swelling hearts.

5.4. The GAA widened the horizons of the young men and made them proud of their country, giving them a new interest in it. By the strict enforcement of rule on the field, it disciplined the fierce and tumultuous spirits among them. The brawls and fights so common heretofore disappeared from our midst. The young learned that skill and self control were better and nobler than quarrelling and fighting, and that deft handling of the camán was more to be admired than to trounce a brother Irishman with fist or cudgel.

6. Parnell and the GAA, December 1884

6.1. *Introduction.* Charles Stewart Parnell, leader of the Irish Parliamentary Party, was chosen as one of three patrons of the GAA to win the approval of constitutional nationalists. He wrote from the Irish Parliamentary Offices at 9 Bridge Street in London on 17 December 1884, accepting the invitation to be a patron. Although Parnell was preoccupied with politics and gave little time to the GAA, his support – even as good wishes – was extremely valuable and lent the new movement respectability. SOURCE: 'The Gaelic Athletic Association', *Freeman's Journal*, 24 December 1884.

6.2. Dear Sir, I have received your letter of the 11th instant. It gives me great pleasure to learn that a 'Gaelic Association' has been established for the preservation of National Pastimes, with the objects of which I entirely concur. I feel very much honoured by the resolution adopted at the Thurles meeting and I accept with appreciation the position of patron of the Association which has been offered to me. I need not say that I shall do anything I can to render the working of the movement a success.

I am, yours very truly,

Charles S. Parnell.

7. Archbishop Croke appeals for the abolition of the ban

7.1. *Introduction.* The GAA held its first annual general meeting on 31 October 1885 in Thurles. The day before the AGM, the *Freeman's Journal* had published an article appealing for reconciliation between the GAA and the Irish Amateur Athletic Association (IAAA), and urged both organisations to abolish their exclusion rules and to allow athletes to compete at meetings under the rules of either. Croke appealed strongly for an end to the ban on GAA athletes from playing other games. Cusack responded, in the same issue of the newspaper, that Archbishop Croke's request would be submitted for approval to the Executive Committee of the GAA, and that the ban would be removed in the interim. SOURCE: *Freeman's Journal,* 2 November 1885.

> **7.2.** When I ventured to connect my name with the GAA I really felt pained at seeing all our fine national sports and pastimes dying out one by one and English and other non-native games introduced and almost universally patronised instead … It did not occur to me when becoming a patron of the GAA that there was to be any substantial much less bitter and persistent antagonism … between it and any similar body already in existence or that may be called into existence afterwards. All I wanted and aimed at was to encourage national sports and thus revive them; but it did not strike me at all at the time, nor does it strike me now, or form any part of my design, absolutely to discharge, and even denounce, all sports and pastimes that are not national. As a patron of the GAA, a lover of fair play all round and the enemy of every species of needless strife and estrangement among Irishmen, I would respectfully suggest to the Committee of management of the GAA the advisability of modifying their rules in the above particular, so as to allow all qualified athletes to compete for their prizes.

8. GAA game rules, 1885

8.1. *Introduction.* A second meeting to promote the newly-formed GAA was held in the Victoria Hotel, Cork on 27 December 1884. A large crowd attended, including leading athletes from clubs in Cork and Dublin. Alderman Madden, Cork's mayor-elect, read letters of acceptance from Croke, Parnell and Davitt. Cusack told the group that the nationalist MP, William O'Brien, had offered the GAA space in his newspaper, the *United Ireland,* for weekly reports. The meeting passed a resolution that the governing body of the GAA was to consist of those officers already elected, the committee of the National League, and two representatives from every athletic club in the country. Another important meeting was held at Hayes' Hotel, Thurles, on 17 January 1885, at which the decision was taken to ban members of any other sporting organisation from joining the GAA. It was decided to form a club in every parish. Rules were drawn up to regulate sports. The rules for hurling and football, given below, were published in *United Ireland* on 7 February 1885, those for weight-throwing on 14 February and those for athletics (also given below) and for GAA sports in general, were published on 21 February.

SOURCE: Michael Cusack, 'Address to the Irish people', 4 Gardiner's Place, Dublin, Candlemass Day 1885 [introduction to the rules], *United Ireland*, 7, 21 February 1885.

8.2. Brethren – John Augustus O'Shea says that the Archbishop's letter, which is here printed, ought to be read, as an order of the day, at every annual meeting of the Athletic Clubs in Ireland. He says 'it is as Irish as an open smile and as stirring as brass music'.

8.3. I agree with Mr J.A. O'Shea. I believe that the Irish People laid aside a powerful weapon for the cultivation of the intellect when they gave up the free use of their National Language; and I very much fear that the profound depth of religious feeling which so generally prevailed among our Irish-speaking ancestors could scarcely be paralleled among those who habitually speak English at the present day. But whether it is granted or not that with the decline of the Irish language came a decline of religion, of morals, and of intellect, I am sure no sensible person will deny that, as a nation, we have very considerably declined physically since we gave up our national game of HURLING.

8.4. The game is called 'báire', in Irish, and the hurley is called 'camán'. The goal-keeper is 'cúl-báire'. The game is probably the oldest game extant. There is not a shadow of doubt that it was played in Ireland two thousand years ago. It was the training of the hurling field that made the men and boys of the Irish Brigade. Guard the game well. But in doing so it will be necessary to play without anger or passion. Irishmen have endured many agonies for the sake of their country without going mad. Why, then, should we gratify our enemies by getting up an unseemly row because one of us get an accidental crack of a stick from a fellow-workman? …

8.5 The following are the rules for hurling and football adopted at the meeting held at Thurles:

HURLING RULES

1. The ground shall, when convenient, be at least 200 yards long by 150 yards broad, or as near to that size as can be got.

2. There shall be boundary lines all around the ground, at a distance of at least five yards from the fence.

3. The goal shall be two upright posts, twenty feet apart, with a cross-bar ten feet from the ground. A goal is won when the ball is driven between the posts and under the cross-bar.

4. The ball is not to be lifted off the ground with the hand, when in play.

5. There shall not be less than fourteen or more than twenty-one players at the side in regular matches.

6. There shall be an umpire for each side and a referee who will decide in cases where the umpires disagree. The referee keeps the time and throws up the ball at the commencement of each goal.

7. The time of play shall be one hour and twenty minutes. Sides to be changed at half-time.

8. Before commencing play hurlers shall draw up in two lines in the centre of the field opposite to each other and catch hands or hurleys across, then separate. The referee then throws the ball along the ground between the players or up high over their heads.

9. No player to catch, trip or push from behind. Penalty, disqualification to the offender and free puck to the opposite side.

10. No player to bring his hurley intentionally in contact with the person of another player. Penalty same as in Rule 9.

11. If the ball is driven over the side-line it shall be thrown in towards the middle of the ground by the referee or one of the umpires; but if it rebounds into the ground it shall be considered in play.

12. If the ball is driven over the end-lines and not through the goal, the player who is defending the goal shall have a free puck from the goal. No player of the opposite side to approach nearer than twenty yards until the ball is struck. The other players to stand on the goal-line. But if the ball is driven over the goal-line by a player whose goal it is, the opposite side shall have a free puck on the ground twenty yards out from the goalposts. Players whose goal it is to stand on the goal-line until the ball is struck. NB: Hitting both right and left is allowable.

The hurley may be of any pattern fancied by the player.

FOOTBALL RULES

1. There shall not be less than fifteen or more than twenty-one players a side.

2. There shall be two umpires and a referee. Where the umpires disagree, the referee's decision shall be final.

3. The ground shall be at least 120 yards long by 80 in breadth and properly marked by boundary lines. Boundary lines to be at least 5 yards from the fences.

4. Goal-posts shall stand at each end in the centre of the goal-line. They shall be 15 feet apart, with cross-bar 8 feet from the ground.

5. The captains of each team shall toss for choice of sides before commencing play and the players shall stand in two ranks opposite each other, until the ball is thrown up, each man holding the hand of one of the other side.

6. Pushing or tripping from behind, holding from behind, or butting with the head shall be deemed foul and players so offending shall be asked to stand aside and may not afterwards take any part in the match, nor can his side substitute another man.

7. The time of actual play shall be one hour. Sides to be changed at half time.

8. The match shall be decided by the greater number of goals. If no goal be kicked, the match shall be deemed a draw. A goal is when the ball is kicked through the goal-posts under the cross-bar.

9. When the ball is kicked over the side-line it shall be thrown back by a player of the opposite side to him who kicked it over. If kicked over the goal-line by a player whose goal-line it is, it shall be thrown back in any direction by a player of the other side. If kicked over the goal-line by a player of the other side, the goal-keeper whose line it crosses shall have a free kick. No player on the other side to approach nearer than 25 yards of him till the ball is kicked.

10. The umpires and referee shall have, during the match, full power to disqualify any player or order him to stand aside and discontinue play for any act which they may consider unfair as set out in Rule 6.

No nails or iron tips allowed on the boots. Strips of leather fastened on the soles will prevent slipping.

The dress of hurling and football to be the knee-breeches and stockings and boots or shoes.

It would be well if each player was provided with two jerseys, one white and the other some dark colour. The colours of his club could be worn on each. Then when a match was made, it could be decided the colours each side should wear.

ATHLETICS RULES

1. Every competitor must wear complete clothing from the shoulders to the knees, e.g. sleeved jersey and loose drawers.

2. Any competitor maybe excluded from taking part in the sports except properly attired.

3. Competitions must be limited to amateurs, except in cases where committees put on events for money prizes. No person competing for a money prize can afterwards compete as an amateur.

4. All betting must be put down if possible. It was further decreed that the Central Committee could suspend anyone guilty of any malpractice connected with athletics.

5. All entries must be made in the real name of the competitor.

9. Opposition to the GAA

9.1. *Introduction.* The meeting of the Irish Cyclists' Association, held in Dublin on Thursday, 22 January 1885 decided 'to discuss some matters relative to the Gaelic Athletic Association, which had recently come into existence'. The members agreed to oppose Cusack's sporting organisation which, in their opinion, was highly political. It had been set up by Cusack to dominate Irish athletics, and they refused to be bound by its rules. The chairman of the Association, J.A. Christian, sent a circular to members announcing that 'matters of the most urgent and pressing importance to the athletic community in Ireland' would be discussed at a meeting on Saturday 24 January 1885. The *Freeman's Journal* carried a report of the meeting next day. It criticised members of the Cyclists' Association for going against such influential people as Croke and Parnell. SOURCE: 1. 'Cyclists' meeting'; 2. '*Freeman's Journal's* response', *Freeman's Journal*, 25 January 1885.

I

CYCLISTS' MEETING, 24 JANUARY 1885

9.2. The Chairman, Mr J.A. Christian, said they … were strongly opposed to this body newly formed attempting to govern Irish athletics. They wanted to govern and manage their own sports and let the Gaelic Athletic Association govern and draw up rules applicable to the sports and pastimes they wished to revive, and which everyone wished to see successful. At any rate they could not allow themselves to be dictated to, or bossed in the way proposed.

9.3. Mr T. Ashley (Dundalk) proposed the following resolution: – That whereas a self-constituted body, calling itself the Gaelic Athletic Association has been formed; and whereas this Association has for its Hon. Sec. Mr Michael Cusack, and is formed on political lines; and whereas this association at a meeting held at Thurles on the 17th instant, at which seven gentlemen were present, passed rules presuming to dictate to the whole body of Irish athletes, it is now resolved that in the opinion of this meeting, the Gaelic Athletic Association does not command the confidence of Irish athletes, and that this meeting refuses to recognise the right of such an unrepresentative meeting to make laws governing athletes in Ireland. It appeared a monstrous thing, he said, that seven gentlemen should go and pass rules at Thurles for the athletes of Ireland. Mr J.S. Berry seconded the resolution which was adopted unanimously …

9.4. Mr J.C. Beatty then proposed: That in the opinion of this meeting of hon. secs. and representatives of Irish athletic clubs, it is necessary that an Amateur Association be immediately formed, and that the hon. secs. of the meeting be instructed to write to the hon. secs. of each athletic club in Ireland, requesting him to send representatives of his club to a meeting to be held on a date fixed by the committee for the purpose of forming such an association in Ireland. In seconding the resolution, Mr Christian said that they had been forced to take the present steps. The GAA, he said, went directly contrary to the Amateur Athletic Association in allowing amateurs and professionals to compete at the same meetings. There was the fundamental axiom that the laws should be made by the people to be governed by them, but the GAA had the audacity to come forward and make laws, forcing them on Irish athletes, and anyone who did not conform to the rules laid down by the ... meeting at Thurles would not be allowed to compete after the 17th March. If such a thing were allowed to go on, athletics would soon die. The GAA was formed on what must be called national lines, but they had an objection to sport being mixed up with athletics. He had no objection to the GAA in its proper sphere.

II

FREEMAN'S JOURNAL'S RESPONSE, 25 JANUARY 1885

9.5. We do not know that it [the GAA] seeks to interfere with any other association, but if the bicyclists of Dublin imagine that they are going to quash the Archbishop of Cashel, Mr Parnell, and Mr Davitt, because these gentlemen desire to promote Irish athletics, and to secure a due recognition in athletic programmes of those manly exercises in which Irishmen have from time immemorial excelled, we take the liberty of telling them that they are very much mistaken.

10. GAA Central Committee meeting, July 1885

10.1. *Introduction.* At a meeting in Thurles on 18 July 1885, the Central Committee of the GAA voted congratulations to Michael Davitt on the end of his 'ticket-of-leave', a remand period for convict prisoners who are released early, and after which time they are officially declared free. The Committee voted another resolution immediately afterwards, however, to declare that the organisation was not political but national. This reflected tensions within the GAA between constitutional and the more militant nationalists. SOURCE: 'The Gaelic Athletic Association', *Freeman's Journal*, 19 July 1885.

10.2. That we take this, the earliest opportunity, of expressing our gratification at the fact that, with reason unimpaired, Mr Michael Davitt, one of the patrons of the Gaelic Athletic Association and the sterling friend of the national language, as well as of the national pastimes, has survived the fifteen years of horror and physical and mental suffering which ended yesterday, and our best wishes for his success in his unceasing efforts to infuse an intense national life into the hearts of the Irish people that they may develop not only the resources of the country, but their own physical, moral, and intellectual powers to the fullest extent of which they are capable.

10.3. That we hereby declare that the Gaelic Athletic Association is not a political association, although it is a thoroughly National one: that our objects are ... the preservation and cultivation of national pastimes, that our platform is sufficiently wide for Irishmen of all classes and creeds; that whilst we welcome assistance from every quarter, we do not stand in need of any support from any organisation external to our own; and that we emphatically disclaim any intention of interfering with, or using to its disadvantage, or injuring in any respect, any existing Irish National organisation.

11. GAA sporting events

11.1. *Introduction.* Cusack's initial focus was on Irish athletics and the revival of hurling. Rugby and hurling was never really an option for working men whose leisure time was on Sundays and people on small incomes and of low social standing would not have made have been welcomed by those in control of cricket or athletics (then under the sponsorship of the Irish Amateur Athletic Association). The press report below suggest something of the energy and excitement at these early GAA events. Cusack himself wrote many of the reports on GAA events for the *United Ireland*. SOURCE: 'Hurling in the Phoenix Park, Dublin', *United Ireland,* 27 February 1886.

11.2. Those who frequent the Phoenix Park on Sundays now find almost every available patch of ground swarming with football-players and hurlers. Even the Phoenix cricket ground has been invaded by the hitherto neglected working people of the city. The grounds of the Metropolitan Hurling Club, the Polo-grounds, the Fifteen Acres, etc. were last Sunday crowded with ardent supporters and admirers of the open-air pastime recommended by the Gaelic Athletic Association. On the Nine Acres, the Grocers' Assistants Gaelic Athletic Club had a splendid practice match in which those who are to play the representatives of the Dalkey branch of the GAA next Sunday week took part. On the Fifteen Acres, the Michael Davitt branch fought a stubborn fight against the Faugh a Ballagh Branch from half past eleven to half past twelve o'clock and were defeated by only one goal, notwithstanding that their men were younger and that they had evidently less training than their opponents. The honorary secretary of the GAA [Cusack] acted as referee.

12. The GAA ban and the Executive

12.1. *Introduction.* Members of the Crown forces and the police were barred from participating in GAA games. The ban was later extended in the early 1900s to include military pensioners and merchant seamen serving in British-registered ships. Nationalism was also used to 'enhance the appeal of the organisation'. Others within the GAA believed that military men were simply too well trained and when they did play, they were too successful. The anonymous letter below argues eloquently against the ban. SOURCE: *The Celtic Times*, 2 April 1887.

To the editor of *The Celtic Times,*

Cashel, Co. Tipperary.

21 March 1887.

12.2. Sir … No one will deny that the Gaelic Athletic Association is a movement so grand in its conception, so Celtic in its character, and so essentially popular in its organization, that, perhaps, it surpasses all other existing organizations, both in what it has done and what it is yet destined to do, to elevate a nation, physically as well as morally …

12.3. Indeed, well may its founder contemplate his beautiful structure with pride and admiration; but at the same time he, in common with all true Gaelic men, must deprecate any attempts, such as have recently been made by the Executive, to cast discredit on a movement which, up till then, went on remarkably well, and for the simple reason that it was left for the most part to take care of itself …

12.4. No one expected that this body was capable of exhibiting much wisdom; but on the other hand neither was anybody prepared to give them credit for such suicidal tendencies, as certain resolutions which passed at their present meeting in Dublin exhibited. One in particular which has caused widespread indignation in this locality. I refer to the one which excludes members of the Royal Irish Constabulary from competing under the rules of the GAA. Now, this resolution is inconsistent with the liberality of the thing called the Executive. There are no just grounds on which members of the RIC can be thus boycotted. It is a body principally composed of small farmers, and which can count within its ranks men in whose bosoms there burns the fire of patriotism no less brilliant and no less intense than is to be found in the breast of any man who ever swore fidelity to the cause of Ireland. The brutality of the force on certain trying occasions was the exception, not the rule, and instances are on record in which kind-hearted members of the police contributed to the support of impoverished tenants whom they reluctantly helped to exterminate …

12.5. This resolution is untenable, indiscriminate, and unjust, and every liberal-minded Gaelic man should raise his voice in protest, and loudly demand to have it rescinded. It will, otherwise, have the effect of excluding some of our best men from the arena of Gaelic Athletics – an arena into which all true Irishmen, irrespective of creed, class, or occupation should be welcomed with open arms … I would not feel it a bit degrading to take my stand, side by side, in a Gaelic contest with a member of the RIC …

12.6. Having thus seen the many blunders made, by the present Executive (for which its respected President [Davin] is no way responsible), I think every effort should be made to rescue the Association from their hands, and to place it in the hands of men who will be competent to guide it properly …

13. GAA Convention of 1889

13.1. *Introduction.* The IRB took substantial control of the Association at a Convention held in Thurles on 9 November 1887. The meeting was both noisy and violent. E.M.

Bennett of Ennis, the IRB candidate, defeated Maurice Davin by 316 votes to 210. Archbishop Croke quickly dissociated himself from the new executive. In order to prevent a split in the GAA, a 'reconstruction convention' was called for 4 January 1888, when extreme nationalists were outnumbered and Maurice Davin was again relected as President. The following year, however, the GAA found itself in heavy debt and much of the blame fell on Davin. The extract below recounts the Convention of 24 January 1889. Divisions were clearly evident and disorder soon broke out. A walk-out by Davin was interpreted as a resignation from office, and delegates from sixteen counties elected the IRB man Peter Kelly as president. The Davin executive was replaced by a new council dominated by members of the IRB. Control of the GAA was to remain in Fenian hands for many years. Davin never again actively participated in the Association. SOURCE: 'The GAA Convention, Thurles, 1889', *The Times* (London), 24 January 1889.

> **13.2.** The annual convention of delegates of the Gaelic Athletic Association was held today at Thurles. There was a very large attendance, including a number of Catholic clergymen. The association consists of a central council and a Board in each county. Mr Frinell, MP, Mr William O'Brien, MP, an Archbishop Croke being patrons. The convention held today was for the purpose of electing members to form the central and county boards. The president, Mr Maurice Davin … was constantly interrupted while speaking, the proceedings being of a most disorderly character. Several delegates jumped on the platform and attempted to address the meeting, but were unable to do so owing to the continuous uproar and shouting. Eventually the president left the chair, and, accompanied by the clergymen present with some others forming the moderate section of the association, retired to an ante-room, where they passed a resolution abolishing the central council. Meanwhile the extreme or Fenian section of the association elected officers for the ensuing season. Both parties left the hall without coming in contact with each other.

14. Drink and the GAA: letter from Archbishop Croke

14.1. *Introduction.* Archbishop Croke was a lifelong opponent of intemperance. Even though the Home Rule Party had strong links with the drink industry, the Catholic Church, revived the issue of teetotalism in the 1880s. In 1898 the Jesuit, Fr James Cullen, founded the Total Abstinence Association of the Sacred Heart. The Sale of Liquors on Sunday (Ireland) Act, 1878 brought in complete Sunday closing, although the larger cities of Dublin, Cork, Limerick, Waterford and Belfast were exempted. However, the act was ineffective in practice. As patron of the GAA Croke urges delegates to encourage moderation in drinking and not to schedule sporting events during mass time. However, Croke's message fell on deaf ears. SOURCE: *The Gael*, the official Journal of the Gaelic Athletic Association, Saturday, 7 January 1888.

1. Photograph of Parnell *c.*1880 by his nephew, Henry Thomson. (Courtesy of the National Library of Ireland.)

2. Members of the Irish Parliamentary Party. *Illustrated London News*, 10 April 1886.

3. Cartoon: 'The political graveyard.' *Weekly News*, 12 November 1885. In the December 1885 general election, the Irish Parliamentary Party secured 86 seats at the expense of the Liberal Party, and the Conservatives won just 16 seats, almost all in Ulster. The Irish Loyal and Patriotic Union which was founded in May 1885 to galvanise resistance to Home Rule, took just one seat, Trinity College, Dublin.

4. Cartoon: 'Lord Randolph Churchill leads on the Demon of religious strife to do the work of Hell in the North of Ireland.' *Weekly News*, 27 February 1886. This cartoon proved quite prophetic, for later that year Belfast witnessed the worst sectarian violence of the century.

5. 'Land League Cruelty.' Facsimile of a propagandist poster, of uncertain date and provenance, denouncing the inhumanity of the Home Rule movement. (Courtesy of the Public Record Office of Northern Ireland, D.2733.)

6. A large crowd at the Ulster Convention at Balmoral, Belfast, 17 June 1892. Over 12,000 Unionist and Liberal Unionist delegates resolved 'to have nothing to do with' any Home-Rule Parliament. The formation of Lord Templetown's (1853–1939) network of Unionist Clubs and the Ulster Defence Union (UDU) in 1893 kept up the momentum. (Courtesy of the Public Record Office of Northern Ireland.)

Ulster's
Solemn League and Covenant.

Being convinced in our consciences that Home Rule would be disastrous to the material well-being of Ulster as well as of the whole of Ireland, subversive of our civil and religious freedom, destructive of our citizenship and perilous to the unity of the Empire, we, whose names are underwritten, men of Ulster, loyal subjects of His Gracious Majesty King George V., humbly relying on the God whom our fathers in days of stress and trial confidently trusted, do hereby pledge ourselves in solemn Covenant throughout this our time of threatened calamity to stand by one another in defending for ourselves and our children our cherished position of equal citizenship in the United Kingdom and in using all means which may be found necessary to defeat the present conspiracy to set up a Home Rule Parliament in Ireland. ¶ And in the event of such a Parliament being forced upon us we further solemnly and mutually pledge ourselves to refuse to recognise its authority. ¶ In sure confidence that God will defend the right we hereto subscribe our names. ¶ And further, we individually declare that we have not already signed this Covenant.

The above was signed by me at *Belfast.*
"Ulster Day," Saturday, 28th September, 1912.

Edward Carson

——— God Save the King. ———

7. Facsimile of a copy of Ulster's Solemn League and Covenant, signed by Sir Edward Carson, 28 September 1912, pledging opposition to Home Rule. (Courtesy of the Public Record Office of Northern Ireland, D.1496/3.)

8. 'Ulster's Solemn Covenant'. A postcard issued to commemorate the signing of the Solemn League and Covenant on 'Ulster day', 28 September 1912.

9. Second Reading of the Government of Ireland (Home Rule) Bill, House of Commons, 10 May 1886. Parnell is seated in the second row on the right; to his right are T.M. Healy, T.P. O'Connor, John Redmond and Joseph G. Biggar. *Weekly News*, 15 May 1886.

10. John Devoy photographed in prison clothes, 1866. In 1865 John Devoy was appointed Chief Organiser of Fenians in the British Army in Ireland. The government got wind of his plans to recruit Irish soldiers into the IRB and he was arrested in February 1886 and interned at Mountjoy Gaol. He was tried for treason and sentenced to 15 years penal servitude. (Courtesy of the National Museum of Ireland.)

11. Cartoon: 'Drive him under the surface' – His Ex. [Lord John Poyntz Spencer, Lord Lieutenant] – "Down! and forever be silent"; English Press – "Bravo! That's right, my Lord; Cudgel him, whether he is acting lawfully or unlawfully"; Irishman – "Mind, it's not my desire to be thrown amongst these things again, but if I am, you know that it's yourselves is to blame." Supplement, *Weekly Freeman*, 6 October 1883.

12. Arthur James Balfour, Chief Secretary of Ireland, 1895–1900, photographed c.1892. Balfour increased the amount of money available for land purchase and oversaw the Local Government Act of 1898. However, the measures failed to silence the nationalist demand for Home Rule. (Courtesy of the National Portrait Gallery, London.)

13. Herbert H. Asquith, Liberal Prime Minister of Great Britain, 1908–16.
(Courtesy of the National Portrait Gallery, London.)

14. Photograph of Michael Davitt *c.*1886, the driving force behind the Irish National Land League and architect of the Land War, 1879–82.

15. John Redmond photographed with members of the Irish Volunteer Force, September 1914. A few weeks later the movement split. A smaller group of some 12,000 men, among them Eoin MacNeill, Patrick Pearse and Thomas MacDonagh, formed the IRB-led Irish Volunteers, while as many as 180,000 supported Redmond and became known as the National Volunteers. (Courtesy of George Morrison.)

16. Cartoon: 'Second Thoughts' – John Redmond: "Full shteam ahead! (*aside*) I wondher will I lave this contrairy little divil loose, he'd come back by himself aftherwards? [*sic*]" Partridge, *Punch*, 8 October 1913. While four of the five pigs obediently enter the Home Rule pen, the N.E Ulster pig tries to break away. The nationalist leader's 'second thoughts' is a reference to Lloyd George's proposal that Ulster be excluded from Home Rule for a period of six years.

17. Men dressed and masked as women at an anti-suffrage demonstration in Strabane, Co. Tyrone, *c*.1910. Neither the Unionist or Nationalist leaders supported female suffrage. Suffragists were often described as 'degenerates' who posed a threat to family life. Heckling and physical assaults by angry mobs were not uncommon. (Courtesy of the Public Record Office of Northern Ireland.)

18. The first nine women to be awarded degrees from the Royal University of Ireland, Dublin, 1884. The women would have studied for their exams at unendowed private colleges. Full and equal rights for women in higher education only came with the Universities (Ireland) Act of 1908. (Courtesy of Alexandra College, Dublin.)

19. Michael Cusack photographed *c.*1880s. Cusack promoted the idea of a national organisation for the preservation and promotion of traditional Irish games. The Gaelic Athletic Association (GAA) was formed at a meeting in Hayes' Hotel, Thurles, Co. Tipperary, 1 November 1884. (Courtesy of the National Library of Ireland.)

20. Douglas Hyde, scholar, author and later President of Ireland (1938–45), photographed at the Gap of Dunloe, Co. Kerry, September 1914. After four days' sightseeing he wrote that he had 'never seen the likes of that scene ever.'

21. Facsimile of a page from *An Claidheamh Soluis* (1899); it was the official organ of the Gaelic League and was edited by Eoin MacNeill.

22. Photograph of the National Library (with Leinster House on the right), *c*.1890. On 10 April 1885, the Prince and Princess of Wales laid the foundation-stone of both the National Library and the nearby Science and Art Museum. The architect was Thomas Newenham Deane (1828–99). Both buildings were opened on 29 August 1890. (Courtesy of the National Library of Ireland.)

23 The great poet and dramatist William Butler Yeats *c.*1923. (Courtesy of the National Library of Ireland.)

24. Victoria Channel and Queen's Island, Belfast, 1911. The latter part of the nineteenth century saw wooden sailing ships replaced by larger and faster metal ships powered by steam. An older wooden schooner lies moored in Victoria Channel, at Queen's Island in the background, the huge steel hull of *SS Titanic* is being readied for launching. (Courtesy of the Ulster Folk and Transport Museum.)

25. Tenement building in Fade Street, Dublin *c*.1890s. (Courtesy of the Irish Architectural Archive.)

To the Delegates of the GAA Convention, Thurles.

The Palace, Thurles,

Co. Tipperary.

January 4, 1888.

14.2. GENTLEMEN – Allow me to congratulate you on the very satisfactory results, as far as I know, that have hitherto attended your desire to reconstruct the Gaelic Athletic Association and place it on a solid and satisfactory basis … I have no desire, gentlemen, nor have I a right, to interfere in any way with your deliberations; but it can hardly be said that I am entering on a province that does not belong to me as patron of your society if I venture to offer, as I do, a few facts for your consideration, and a few practical suggestions thereon. First, then, I beg to call your serious attention to the grave matter of *drink* in connection with our Gaelic sports.

14.3. … I would respectfully suggest that it be ruled somewhat as follows: –

1. That the sale of porter and ale, and of course of all alcoholic drinks, be strictly prohibited on, and as far as possible even near, the field in which athletic sports are held.

2. That in selecting the locality for such sports, the immediate neighbourhood of public houses be specially avoided.

3. That no prizes be henceforth accepted from publicans – at least, when there is good reason to believe, as there nearly always is, that they have offered them solely, or chiefly, with a view of attracting customers to their shops.

4. That no tournament, no county or district games, be held on Sundays or holidays of obligation (if that be at all practicable), and that even parochial or inter-parochial competitions be not begun on such days before two o'clock.

14.4. I have good reason to believe that the country at large expects you will substantially make such regulations as I now suggest; and I pray you, therefore, either now or at some future, but not distant time, to give them practical effect in your respective counties.

I have the honour to remain, gentlemen, your very faithful servant,

+ T.W. CROKE, Archbishop of Cashel

15. Pastoral letter of Archbishop Logue of Armagh

15.1. *Introduction.* Archbishop (later Cardinal) Michael Logue (1840–1924) of Armagh and Primate of All Ireland (from December 1887) denounced the working of the GAA in 1889 and its 'demoralising effects' on its members. He was a supporter of the total abstinence movement and he also preached against the evils of poitín [illicit whiskey]. Although the Catholic Church tolerated games on Sundays, Protestant Sabbatarianism ruled them out. And in general, cricket, soccer and rugby also barred Sunday play. However, many Catholics travelled to GAA matches on Sunday, their only day of rest. Major matches often offered additional entertainments: Irish dancing competitions, poetry readings, parades etc. The question of games on a Sunday was, therefore, a more pressing matter in the north of the country where Sabbatarian Protestants were numerous. Football, hurling, and athletics usually took place after mass. Archbishop Logue is critical of those who would seek to draw men and boys out of the Church and into the playing field. He encourages clergy to speak out strongly against such practices. SOURCE: *Freeman's Journal*, 13 February 1888.

> **15.2.** … There is however, one abuse lately sprung up and daily growing which, as bishop charged with the grave responsibility of promoting among the youth of my flock a spirit of religion and habits of temperance, I can no longer pass over in silence.

> **15.3.** Some time since a movement was set on foot to revive the old Irish games and thereby develop the manhood and national spirit of our young countrymen. This movement and its motives have my heartiest sympathy and would merit any countenance and encouragement. But laudable as the object may be, if it can be gained only by the sacrifice of Sunday's duties, of the spirit of religion and the habits of temperance among our young men, it is not worth the price.

> **15.4.** Lately a great prelate [Archbishop Croke] whose voice seldom appeals in vain to the hearts of Irishmen, procured the adoption by the Gaelic Athletic Association of a rule which would go far to remove the abuses to which I refer, but I am sorry to learn that in parts of this archdiocese little heed has been paid to the rule in question. Young men assemble early on Sundays, sometimes to practise, sometimes to play set matches outside their own parishes. Of these, many have no opportunity of hearing mass before leaving and even those who have, few I fear take precautions to do so; none of them can by any chance hear any instruction. Instances even have occurred in which football matches have been played quite close to the church at the very time when the people were assembled to assist at the Holy Sacrifice, thus disturbing by unseemly noise and excitement a congregation engaged in the discharge of a most sacred duty.

> **15.5.** Nor is the evil confined to those actually engaged in the game. They draw after them the children of both sexes, thus depriving them of instruction in the Catechism. Yes and they draw after them too foolish old men who would be better employed telling their beads in a quiet corner of the church and praying for the end which is so close upon them. They furnish moreover, especially by their inter-parochial matches,

an excuse for the keeping open of public houses on Sundays, thus exposing themselves and the spectators to the dangers of intemperance. It is very evident such a profanation of the Sunday and turning of the people away from the religious duties, to which the chief part of the day should be devoted, can no longer be tolerated.

15.6. Hence I exhort the clergy to set their faces against this abuse and neither to countenance, nor as far as in them lies, tolerate any athletic club in their parishes that will not keep, at the very least, within the lines of the rule laid down by his Grace, the Archbishop of Cashel.

16. Special Branch reports on the GAA between 1889 and 1891

16.1. *Introduction.* Shortly after its foundation, the GAA had been heavily infiltrated by the IRB. From 1887 onwards the RIC in various parts of the country closely monitored its activities. These reports are an invaluable source for the local history of the GAA at this time. They were written monthly and annually by the District Inspectors and sent to Dublin where the Inspector General would add his comments. SOURCE: 1. 'Extract', *Special Branch Reports Northern Division* (National Archives of Ireland, CBS 2701/S); 2. District Inspector W. Reeves, *Special Branch Reports Northern Division* (National Archives of Ireland, CBS 2010/S); 3 & 4. District Inspector William Jones, *Special Branch Reports Southern Division* (National Archives of Ireland, CBS 181/127 S).

I

Table 1: Extract from reports on the GAA, 1890–1 by the RIC – Northern Division

---

County of Louth
List of GAA clubs in above County and Officers of each

No.	Name of Club	Names of Officers	Position	Approx. No. of members in each club	Remarks
5	Tullyallen 'Tars'	Patrick Pentony	President	60	IRB
		Michael Walsh	V.P.		IRB
		Thomas Downey	Captain		
		Jason Brannigan	Treasure		
		Jason Carther	Secretary		IRB
	Sandpit 'T.P. Gills'	Patrick McKeown	President	40	IRB
		Hugh Woods	Captain		
		Laurence McKeown	Secretary		IRB

II

SPECIAL BRANCH REPORTS ON THE GAA IN 1889–90 – NORTHERN DIVISION

4 January 1889

16.2. The principal business which the IRB seems to have been engaged in for some time past is the enrolment in their ranks of members of the GAA. This is not only confirmed by the informants but in places the Roman Catholic priests have spoken of it openly. In one instance, the Parish priest of Clones [Co. Monaghan] recently condemned the GAA in strong language in chapel and gave it as his opinion that the Association was a secret one and must eventually lead to evil results …

24 April 1890

16.3. The GAA is becoming very weak in this Division. There are in all but 85 branches, 30 of which are not affiliated with the central branch and the Association is continuously losing ground. About this time last year there were 154 branches in the Division. The Society has been held up to so much public condemnation by the Roman Catholic clergy throughout the North on account of its connection with the IRB that it could not withstand the attacks and its final break-up is only a matter of time …

III

SOUTHERN DIVISION

CRIME DEPARTMENT – SPECIAL BRANCH

SUBJECT: Modus operandi of seducing one of the GAA into the IRB society

Cork, 14 April 1890

16.4. Hints are given to the member of the GAA intended to be practised on that the person addressing him belongs to a higher club. The Manchester Martyrs are eulogized, and other 'patriots' praised up – such Emmet, Lord Fitzgerald etc. At the same time a close watch is kept on the patient to observe how the bait takes. It is appears successful the next step is to ask him if he would not wish to do likewise. If the answer is in the affirmative the questioners then admits he is a follower of the 'patriots'. The candidate is then tested to see if he would 'blab'. He is treated to plenty of drink, and tested whether he can hold his tongue. If found all right, he is requested to accompany the person who first broached the subject to a place named to meet a person unknown to him. The place is always dark, and when there he is asked by the unknown whether he is satisfied to join the IRB and fight for the republic when called on. On answering in the affirmative, he is duly sworn in.

William Jones

District Inspector of Constabulary

IV

SUBJECT: Yearly Report of Crime & Special Work in above Division during the year 1891

Cork, 16 January 1892

16.5. District Commissioner, I have to report that during the past year in Cork City the IRB organisation has played a considerable part in political affairs. With very few exceptions all the prominent members have taken the Parnellite side in the split, and have worked steadily to further the interests of that section of the Nationalist party … The GAA which promised in 1887 and 1888 to be a considerable factor in the political history of Ireland. Is at the present moment tottering to its fall. It is torn by dissensions, and in finance has been the victim of fraud. The clerical wing particularly seems to have gone out of hand, and to be completely disorganized. However, in Cork there is much talk amongst the IRB section of reorganizing the Association, training it purely as a Fenian branch. This may work for a time in the larger cities, but in rural districts will end in failure. We have now 44 Branches in the Division as compared with 72 last year under clerical influence, and 50 as compared with 63 under Fenian control, showing in all a decrease of 41 branches.

17. The Parnell split and the GAA

17.1. *Introduction.* The GAA as a body supported Parnell when the split in the Irish Party took place. At a meeting held in the Rotunda in Dublin on 23 July 1891, attended by delegates from sixty-five clubs (one-third of them from Dublin), a resolution was passed: 'That this convention is resolved to support the policy of independent opposition and freedom of opinion under the leadership of Mr Charles Stewart Parnell'. In February the Dublin board had given its full backing to a successful demonstration by Gaelic players and athletes of the city and county. As a result, the support of the clergy largely evaporated and many members left the Association. In many counties the GAA ceased to exist and competitions lapsed. When Parnell died, the funeral at Glasnevin was a joint GAA-IRB affair. It is estimated that 2,000 GAA players were in attendance, each carrying a hurley draped in black and held in reverse to resemble a rifle. The entire Central Council of the GAA also attended. The extracts below show the depth of GAA support for Parnell during 1890–91. It would take years, however, for the Association's membership to recover. SOURCE: 1. 'Parnell in Galway', *The Times*, 16 March 1890; 2. 'Parnell in Killarney', *The Times,* 26 December 1890; 3. 'Parnell in Thurles', *The Times*, 12 January 1891.

I

17.2. Mr Parnell arrived here this morning by special train … Mr Parnell was accompanied to Galway city by a large body of people from different parts of the county

Galway … and other places. The reception at Galway was very enthusiastic, although there were isolated cries of dissent sad one or two counter cheers for Kitty O'Shea. Colonel Nolan, MP, and Mr P. Mahony, MP, received Mr Parnell, and, after a short delay, the party proceeded in a wagonette through the town, accompanied by several bands and by about a thousand persons. A number of flags were carried. A stop was made at the gaol and cheers were given for Messrs. O'Brien and Dillon who are at present incarcerated in that institution. The speaking took place from a platform in Eyre Square. In front of the platform were the words, 'Where Parnell leads Galway will follow', affixed to the railings … There were a large number of members of Gaelic Athletic Associations in their uniform, and a considerable number of men on horseback. Between three and four thousand spectators assembled at the platform. The proceedings were unanimous. Colonel Nolan, MP, who presided, said that Mr Parnell was the best leader they could get. If they dismissed him it would be 50 years before they could obtain an honest leader. On the motion of Mr Ashe, seconded by Mr Sullivan, a resolution expressing the fullest confidence in the honesty and sagacity of Mr Parnell was passed unanimously on a show of hands amid great enthusiasm … Mr Parnell was subsequently presented with a large number of addresses from different Nationalist bodies … Mr Parnell, in replying, said the institutions that the addresses represented were no mushroom institutions. He was sure the Gaelic Athletic Association wore longing for a general election in order to show the stuff they were made of. (*Loud cheers*) He knew that wherever the Gaelic Association was strong the constituency was safe. They would know how to keep public opinion right and on the straight road to Irish nationality. They had acted in the face of unexampled intimidation, but as long as they stood by him he was not a bit afraid of the whole of those against him. (*Cheers*) They must not allow any defeat to discourage them … Time was against their enemies, because they had nothing to rest upon except a foundation of lies and misrepresentation.

II

17.3. A meeting of the Dr. Croke branch of the Gaelic Athletic Association was held in Killarney on Sunday night, at which there was a decided difference of opinion. A resolution was proposed expressing approval of the action of their president, Mr Sheehan, MP, in opposing Mr Parnell's leadership. An amendment was proposed that the club refused to endorse Mr Sheehan's action. A heated discussion ensued, and eventually the amendment was rejected. The meeting then broke up with some loudly cheering for Parnell, while others cheered for Dillon and O'Brien. …

III

17.4. The train was met at Thurles by about 200 people, and Mr Parnell was accorded a very warm reception. When the cheering had subsided he was presented with two addresses – one on behalf of the local branch of the Irish National Foresters' Association, and the other on behalf of the Thurles branch of the Gaelic Athletic Association. Mr Parnell, in reply, said, 'Men of Thurles, I am proud to be with you tonight and to find that the number of my supporters in Thurles has not diminished, but, on the contrary, has increased. (*Cheers*) I am glad to be able to assure you, as I did on the last occasion I had the honour of meeting you, that your confidence in me and in the success of our cause is not a mistaken or misguided one. (*Cheers*) I pledged you that then I renew the same pledge to night; and leave you asking you to rely on me (*cheers*), to depend that in every thought and action I shall regard and look to only the future prosperity and the nationality of Ireland. (*Cheers*) There are times, fellow-countrymen, when the wheat is separated from the chaff (*cries of 'Tim Healy'*), and when parties are weighed, not by their numbers, but by their quality and determination. (*Cheers and cries of 'Judas Healy'.*) I am proud to recognise in you the same men who stood around me when I first came into your gallant country ... With that confidence, my friends, with your help, I go forward, fearing nothing, knowing the honesty of my own heart, knowing my own determination, and, above all, recognizing and feeling sure of your honesty and unconquerable courage.' (*Cheers*) The train moved off amidst great cheering ...

GILLIAN M. DOHERTY AND TOMÁS O'RIORDAN

CHAPTER 8

Dublin, 1913 – strike and Lockout

1. Introduction

1.1. In Britain and Ireland, the divisions between the labour movement and employers had deepened greatly in the early years of the twentieth century. Strikes had occurred frequently in many places, although Dublin had escaped major labour unrest. The Dublin Chamber of Commerce noted rather optimistically in 1900 the 'the growing disposition of all classes to unite in promoting the best interests of our country'. This harmony did not last, and in 1913 workers in the city became involved in a serious conflict with the employers, known as the 'Lockout'. It was a dispute to rival any in Europe in the first quarter of the twentieth century. Although for the most part a trade union and industrial dispute, it was closely associated with the political and social conditions of the period – it was a struggle for jobs, housing and health. It was also a fierce, determined battle between two stubborn and passionate men: the labour leader, James Larkin and, the powerful business leader, William Martin Murphy.

2. A tenement city

2.1. There was good reason for discontent in Dublin in 1913. As early as 1841, Dublin had ceased to be the 'second city of the empire' having been overtaken by Glasgow and Liverpool. The city's working class were the worst paid and worst housed in the United Kingdom. The death rate in Dublin (22.3 per 1,000) was as bad as Calcutta, and the city's slums were among the worst in Europe. The census of 1911 recorded 90,000 adult males living in the city. While the population of the country as a whole had dropped by 315,000 since 1891, the population of Dublin had increased by 55,000 by 1911. Overcrowding in the city's tenements was a serious problem, and bred disease and infection. Malnutrition was common. The same census revealed that a total of 835 people were living in the 15 houses of the formerly prosperous Henrietta Street. In one house alone, there resided members of 19 different families. Nearly 26,000 families in the city centre lived in tenements, with over 20,000 of these families in single-room dwellings. Some families even took in lodgers. Men, women and children were living in buildings that were considered unfit, or near unfit, for human habitation. There were often more than ten families in town houses that had been built for one upper-class family in the eighteenth and nineteenth centuries. These houses became dilapidated with the flight of the wealthy elite to the suburbs. The houses were often taken over by landlords who rented them out, room by room, to poor families, and they quickly became slums. There was little privacy. Facilities for cooking, cleaning, and washing were wholly inadequate.

Sanitary conditions were even worse. Many tenement buildings shared just one lavatory in a yard. People like James Connolly (a leading socialist who returned to Ireland from the United States) were well aware of such conditions:

> Ireland is a country of wonderful charity and singularly little justice. And Dublin, being the epitome of Ireland, it is not strange to find that Dublin, a city famous for its charitable institutions and its charitable citizens, should also be infamous for the perfectly hellish conditions under which its people are housed, and under which its men, women and children labour for a living.

2.2. In 1913, events occurred which made clear the dreadful conditions of poverty in Dublin. On the evening of Tuesday, 2 September 1913, at about 8.45 p.m., two houses owned by Mrs Ryan on Church Street suddenly collapsed, burying the occupants. The buildings were four storeys high, with shops on the ground floor. The 16 rooms upstairs were occupied by about 10 families, over 40 people. Rescuers worked through the night digging people out. Seven people were killed and many more were badly injured. Most people were shocked that such an event could occur. Others were less surprised. Mr R.G. Pilkington of the Dublin Citizens' Association Committee on Housing wrote in the *Irish Times* that 'the mass of the citizens are in ignorance of the real wants of the city ... We have evidence to show that (owing to dilapidation) what recently happened in Church Street may occur in other parts of the city.'

2.3. After the Church Street disaster, a Committee of Inquiry was set up by the government to study housing in the city. The Committee reported disturbing findings in 1914. It found that 16 members of the City Corporation owned tenements and it was clear that its members had deliberately prevented enforcement of regulations against their properties. Of the 400,000 people living in Dublin, 87,305 lived in tenements in the centre of the city. Eighty per cent of these families occupied only one room each. The Committee defined 'tenement houses' as:

> Houses intended and originally used for occupation by one family but which, owing to change of circumstances, have been let out room by room and are now occupied by separate families, one in each room for the most part.

2.4. Reporting on the conditions in the tenements, the Committee said:

> There are many tenement houses with seven or eight rooms that house a family in each room and contain a population of between forty and fifty souls. We have visited one house that we found to be occupied by 98 persons, another by 74 and a third by 73. The entrance to all tenement houses is by a common door off a street, lane or alley, and in most cases the door is never shut day or night. The passages and stairs are common and the rooms all open directly off either the passages or landings. Most of these houses have yards at the back, some of which are a fair size, while others are very small, and some few houses have no yards at all. Generally the

only water supply of the house is furnished by a single water tap which is in the yard. The yard is common and the closet accommodation is to be found there, except in some few cases in which there is no yard, when it is to be found in the basement where there is little or no ventilation. The closet accommodation is common as the evidence shows not only to the occupants of the house, but to anyone who likes to come in off the street, and is of course common to both sexes. The roofs of the tenement houses are as a rule bad … Having visited a large number of these houses in all parts of the city, we have no hesitation in saying that it is not an uncommon thing to find halls and landings, yards and closets of the houses in a filthy condition, and in nearly every cases human excreta is to be found scattered about the yards and in the floors of the closets and in some cases even in the passages of the house itself …

2.5. The tenement rooms were poorly furnished. The basic items were bedsteads, bed-clothes, tables and chairs (boxes were often used instead of the last two). David Alfred Chart (1847–1919), was an eminent Irish historian and social scientist. He addressed the Dublin Social Inquiry and Statistical Society about poverty and slum housing in Dublin on 6 March 1914. He noted during one of his visits that:

> … in some tenement rooms the bedstead is not to be seen in its usual place in the corner, but in its stead there is spread on the floor a mysterious and repellent assort-ment of rags, which few inquirers have had the hardihood to investigate and which is believed to serve as a bed.

2.6. The contrast between the squalor of life in the city slums and the beautiful coun-tryside only a few miles from the city could not have been greater. Visits to the coun-tryside were a rare treat for slum children.

2.7. Many families were forced to pawn what little they had in bad times, and times were nearly always bad. One observer noted that the 'the number of articles pawned in Dublin is very large. From inquiries which I made some years ago, I ascertained that, in a single year, 2,866,084 were issued in the city of Dublin'. Family belongings were com-monly pawned at the beginning of the week and redeemed at the end of the week when some money came in.

3. Human conditions in the city

3.1. The evil effects of overcrowding, physical and mental, were obvious. Chart visited various tenements in the city and recalled the depressing scenes:

> I entered a 'front-drawing room' on a sultry day in August. A child lay ill with whooping cough and was lying exhausted on the bed after a paroxysm [convulsion] of coughing. Flies were numerous in the room (it was a hot summer) and were pass-ing and repassing from the food on the table to the face and body of the sick child.

3.2. He also recalled a father:

> ... who appealed to me, as one in temporary authority, to procure the ejection of a suspected 'unfortunate' from the room above his own. He said he was trying to 'bring up his children dacint [decent]' and how could he do it with women like that in the house. ...

3.3. Because of bad housing, poor sanitation and bad diet there were major health problems in the tenements. The most common and dreaded of the 'killer diseases' was TB [tuberculosis] or 'consumption', as it was commonly known. Diseases such as measles and whooping cough were highly contagious, and very dangerous to undernourished children. Bronchitis, gastro-enteritis, diarrhoea, and pneumonia also often proved fatal. Overcrowding and poor hygiene meant that disease was everywhere. Sexually transmitted disease was also a serious health problem. Children accounted for nearly seven out of ten deaths recorded from syphilis and gonorrhoea. Infant mortality was most alarmingly high. The 1911 census reveals that nearly half of the children in some larger families died in childhood. Sir Charles Cameron, the Medical Inspector for Dublin, said: 'It is certain that infants perish from want of sufficient food ...' About 20 per cent of all who died in the city (1,808 in 1911) were children less than a year old and nearly all those occurred among the poorest classes. The death rate in the city was not helped by the presence of livestock in cattle yards near the tenements. Private slaughter-houses often illegally disposed of offal and other substances on the city streets. Such appalling living conditions also led to other social problems. Alcohol played a very large role in the lives of many. It offered an easy escape from the dreary everyday troubles of life in the tenements. Workers who drank had little or no money to spend on their families. The problem was made worse by the custom, in some areas, of paying workers their wages in pubs. James Larkin tried to target the problem of heavy drinking. He was a teetotaller, and was firmly opposed to alcohol. His newspaper, the *Irish Worker,* often warned its readers of the dangers of drink. In 1913, reflecting on the appalling conditions that existed in Dublin, he said:

> When I came to Dublin, I found that the men on the quays had been paid most of their wages in public houses, and if they did not waste most of their money there, they would not get work the next time. Every stevedore [worker employed in the loading or unloading of ships] was getting 10 per cent of the money taken by the publican from the worker, and the man who would not spend his money across the counter was not wanted.

3.4. Because of his anti-alcohol campaign, Larkin was greatly admired by wives and mothers who suffered most from the heavy drinking of their menfolk.

3.5. Crime was widespread in the city, and often connected with drunkenness. The figures for serious crimes – murder, rape and larceny – were 100 crimes for every 10,000 people (higher than most large cities in Britain at the time).

3.6. The high rate of prostitution was another great social problem. Indeed, Dublin had the highest incidence of prostitution of any city in the United Kingdom, and it had one of the biggest red-light districts in Europe. The presence of thousands of troops in various Dublin barracks encouraged the trade. This enraged many nationalists, and Arthur Griffith frequently lamented the fate of Dublin as an 'extended brothel' for His Majesty's forces in Ireland. Dire poverty forced many women into a life on the streets: for most it was the only option open to them. The Dublin Metropolitan Police (DMP) estimated that over 1,600 women were engaged in prostitution in 1900 – nearly 1 in 50 women in the city. In 1912, there were over 1,000 arrests for prostitution in the city, an increase of more than one third on previous years. Sackville Street (O'Connell Street), Harcourt Street, St Stephen's Green and Grafton Street were notorious areas for prostitutes. Some of the best-known brothels in the city were to be found in the Montgomery ('Monto') Street district, around Gloucester Street, around the docks and in the south inner city. Indeed, the custom in Sackville Street was that one side of the street was frequented by 'respectable' people and the other by prostitutes. Larkin speaking to trade unionists in Dublin in 1907, had asked, 'Why did they not put a stop to the disgraceful scenes in O'Connell Street, when fellows from the slums of London, in red uniform, were coming along with Irish girls on their arms, whom they would ruin in body and soul?' A girl of a tenement family was forced to grow up quickly and was often a surrogate mother to her younger brothers and sisters. Religious organisations established Magdalen asylums to save some of the 'fallen' women who worked the city streets, but they enjoyed only limited success. The closure of many brothels forced many women into an even more precarious existence on the city streets.

4. Employment in Dublin

4.1. While Dublin remained an important political, commercial and cultural centre in 1913, the city was in industrial decline. The industrial powerhouse of Belfast was now the largest city in Ireland. Improvements in transport had assisted the middle-class flight to the suburbs. The lack of manufacturing in the city, a direct consequence of imperial policy, meant that there were an unusually high number of unskilled labourers in various jobs. In 1901, only 9,400 of the 40,200-strong male labour force were engaged in industry – brewing, tanning, engineering, printing etc. Over 7,600 men were employed as carters (distributing and transporting goods) and over 23,000 others were employed as labourers in the building and general trades. These jobs were very often 'casual'. Some employers felt that tenement-people were bad workers because they were physically weak. The English journalist, Arnold Wright, wrote that 'the very nature of their mode of living tends to reduce their value to the labour market ... they speedily lose, not merely their sense of self-respect, but their capacity for sustained exertion'.

4.2. The naturally growing population of the city was swelled by others coming from the countryside. As a result there were always more workers available than jobs. The unemployment rate was sometimes as high as 20 per cent. With such competition for jobs, unskilled workers were in a very weak position to demand better pay and conditions. While Dublin tradesmen had been able to maintain their craft privileges, most Irish workers lacked the power and confidence of organised, skilled workers, common in Britain and Europe. Trade Unions in Dublin were very weak and many workers found themselves at the mercy of their employers. The Report of Inquiry into Dublin Housing in 1913 found that most heads of families in Dublin took home between 15 and 20 shillings in wages per week, and, Board of Trade figures reproduced below show that Irish workers, especially labourers, generally earned less than workers in other large cities:

Table 2: Board of Trade wage figures, November 1913				
City	*Dublin*	*Belfast*	*London*	*Manchester*
(Cost of living index)	100	105	100	100
bricklayers (per hour)	8½d.	8½d.	10½d.	10d.
builders & labourers	4½d.	4½d.	7d.	7d.
carpenters	8½d.	8½d.	10½d.	8½d.
masons	8½d.	8½d.	10½d.	8½d.
engineers (per week)	33s.	39s.	40s.	37s.

4.3. Women fared even worse than men. While the average labourer's wage was less than one pound a week, the average female earned about half that. Most women who worked were in domestic service in the homes of the wealthy. Women also found work in laundries or in manufacturing and on the farms on the outskirts of the city. Others tried to make a living selling fish, flowers, clothes, fruit etc., on the sides of streets. There were few other jobs to be had.

4.4 The situation for children was even worse. Thousands of children wandered the streets of Dublin trying to sell their wares. A 1902 report into the problem found that many children were homeless or from broken families, and nearly one in six children were orphans or came from one-parent families. Many children, particularly boys, ended up in prison or industrial schools like Artane.

5. James 'Big Jim' Larkin and the rise of the ITGWU

5.1. The 1913 Lockout is often seen as a clash between two influential men: James 'Big Jim' Larkin, founder and head of the Irish Transport and General Workers Union (ITGWU), and William Martin Murphy, one of the city's most wealthy and powerful industrialists, and the main force behind the Dublin Employers' Federation Ltd. Both were very important as the representatives of workers and employers: Larkin with support of thousands of urban workers, and moral force, behind him; Murphy with wealth, influence and the support of a privileged elite.

5.2. Larkin, the Liverpool-born son of poor Irish immigrant parents, worked at various jobs before becoming involved with the National Union of Dock Labourers (NUDL) that was established there in 1889. James Sexton (1856–1938), another son of Irish parents, was elected general secretary of the NUDL in 1893. Having already served his time as a branch officer and trades council delegate, Sexton proved himself to be very competent manager and administrator. When Larkin led his men out on a strike in the summer of 1905, the NUDL offered him £4-a-week job as a full-time organiser. Assisted by his personal charisma and oratorical skills, he proved himself more than capable. Larkin succeeded in recruiting hundreds of dock workers to the Union when he organised the Scottish ports. He was then assigned to do the same in the Irish ports. He arrived first in Belfast, where he organised the unskilled workers. Larkin went on to lead a successful strike for recognition of the union and for higher wages. He tried to use the same tactics in Cork, Dublin and Waterford but the executive of the NUDL was reluctant to support unofficial strikes. Larkin was later prosecuted by the NUDL for diverting union funds to pay striking Cork workers.

5.3. Tensions about leadership soon arose between Larkin and Sexton and in 1908 Larkin was sacked from the Union. He remained committed to building up a strong union among the city's workers and he founded the Irish Transport and General Workers Union (ITGWU) in late 1908 (now known as the Services Industrial Professional & Technical Union – SIPTU). He managed to take most of the Irish NUDL members with him. Larkin became the union's secretary and edited its paper, the *Irish Worker and People's Advocate*. He wanted this weekly newspaper to speak out for the workers of the city. It had a circulation of over 90,000. Liberty Hall at the corner of Eden Quay and Beresford Place (formerly the Northumberland Hotel) became the headquarters of the ITGWU and the centre of all the Union's activity.

5.4. Many of the founding members were influenced by syndicalism: the idea that advocates bringing industry and government under the control of federations of labour unions through the use of direct action, such as general or 'sympathetic' strikes, public demonstration, sabotage, or revolutionary violence and who then manage them for the public good. A 'sympathetic strike' was when workers supported striking workers by refusing to deal in any way with firms whose employees were on strike. Many syndicalists wanted, ultimately, to overthrow the capitalist system, and to establish socialism, that is, that all workers would be equal, would share responsibilities equally and receive equal pay.

5.5. Due in the main to Larkin's own personal appeal, membership of the ITGWU grew to around 10,000 within a few years and nearly 18,000 by 1918. His tremendous ability as a speaker and his obvious compassion for the oppressed made him the hero of thousands of workers. In the words of a British Trade Union Congress delegation:

> … the ITGWU had considerably raised the wages of the various sections of industry that it had organised. The union had brought hope to thousands of lower paid workers in Ireland by … adopting a very aggressive policy … extending the use of the sympathetic strike.

5.6. Among his own colleagues he was admired but not always liked personally. James Connolly (who became an official of the new Union), Thomas McPartlin, William P. Partridge and others worked hard with Larkin in building up the Union, but they often resented his strong personality and fiery manner. He was impulsive, extremely sensitive to criticism and was never an easy man to work with. James Connolly said that Larkin was 'consumed with jealousy and hatred of anyone who will not cringe to him'.

5.7. Connolly had been reared in dire poverty in an Edinburgh slum, and had taught himself to read by the light of a coal fire. He spent some time in the United States and he returned to Ireland with a passionate interest in labour politics and socialism in general. He sought to apply Marxist thought to the Irish situation. He argued that the Irish working classes had been historically exploited by their fellow Irishmen and by British capitalists. Prior to the events of 1913 and after, Connolly argued for a socialist revolution in Ireland, a revolution which would bring his beloved dock-workers and urban slaves to political power.

5.8. From its foundation, the Union organised successful strikes of carters, dockers and railwaymen. One of these took place in Wexford in 1911, when two foundries, Pierce and Star Works, prohibited staff from joining the ITGWU. Workers protested, and employers locked out 550 union members who refused to accept their terms in August 1911. Strike-breakers (referred to as 'scabs' and 'blacklegs') were imported to break the strike and violent clashes followed. One worker, Michael Leary, died following a police baton charge. The strike lasted six months, but employers relented in the end, and agreed to improved working conditions. They demanded, in return, that workers form a different union: this was called the Irish Foundry Workers' Union but it remained affiliated to the ITGWU. In 1911, Delia Larkin established the Irish Women Workers' Union after a strike by 3,000 women workers in Jacob's Biscuit Factory. In Belfast, Connolly drew attention to the appalling conditions in which women worked in the city's textile mills and organised them into a branch of the ITGWU. Success in Wexford, and elsewhere, encouraged ITGWU leaders to call more strikes in Galway and Sligo, and then Dublin where there were over 30 between January and August 1913.

6. 'A most formidable foe' – William Martin Murphy

6.1. William Martin Murphy was the son of a Cork building contractor. His father died when he was nineteen years old. Young Murphy had a natural talent for commerce and he guided the family business through years of immense growth. He became very wealthy through shrewd business dealings extending from London to Africa. By the early 1900s, he had become the foremost Irish businessman. His wealth and fame lay in his ownership of, or interest in, such enterprises as Clery's Department Store, the Imperial Hotel, the *Irish Independent* newspaper and the Dublin United Tramways Company (DUTC). Murphy was a strong, aloof man. Wealthy, charitable, just and able, he was a loyal friend and a ruthless enemy.

6.2. Because of his powerful position in business, Murphy had immense influence. He was greatly respected by his fellow employers in the Dublin Chamber of Commerce. The ITGWU's success in winning concessions from employers was mainly because of the use of sympathetic strikes. In 1911, frustrated at their seeming powerlessness, employers responded to a call by Murphy to form a federation to break the ITGWU. The Dublin Employers' Federation Ltd, led by William Martin Murphy, refused to recognise the ITGWU. A Cork Employers' Federation had already been successful against Larkin in 1909. Murphy had the reputation of being a good employer who gave his workers fair wages. However, he would not tolerate dissension and refused to employ anyone who was a member of the ITGWU. He was well known for his personal charity. One woman wrote in 1913:

> Mr Murphy is a just and kind employer. Outsiders know little of his real goodness – I experienced it myself when my husband died after a long and expensive illness. The first letter I received was from Mr Murphy enclosing a cheque for £30 – 'as my needs might be pressing' – and just asking me to say a prayer for the soul of his son who died a year before my husband, although he had never laid eyes on me or my children.

7. The 'Titanic struggle' begins

7.1. Matters between Murphy and the ITGWU came to a head in the summer of 1913. Murphy refused to employ ITGWU members on the staff of his *Irish Independent* newspapers and in July 1913, he forbade staff in the Tramways Company to join the Union. On Saturday, 27 July 1913, Murphy called a meeting of his employees in the Tramways Company. He warned his workers of the consequences of strike:

> I want you to clearly understand that the directors of this company have not the slightest objection to the men forming a legitimate Union. And I would think there is talent enough amongst the men in the service to form a Union of their own, without allying themselves to a disreputable organisation, and placing themselves under

the feet of an unscrupulous man who claims the right to give you the word of command and issue his orders to you and to use you as tools to make him the labour dictator of Dublin ... I am here to tell you that this word of command will never be given, and if it is, that it will be the Waterloo of Mr Larkin. A strike in the tramway would, no doubt, produce turmoil and disorder created by the roughs and looters, but what chance would the men without funds have in a contest with the Company who could and would spend £100,000 or more. You must recollect when dealing with a company of this kind that every one of the shareholders, to the number of five, six, or seven thousands, will have three meals a day whether the men succeed or not. I don't know if the men who go out can count on this.

7.2. The following month, on 21 August, about 100 employees in the Tramways Company received a dismissal notice:

As the Directors of the Tramways Company understand that you are a member of the ITGWU whose methods are disorganising the trade and business of the city, they do not further require your service.

7.3. This was a direct challenge to the ITGWU. There could only be one reply to Murphy. He and his fellow directors had started a Lockout: the workers could only respond with a total withdrawal of labour. Larkin saw the dispute with Murphy very much in personal terms: 'The employing class have determined in the interests of themselves and all the capitalist class that one individual [Larkin] must be broken and the organisation he represents must be smashed into chaos'. Larkin carefully chose the moment to strike in order to cause the maximum disruption. Shortly before 10.00 a.m. on Tuesday, 26 August 1913 – the first day of the Dublin Horse Show, one of the city's busiest events – drivers and conductors stopped their trams and abandoned them in protest. About 700 of the 1,700 Tramways Company's employees went on strike. The city was filled with tension on the days following. Strikers resented the workers who continued to operate the trams, and fights often took place between them. Workers who usually distributed the *Irish Independent* [owned by Murphy] – though not employed by Murphy – refused to handle it in protest. Messrs. Eason and Co., the large city newsagents, were asked by Larkin not to sell the paper. They refused. As a result dockworkers at Kingstown (now Dún Laoghaire) refused to handle any Eason and Co. goods from England or addressed to England. Thousands of railway workers in the Midlands and north-west refused to handle goods until they were ordered back to work by National Union of Railwaymen (NUR) leaders.

7.4. Many clashes with the police took place, and fierce baton charges resulted in numerous injuries. Father Michael Curran left the Archbishop of Dublin well supplied with information about the strikers, he believed that it was 'no longer a question of a tram strike. It is simply the scum of the slums versus the police'. On Saturday night, 30 August, police officers again baton-charged strikers, injuring many people and leaving one man, James Nolan, fatally injured. Stephen Gilligan, who was at the scene of the charge, described what he saw:

> I was going down to the post office with a telegram. As soon as I landed outside I saw the charge of the police. The people were talking in threes and fours, and got no chance of moving. The first thing they knew was the batons coming down on them. I heard a voice saying, 'Now give it to them, boys!' I pretended I was a reporter and got safe. I saw the police charge the doorway and smash the sidelights. They charged round Eden Quay. The people for the most part kept to the quayside. I stood in the shadow of the Corporation weigh-house and saw poor Nolan trying to get away. I saw a police constable, 224C, Constable Bell, strike him with a baton. I saw him fall on his knees. The constable ran on, and then 149C struck him across the neck. I went back towards the Butt Bridge.

7.5. Larkin and the ITGWU saw the sympathetic strike as the finest example of workers' solidarity. In their eyes, the bosses were always united – 'the employers know no sectarianism', Larkin said, 'the employers gave us the title of 'the working class'. Let us be proud of the name'. That pride could best be shown by the principle of 'one out, all out'. The sympathetic strike had the great strength of immediately showing the employers the power of the working class, and making it clear that no section could be bullied without taking on the whole class of workers. 'The sympathetic strike', James Connolly wrote, 'is the recognition by the working class of their essential unity'. Professor Thomas Kettle, a young MP, a neutral observer of the battle between the employers and workers, was fairly sympathetic to the workers. However, he disapproved strongly of the sympathetic strikes referring to them, as 'strikes-by-telephone'.

8. The strike intensifies

8.1. On 28 August, Larkin and four of his comrades had been arrested on charges of libel and conspiracy. They were soon released on bail. It had been announced that Larkin would address a meeting in Sackville Street on Sunday 31 August, but the authorities issued an order prohibiting the meeting. Larkin subsequently burned a copy of the order and encouraged his listeners to fight any attempt to stop the meeting. On Sunday, Larkin, disguised as a bearded priest, entered Murphy's Imperial Hotel and appeared on a balcony on the first floor. He spoke briefly to the crowd before being promptly arrested. The police baton-charged the excited crowd on Sackville Street. Dublin was in a state of great unrest for the next week. Violent clashes between labour supporters and police broke out in other parts of the city – Gardiner Street, Sheriff Street, North Wall, Henry Street, Mary Street, South Wall, Christ Church, and Inchicore. Police conduct was much criticised by politicians and journalists. This led to a government inquiry into allegations of police brutality. The committee summed up its findings, as follows:

We desire to report in conclusion that in our opinion the officers and men of the Dublin Metropolitan Police and the Royal Irish Constabulary as a whole, discharged their duties throughout this trying period with conspicuous courage and patience. They were exposed to many dangers and treated with great brutality … The total number of constables injured during these riots exceeded 200.

8.2. News of events in Dublin soon reached delegates to the British Trade Union Congress (TUC) which was held in Manchester on 1 September. A number of delegates travelled over from Dublin. The conference condemned 'in the most emphatic manner' the actions of the authorities in Dublin and sent a delegation to Dublin in an attempt to mediate between workers and employers. William Partridge said that is was 'not an attack upon Larkin which we are witnessing, but an attack upon the entire trade union movement of Ireland'. Meetings of workers were held around the city, especially at Liberty Hall, the nerve-centre of the workers' movement. The TUC delegation reasserted the right to hold public meetings but its attempts to hold meaningful negotiations between the two sides proved fruitless. The funeral of James Nolan, who died after being stuck by a police baton, was held on Wednesday, 3 September, and was attended by thousands of sympathisers. Keir Hardie, the British Labour leader, who supported the striking workers, gave the funeral address because Larkin was being held in Mountjoy Jail. On behalf of the British Unions, Hardie expressed solidarity with the locked-out workers, and urged the strikers to stay the course.

8.3. Murphy, also appealing for support, issued a statement on behalf of over 400 employers that repeated his opposition to the ITGWU. The employers drew up a pledge for workers, which stated that they were not, and would not become, members of the proscribed Union:

> I hereby undertake to carry out all instructions given to me by or on behalf of my employers, and further, I agree to immediately resign my membership of the ITGWU (if a member) and I further undertake that I will not join or in any way support this union.

8.4. Those who refused to sign would be dismissed. Angered by this document, 20,000 workers refused to sign. Many who were not even members of the ITGWU, refused to sign it as a matter of conscience, even though they had no dealings with Larkin or his Union.

8.5. Within a few weeks many striking workers were getting very distressed. The TUC undertook to provide food for the families of the striking workers. Although the ITGWU paid strike wages, these were inadequate for workers who were already deeply impoverished even before the strike began. The situation in the city was getting desperate: hunger was widespread in the tenements. The TUC reported back to London on 23 September. On Saturday, 28 September a ship, *The Hare*, arrived in Dublin. On board were 60,000 'family boxes', each box holding enough food for five people. Thousands of people lined up outside Liberty Hall, holding vouchers ready to be exchanged for their boxes. The food ship had a great effect on the morale of the strikers. It showed them that the workers of Britain would support them to a degree. But there was to be no large-scale sympathetic strikes movement or boycott of Irish goods. By the time the dispute ended nearly £150,000 (approx. €12.5 million at 2009 values) of food etc., had been sent to striking Irish workers and their families. Food kitchens were set up in Liberty Hall and, after all the British family boxes had been given out, bread and soup became the usual fare for the starving Dubliners.

8.6. On his release on bail from Mountjoy Prison, Larkin went to England to get as much support there as he could. Speaking at huge meetings, he got a rousing response from English workers. Sympathetic strikes continued in Manchester, Liverpool and Birmingham. Larkin and Connolly attempted to push the British trade unions into a general stoppage of work in support of the Dublin workers. However, the union leaders, were not prepared to go so far. This failure was something that Larkin and Connolly never forgave, and it left them bitterly disappointed.

9. The Askwith Inquiry

9.1. Many attempts were being made to solve the dispute. A Peace Commission headed by Professor Thomas Kettle failed to get anywhere. As the strike worsened, a Board of Trade Inquiry known as the Askwith Inquiry, was set up to meet representatives of employers and of workers, and in an attempt to bring about a resolution to the dispute. The government appointed three officials to run this: Sir George Askwith, Sir Thomas Ratcliffe Ellis (an expert in mining matters who helped resolve an earlier dispute in 1911), and J.R. Clynes (MP and labour representative). They were instructed to 'to enquire into the facts and circumstances of the disputes now in progress in Dublin, and to take such steps as may seem desirable with a view to arriving at a settlement'.

9.2. The Inquiry began on Monday, 29 September, and the officials presented their report on 5 October. Speaking at the Commission of Inquiry on behalf of the employers, T.M. Healy stated that the employers were fighting for 'the industrial freedom of the city, which had been so gravely imperilled in the previous three years by the Larkinite movement'.

9.3. Employers who gave evidence at the Inquiry emphasised that they were not opposed to unions, but to the ITGWU alone, which they described as 'a menace to all trade organisations' because of its use of 'sympathetic strikes', that is, calling all members of their union to go on strike to support one group of workers.

9.4. In their report, the Commissioners joined with employers in criticising the 'sympathetic strike', which, they believed, injured workers and employers because it spread far beyond the original dispute and involved many people who had nothing to do with the original grievance or had no interest in it. The 'sympathetic strike' would, in the Commissioners' opinion, embitter relations between workers and employers, and make it far more difficult to resolve industrial disputes because reprisals on one side were met by reprisals on the other 'in such rapid succession as to confuse the real issues'. The Report concluded that:

> No community could exist if resort to the sympathetic strike became the general policy of Trade Unionism, as, owing to the interdependence of different branches of industry, disputes affecting even a single individual would spread indefinitely.

9.5. Though the Commissioners criticised the ITGWU for using the sympathetic strike, they also condemned the 'employers' agreement' that forbade membership of the union, and that threatened to dismiss workers who refused to comply as being 'contrary to individual liberty'. The document 'would force people to work under conditions which no workman or body of workmen could reasonably be expected to accept'. The Commissioners did not object to strikes or Lockouts in principle, but said that before these methods were used, there should be an opportunity for independent inquiry to try to find a solution. They suggested that workers and employers should elect representatives to form a Conciliation Committee to discuss problems before taking drastic action.

9.6. Much to the surprise of *The Times*, the employers replied to the Commission, saying that they could not accept its proposals. 'Larkinism' had to be crushed, once and for all. They claimed that, while they favoured the principle of trade unionism, they could not accept the Larkin style of operation. Their lawyer summed up their attitude when he first addressed the Commission:

> Trade Unionism in the mouths of these people [Larkin and his comrades] is a mockery; it exists only in name. The men are puppets in the hands of three or four of the leaders. Mr Larkin acts the part of a Napoleon; he orders this or that, and the men obey him, and that is what brought about the strikes.

9.7. While the workers were willing to enter talks, the employers refused. They did not trust the Union to give up sympathetic strikes, and they were not prepared to reinstate all workers, and to dismiss those who had taken their places. The dispute continued.

10. 'Save the kiddies': deepening hostilities

10.1. In October 1913, many families had no food for their children. Larkin and Irish labour leaders decided to send the children of the worst-affected families to sympathetic homes in England for a holiday until the strike was over. The idea appealed to Larkin because it was so daring and he set about organising it. However, the Catholic Archbishop of Dublin, William J. Walsh, was strongly opposed because he believed the faith of Catholic children might be at risk in non-Catholic families. He declared that their mothers would 'no longer be worthy of the name Catholic if they so far forgot their duty as to send away their little children to be cared for in a strange land'. Catholic priests and comfortable middle-class people picketed the ships that were being used for the 'abduction' of the children to a 'pagan land'. There were clashes at the docks when children started to board. More than any other event in the three-month old dispute, the sending away of the children raised the wildest emotions in people. James Connolly replied to the Archbishop, on behalf of the ITGWU: 'Nobody wants to send the children away – the Irish Transport and General Workers Union least of all desires such a sacrifice. But neither do we wish the children to starve'.

10.2. There was too much opposition and anger, and the plan was dropped. The children remained in Dublin to share the miserable conditions as their parents. The Chief Secretary, Augustine Birrell, reported on the affair to the Prime Minister:

> It certainly was an outrage. For in the first place, there are no starving children in Dublin, and in the second place, the place swarms with homes for them. It was a new advertising dodge of a few silly women, but it has broken the strike.

10.3. Birrell's report was not true on several counts, but the 'save the kiddies' campaign, lost the workers a great deal of public sympathy.

10.4. The Irish Parliamentary Party, whose members were mostly middle class and drew their support from the farming community, was largely hostile to the strike. Even those who felt sympathy for the plight of the striking workers feared that the strike and Lockout would distract attention from what, to them, was the much more serious struggle with Carson's Ulster Unionists. Stephen Gwynn was the only sitting Irish nationalist MP to declare publicly his support for the cause of labour during the Lockout. Others like Donegal MP Hugh Law called for a living wage for labourers and public housing assistance for the urban population. However, long before the Lockout, a substantial number of nationalist MPs had ignored the plight of workers and perceived Irish labour radicalisation under Larkin as a threat. John Dillon, Redmond's second-in-command, expressed the party's exasperation with the Lockout when he wrote that 'Murphy is a desperate character, Larkin is as bad. It would be a blessing for Ireland if they exterminated each other'.

10.5. Nationalist newspapers like *Liberator* and *The Toiler* attacked Larkin and the ITGWU. The editor of *The Toiler*, Patrick McIntyre, mounted a sustained attack on the union, Larkin, and socialism. It spoke on behalf of workers who did not side with Larkinism. The weekly newspaper *Liberator* strongly defended employers and strike-breakers. Larkin and other labour leaders were denounced as greedy communists and atheists. Despite the attack from these and other newspapers, support for Larkin and the ITGWU grew steadily during the conflict.

10.6. The dislike that grew between Larkin and Arthur Griffith was almost as intense as that between Larkin and Murphy. Griffith frequently attacked Larkin, calling him a 'strike organiser', and the 'representative of English trade-unionism in Ireland'. He had little sympathy for the workers and he saw the foodships from England as a dangerous bribe. He strongly opposed the 'save the kiddies campaign' saying that 'the number of Dublin parents who would consent to send their children to be nurtured in the homes of the enemies of their race do not form five per cent of the parents affected by the strike'.

10.7. When the scheme was finally abandoned, Connolly suspended free dinners at Liberty Hall and sent the children instead to the Archbishop's palace.

11. The 'fiery cross' campaign and the breaking of the strike

11.1. Larkin had travelled to England on 10 October. He attacked the tame response of the TUC leadership to events in Dublin, telling a *Daily Herald* rally:

> The official labour leaders are standing in our road, and like the engine to the cow, we've got to bump them out of it. The Labour Party could wrap themselves up in cloth tomorrow and they would be just as useful as mummies in the museum. These damnable hypocrites get up and tell you, you must not use the sympathetic strike because you are going to discommode the public. If our mates are injured aren't we injured too?

11.2. Relations with Larkin and the Dublin strike committee had become strained. Larkin told the Dublin workers that while he 'did not wish to cast any reflection upon our friends across the channel, this fight must be settled by the men here at home in our own union'. Larkin was sentenced to seven months' imprisonment for 'incitement' on 28 October 1913 by Magistrate Swift (who owned shares in Murphy's tram company). James Connolly organised the strikers in Larkin's absence and managed to close the port of Dublin when dockers walked off the job. In England, workers were encouraged to vote against the Liberals at all by-elections in an attempt to secure Larkin's release. The government caved in and Larkin was released on 13 November 1913. He immediately left on another tour of England to rally support for the suffering workers. The 'fiery cross' campaign, as he referred to his series of torch-lit meetings, caught the imagination of the British workers. He issued a joint manifesto with Connolly calling on British workers 'to strike while the iron of revolt is hot in our souls'. Although his meetings attracted large crowds, he failed to bring about a general stoppage in Britain. The TUC parliamentary committee had a raucous meeting with Larkin on 18 November and agreed to schedule a special conference for December.

11.3. When two train drivers in Wales refused to handle goods bound for Dublin and were dismissed in early December 1913, 30,000 men went on sympathetic strike. The National Union of Railwaymen (NUR) official and Labour MP, James Henry Thomas, intervened and ordered all members back to work. To make matters worse he allowed NUR members to fill the jobs left vacant by the sacked workers who were members of the Associated Society of Locomotive Engineers and Firemen (ASLEF).

11.4. Larkin was met with a hostile reception at the Trade Union Congress conference on 9 December. Many of the appointed delegates expressed their anger at his open criticism of the Trade Union leadership. Larkin was jeered when he responded that 'your money is useful but money never won a strike'. A resolution by Jack Jones to blockade Dublin was overwhelmingly defeated by 2 million votes to 200,000. The conference instead agreed to focus their efforts on negotiating a settlement. The *Daily Herald* concluded that:

> … officialism has had its inglorious day. It is now the turn of the real men and minds to retrieve the situation. Officialism can only prevail so long as you tolerate it. In the last analysis it is your servant. Sweep it aside and act.

11.5. Larkin's calls on English unions to 'black' ships sailing into Dublin Port and to prevent English dockers from working in Ireland fell on deaf ears. He denounced the reponse in strong terms and as a result no further aid was sent to Ireland. Sailings started again from Dublin Port with the assistance of the National Sailors' and Firemen's Union whose members were condemned as 'scabs'. The trade unionist Havelock Wilson produced a pamphlet which claimed that Larkin 'alone, stands in the way of a proper settlement'. Tom Kettle MP felt that 'the critical moment has come. There is a limit to human endurance, and a point beyond which the belt cannot be tightened'. On 16 December, Connolly urged men to return to work wherever they could do so without signing the pledge. Most companies, with the exceptions of Murphy's and Jacob's, had agreed to do this. However, some companies only took back some of their workers. The workers had a bleak Christmas in 1913. The food ships from England could no longer be depended on.

11.6. In early January the TUC informed Dublin leaders that there was only one week of strike pay left in the fund. Most of the remaining strikers had lost all hope. With the failure of the British Trade Unions to come out in sympathetic strike, the cause was doomed. The choice was gradually becoming clearer to each worker – surrender or starve. The ITGWU leadership met secretly on 18 January 1914, and decided to end the strike. They advised members to return to work but not to sign the employers' document, if possible. By 21 January, 8,000 ITGWU members and 1,200 builders' labourers were still locked out. In early February, the Builders' Labourers' Union (about 3,000 men) agreed to sign the document and returned to work. Other workers throughout the city gradually followed. The strikers had realised that they could not win this battle on the terms set by Larkin. Within weeks, Murphy and the Employers' Federation claimed victory and they had, indeed, broken the strike. They claimed that 'Larkinism' was completely defeated within the city. As the tram workers settled back into their jobs, they pledged not to join Larkin's hated ITGWU under any circumstances. The workers had been defeated by the employers' Lockout. Many of them remained convinced that there would be further conflict between capital and labour. This failure did not, however, destroy the ITGWU.

11.7. James Connolly wrote with great bitterness:

> And so we Irish workers must go down into Hell, bow our backs to the lash of the slave driver, let our hearts be seared by the iron of hatred, and instead of the sacramental wafer of brotherhood and common sacrifice eat the dust of defeat and betrayal. Dublin is isolated.

11.8. Larkin and Connolly now directed their anger at the leaders of the British trade unions who refused to come out in support of their colleagues in Dublin. As the months went by, however, it became clear that the employers had not won a total victory. Workers who had promised never to join the ITGWU slowly began to drift back. Within a short time, the ITGWU was once more the largest and most influential union in the city. No employer was willing to sack large numbers of his workforce and face a second Lockout.

11.9. In June 1914, all the Irish trade unions came together for their Annual Congress. Larkin gave a long speech to the delegates there, and he referred proudly to the events of the previous year:

> The Lockout in 1913 was a deliberate attempt to starve us into submission and met with well-deserved failure … The employers claim a victory but the employers did not beat back organised labour in the city. I admit we had to retreat to base, but that was owing to the treachery of leaders in affiliated unions and betrayal in our own ranks.

11.10. William Martin Murphy and the employers believed that Larkinism had been decisively defeated at last. The *Irish Times* saw the position differently:

> The very necessary business of 'smashing Larkin' is successfully accomplished; but that is very far from being the same thing as 'smashing Larkinism'. There is no security whatever that the men who are now going about their work brooding over the bitterness of defeat will not endeavour to re-organise their broken forces and, given another leader and another opportunity, strike a further and a more desperate blow at the economic life of Dublin.

12. Connolly and the aftermath of the Lockout

12.1. The Lockout failed to crush the ITGWU, which still had 22,935 members at the end of 1913. However, the strike had decided nothing: future relations between employers and workers remained unclear. Looking back over the whole episode in November 1914, James Connolly wrote:

The battle was a drawn battle. The employers were unable to carry on their business without men and women who remained loyal to their union. The workers were unable to force their employers to a formal recognition of the union and to give preference to organised labour. From the effects of this drawn battle both sides are still bearing scars. How deep these scars are none will reveal.

12.2. The Lockout left a deep legacy of bitterness between employers and workers, and between workers and police. This manifested itself in the Irish Citizen Army, an armed defence force founded by Connolly to protect workers during the Lockout. It remained, grew in strength afterwards, and played a role in the 1916 Rising. The bitterness surrounding the 1913 Lockout had a great effect, personally and politically, on many figures who would come to dominate Irish politics in the following years.

12.3. Connolly and William O'Brien set about rebuilding the ITGWU and carefully avoided confrontation with the employers. Connolly saw the strike as a symbol of things to come. He came to believe that socialism could only succeed in Ireland if it allied itself with nationalism, and more particularly with Irish Republicanism. The strike had taught Connolly that Marxism had a limited attraction for the Irish masses, given their devout Catholicism and their conservatism about land and property, particularly in the countryside. Connolly's most important contribution to Irish political thought was his argument that Irish Republicanism and socialism could be easily reconciled. By the beginning of 1915, his Irish Citizen Army had joined forces with the radical nationalists of the Irish Republican Brotherhood. The result was the 1916 Rising and its complicated rhetoric of Catholic national liberation on the one hand, and international socialism on the other. Connolly felt that the workers' campaign:

> … caught the imagination of all unselfish souls, so that the skilled artisan took his place also in the place of conflict and danger, and the men and women of genius, the artistic and the *literati*, hastened to honour and serve those humble workers whom all had hitherto despised and scorned.

12.4. He saw signs of hope in the actions of the British working classes during the months of the Lockout. Connolly and Larkin fell out with the leadership of the British Labour Party when they refused to order their members to go on sympathetic strikes in Britain for the duration of Larkin's campaign. But Connolly had nothing but praise for the rank-and-file of the labour movement in Britain. In February 1914 he said that:

> … in its attitude toward Dublin the Working Class Movement of Great Britain reached its highest point of moral grandeur – attained for a moment to a realisation of that sublime unity towards which the best in us must continually aspire.

12.5. It is clear that Connolly did not think that the employers or the imperial capitalists had won the day. He pledged himself to listen to any group who shared his basic vision of a new society arguing that 'because I realise human nature is a wonderful thing, I try to preserve my reception towards all manifestations of social activity'.

13. Patrick Pearse

13.1. Prior to Lockout, Pádraig Yeates argued that 'A Generation of working class activists oscillated between radical nationalism and socialist politics'. The defeat of the workers ensured that Irish politics turned from socialism to questions of Irish governance, thereby setting the stage for 1916. The Lockout had an important influence on the thinking of the poet and romantic nationalist, Patrick Henry Pearse. A respectable middle-class Dublin schoolmaster in many ways, Pearse was mainly interested in cultural nationalism and the Gaelic League. He looked forward to the passing of the Home Rule Bill and the establishment of an Irish parliament. From 1913, he became more of a political nationalist. He criticised the British government for destroying the national spirit in Irish children through their school system. After the Lockout and the shocking scenes on Sackville Street where police baton-charged hundreds of civilians, Pearse began to develop an economic critique of British imperialism. Commenting in 1913 at the height of the Lockout, Pearse wrote in *From a Hermitage*:

> Twenty thousand Dublin families live in one room tenements. It is common to find two or three families occupying the same room; and sometimes one of the families will have a lodger! There are tenement rooms in Dublin in which over a dozen persons live, eat and sleep. High rents are paid for these rooms, rents which in cities like Birmingham would command neat four-roomed cottages with gardens. These are among the grievances against which men in Dublin are beginning to protest. Can you wonder that protest is at last made? Can you wonder that the protest is crude and bloody? I do not know whether the methods of Mr James Larkin are wise methods or unwise methods (unwise, I think, in some respects), but this I know, that here is a most hideous wrong to be righted, and that the man who attempts honestly to right it is a good man and a brave man.

13.2. Pearse was now conscious of the same social problems that drove Connolly and Larkin. He sought a national and cultural revolution in Ireland. The country could only born anew by a Christ-like sacrifice of blood. After the Lockout, Connolly sought a material and social revolution in Ireland. Both men were to find common ground in the General Post Office a few years later.

14. The Lockout remembered

14.1. The Lockout was the last great surge of labour unrest before the outbreak of the Great War. It lasted for over six months, involved over 20,000 men and 1.7 million working days were lost. Nearly 700 trade Unionists were arrested during the dispute and five were killed by police or strikebreakers. The brutality and suffering of the 1913 Lockout left a deep impression on many generations of thinkers and agitators in Ireland. Two of Ireland's greatest poets in the twentieth century celebrated the activities of the workers during those terrible months in 1913 and 1914.

14.2. William Butler Yeats (1865–1939) wrote an angry critique of the petit bourgeois employers who had starved the tramworkers and their families into defeat. His poem, 'September 1913', was written in part as an attack on William Martin Murphy's interference with plans to find a permanent home for Sir Hugh Lane's Art Gallery and its many fine paintings. Yeats used a series of phrases that Larkin and Connolly might well have approved of, particularly in his description of the selfishness of Murphy and his supporters. Contrasting the heroism of Irish patriots with the narrow-minded materialism of the Dublin employer class, Yeats asked:

> What need you, being come to sense,
> But fumble in a greasy till
> And add the ha'pence to the pence
> And prayer to shivering prayer, until
> You have dried the marrow from the bone,
> For men were born to pray and save?
> Romantic Ireland's dead and gone,
> It's with O'Leary in the grave.
>
> [W.B Yeats, *Responsibilities and other poems* (London, 1916)]

14.3. Patrick Kavanagh (1904–67) wrote a piece celebrating the achievements of James Larkin shortly after the trade unionist's death in 1947. Kavanagh used deliberately heroic and exaggerated imagery and phrases in the poem to portray the courage of Larkin's many campaigns. Kavanagh particularly admired Larkin's determination and his idealism during the 1913 Lockout. His elegy written in 1947 was entitled 'Jim Larkin':

> Not with public words now can his greatness
> Be told to the children, for he was more
> Than a labour-agitating orator –
> The flashing flaming sword merely bore witness
> To the coming of the dawn. 'Awake and look!'
> The flowers are growing for you, and wonderful trees,
> And beyond are not the serf's grey docks, but seas –
> Excitement out of the creator's poetry book.
> When the Full Moon's in the River the ghost of bread
> Must not haunt all your weary wanderings home.
> The ships that were dark galleys can become
> Pine forests under the winter's starry plough
> And the brown gantries will be the lifted hand

Of man the dreamer whom the gods endow.'
And thus I hear Jim Larkin shout above
The crowd who wanted to turn aside
From Reality coming to free them. Terrified,
They hid in the clouds of dope and could not move.
They ate the opium of the murderer's story
In the Sunday newspapers; they stood to stare
Not at a blackbird, but at a mllionaire
Whose horses ran for serfdom's greater glory.
And Tyranny trampled them in Dublin's gutter,
Until Larkin came along and cried
The call of Freedom and the call of Pride
And Slavery crept to its hands and knees,
And Nineteen Thirteen cheered from out the utter
Degradation of their miseries.

> ['Jim Larkin' by Patrick Kavanagh is reprinted from *Collected poems*, edited by Antoinette Quinn (Allen Lane, 2004), by kind permission of the Trustees of the Estate of the late Katherine B. Kavanagh, through the Jonathan Williams Literary Agency.]

14.4. The Lockout also inspired the writing of James Plunkett's historical novel *Strumpet city* (1969) which was made into a successful television series (1980) by Radio Telefís Éireann. The events of 1913 were also the subject of a fine Radio Éireann play; James Plunkett's play *Big Jim* was first broadcast in 1955.

15. Outcomes

15.1. One of the most important effects of the dispute was to make people more aware of the urgent need to improve living conditions in Dublin. Prompted by Lady Aberdeen (wife of the Lord Lieutenant of Ireland), a Civic Exhibition was held in July 1914. Among the most important items of the exhibition were a section on town-planning and a competition for a 'Dublin Development Scheme'. This was now an important issue, of concern to many citizens. More attention was paid to improving housing, health and sanitary conditions. No longer could the wealthy ignore the poverty of their own city.

15.2. The principal characters of 1913 – William Martin Murphy and James Larkin – never again reached the same degree of public influence. During the Great War, Murphy recruited for the British army; and even suggested to employers that they sack able-bodied men to force them to enlist. He went on to chair the Finance and General Purposes Committee of Dublin Corporation. He died in 1919, leaving a personal estate of £264,005 (approx. €10.5 million at 2009 values).

15.3. In October 1914 Larkin went on a fundraising lecture tour of the United States. He soon became involved with the American socialist and labour movement. He was arrested for membership of the Communist Labour Party in November 1919 and sentenced to five to ten years' imprisonment on 3 May 1920. He was pardoned by Governor Al Smith of New York on 17 January 1923. He came back to a hero's welcome in Dublin on 30 April that year.

15.4. Larkin found a country very different from the one he had left. He disagreed with Connolly's participation in the 1916 rising and was shocked that the party of his old enemy, Arthur Griffith, now held power in Ireland. He found himself out of favour with many of his old colleagues in the ITGWU and he went on to found a new union, the Workers Union of Ireland. He died a disillusioned man in 1947.

15.5. Through the sufferings of the workers of Dublin and the tireless efforts of men like Larkin and Connolly, the Irish Labour Movement had come of age. The great upheaval in Dublin in 1913 had without doubt started a process which brought about great changes in the living standards of the poor. As the American historian, J.D. Clarkson, later wrote:

> In the deepest sense, 'Larkinism' had triumphed. The Dublin struggle had fired the hearts and minds of the working classes throughout the length and breadth of Ireland … Most significant of all, the most helpless of all classes had learned the lesson of its power and in the learning had proved itself worthy of Ireland's bravest traditions.

JOHN PAUL McCARTHY AND TOMÁS O'RIORDAN

CHAPTER 9

Dublin, 1913 – strike and Lockout: documents

1. Impressions of a Dublin Medical Officer

1.1. *Introduction.* At the beginning of the twentieth century, Dublin had some of the most appalling slum conditions in Europe. In 1882, the Corporation of Dublin placed the whole of their sanitary department under the direction of Sir Charles A. Cameron (1830–1921), the newly appointed Chief Health and Medical Officer of Dublin. Cameron had studied medicine in Dublin and Cambridge University. His most important work was in the area of public health and he worked hard to improve sanitation and living conditions in the city. His administration of the sanitary affairs of Dublin led to the closing of nearly 2,000 houses considered unfit for human habitation. The condition of thousands of other houses was greatly improved. He reduced the death rate (one of the highest in Europe) by nearly a quarter between 1901 and 1911. Cameron was very sympathetic to the plight of the poor. In the harrowing account below, he describes their hardships. There were more families in one-roomed dwellings in Dublin than any other city in the United Kingdom. Unemployment rates (for men and women) were very high. Unemployment forced people into the cheapest accommodation: cold, damp, overcrowded and dirty rooms with bad cooking facilities and worse sanitation. Children were often malnourished, badly clothed and barefoot. Poor living conditions bred infection and disease that affected all. He describes how many poor people depended on pawnbrokers for survival. They pawned basic necessities to buy food or fuel (though they hoped to redeem them). Pawnbrokers charged very high rates of interest, and their customers were often in debt. He praised the generosity of the poor to each other, but he was critical of those who spent money on drink. He did not think it was possible for the authorities to end poverty completely or provide jobs for all. However, he believed that the Corporation could, and should, help the poorest people, especially unskilled labourers, by providing at least one meal a day and good accommodation at cheap rents. This, he argued, would be money well spent. Cameron was knighted for his work in 1885, and was made a Freeman of the City of Dublin in 1911. SOURCE: Charles A. Cameron, 'How the poor lived in Dublin', *Reminiscences of Sir Charles Cameron* (Dublin & London, 1913).

1.2. During the 32 years that I have been the Chief Health Officer of Dublin, I have seen much of life amongst the poor and the very poor, and I have many remembrances of painful scenes that I have witnessed in their miserable homes. I have long been of opinion that the proportion of the population belonging to the poorest classes is greater in Dublin than it is in the English and Scotch towns. There are many proofs of the poverty of a considerable proportion of the population of

Dublin. For example, in 1911, 41.9 per cent of the deaths in the Dublin Metropolitan area occurred in the workhouses, asylums, lunatic asylums, and other institutions. In the English towns the average proportion of the deaths in institutions is about 22 per cent. Another proof of poverty is the large number of families who reside each in a single room – 33.9 per cent of the total families. [Census of 1911] In Belfast, with few exceptions, each family occupies more than one room. In many of the English towns not more than 10 per cent of the families occupy but one apartment.

1.3. ... Dr Russell, Medical Officer of Health, has shown that the dwellers in these tenements (or 'houses' as they are termed in Scotland), consisting of a single apartment, have a much higher death rate than is the case of those who have two or more rooms. It has also been proved that the one-room denizens suffer more from tuberculosis of the lungs.

1.4. ... I have been far more anxious about the condition of the labourers and other workers at small wages. I have always maintained that it is only for these workers that municipalities should provide dwellings, even at some cost to the ratepayers. The expenditure of public money in the erection of dwellings to be let at from 3s. 6d. to 7s. 6d. per week does not benefit the whole community. The persons who are able to pay such rents should be allowed to deal with the ordinary house owners. In the case of one-room tenements, the occupants are usually very poor, and unable to pay for more accommodation. The wages of unskilled labourers are rarely more than £1 per week; many earn only from 15s. to 18s. weekly. Even when the labourer is a sober man, and has a small family, he cannot enjoy much comfort on the higher rate of wages. When he is of the inferior order, has a large family, and precarious employment, it is easy to imagine his deplorable condition. Now, if the Municipality provided for this class of worker a two-apartment dwelling at 2s. 6d., or if possible 2s., per week, though at some expense to the ratepayers, the general public would at least be benefited from a health point of view.

1.5. In the homes of the very poor the seeds of infective disease are nursed as it were in a hothouse. They may spread from the homes of the lowly to the mansions of the rich. Unsanitary homes cause illness and consequent poverty, and poverty causes the poor's [death] rate to go up. The poverty of a considerable proportion of the population is shown by the large number of persons who are obliged to resort to the pawnbroker – 'the banker of the poor'. No inconsiderable number of the poor get out of their beds, or substitutes for them, without knowing when they are to get their breakfast, for the simple reason that they have neither money nor credit. They must starve if they have got nothing which would be taken in pawn. But articles of very small value will be accepted by the pawnbroker, and some item or items of a slender wardrobe are exchanged for the price of one or more meals. So small a sum as 6d. may be obtained in this way. When work is procured the articles are, as a rule, released from pawn … Some families pawn their clothes regularly every week, thus living a few days in advance of their income.

1.6. The ordinary money-lender may charge any amount of interest on his loans – 60 per cent is not uncommon; but the interest charged by the pawnbroker is limited by law to 5*d*. per £1 per month for sums under £10. A month's interest may be charged though the article may be redeemed within a shorter period. The general state of things is the following:

1.7. The artisan or labourer is out of employment, perhaps for a week or a few weeks. How is he and his family to live until he regains employment? He may not be able to get credit with the food purveyors, and if he does he will, as a rule, be charged more on credit than he would for ready money. To persons so situated the pawn-broker is often the only 'friend in need', failing whose assistance the resource might be the workhouse. …

1.8. I have rarely met a poor man of mature age who was a celibate. A man's desire for matrimony appears to be inversely to his means for maintaining a family. It is rich men who remain in so-called 'single blessedness'.

1.9. Dublin is not much of a manufacturing city … There is comparatively less work for females in Dublin than in most English towns. The disadvantage of want of employment for women is the smaller average earnings of families, with consequent lower standard of diet, lodging and clothing.

1.10. Amongst the labouring population the children are worst off for proper clothing. They rarely get new articles to wear, and are frequently clothed in the worn-out garments of their parents, ill-adjusted to the size of their new wearers. Thousands of children go with naked feet even in the height of winter. The want of warm clothing in winter often lays the foundation of future delicacy [poor health], and renders them less liable to resist the attacks of disease. The want of good food and warm clothing often causes the fatal sequel to attacks of measles. Amongst the rich this disease is rarely fatal; but the children of the poor offer up many victims to it – not so much during the attack, but in bronchial and other affections which supervene as consequences of neglect, insufficient clothing and nourishment. The Police-Aided Society for Providing Clothes for Poor Children performs good work in Dublin, and deserves more support than it receives from the general public. A humorist once said that half the population of Dublin are clothed in the cast-off clothes of the other half. This is true to a large extent.

1.11. The diet of the labourers, hawkers, and persons of the same social position is generally very poor and insufficient. The constant items are bread and tea. Butter is not always obtainable. Cocoa is largely used; coffee, never. Very little home-made bread is used. The bakers' bread is of good quality, for even the very poor will not purchase inferior bread. Oatmeal porridge is not so generally used as it ought to be ... Beef and mutton are not often found on the tables of the poor. When they are it is generally for the breadwinner of the family. They are fried or boiled, for there is no way of roasting them. Pork is not much in demand, except in the form of 'crubeens', or feet of the pig. Bacon is largely used, sometimes as rashers, but more frequently it is boiled with cabbage. The inferior American kind is, owing to its cheapness (5*d.* or 6*d.* per lb.), mostly in use. Puddings, pies, and tarts are practically unknown. There are no ovens to bake them in, nor, as a rule, any knowledge of how they should be made. In very few of the primary schools for girls is cooking taught. As regards vegetables, few kinds, except potatoes and cabbage, are used. Peas and beans are rarely seen on the table of a labourer's family ... Not much fruit appears on the tables of the poor. Oranges and apples are sometimes given as a treat to their children. They also get inferior kinds of sweetmeat. Amongst the very poor fruit and sweets are practically unknown.

1.12. As is well known, there is a large consumption of whiskey and porter amongst the labouring classes. In many instances an undue proportion of their earnings is spent on these beverages, with consequent deprivation of home comforts and even necessaries. The workman is blamed for visiting the public-house, but it is to him what the club is to the rich man. His home is rarely a comfortable one, and in winter the bright light, the warm fire, and the gaiety of the public-house are attractions which he finds it difficult to resist. If he spends a reasonable proportion of his earnings in the public-house, is he more to be condemned than the prosperous shopkeeper or professional man who drinks expensive wines at the club or the restaurant, spends hours playing billiards or cards, and amuses himself in other expensive ways? At the same time, it cannot be denied that there is, too much intemperance amongst the working classes, and that the women, who formerly were rarely seen intoxicated, are now frequently to be observed in that state. The publicans themselves dislike drunkards. Their best customers are the men who spend a moderate proportion of their wages in drink, for the drunkards lose their situations, or, if tradesmen, neglect their work, and thereby reduce their incomes.

1.13. It is not in the power of the Sanitary Authorities to remove many of the evils from which the poor suffer. They cannot augment their deficient earnings: they can only employ a very small proportion of them as labourers in the various civic departments. They can, however, soften the hard conditions under which the poor, especially the very poor, exist. How? By providing them with homes superior to those they now have, without increasing their rents. The most urgent want of the labourers and the poorer tradesmen is better dwellings. This is a measure that should be carried out liberally. Consumptives are not kept for any length of time in the general hospitals, and but very few gain admission to the Consumption Hospital at Newcastle. They are, therefore, obliged to live with their families, sleeping in the same room with other persons, and infecting them. The operation of the Insurance Act now provides treatment for the poor consumptives.

1.14. If it were possible to provide the very poor children, who are now obliged to go to school, with a meal, much good would result. There is little doubt that many of the school-children have to learn their lessons on empty stomachs. Madame Gonne has recently organised a society with the object of providing a daily meal for poor children. I would like to bear testimony to the wonderful kindness which the poor show to those who are still poorer and more helpless than themselves.

2. The state of the poor

2.1. *Introduction.* David Alfred Chart (1878–1960), an eminent Irish historian and social scientist, addressed the Statistical and Social Inquiry Society of Ireland about poverty and slum housing in Dublin on 6 March 1914. He describes the terrible poverty of the most deprived class in Dublin – the unskilled labourers. There was a huge gulf between rich and poor in the city. The wealthy had long since fled to the suburbs but most of the city's labourers lived in filthy run-down tenement housing. He explains the origins of tenements, most of which were formerly the luxurious four- and five-storey Georgian townhouses of wealthy families. These were later bought by slum landlords who tried to maximise the rent. They usually let out the houses, room by room, to the poor. They did little or nothing to maintain them. There was great demand for housing because of the city's rising population, and once-grand houses quickly deteriorated due to overcrowding and neglect. People could not be expected to clean the stairs, halls, kitchens, outdoor toilets, and yards that they shared with 20 or 30 other people. These buildings quickly became filthy and breeding grounds for disease. Sanitation was deplorable. Many houses had a single toilet and one kitchen, generally on the ground floor and shared by all. Most of the poor had little or no money for clothing, furniture or food. Frequent unemployment meant great hardship for families that were already living on the breadline. Many people depended on charity. Although he sympathised with the plight of tenement families, Chart, wealthy and privileged himself, shared some of the prejudices of his class. He praised the devout faith, kindness, and friendliness of the poor. He thought poverty lowered their standards of cleanliness and decency (for example, prostitutes lived in the same houses as families with young children). He claims that the poor were partly responsible for their own condition because they accepted their lot in life passively, were politically unaware and elected slum landlords to public office. These landlords added to their misery by charging excessive rents and failing to maintain houses that should now be condemned. SOURCE: David Alfred Chart, 'Unskilled labour in Dublin: its housing and living conditions', *Journal of the Statistical and Social Inquiry Society of Ireland*, 94 (1914), 160–81.

2.2. Large numbers of the population live starved and stunted lives … Glaring social evils stare us in the face, yet the problems connected with them must be approached very warily, lest the effort to do good may bring about a greater harm. If we are to play the surgeon, we must study the anatomy of the body politic. The paper to be read this evening will illustrate a phase of life in the city of Dublin, the life of the class generally described as unskilled labour ... The great mansions of the eighteenth-century aristocracy, forsaken by the class which designed them, have been occupied in quite a different manner by quite a different class of people. Instead of one family occupying a ten-roomed house, there is a family in every room, each paying from 2*s.* to 3*s.* a week for accommodation. ...

2.3. Where they [poor families] do not inhabit the old mansion cut up into one-roomed tenements, as shown above, they will probably be found living under even worse conditions in airless courts and alleys or in the tumble-down death-traps of the Church Street district and the Liberties ... Families living under such conditions as these are manifestly overcrowded and, as a result of such overcrowding, have to make continual sacrifices of comfort, decency, and health. Moral and physical contagion are ever present ...

2.4. Again, to consider merely physical conditions, how is absolute cleanliness possible, even with the best intentions, when some thirty or more people of both sexes and all ages and belonging to different families have to share the same water supply and the same sanitary accommodation, both on the ground floor of a four or five story house? Is there not a temptation to be dirty, when cleanliness involves the descent and ascent of perhaps eight flights of stairs and the carrying of heavy cans of water? Even the cleanest of us is not willing to clean up other people's dirt, and so the common hall and staircase become exceedingly foul, while the state of the common yard frequently beggars description.

2.5. The sanitary officers do their duty, no doubt, but they cannot go into the house every day, and so evils often go for a long while undetected and unchecked. Again just consider such overcrowding as is shown in Case No. 27, seven people in one room, eating, sleeping, cooking, being born, as like not dying, all within the compass of the same set of walls. Dirt fosters disease, overcrowding leads directly to tuberculosis, to infantile mortality and many other evils. Can it be wondered then, considering that at least a quarter of our population live in dwellings of the type illustrated, that of all the cities of the United Kingdom, Dublin, year after year, has the highest death-rate ...

2.6. When the rent has been paid and the four or five hungry mouths fed for the week, there is little over to provide clothes, furniture, fuel and the like. The way of spending the money varies, of course, with different individuals, but a typical budget would perhaps be as follows:

Rent 2*s.* 6*d.*
Fuel and light 2*s.* 0*d.*

Bread 4*s.* 0*d.*
Tea 0*s.* 9*d.*
Sugar 0*s.* 8*d.*
Milk (usually condensed) 0*s.* 6*d.*
Butter (dripping, margarine) 1*s.* 6*d.*
Potatoes or other vegetables 1*s.* 0*d.*
Meat, fish, bacon, etc. 2*s.* 0*d.*
Total 14*s.* 11*d.*
Balance 3*s.* 1*d.*
Wages for week 18*s.* 0*d.* ...

2.7. It will be seen from the typical budget quoted that there is only a balance of three shillings and one penny for provision of clothes, furniture, insurance, amusements, etc. It is a standing wonder that this scanty and precarious balance can be made to provide for the innumerable small needs of a household.

2.8. Clothes are a continually recurring item, and the usual practice is that already mentioned in connection with housing, the adaptation to the labouring class of the discarded possessions of the well-to-do. Husband and wife probably wear second-hand clothes purchased in Little Mary Street or elsewhere for a few shillings. The children go hatless and barefoot, and are frequently dressed in the worn-out clothes of their parents, rudely cut down to fit, thus producing that characteristic Dublin figure, the street child with its tousled head, its bare legs and the quaintly fluttering rags of its wardrobe. ...

2.9. Furniture too, is usually bought second-hand and is confined to the barest necessities. Bedsteads, bedclothes, tables and chairs will be found in these households, but may be dispensed with at need. Boxes may be substituted for tables and chairs. If there is no bedstead or bedclothes the family may have to huddle in a corner and cover themselves with their united wardrobes. In some tenement rooms the bedstead is not to be seen in its usual place in the corner, but in its stead there is a spread on the floor in a mysterious and repellent assortment of rags, which few inquirers have had the hardihood to investigate and which is believed to serve as a bed. When hard times come, the furniture goes, and probably most of the clothes. ...

2.10. 'Hard times' are unfortunately of frequent occurrence, and are usually caused by sickness or unemployment. Sickness, as has been said, is an inevitable result of the conditions of life, and periods of unemployment are characteristic of the life of the unskilled labourer ... If the breadwinner has to enter a hospital or is unable to get work, the wife goes out 'sharing', or obtains outdoor relief, or, more probably, assistance, from some charity or other. The clothes and furniture are pawned, the rent falls into arrears, and the financial equilibrium, always unstable, is completely disturbed. Furthermore, the evil effects of periods of destitution are not always forgotten when comparative prosperity is restored. Debts have been contracted, possessions which have been sold or pawned must be replaced, and by the time all this has been done the wolf may be prowling around the door again. ...

2.11. From the continual financial stress, which turns the laughing girls of the poorer Dublin streets into the weary-eyed women of the tenement houses, no real relief comes until the children begin to grow up and contribute some part of their earnings to the family exchequer. By the time the boys and girls are fourteen or fifteen they are old enough to go out and earn a few shillings ... However, later on, when the boys and girls grow up and marry, the parents, now growing old, are thrown on their own resources and, though they have no one but themselves to clothe and feed, sometimes pass through a period of considerable penury before the Old Age Pension, 'God's Bounty', as some of the poor call it, descends on them at the age of 70 ...

2.12. The Dublin labouring class ... exhibits in a marked degree the social virtues of kindness, cheerfulness, and courtesy. The inquirers of the Housing and Town Planning Association, though they went into hundreds of dwellings during a great strike and asked a number of very pointed and delicate questions, rarely encountered suspicion or incivility. Mentally and morally this class is probably on a higher level than the labouring classes of most cities. It is on the physical and economic sides that Dublin falls so far behind. ...

2.13. It will be said, doubtless, that the blame for the state of the slums lies with the slum dwellers themselves, that the tenant of unsanitary habits makes the house noisome [stinking], and so on, and that such people, if admitted to a palace, would soon turn it into a pigsty. We all know the stories of the bathroom used as a coal cellar and the water closet turned into a fowl-house.

2.14. Undoubtedly there is a long educative process before those who would try to raise the standard of life of the Dublin labourer. His worst fault is his too easy acquiescence in a shameful and degrading position. He accepts the one-roomed tenement, with all that the one-roomed tenement implies, as his natural lot and often does not seem to think of, or try for anything better. If he had any real resentment against that system, he would not have elected so many owners of tenement houses as members of the Corporation.

3. The problem of Dublin slums: a Catholic view

3.1. *Introduction.* J.R. O'Connell, a director of the Association for the Housing of the Very Poor and a somewhat pompous but sincere lay Catholic spokesman, addressed the Catholic Truth Society on the housing of the Dublin poor. He condemned the filthy accommodation of the poor in Irish towns and cities – the most serious social and moral issue in modern Ireland. He accuses Corporations and Councils of failing in their duties. He quotes the social teachings of Pope Leo XIII (1810–1903). O'Connell cites a letter from a parish priest describing the horror and rampant diseases of overcrowded tenement houses. He contrasts the conditions of the working classes in urban and rural Ireland. Housing in the countryside was greatly improved by government action but hardly anything was done for the city poor. He warned the authorities that it was in their own interest to improve the living conditions of the urban poor that led to immorality, disease, drunkenness, laziness and crime. His appeal to the Catholic middle classes mostly fell on deaf ears, clerical and lay. SOURCE: J.R. O'Connell, *The problem of the Dublin slums* (Dublin, 1913), pp 2–5.

3.2. … It is without any hesitation that I say that at the present time there is no question more urgently demanding the attention and study of the Catholic public of Ireland, both lay and clerical, than the deplorable conditions under which the poor are housed in our cities and large towns, and especially in this City of Dublin.

3.3. … It is, of course, obvious that the essential mission of the Church is the spiritual uplifting of the Faithful, but the Church of God has ever been mindful of the material well-being of her children …

3.4. Pope Leo XIII, in his Encyclical Letter, dated 15th of May, 1891, on 'The Condition of the Working Classes', declared:

'Neither must it be supposed that the solicitude of the Church is so preoccupied with the spiritual concerns of her children as to neglect their temporal and earthly interests. Her desire is that the poor, for example, should rise above poverty and wretchedness, and better their condition in life, and for this she makes a strong endeavour. By the very fact that she calls men to virtue and forms them to its practice she promotes this in no small degree'.

3.5. These words of our late Sovereign Pontiff impress upon us how deeply the Church has been concerned for the welfare and upraising of the poor, and they encourage me to ask your consideration of one of the questions most vitally affecting their moral and physical welfare at the present time in Ireland – the problem of the decent, healthy housing of the poorer classes. This is a matter on which no Irishman possessed of what Leo XIII called 'the social conscience' can be apathetic … because it is unquestionable that the Catholic poor are very largely in the majority in the number of those who suffer most from the present deplorable conditions of ill-housing in the cities and towns of Ireland.

3.6. Undoubtedly this is a problem the solution of which must rest largely in the hands of municipal and other local bodies … Many local Councils still hesitate to avail to the full extent of the powers conferred upon them under the Housing of the Working Class Acts, and even when housing schemes are undertaken they are sometimes administered in a very half-hearted fashion.

3.7. ... As to the urgency of this question, a sad and striking proof has been supplied in our city ... In a street in the very heart of Dublin, within a hundred yards of the Courts of Law, and near other public buildings of importance, without a moment's warning two houses crumble into dust, covering in their ruins many people, of whom six were killed and at least seven very seriously, injured. These houses had been under the observation of the Municipal Sanitary Authority, which regarded them as reasonably safe, and there is no reason for thinking that this opinion was not fully justified; but this occurrence ... must bring home to us in a very impressive way the fact that in this city there must be large numbers of houses, even perhaps entire streets, in which the poor are crowded together, which are so unsuitable and dangerous as dwelling-places as the two houses in Church Street which so suddenly crumbled into dust.

3.8. May I be permitted to read for you a letter which I have received from a well-known Dublin Parish Priest ...

'When the plebiscite on this question was taken a few years ago I wrote very strongly from my twenty-one years' experience in the Pro-Cathedral Parish, but all our pleading perished before the slum-owners' widespread influence and interest. I recall with clinging realism my countless visits, at all hours of the night, to the pestilent slum-rooms, in each of which five or six poor creatures, and often more, would be found inhaling, through their sleep, the night through, the foul and fetid air that worsened hour by hour. It is only one who comes from out of the fresh air of the midnight streets into the crowded slum-room that at all realises the intolerable and prostrating smells in which the poor must take their unrefreshing slumbers. How dreadfully is this aggravated when some pitiable, emaciated, far-spent consumptive, coughing through the hours, adds to the horror. I came by long experience to know the consumptive smell that comes to abide in many tenement rooms. It is only less overwhelming than the nameless stench of cancer. There is no escape from infection in these seed-plots of disease'.

3.9. ... Let me summarise in a few words the present condition of the poor in our own city. There are roughly about twenty thousand families, comprising about 100,000 individuals, living in one-room tenements in Dublin. According to the Census of 1901, of 59,263 families or occupiers of distinct dwellings, 21,702, or 36.6 per cent, or nearly two-fifths of all the families, occupied each only a single room; and according to the Census of 1911 this state of things has but very slightly improved.

3.10. It appears from the report, for the Year 1912 ... that there were in the City of Dublin last year, 21,133 tenements of one room, 3,604 of which were occupied by one person each, 5,310 by two persons, 3,893 by three persons, 3,074 by four persons, 2,267 by five persons, 1,488 by six persons, 854 by seven persons, 431 by eight person,

146 by nine persons, 45 by ten persons, 16 by eleven persons, and 5 by twelve and upwards. There were 40 families occupying part of a room, 21,113 occupying one room, 13,087 occupying two rooms, 6,577 occupying three rooms, and 6,475 occupying four rooms. Nearly one-third of the Dublin population – according to Sir Charles Cameron – including the whole of the Metropolitan registration area, is composed of labourers, hawkers, porters, etc., and the death-rate amongst this class is about 31.9 per 1,000. ...

3.11. Serious as the conditions of the housing of the poor are from the point of view of the sanitarian and of the statistician, they are infinitely more serious from the point of view of anyone in whom abides 'the social conscience'. If it be true that the slum dwelling is the hotbed and propagating ground of disease, of cancer, of tuberculosis, of bronchitis, and rheumatism, and many other pulmonary and infectious diseases, it is certainly not less true that it causes and confirms the vices of drunkenness, immorality, idleness, thriftlessness, turbulence in all their forms. We profess to deplore the drunkenness ... but how can we expect any reform until our poor are provided with decent, cleanly, wholesome sanitary homes? How can we expect any improvement while the only alternative to the glitter and the glamour of the gin-palace is the pestilential and fetid room in an unsanitary slum, shared by the worker with a wife and perhaps half-a-dozen sickly children?

3.12. ... Again, how can it be expected that immorality shall not spread and increase when perhaps a dozen or twenty families are crowded into one house, originally planned as the residence of one single household, where all must meet and mingle on the common hallway of the stairs, and yard and passages, and in which a family of persons of different ages and sexes is packed into each room at night regardless of the most elementary conditions of decency and morality ... the life of the tenement in its absolute impossibility of privacy or reticence, bringing as it does all the most degraded into association with their neighbours, has the most deplorable results on the self-respect and decency even of those who come to it fresh from the healthful atmosphere of the country. In such conditions all inducement and encouragement to cleanliness, thrift and progress vanish, and the tendency is to sink to the level of the most degraded ...

3.13. Perhaps, however, the saddest aspect of this question is its destruction, moral as well as physical, of child life ... the exceptionally high death-rate amongst the children of the poor in the slum areas is appalling. Vast sums are being spent every year, and necessarily and wisely spent, in better and brighter schools, much thought and care is being devoted to our system of education; but all this money and care and thought will have little effect on the future lives of the children of the poor if they are condemned to live their miserable childhood in the slum area. I do not hesitate to say that the children of the poor, that future generation on which so much depends, whose future, so often in peril, so constantly neglected, is our greatest national asset, are being sacrificed in soul and body, and mind in the present and in the future because nobody of Irishmen grapple seriously with the financial and other difficulties which impede, though I am sure they cannot prevent, the solution of this problem. Happily the problem of the housing of the poor in the country districts his been solved, or is at least on the path to solution …

3.14. When we turn from the country to the cities and towns of Ireland we find ourselves face to face with a different and much more difficult set of problems … In the difficulty in obtaining sites and the expense of purchasing sites, of clearing areas and compensating acquired interests, consists the problem of the housing of the poor in cities and large towns … Owing to one cause or another there are a very large number of derelict spaces in Dublin. A Municipal report of this present year shows that there are 1,166 vacant houses and 54 vacant spaces of varying dimensions within the city … I suggest that powers might again be sought by the Corporation to take possession of any derelict house or vacant space the rates of which have not been paid for a period of not less than six years. These plots might then be utilised for the erection of sanitary dwellings for the poor, if large enough …

3.15. … Up to the present time the Corporation of Dublin has spent £352,082 in various housing schemes … there are still at least 12,200 families living in single-room tenements, who by reason of the size or other circumstances of the family, ought to be housed in a three-roomed tenement, the average cost of which would be £150. The cost, therefore, of housing these 12,200 families would be something like £1,830,000, which would probably mean an annual loss to the ratepayers of between £75,000 and £80,000 per annum. A deficit so startling as this could only be bridged … by the State lending part of the money …

3.16. … In conclusion, I would wish to call attention to the fact that expert opinion on the housing question … has even within the last few years passed through several distinct phases. The first phase may be said to have been arrived at when public opinion realised the degradation of the slum tenement houses and the disgraceful conditions under which whole families were allowed to exist in cellars, stables, and damp and dreary underground kitchens, and when, as a consequence, the Legislature stepped in to regulate tenement dwellings. The second stage was reached when the erection of Artisans' Dwellings was undertaken by Municipal effort and by various philanthropic and benevolent agencies, the result of which has been that a great deal has been done by Corporations and Local Bodies throughout Ireland to provide improved dwellings for the labouring classes … in Dublin alone over seven thousand sanitary dwellings have been provided by various agencies, Municipal, Commercial and Philanthropic, and over 32,000 individuals are housed in these dwellings.

4. Workers' resentment towards employers

4.1. *Introduction.* This article, printed in the Labour movement's newspaper, the *Irish Worker*, shows the growing anger towards employers. It threatens them with the same fate as the landlords before them. SOURCE: 'Employers' secret society unmasked', *Irish Worker*, 29 July 1911.

4.2. Some of these gentlemen seem to have forgotten that we had a land problem in Ireland, and that a few individuals, who claimed they owned the land, were taught a lesson. In the beginning of that struggle a large number of the dispossessed farmers blamed the tools of the landlords and dealt in a very summary way with them. Later on men arose in the land who made it clear to the minds of the exploited that it were foolish to blame the tools, the emergency men, and the grabber; the people who were responsible were the alien landlord class, and in a few short years the problem was solved – as regards the tenant farmers. Some of the landlord class tried the self-same tricks that you in Dublin intend playing. Well, some of them found themselves lying behind a ditch suffering from want of breath, and don't forget we are the sons of those men who enjoyed the gaol and trod the scaffold. Do you think we will be less worthy than they who went before? You will conspire; your tools will perjure their dirty souls; you will intimidate, you will starve us into submission; you threaten us and our wives and children with the whiplash of hunger. Eh! That is your game. Do you think there are no brains, or muscle left in this land among the working class?

5. Larkin addresses the workers

I

5.1. *Introduction.* The strike began on 26 August when tramworkers from William Martin Murphy's company walked out in protest when he forbade them to join the ITGWU. Later that day, James Larkin addressed a crowd of strikers and supporters, condemned police brutality, urged people to defend themselves and told them to be prepared to fight if necessary. He referred to the prominent Unionist Edward Carson's advice to the men of Ulster to resist Home Rule by force, and said that Dublin's workers might have to resort to violence to achieve their objectives. Larkin was arrested but released a few days later. SOURCE: Cited in Arnold Wright, *Disturbed Dublin: the story of the great strike of 1913–14 with a description of the industries of the Irish capital* (London, 1914), pp 124–5.

5.2. If it is right and legal for the men of Ulster to arm, why should it not be right and legal for the men of Dublin to arm themselves to protect themselves? You will need it. I don't offer advice which I am not prepared to adopt myself. You know me, and you know when I say a thing I will do it. So arm, and I'll arm. You have to face hired assassins. If Sir Edward Carson is right in telling the men of Ulster to form a

Provisional Government in Ulster, I think I must be right, too, in telling you to form a Provisional Government in Dublin. But whether you form a Provisional Government or not, you will require arms, for Aberdeen [Lord Lieutenant of Ireland] has promised Murphy not only the police but the soldiers, and my advice to you is to be round the doors and corners, and whenever one of your men is shot, shoot two of theirs. Now we will hold our next big meeting in O'Connell Street, come what may, and we will show them that we can use the property for which we pay.

II

5.3. *Introduction.* Larkin spoke to nearly 10,000 people in Beresford Place, on 29 August 1913, at which he burned the government proclamation prohibiting the gathering, and warned the authorities not to curtail the rights, or abuse the liberties, of the people. He questioned the King's right to interfere with the right of people to meet in public. He was later tried for incitement. SOURCE: Cited in Arnold Wright, *Disturbed Dublin: the story of the great strike of 1913–14 with a description of the industries of the Irish capital* (London, 1914), pp 127–8.

> **5.4.** I care as much for the King as I do for Mr Swifte the magistrate. People make kings and people can unmake them; but what has the King of England to do with stopping a meeting in Dublin? If they like to stop the meeting at the order of Mr Murphy, Mr Wm. Murphy will take the responsibility; and, as I have previously told you, for every man that falls on our side two will fall on the other. We have a perfect right to meet in O'Connell Street. We are going to meet in O'Connell Street, and if the police or soldiers are going to stop or try to stop us, let them take the responsibility. If they want a revolution, well then, God be with them.

6. On the eve of the Lockout

6.1. *Introduction.* Larkin addressed a mass meeting in Sackville Street [now O'Connell Street] on 27 August, and urged crowds to support the striking tramworkers. Another huge crowd gathered on the same street on 30 August 1913 to see him. In spite of a large police presence, Larkin showed up, in disguise. He appeared briefly in the window of the Imperial Hotel, and was promptly arrested as the crowd cheered wildly. Police were increasingly nervous about the mood and size of the crowd, and when given the order to disperse the gathering, a riot ensued. James Connolly wrote the article below in the *Irish Worker*, newspaper of the ITGWU. He encourages people to take a stand against employers in solidarity with the strikers, and to demand their right to join whichever union they chose. He writes in response to newspaper reports that supported William Martin Murphy's actions against the tramworkers. Connolly praises the ITGWU for encouraging workers to challenge their employers, for giving them pride, and for telling them that while they might be poor and powerless, they could become strong if they were united. He welcomes the possibility of an all-out-lockout. Connolly believes it would show clearly how society was divided between rich and poor. It would also help to persuade the poor to fight against injustice. He says that the working classes had been exploited by social and political elites since the arrival of the English in the twelfth century. Workers were brainwashed into believing that they were less valuable and less worthy than employers and governors. SOURCE: James Connolly, 'The Dublin Lockout: on the eve', *Irish Worker*, 30 August 1913.

6.2. Perhaps before this issue of the *Irish Worker* is in the hands of its readers the issues now at stake in Dublin will be brought to a final determination. All the capitalist newspapers of Friday last, join in urging, or giving favourable publicity to the views of others urging the employers of Dublin to join in a general lockout of the members of the Irish Transport and General Workers' Union. It is as well. Possibly some such act is necessary in order to make that portion of the working class which still halts undecided to understand clearly what it is that lies behind the tyrannical and brow-beating attitude of the proprietors of the Dublin tramway system.

6.3. The fault of the Irish Transport and General Workers' Union! What is it? Let us tell it in plain language. Its fault is this, that it found the labourers of Ireland on their knees, and has striven to raise them to the erect position of manhood; it found them with all the vices of slavery in their souls, and it strove to eradicate these vices and replace them with some of the virtues of free men; it found them with no other weapons of defence than the arts of the liar, the lickspittle, and the toady, and it combined them and taught them to abhor those arts and rely proudly on the defensive power of combination; it, in short, found a class in whom seven centuries of social outlawry had added fresh degradations upon the burden it bore as the members of a nation suffering from the cumulative effects of seven centuries of national bondage, and out of this class, the degraded slaves of slaves more degraded still – for what degradation is more abysmal than that of those who prostitute their manhood on the altar of profit-mongering? – out of this class of slaves the labourers of Dublin, the Irish Transport and General Workers' Union has created an army of intelligent self-reliant men, abhorring the old arts of the toady, the lickspittle, and the crawler and trusting alone to the disciplined use of their power to labour or to withdraw their labour to assert and maintain their right as men.

6.4. To put it in other words, but words as pregnant with truth and meaning: the Irish Transport and General Workers' Union found that before its advent the working class of Dublin had been taught by all the educational agencies of the country, by all the social influences of their masters, that this world was created for the special benefit of the various sections of the master class, that kings and lords and capitalists were of value; that even flunkeys [lackeys], toadies, lickspittle and poodle dogs had an honoured place in the scheme of the universe, but that there was neither honour, credit, nor consideration to the man or woman who toils to maintain them all ...

6.5. If the value of a city is to be found in the development of self-respect and high conception of social responsibilities among a people, then the Irish Transport and General Workers' Union found Dublin the poorest city in these countries by reason of its lack of these qualities. And by imbuing the workers with them, it has made Dublin the richest city in Europe to-day, rich by all that counts for greatness in the history of nations.

6.6. It is then upon this working class so enslaved, this working class so led and so enriched with moral purposes and high aims that the employers propose to make general war.

6.7. Shall we shrink from it; cower before their onset? A thousand times no! Shall we crawl back into our slums, abase our hearts, bow our knees, and crawl once more to lick the hand that would smite us? Shall we, who have been carving out for our children a brighter future, a cleaner city, a freer life, consent to betray them instead into the grasp of the blood-suckers from whom we have dreamt of escaping? No, no, and yet again no!

6.8. Let them declare their lockout; it will only hasten the day when the working class will lockout the capitalist class for good and all. If for taking the side of the Tram men we are threatened with suffering, why we have suffered before. But let them understand well that once they start that ball rolling no capitalist power on earth can prevent it continuing to roll, that every day will add to the impetus it will give to the working class purpose, to the thousands it will bring to the working class ranks and every added suffering inflicted upon the workers will be a fresh obstacle in the way of moderation when the day of final settlement arrives. Yes, indeed, if it is going to be a wedding, let it be a wedding; and if it is going to be a wake, let it be a wake: *we are ready for either*.

7. An 'orgy of anarchy'

7.1. *Introduction.* Arnold Wright, an English writer visiting Dublin, put the blame for riots entirely on the protestors, not the police. Here, he describes the serious riots of 30 August, when, police baton charged the crowds and injured many protestors. Two men caught up in the riots, James Nolan and John Byrne, died from the injuries. He defended police actions as necessary and courageous. He denies that the protestors were innocent victims of police brutality, moreover, he argues that the police were the victims of simple mob aggression, even though they were attempting to protect life and property. SOURCE: Arnold Wright, *Disturbed Dublin: the story of the great strike of 1913–14 with a description of the industries of the Irish capital* (London, 1914), pp 133–8.

7.2. The opening scene, in what was to prove a prolonged and sanguinary drama, was enacted in the Ringsend district. In his speech on Friday night Mr Larkin had referred to a football match which was to be played on Saturday on the Shelbourne Ground at Ringsend between two local clubs. 'There are "scabs" in one of the teams, and you will not be there except as pickets', he said, in language whose menacing character was understood by those who heard him.

7.3. In obedience to the implied command, a large body of members of the Transport Workers Union gathered at the time announced for the match near the entrance to the grounds. The Larkinites vigorously hooted the teams as they passed in; but, apart from this and an occasional scuffle between the pickets and those who entered the enclosure, there was no actual disturbance of the peace. A little later the temper of the demonstrators underwent a change. They gathered in considerable numbers on a bridge in the locality and indicated a clear intention to resort to violence against those who had excited their animosity.

7.4. The small force of police present attempted to disperse them, but without success. Shortly afterwards, when reinforcements arrived, including a body of mounted officers, the attempt was renewed and the bridge was cleared ... A flower-pot thrown at the police from an adjacent house was a signal for a regular outbreak of violence. Tramway cars, crowded with passengers, were attacked by a howling mob, who broke the windows and assaulted the drivers and conductors. One occupant of a car, who had been struck by a stone, jumped off into the roadway and threatened the rioters with a revolver – a course which, in that instance, produced a cessation of hostilities. But soon the fight was raging as fiercely as ever.

7.5. The police, finding that the crowd was rapidly getting out of hand, drew their batons and charged. They were, however, too few in number to make any great impression on the mob, which had been augmented by new arrivals ... At one point there seemed a danger of the rioters getting the upper hand. A ruffian seized an inspector's sword, drew it from its scabbard, and was about to use it upon the police when the weapon was recaptured and the daring individual was arrested for his pains. Scenes of wild disorder followed. The police were savagely attacked and a number of them were injured by the missiles thrown by the crowd.

7.6. A substantial reinforcement of police, sent to the scene of the disturbances about six o'clock, had to fight their way through masses of rioters at strategic points; and when, later, prisoners arrested in the various encounters were sent to the College Street police station, the escort were stoned from the side streets ... About an hour later Brunswick Street became the scene of a hot encounter between the police and the rioters, owing to attacks made on the tramway cars. It was only after a series of baton charges that the street was cleared. Nightfall brought an addition to the anxieties of the harassed guardians of order. Excitement increased every moment, and it was manifest that a spirit of lawlessness was abroad which would not be easily quelled.

7.7. Beresford Place now became the centre about which the conflict raged. Here, about eight o'clock, a crowd gathered in anticipation of a meeting announced for that hour. Liberty Hall, with its doors heavily barricaded and its windows mostly in darkness, presented an ominous appearance of calm. About twenty policemen were on duty in the vicinity of the square at the time, and, as the outlook was apparently peaceful, the officer in charge considered that he might safely dispense with half his force.

7.8. The detachment thus relieved had not long quitted the square before a fierce attack was made upon the squad left on duty. Stones and bottles were thrown at them, some from the crowd, but the larger number from the windows of the Transport Workers' Union building, which offered a safe vantage-ground for an attack of this kind. The police were ordered into the open by their superior officer, Inspector Campbell, and the word was given to charge the mob. One constable in the mêlée received a bad wound from a stone thrown from the window of Liberty Hall, and a bottle projected from the same quarter, doubtless intended for a constable, felled a rioter with whom he was engaged in conflict. Inspector Campbell himself was wounded in the face by a bottle and had to go off duty.

7.9. Repeated charges were necessary before the rioters were dispersed; and, so desperate was the fighting while it lasted, that the ambulances were kept busy for some time in removing the injured to the hospital.

7.10. The outbreak in Beresford Square was quickly followed by a still more dangerous disturbance near the Abbey Theatre. A riotous crowd which had assembled here was driven off by police charges, but the mob again collected in more formidable dimensions in Abbey Street. Sir John Ross, the head of the executive, who arrived on the scene at this juncture, impressed with the seriousness of the position, gave orders for the street to be cleared.

7.11. The police in great force charged down the thoroughfare against the dense mass of rioters. At first the ground was stubbornly contested, viragos from the slum districts actively assisting the men in assaults on the hated representatives of the law. A number of constables dropped out of the attacking line with nasty wounds inflicted by the flying missiles. Disciplined force, however, eventually carried the day to the extent of dislodging the mob from the position it had taken up.

7.12. For some time the contest raged in adjacent localities. One particularly violent ebullition occurred as three injured constables, whose wounds had been dressed in hospital, were being escorted by their comrades back to the Store Street station. They were set upon in a most cowardly fashion by a howling mob of both sexes, who assailed them with volleys of stones and broken bottles.

7.13. A small body of policemen emerged from the Store Street station and attempted to clear the street. Their appearance was the signal for a renewal of the attack with increased violence. Under the concentrated fire of glass and stone the little band quailed and eventually retired. A shriek of triumph went up from the frenzied mob. Another charge and another repulse, and another wild howl from the rabble. 'So furious was the rain of bottles – broken and whole – and bricks', says a newspaper representative who was a spectator of the scene, 'that the place seemed more like the haunt of howling demons than a Dublin street within a few hundred yards from the cathedral. The shameful, filthy expressions, shouted at the top of women's voices, formed a very painful feature of the melancholy exhibition'.

7.14. A baton charge down Talbot Street by Inspector Campbell with twelve or fourteen constables sent the mob down Mabbott Street towards Tyrone Street. 'To the accompaniment of hoarse, ribald execrations and shrieks from the rioters', says the writer, to whose exceedingly graphic account I am indebted for these details, 'the combined police force charged up towards Tyrone Street, but had to withdraw owing to the hail of bottles and stones.

7.15. Each time the police drew back, the howling rabble followed them and made havoc in their ranks with the hail of missiles that poured on them from all directions. The little barefoot urchins – girls and boys – more daring than their elders, rushed out every now and then and gathered up fresh stores of 'ammunition' for the mob. Darting out into the street, they had little trouble in finding plenty of broken bottles and bricks which had been used on the police a moment before.

7.16. Women, with dishevelled hair and looking like maniacs, were even more persistent than the men and youths in belabouring the police. One of them would rush out of the mob with a shriek and fling a bottle high in the air to drop on the head of a policeman or one of the foolish crowd of onlookers, or to fall with a crash on the street'. So great was the fury and determination of the mob, and so slender, comparatively speaking, were the resources of the police, that it looked at one time as if authority would be deposed.

7.17. It was only towards midnight that the situation was got well in hand and that a proportion of the exhausted constables could be sent home to secure a much-needed rest. When the tale of casualties came to be made out, it was found that hundreds of people had received injuries. The wounds in some instances were serious; and one man, named James Nolan, died in the early hours of Sunday morning from the effects of a fractured skull received in the street fighting. A second individual, named John Byrne, subsequently succumbed. Eloquent evidence of the fierceness of the fray is supplied by the fact that over thirty constables received injuries which necessitated medical treatment. The circumstance deserves to be borne in mind in view of the allegations afterwards made by the Larkinites as to the inoffensiveness of the crowds with whom the police dealt.

7.18. No need exists to emphasise the highly dangerous situation which by this time had been developed in Dublin. Lawlessness was everywhere rampant. The mob had tasted blood, and they were ready for a display of violence at the smallest provocation and in any direction that a favourable opportunity might offer. For the moment the police had triumphed, but it had been by so slender a margin of force that the dangerous lesson had been given of the tremendous power of a determined mob operating from several points. Not without many forebodings must the authorities have awaited the events of that fateful Sunday, August 30.

8. Report of the Dublin Disturbances Commission, 1914

8.1. *Introduction.* There was much industrial strife in Dublin in 1913: some 30 strikes from January to August 1913. Those who continued to work or who took the jobs of strikers were intimidated and attacked, and there were frequent clashes between strikers and police. When the workers in the Dublin Tramways Company went on strike in August 1913, the company hired additional staff and kept operating. Because of attacks on trams and tram drivers the Dublin Metropolitan Police and Royal Irish Constabulary provided a guard for each tram. Several of the riots on Saturday 30 August and Sunday 31 August resulted from attacks on tramcars. As tensions rose in the weeks that followed, riots broke out sporadically all over the city The government appointed a Commission on 19 December 1913 to inquire into the rioting and to investigate allegations of 'the use of excessive and unnecessary force' by police officers. The Inquiry began on Monday 5 January 1914 in the Four Courts. It sat for 18 days and heard 281 witnesses, comprising 202 members of the Dublin Metropolitan Police and 79 civilians. It concluded that the police were not guilty of starting the riot in Sackville Street [now O' Connell Street] on 31 August or of gross brutality in trying to contain it. It praised the courage and patience of the police, in particular, when provoked or threatened by people they described as forming a 'desperate criminal band'. SOURCE: *Report of the Dublin Disturbances Commission* (London, 1914).

BERESFORD PLACE, TALBOT STREET, MARLBOROUGH STREET, EARL STREET, EDEN QUAY, AND BURGH QUAY, SATURDAY, 30 AUGUST 1913

8.2. The stone-throwing continued, and charges were made during the night along Eden Quay, across Butt Bridge, on Burgh Quay, and in Beresford Place. During part of the disturbance Superintendent Quinn was in charge of a party of men on Butt Bridge, and a number of his men were injured, at least one having to be removed to hospital. This constable, who was hit with a bottle on the head, was unable to return to duty for three weeks. The riot in this locality went on for a long time, and while it lasted, the throwing of stones and bottles was almost continuous, and many injuries were inflicted. We regret to say that, as far as we can ascertain, two deaths are attributable to injuries received as a result of baton charges which took place.

8.3. At Eden Quay, a man called James Nolan, of 8, Spring Garden Street, North Strand, sustained a fracture of the skull, which resulted in his death at Jervis Street Hospital on the morning of Sunday, the 31st. The jury at the inquest found that death was caused by fracture of the skull, and compression of the brain. They also found that the injuries were caused by the blow of a baton, but that the evidence was too conflicting to say by whom the blow was administered. It was proved before us that before the baton charge in question took place, the crowd at the spot in question had been very disorderly, stones had been thrown, and it was quite obvious to any peaceable person that a riot was in progress for some time. No evidence was given before us as to the circumstances under which Nolan became a member of the crowd, but it was beyond all doubt a riotous one.

8.4. On the same night a labourer named John Byrne, residing at 4, Lower Gloucester Place, was treated at Jervis Street Hospital for a wound on his head. He died on the 4th September, and the jury at the inquest found that John Byrne died from fracture of the skull and haemorrhage. They further found that they had no evidence to show how the deceased received his injuries. No person gave evidence at the Inquest, or before us, as to the circumstances under which John Byrne sustained the injuries which resulted in his death, and the only account available was the statement made by him to his wife, that he had been struck with a baton at Burgh Quay. It was proved before us that a baton charge had taken place at Burgh Quay on Saturday night, and that the crowd against which this charge was directed was very disorderly and violent, and we have little doubt that in the course of this charge Byrne received the injury which led to his death. We are of opinion that in the case of both these crowds their conduct towards the police clearly showed to any peaceable persons the danger that they ran by remaining members of them.

8.5. Later on the same night riotous crowds assembled in Marlborough Street, Talbot Street, and Earl Street, and damage was done in many instances to shops and houses. The rioters gathered at the corners of streets, and when charged by the police rushed away, to re-assemble later on and again indulge in stone-throwing. In fact during the greater part of the night continuous disturbances existed in this area, and the force engaged were kept busy in dispersing crowds. Unless the officers in charge were prepared to abandon possession of the streets to rioters, they had no alternative but to give the orders to clear the various streets that they did.

SACKVILLE STREET [O'CONNELL STREET], SUNDAY, 31 AUGUST 1913.

8.6. The immediate cause of the riot in Sackville Street on Sunday afternoon, the 31st August, 1913, was the appearance of James Larkin outside the Imperial Hotel in Sackville Street, for the purpose of addressing a public meeting, which had been proclaimed by the Chief Magistrate of the City of Dublin. Larkin was arrested, and committed for trial on the 28th August, 1913, and was admitted to bail on the same day. After his admission to bail Larkin publicly expressed his intention of holding a public meeting in Sackville Street on Sunday, the 31st of August.

8.7. On the 29th of August a Proclamation, which was extensively posted and circulated in the city, was issued by the Chief Magistrate, prohibiting this meeting. On the evening of the 29th of August, Larkin burned a copy of this Proclamation at a meeting in Beresford Place, and again expressed his intention of holding a meeting in Sackville Street on Sunday, the 31st of August. In these circumstances a warrant was issued for the re-arrest of Larkin, and it became necessary for the police authorities to take steps for the purpose of preventing and dispersing the meeting if an attempt were made to hold it in Sackville Street, on the Sunday.

8.8. ... Mr Harrell met all the Superintendents at Head Quarters on Saturday, the 30th of August, and directed them to assemble at 11.30 a.m. on the Sunday in Sackville Street a force of police ... to instruct their officers and men that while persons were to be allowed to pass freely along the street about their lawful business, no assembly of persons was to be permitted; that the police were to advise persons to pass along, and not to remain about; that small parties of police consisting of a sergeant and a few constables were to move along the sections of the street allotted to each Superintendent to keep the people moving when necessary; that no organised bodies of people were to be allowed to enter the street at any point; and that James Larkin was to be arrested if he appeared.

8.9. The Superintendents to whom these instructions were given are all men of long experience in the force ... Up to 12.30 on the Sunday the state of affairs was normal in Sackville Street; but from that hour the number of persons in the street increased rapidly until about 1.25 p.m., when there was a considerable though unformed crowd in the street, particularly in the neighbourhood of the General Post Office.

8.10. About 1.25 p.m. Larkin appeared on the balcony of the Imperial Hotel, and appears to have uttered some words, and to have then retired into the hotel. As soon as he was observed by the people in the street, there was a rush by a crowd numbering 300 to 400, and waving hats and sticks, from the neighbourhood of the General Post Office towards the Imperial Hotel. In order to prevent the rush of this crowd on the hotel, Inspector McCaig with a sergeant and ten men ... doubled out into the carriage way ...

8.11. ... Inspector McCaig and his party of police had been ordered to enter the Imperial Hotel for the purpose of effecting the arrest of Larkin, leaving Sergeant Butler and his men guarding the door of the hotel. As soon as the police were seen entering the hotel, there was a second rush by the crowd, which had greatly increased in numbers, from the direction of the General Post Office towards the hotel. During this rush sticks were brandished, and a missile was thrown from the crowd, which broke a large plate glass window a few feet from the hotel door.

8.12. Believing that the object of the crowd was to prevent the arrest of Larkin, the police who were guarding the door of the hotel drew their batons, with the result that the rush was stopped, and the crowd again retreated in the direction of the General Post Office, where they again seem to have reformed. In this instance also no batons were used by the police, and none of them came in contact with the crowd.

8.13. A few moments later Larkin was removed from the hotel under arrest, and, guarded by an escort, was taken to College Street Police Station. As soon as Larkin appeared in the street under arrest a third rush was made by the crowd from the direction of the General Post Office and Prince's Street, diagonally across the street in the direction of the escort. Fearing that the object of the crowd, who were shouting, brandishing sticks, and throwing stones, was to rescue the prisoner, orders were given by Inspector Barrett and other responsible officers to the police to put back and disperse the crowd. In our opinion these orders, and the baton charge by which they were carried out, were justified by the circumstances.

8.14. The crowd was dispersed by three bodies of police, numbering in all about fifty, who moved out into the street, one from the corner of Lower Abbey Street, another from O'Connell Bridge, and the third from the neighbourhood of the Metropole Hotel. These three bodies of police effectually prevented the crowd from approaching the escort which was guarding Larkin, and turned the crowd back – dispersing them in the direction of the Nelson Pillar and the General Post Office. In the course of the charge by means of which this crowd was dispersed batons were used by many of the police, and a number of civilians were knocked down in the rush back along and across the street, some as the result of blows from batons, and some as the result of collision with and tripping over each other ...

8.15. ... During the dispersal in Sackville Street of the crowd which had followed the escort which was guarding Larkin, a large number of persons rushed round the corner of the Metropole Hotel into Prince's Street, cheering and throwing stones at the police in Prince's Street, many of whom were struck. In pursuance of the orders which they had received the sergeant and nine men who were stationed near the office of the *Freeman's Journal* prevented the crowd from going down Prince's Street, and turned them back towards Sackville Street, using their batons for the purpose. ...

8.16. Unfortunately this crowd, as it was being driven back out of Prince's Street, was met by another crowd rushing into Prince's Street and away from the police in Sackville Street, and the two crowds collided, filling up the entrance to Prince's Street, and becoming mixed up with the police who were near the corner of the Metropole Hotel ... a large number of people must have received injuries, not only from the pressure and struggle of the crowd, but also from the blows of batons.

8.17. As frequently happens in incidents of the kind, there seem to have been several peaceable citizens swept into and along by the riotous mob; and we have no doubt that some of them were injured during the clearing of the street. In one regrettable instance, that of Mr O'Donnell, a respectable gentleman carrying on business in Lower Sackville Street received very severe injuries at the hands of the police. There were thirteen police injured during the course of this riot (including the sergeant and nine men who were stationed in Prince's Street – all of whom were injured in discharging their duty).

8.18. In dealing with the conduct of the police during this riot it must be borne in mind that the riot was a matter of a few minutes. All the incidents we have described from the appearance of Larkin on the balcony of the Imperial Hotel until quiet was restored in Prince's Street, took place within three or four minutes. So far as the movements of the police which turned and dispersed the crowd which was rushing in the direction of the escort are concerned, although batons were freely used, there is no evidence of the use of unnecessary or excessive force up to the moment of the collision of the two crowds at the entrance to Prince's Street. In the confusion of this moment there may have been, and we think that in isolated instances there was, the use of force which in fact was unnecessary.

8.19. … To the police it very naturally appeared to be a renewed and determined effort by a suddenly and greatly increased crowd to force a passage through Prince's Street, and they dealt with it accordingly. Any unnecessary or excessive force used by the police during the suppression of this riot was due to this misunderstanding.

8.20. As some suggestions have been made that the crowd in Sackville Street was driven into Prince's Street for the purpose of being caught and batoned there, we think it right to say that, in our opinion, there is no foundation for these suggestions. As suggestions were made in cross-examination of the police that some members of the force were seen smoking, and that others of them were under the influence of drink, while on duty in Sackville Street on Sunday, the 31st August, 1913, we also think it right to say that both these charges were indignantly denied by the police, that there is no evidence whatever to support either of them, and that they are without foundation.

8.21. … We desire to report, in conclusion, that in our opinion the officers and men of the Dublin Metropolitan Police and the Royal Irish Constabulary, as a whole, discharged their duties throughout this trying period with conspicuous courage and patience. They were exposed to great dangers, and treated with great brutality, and in many instances we were satisfied that, though suffering from injuries which would have fully justified their absence from duty, they remained at their posts under great difficulties until peace had been restored.

8.22. The total number of constables injured during these riots exceeded 200. Notwithstanding the extent and violence of the disturbances, in no case, save one, and then only for the purpose of protecting two tram cars, was the assistance of the military called for. The riots were dealt with and suppressed by the police, and by the police alone, and had it not been for their zeal and determination, the outburst of lawlessness which took place in the months of August and September would have assumed more serious proportions, and been attended with far more evil results. We have the honour to remain,

Your Excellency's obedient servants,

DENIS S. HENRY,   S.L. BROWN.

THOMAS PATTON,

9th February, 1914. Secretary.

9. Larkin vows to fight

9.1. *Introduction.* ITGWU leaders were in serious financial difficulty after just a few weeks. English unions had promised support in speeches and statements, but donated little money. Larkin went to England to appeal for help, moral and financial. He made the following speech, reported in the *Manchester Guardian*, at an open air rally in Manchester on 14 September 1913. He declares that he would stop at nothing to force employers to improve the working conditions of the unskilled classes. He claims that he would happily accept the permanent hostility of social and clerical elites, even eternal damnation, if he could improve the circumstances of Dublin's most wretched. SOURCE: 'Larkin to fight on', *Manchester Guardian*, 15 September 1913.

9.2. 'I am out', he said, 'to save William Martin Murphy and those associated with him from eternal damnation.' 'I care for no man or men', Mr Larkin went on. 'I have got a divine mission, I believe, to make men and women discontented. I am out to do it, and no Murphy nor [Lord] Aberdeen, nor other creatures of that type can stop me carrying on the work I was born for. Some men will say, you should not start to arouse men's minds until they get Home Rule. Home Rule! You have got it in England, and you are making a damn bad job of it. A question of Home Rule?

9.3 No. It is an economic question – a bread-and-butter question. Our whole Trade Union movement is absolutely rotten. If we were the men we think we are, the employing classes would be wiped out in an hour and we should become the employing class'. Another characteristic outburst was in a passage dealing with the attitude of the Church towards labour questions. 'I knelt down', he said, 'in Sligo Cathedral at the feet of a bishop, when he said "Anti-Christ is come to town: it is Larkin". Thank God, for his soul's sake and my own, before he died he understood the problem better. I do not blame him. Better men than I in Ireland have been cursed. I prefer to go to the seventh pit of Dante than to go to heaven with William Martin Murphy. Hell has no terrors for me. I have lived there. Thirty-six years of hunger and poverty have been my portion. The mother who bore me had to starve and work, and my father had to fight for a living. I knew what it was to work when

I was nine years old. They cannot terrify me with hell. Better to be in hell with Dante and Davitt than to be in heaven with Carson and Murphy, not forgetting our good friend the Earl of Aberdeen'.

10. Larkin's speech to the Askwith Inquiry, 4 October 1913

10.1. *Introduction.* Larkin presented the workers' case at the Askwith Commission of Inquiry into the Lockout on 4 October 1913. His address focused on the extreme hardships of the working classes because of miserly wages and desperate working conditions. In response to employers' claims that they were entitled to control their workers as they saw fit, Larkin replied that they had no right to abuse their authority. He accuses them of being interested only in profit, and of denying workers their basic human rights. Like many workers, he too had known hunger and poverty. He was no atheist, as priests had proclaimed from their altars. If anyone made people doubt God, and if anyone acted against God he says, it was not he, but the employers who treated people so shamefully. He eloquently defends his own integrity. SOURCE: *Irish Times*, 6 October 1913.

10.2. I hope you will bear with me in putting before you as plainly as possible a reply somewhat of a personal character, but which I think will cover the matters dealt with during the last few days. The first point I want to make is that the employers in this city, and throughout Ireland generally, have put forward a claim that they have a right to deal with their own; that they have a right to use and exploit individuals as they please; that they have duties which they limit, and they have responsibilities which they also limit, in their operation. They take to themselves that they have all the rights that are given to men and to societies of men, but they deny the right of the men to claim that they also have a substantial claim on the share of the produce they produce, and they further say that they want no third party interference.

10.3. They want to deal with their workingmen individually. They say that they are men of such paramount intelligence and so able in their organising ability as captains of industry, who can always carry on their business in their own way, and they deny the right of the men and women who work for them to combine and try to assist one another in trying to improve their conditions of life. ...

10.4. There must be fair play between man and man. There are rights on both sides, but these men opposite assume to themselves certain privileges, and they deny to the workingmen, who make their wealth and keep them in affluence, their rights.

10.5. Shakespeare it was, who said that: 'He who holds the means whereby I live, holds my life and controls me'. That is not the exact quotation, but I can give it. 'You take my house when you do take the prop that doth sustain my house, you take my life, when you doth take the means whereby I live'.

10.6. It means that the men who hold the means of life control our lives, and, because we workingmen have tried to get some measure of justice, some measure of betterment, they deny the right of the human being to associate with his fellow. Why, the very law of nature was mutual co-operation. Man must be associated with his fellows. The employers were not able to make their own case. Let him help them. They had had all the technique and the craftsmanship, but they have not been able to put their case in proper focus. What was the position of affairs in connection with life in industrial Ireland? Let them take the statement made by their own apologist. Take Dr Cameron's statement that there are 21,000 families – four and a half persons to a family – living in single rooms. Who are responsible?

10.7. The gentlemen opposite would have to accept the responsibility. Of course they must. They said they control the means of life; then the responsibility rests upon them. Twenty-one thousand people multiplied by five, over 100,000 people huddled together in the putrid slums of Dublin, five in a room in cubic space less than 1,000 feet, though the law lays it down that every human being should have 300 cubic feet.

10.8. We are determined that this shall no longer go on; we are determined the system shall stop; we are determined that Christ will not be crucified in Dublin by these men. Mr Waldron was good enough to say yesterday that Larkin had done what was right and just in getting facilities for the workers on the Canal to be enabled to get to Mass on Sundays. Let them go further with the argument and add a little more to the picture. ...

10.9. The argument was used that Larkin came from Liverpool. Well, if that was so, it was time that someone came from some place in order to teach those whom he addressed their responsibilities. What about the gentlemen on the other side? Were they to be asked to produce their birth certificates? Could they all speak as men who represented the Irish race? These men had no feeling of respect for the Dublin workman ... The only purpose and desire they had was to grind out wealth from the poor men, their wives and children.

10.10. Let people who desire to know the truth go to the factories and see the maimed girls, the weak and sickly whose eyes are being put out and their bodies scarred and their souls seared and when they were no longer able to be useful enough to gain their £1 a week, or whatever wage they earned, were thrown into the human scrap heap. These things were to be found in their midst, and yet the people who caused these conditions of wretchedness described workingmen as loafers.

10.11. True it was that Mr Murphy said that the Dublin workman was a decent man; but he would deny the right of the Dublin workmen to work in their city on terms of decency, on the streets or on the quays. He would deny their right to develop their activities and to receive proper and living wages. He was an instrument to bring down the wages. The souls of these men were steeped in the grime of profit-making.

This dispute would do one thing and had already done something in that directions – it would arouse the social conscience. It had done what every man would thank God for. ...

10.12. ... Mr Murphy was absolutely unable to state his own case. He admitted he had no knowledge of the details of his own business. He admitted he had no strikes at any moment during his connection with industry concerns, but had proved that his life had been one continuous struggle against the working classes. I give him credit, too, that in a great many cases he came out on top, because he had never been faced by a man who was able to deal with him; he had never been faced by a social conscience such as now existed, and according to which the working classes could combine to alter the present conditions of labour.

10.13. There was such a thing as human thought, and no one had killed it yet, not even the theologians or the politicians, and Mr Murphy might try to realise during the later hours of his life, before 'he passed hence' that those who gave him affluence and wealth deserved something to encourage them from the lower plane on which they existed to a higher plane on which they might live. He had been an able man, backed up by able men; he was backed up at that inquiry by one of the ablest counsel at the Bar, who used his power relentlessly. That could be seen up to a certain point, but there must be a break. There was a point where all that abuse would meet with its own result, and that result would be that the power wielded by such men would be smashed, and deservedly smashed. ...

10.14. I am concerned in something greater, something better, and something holier – a mutual relation between those carrying on industry in Ireland. ...

10.15. These men with their limited intelligence cannot see that. I cannot help that. I cannot compel them to look at the thing from my point of view. Surely they have a right to realise the work in which I am engaged. It is not to our interest to have men locked-out or on strike. We don't get double wages. They say 'Larkin is making £8 a week', and has made more than £18 a week, but he never got it unfortunately.

10.16. I have lived among the working classes all my life. I have starved because men denied me food. I worked very hard at a very early age. I had no opportunities like the men opposite, but whatever opportunities I got I have availed of them.

10.17. I am called an ant-Christ and an atheist. If I were an atheist I would not deny it. I am a Socialist and have always claimed to be a Socialist. ...

10.18. Can anyone say one word against me as a man? Can they make any disparagement of my character? Have I lessened the standard of life? Have I demoralised anyone? Is there anything in my private life or my public life of which I should feel ashamed? These men denounced me from the pulpit, and say I am making £18 a week and that I have a mansion in Dublin. The men who are described as Larkin's dupes are asked to go back. All this is done two thousand years after Christ appeared in Galilee. Why, these men are making people atheists – they are making them godless. But we are going to stop that.

10.19. When the position of the workers in Dublin was taken into consideration, was it any wonder that there was necessity for a Larkin to arise, and if there was one thing more than another in my life of which I will always be proud it was the part I have taken in rescuing the workers of Dublin from the brutalising and degrading conditions under which they laboured.

10.20. We are out to break down racial and sectarian barriers. My suggestion to the employers is that if they want peace we are prepared to meet them, but if they want war, then war they will have.

11. George Russell condemns the employers

11.1. *Introduction.* George William Russell (Æ) (1867–1935), poet, painter, writer and economist, defended the right of workers to join unions, and criticised employers' opposition. He was joined by other prominent intellectuals such as Patrick Pearse, Pádraic Colum, George Bernard Shaw, and William Butler Yeats. Russell, an influential figure in the co-operative movement, and editor of the *Irish Homestead*, was deeply committed to improving the lives of small farmers, and agricultural labourers. During the Lockout, he made many passionate appeals to the public to address the problem of poverty, and exploitation in Dublin. He wrote this open letter to 'the Masters of Dublin' on 6 October 1913, in which he severely condemned the actions of employers in the Lockout. He advised them strongly to reach a compromise with the workers to safeguard both their interests, and for the sake of justice, and humanity. SOURCE: *Irish Times*, 7 October 1913.

11.2. Sirs, I address this warning to you, the aristocracy of industry in this city, because, like all aristocracies, you tend to grow blind in long authority, and to be unaware that you and your class and its every action are being considered and judged day by day by those who have power to shake or overturn the whole social order, and whose restlessness in poverty today is making our industrial civilisation stir like a quaking bog. You do not seem to realise that your assumption that you are answerable to yourselves alone for your actions in the industries you control is one that becomes less and less tolerable in a world so crowded with necessitous life. Some of you have helped Irish farmers to upset a landed aristocracy in this island, an aristocracy richer and more powerful in its sphere than you are in yours, with it roots deep in history. They too, as a class, though not all of them, were scornful or neglectful of the workers in the industry by which they profited; and to many who knew them in their pride of place and thought them all-powerful they are already becoming a memory, the good disappearing, together with the bad. If they had done their duty by those from whose labours came their wealth they might have continued unquestioned in power and prestige for centuries to come. The relation of landlord and tenant is not an ideal one, but any relations in a social order will endure if there is infused into them some of that spirit of human sympathy, which qualifies life for immortality. Despotisms endure while they are benevolent, and aristocracies, *noblesse oblige* ['with wealth, power and prestige come responsibilities'] is not a phrase to be referred to with a cynical smile. Even an oligarchy might be permanent if the spirit of human kindness, which harmonises all things otherwise incompatible, is present.

11.3. You do not seem to read history, so as to learn its lessons. That you are an uncultivated class was obvious from recent utterances of some of you upon art. That you are incompetent men in the sphere in which you arrogate imperial powers is certain, because for many years, long before the present uprising of labour, your enterprises have been dwindling in the regard of investors, and this while you have carried them on in the cheapest labour market in these islands, with a labour reserve always hungry and ready to accept any pittance. You are bad citizens, for we rarely, if ever, hear of the wealthy among you endowing your city with munificent gifts, which it is the pride of merchant princes in other cities to offer, and Irishmen not of your city who offer to supply the wants left by your lack of generosity are met with derision and abuse. Those who have economic power have civic power also, yet you have not used the power that was yours to right what was wrong in the evil administration of this city. You have allowed the poor to be herded together so that one thinks of certain places in Dublin as of a pestilence. There are 20,000 rooms, in each of which are entire families, and sometimes more, where no function of the body can be concealed ... The obvious duty of you in regard to these things you might have left undone ... but your collective and conscious action as a class in the present labour dispute has revealed you to the world in so malign an aspect that the mirror must be held up to you, so that you may see yourself as every humane person sees you.

11.4. The conception of yourselves as altogether virtuous and wronged is, I assure you, not at all the one which onlookers hold of you. No doubt, you have rights on your side. No doubt, some of you suffered without just cause. But nothing which has been done to you cries aloud to Heaven for condemnation as your own actions. Let me show you how it seems to those who have followed critically the dispute, trying to weigh in a balance the rights and wrongs. You were within the rights society allows you when you locked out your men and insisted on the fixing of some principle to adjust your future relations with labour when the policy of labour made it impossible for some of you to carry on your enterprises. Labour desired the fixing of some such principle as much as you did. But, having once decided on such a step, knowing how many thousands of men, women, and children, nearly one third of the population of this city, would be affected, you should not have let one day pass without unremitting endeavours to find a solution of the problem.

11.5. What did you do? The representatives of labour unions in Great Britain met you, and you made of them a preposterous, an impossible demand, and, because they would not accede to it you closed the Conference: you refused to meet them further: you assumed that no other guarantees than those you asked were possible, and you determined deliberately, in cold anger, to starve out one third of the population of the city, to break the manhood of the men by the sight of the suffering of their wives and the hunger of their children. We read in the Dark Ages of the rack and thumb screw. But these iniquities were hidden and concealed from the knowledge of men in dungeons and torture chambers. Even in the Dark Ages, humanity could not endure the sight of such suffering, and it learnt of such misuse of power by slow degrees, through rumour, and when it was certain it razed its Bastilles to their foundations. It remained for the twentieth century and the capital city of Ireland to see an oligarchy of four hundred masters deciding openly upon starving one hundred thousand people, and refusing to consider any solution except that fixed by their pride. You, masters, asked men to do that which masters of labour in any other city in these islands had not dared to do. You insolently demanded of those men who were members of a trade union that they should resign from that union; and from those who were not members, you insisted on a vow that they would never join it.

11.6. Your insolence and ignorance of the rights conceded to workers universally in the modern world were incredible, and as great as your inhumanity. If you had between you collectively a portion of human soul as large as a threepenny bit, you would have sat night and day with the representatives of labour, trying this or that solution of the trouble, mindful of the women and children, who at least were innocent of wrong against you. But no! You reminded labour you could always have your three square meals a day while it went hungry. You went into conference again with representatives of the State, because, dull as you are, you knew public opinion would not stand your holding out. You chose as your spokesman the bitterest tongue that ever wagged in this island, and then, when an award was made by men who have an experience in industrial matters a thousand times transcending yours, who have settled disputes in industries so great that the sum of your petty enterprises would not equal them, you withdrew again, and will not agree to accept their solution, and fall back again on your devilish policy of starvation. Cry aloud to heaven for new souls. The souls you have got cast upon the screens of publicity appear like the horrid and writhing creatures enlarged from the insect world, and revealed to us by the cinematographer.

11.7. You may succeed in your policy and ensure your own damnation by your victory. The men whose manhood you have broken will loathe you, and will always be brooding and scheming to strike a fresh blow. The children will be taught to curse you. The infant being moulded in the womb will have breathed into its starved body the vitality of hate. It is not they – it is you who are the blind Samsons pulling down the pillars of the social order. You are sounding the death knell of autocracy in industry. There was autocracy in political life, and it was superseded by democracy. So surely will democratic power wrest from you the control of industry. The fate of you, the aristocracy of industry, will be as the fate of the aristocracy of land if you do not now show that you have some humanity still among you. Humanity abhors, above all things, a vacuum in itself, and your class will be cut off from humanity as the surgeon cuts the cancer and alien growth from the body. Be warned ere it is too late.

12. 'Save the Dublin kiddies' campaign

I

12.1. *Introduction.* Labour activists, philanthropists and middle-class sympathisers, were very concerned about the plight of strikers and their families. At a meeting in London, 10 October 1913, Dora Montefiore, an English socialist and feminist, suggested that the children of strikers who were worst affected should be sent to England for the duration of the strike. Larkin supported her idea, and within a week, 300 workers in England and Scotland had offered assistance. Upon arrival in Ireland on Sunday 19 October, Montefiore and other labour activists outlined their plans at a packed meeting in Liberty Hall. Many women at the meeting put forward their children's names for the scheme. The first group of children (six) left for London the next day. On 20 October 1913, the Archbishop of Dublin, Dr William Walsh, wrote a public letter condemning the plan, which, he believed, might endanger the faith of Catholic children. He appealed for an end to the strike, and argued that this would be the best possible way to help the children. SOURCE: *Irish Times*, 21 October 1913.

> **12.2.** Sir, I have read with nothing short of consternation in some of our evening newspapers that a movement is on foot, and has already made some progress, to induce the wives of the workingmen who are now unemployed, by reason of the present deplorable industrial deadlock in Dublin, to hand over their children to be cared for in England by persons of whom they, of course, can have no knowledge whatever.

> **12.3.** The Dublin women now subjected to this cruel temptation to part with their helpless offspring are, in the majority of cases, Catholics. Have they abandoned their faith? Surely not. Well, if they have not, they should need no words of mine to remind them of the plain duty of every Catholic mother in such a case. I can only put it to them that they can be no longer held worthy of the name of Catholic mothers if they so far forget that duty as to send away their children to be cared for in a strange land, without security of any kind that those to whom the poor children are to be handed over are Catholics, or, indeed, are persons of any faith at all.

12.4. … With all my desire to see an end of the strike, I make no difficulty in saying in public, as I have been freely saying in private, that I think the employers have been to some extent justified in hesitating to enter into an agreement for the removal of the present deadlock until some guarantee was forthcoming that any agreement now entered upon would be faithfully kept. For my part, I should like to see guarantees given at both sides.

12.5. Now what is our present position? I have just read a newspaper report of an interview given by one of the leading representatives of the interests of labour, Mr Gosling, in which the following occurs: – 'On the question of guarantees, so insisted on by the employers, he said, if the parties would come together, ample guarantees would be forthcoming to ensure the carrying out of agreements, and the support of English trade unionism and public sympathy would depend upon this'. May I venture to ask why, in the face of this explicit statement, the parties should not come together, and see whether something cannot be done to put an end to a conflict that is plainly disastrous to the interests of both?

II

12.6. *Introduction.* Archbishop Walsh's opposition to the scheme to send striker's children to England caused great controversy in Dublin. Although Mrs Montefiore and other labour leaders argued that the children would be sent only to families that had been approved, many people were influenced by Walsh's opinion and condemned the scheme. Large crowds of protesters, encouraged by Catholic priests, assembled at train stations and ports to prevent the children from being sent to 'the homes of Atheists and Socialists'. Thousands of people marched through the city, singing hymns and shouting praise for the Pope, the Archbishop and the priests, to celebrate their success in stopping the scheme. Labour supporters, in return, heckled the marchers and cheered for Larkin. Those who opposed the scheme believed that it would harm Catholic children's faith because it had been organised by socialists and Protestants. The journalist Arnold Wright was most critical of Larkin and the Dublin workers. He describes how events unfolded at the end of October 1913. SOURCE: Arnold Wright, *Disturbed Dublin: the story of the great strike of 1913–14 with a description of the industries of the Irish capital* (London, 1914), pp 221–5.

12.7. The deportation scheme met with organised resistance from a large body of people who were genuinely and, on the whole, not unnaturally alarmed at this strange new development of Larkinism. On October 22, the day after the appearance of Archbishop Walsh's letter, arrangements were in progress for the despatch of a contingent of about fifty children to follow in the wake of parties that had already been sent forward on two previous days. The youngsters were being washed, preparatory to the voyage, at the Corporation Baths, under the supervision of Mrs Montefiore and the other ladies associated with her, when a body of priests appeared on the scene prepared to contest with the strangers for the possession of their charges.

12.8. Mrs Montefiore declined to be moved from her purpose by the representations made to her by the clerics, but she could not prevent them from taking out of her custody a considerable number of the children. Undaunted by this rebuff, the intrepid lady sent off the remnant of the band – nineteen in number – to Kingstown for embarkation on the outgoing mail steamer. The priests, following in the track of the little voyagers, captured ten of the party before the landing stage was reached, and ultimately induced the remaining nine, after they had gone on board, to come ashore. ...

12.9. The ecclesiastical victory stung Mr Larkin to the quick. The same evening, speaking from his forum at Liberty Hall, he made a bellicose speech assailing the priests in strong terms. He denounced the clergymen who had been actively concerned in preventing the deportation of Mrs Montefiore's charges as 'a disgrace to their cloth'. He said:

12.10. 'Some of the priests ... were afraid of these children going to England for a short stay; they were fearful lest their faith would be interfered with; but the religion which could not stand a fortnight's holiday in England had not very much bottom or very much support behind it. Of course he knew that many of these clergy had shares in the Tramway Company, but while soul-destroying agencies were at work in Dublin for many years there was no protest made against them ... Those clergymen and the employers ... had lighted a fire which it would take more than an hour to extinguish'.

12.11. These insulting words, applied to a class held in the highest respect by the great mass of the people of Dublin, had the effect of stimulating the opposition to the deportation scheme to an extraordinary extent.

12.12. It was no longer a question of priests against Liberty Hall, but of a concerted movement of the whole of the Catholic forces in Dublin against what they regarded as an insidious Socialist attack on the faith. On Thursday, October 23, as the hour approached for the departure of the cross-Channel steamers, immense crowds gathered about the quays at North Wall with the declared intention of preventing the embarkation of any more children. A large number of priests were conspicuous in the throng and took an active part in directing what was in reality a picketing of ships. ...

12.13. Eventually, after the last boat had cast off from the wharf and there was no further possibility of deporting children that night, the great crowd, now numbering many thousands, formed in processional order and marched along the quays bareheaded, singing 'Faith of our Fathers', 'Hail, glorious St. Patrick', and other sacred melodies. Thus they proceeded until they reached College Green, where a halt was called and the assembled multitude were addressed by Father Farrell of Donnybrook, a priest who had taken a conspicuous part in the evening's operations. He said 'Remember ... that this great demonstration was unorganised and unprepared. It shows the love you have for the Catholic children of this city. It is a magnificent protest against the proselytising of our children in the Socialistic homes of England'. The crowd cheered these sentiments with enthusiasm, and then dispersed to their homes with cries of 'Away with the Socialists', and 'Down with Larkin'.

12.14. By general consent it was one of the most remarkable and significant uprisings of Catholics that Dublin had witnessed for many a long day. Apart from the weight of the popular protest, a heavy blow had been dealt at the deportation movement by the institution of criminal proceedings, associated with charges of abduction against Mrs Montefiore and Mrs Rand, an American lady who had been prominently identified with the scheme for the removal of the children. Nevertheless, the Larkinites declined to abandon their project without a further struggle.

12.15. On Friday, October 24, an attempt was made under the direction of Mr Larkin's sister, Miss Delia Larkin, to despatch a party of juveniles to Belfast by rail. They were to have travelled by the six o'clock train in the evening from Amiens Street Station, and their tickets had actually been taken for the journey, when a number of priests, with an escort of youths, appeared upon the scene with the evident determination of preventing the execution of the plan. Miss Larkin stood her ground for a time, but the persistency of the clerics, reinforced by the action of a hostile crowd who blocked the approach to the train, compelled her eventually to retrace her steps to Liberty Hall with her charges.

12.16. Flushed with their fresh victory over the forces of Larkinism, the priests and the other demonstrators marched down to the quays to picket the evening boats. There was, however, no further attempt made to get the children out of the country. After the departure of the last boat there was a repetition of the demonstration of the previous evening. A huge procession, numbering in its ranks thousands of earnest sons of the Church, marched off towards O'Connell Bridge, singing appropriate hymns.

III

12.17. *Introduction.* The plan to send the children of strikers to England was abandoned by the end of September 1913, because public opinion, including influential church leaders, was so strongly against it. Connolly addressed those who supported and those who condemned the plan, and tried to explain the motives of both groups. He believed that those who denounced the scheme were misguided, He urged them to act now to end the strike, and thereby remove the need for such measures. SOURCE: James Connolly, 'The children, the Irish Transport and General Workers' Union and the Archbishop', *Forward,*

1 November 1913: cited in Desmond Ryan (ed.), *Socialism and nationalism: a selection from the writings of James Connolly* (2 vols, Dublin, 1987), ii, pp 305–9.

12.18. Our good friend the *Daily Citizen*, official organ of the British Labour movement, describes the scenes attendant upon the intended departure of some Dublin children to Great Britain, under the auspices of a committee organised there for the purpose of taking care of children of the locked out workers, as 'the most extraordinary scene in this most extraordinary industrial conflict in this country'. We do not wonder at our British friends being surprised, nor at them being horrified, nor at them being scandalised and shocked at the treatment to which they have been subjected, and the vile aspersions cast upon their motives. For ourselves we anticipated it all, and have never been enthusiastic towards the scheme.

12.19. We realised that their children are about all the workers of Dublin have left to comfort them, that amidst the squalor and wretchedness of their surroundings the love of their little ones shines like a star of redemption, and that to part with their dear ones would be like wrenching their hearts asunder. We realised, further, what it is very difficult to make even the most friendly of the British realise, that Great Britain is still an alien country to Ireland, and that even the splendid comradeship and substantial aid of today can hardly expect to obliterate immediately the evil results upon our intercourse of long generations of oppression during the period when class rule stood in Ireland for Great Britain, and symbolised all Britain's relations with Ireland. And we also knew that some of the darkest memories of Ireland were associated with British attempts to stab the heart of Ireland through systematic abduction of the bodies and corruption of the minds of Irish children.

12.20. Therefore we felt instinctively that the well-meant move of Mrs Montefiore and her colleagues would arouse in Ireland hostilities and suspicions they could not conceive of, and would not believe were we to attempt the task of making the matter clear. Hence, while placing no obstacle in the way of its fulfilment, and feeling deeply a sense of gratitude towards the noble British men and women of our class who have so unreservedly thrown open their homes for the purpose of sheltering our stricken little ones, we have nevertheless felt that the scheme was bound to be taken advantage of to our detriment by all the hostile elements who surround us, but usually fear to reveal their hostility. We know that people 'willing to wound, and yet afraid to strike', swarm everywhere on the flanks of the labour movement in Ireland, and we also know that the men and women in charge of that labour movement know how to keep these people disarmed and ineffective; but that the men and women in the British labour movement have none of that knowledge of our enemies nor of our methods for neutralising their hostility.

12.21. But when we have said this we have said all that our own position demands. Having said it, we must protest in the name of the whole labour movement of this country against the foul and libellous accusations brought against the noble-minded ladies who have been in charge of the scheme. One scoundrel in clerical garb is said to have stated on Wednesday that the children were being 'brought to England by trickery, fraud and corruption for proselytising purposes'. Nothing more venomous and unfounded was ever spewed out of a lying mouth in Ireland since the *seoinín* [one who apes English ways] clergy at the bidding of an English politician hounded Parnell to his grave. Mrs Montefiore had given His Grace Archbishop Walsh her assurance that wherever the children went, the local Roman Catholic clergy would be given their names and addresses, and requested to take charge of them, and see that they attended to their duties as Catholic children. His Grace felt that, despite that assurance, and without doubting it in the least, there would still be dangers. But not for one moment did he impugn the motives of the ladies in question. His instincts as a gentleman, and his own high sense of honour forbade. But what these instincts and that honour forbade His Grace to do was unblushingly done on Wednesday by a cleric destitute of both. We leave the gentleman in question to be dealt with by His Grace, who will assuredly see that in his diocese the garb of a priest is not made a shield for the acts and language of a scoundrel.

12.22. The utterances of His Grace the Archbishop on the question at issue deserve and no doubt will receive, the earnest consideration of every thoughtful man and woman in Ireland. Nobody wants to send the children away – the Irish Transport and General Workers' Union least of all desires such a sacrifice. But neither do we wish the children to starve. We love the children of Ireland, we are sacrificing our own ease and comfort in order that the future of these children may be sweeter and happier than the lot of their fathers and mothers. We know that progress cannot be made without sacrifice, and we do not shrink from the sacrifice involved in fighting for freedom now in order that future generations may build upon the results of our toil. But the master class of Dublin calmly and coldbloodedly calculate upon using the sufferings of the children to weaken the resistance of the parents. They wish to place us upon the horns of a dilemma. Either the parents should resist, and then the children will starve, or the parents will surrender, and the children will grow up in slavery, and live to despise the parents who bequeathed to them such an evil heritage.

12.23. Your Grace, we are resolved to fight Death itself – the death some of us have already suffered, the death your humble servant has in the same cause looked in the face without flinching – it would be preferable to surrendering the Dublin workers again to the hell of slavery out of which they are emerging. Your Grace, we will fight! But if Your Grace is as solicitous about the poor bodies of those children as we know you to be about their souls, or even if you are but one tenth part as solicitous, may we suggest to you or your laymen that your duty is plain. See to it that the force of public opinion, that the power of the press, that all the engines at your command are brought to bear upon the inhuman monsters who control the means of employment in Dublin to make them realise their duties to the rest of the community. We have done our part, we have told the Lord Mayor, we have told Sir George Askwith, we have told the Dublin Industrial Peace Committee, that we are ready to negotiate. All of these admit that our position is reasonable, all of them have been spat upon with scorn by the employers, and all of them shrink in cowardice from taking the next logical step and concentrating public feeling and public financial support in favour of the workers, the only party to the dispute that all along has declared its readiness to bow to public opinion.

12.24. These people, we repeat, have shrunk in cowardice from their manifest duty. Will you undertake it? It is your duty equally with theirs. To you we repeat our offer: we are willing to accept the mediation of any party whose functions will be strictly limited to bringing the two parties together in a conference to thrash out their differences. We are prepared to meet the representatives of all the employers, or meet any individual employer, as we have done satisfactorily in many cases already. This is our offer to you. And we repeat to you what we have said to the others: 'If the employers reject your offer of mediation and still declare their contempt for any public opinion they cannot rig in advance, then it is your manifest duty to organise public support for the workers to defeat their soulless employers'.

12.25. We have read Your Grace's character in vain if you shrink from that task, or fail in that duty. The plight of the children, and your concern for them should be your warrant for acting, if any warrant other than your high position was needed. Meanwhile, come weal or woe, in good repute or evil, we are prepared to fight, because we feel that this fight is a fight for the future, a brighter future for: – 'The children who swarm and die, In loathsome dens where despair is king; Like blackened buds of a frosty spring that wither, sunless, remote they lie, From the hour that quickens each soul and whilst vice and hunger and pestilence – breastpoisoned nurses – the babes drain dry'.

13. James Connolly urges strikers to stand their ground

I

13.1. *Introduction.* Connolly was imprisoned for riotous conduct during the strike. He met many people who had been jailed for membership of the Irish Transport and General Workers' Union. He urged the unions to put all their energy and money into winning the strike to protect the rights of each individual. He hoped that all-out industrial conflict would change the nature of politics by dividing society into workers and employers, and in the event of a workers' victory, lay the foundation for a reorganisation of society along socialist lines. SOURCE: Cited in Desmond Ryan (ed.), *Socialism and nationalism: a selection from the writings of James Connolly* (2 vols, Dublin, 1987), ii, pp 300–4.

13.2. To the readers of *Forward* possibly some sort of apology is due for the non-appearance of my notes for the past few weeks, but I am sure that they quite well understand that I was, so to speak, otherwise engaged. On the day I generally write my little screed, I was engaged on the 31st of August in learning how to walk around in a ring with about forty other unfortunates kept six paces apart, and yet slip in a word or two to the poor devil in front of or behind me without being noticed by the watchful prison warders. The first question I asked was generally 'say, what are you in for?'

13.3. Then the rest of the conversation ran thus:
'For throwing stones at the police'.
'Well, I hope you did throw them and hit'.
'No, by God, that's the worst of it. I was pulled coming out of my own house'.
'Pulled' is the Dublin word for arrested. It was somewhat mortifying to me to know that I was the only person apparently in prison who had really committed the crime for which I was arrested. It gave me a sort of feeling that I was lowering the moral tone of the prison by coming amongst such a crowd of blameless citizens.
But the concluding part of our colloquy was a little more encouraging. It usually finished in this way:
'Are you in the Irish Transport and General Workers' Union?'
'Of course I am'.
'Good. Well if they filled all the prisons in Ireland they can't beat us, my boy'.
'No, thank God, they can't; we'll fight all the better when we get out'.

13.4. And there you have the true spirit. Baton charges, prison cells, untimely death and acute starvation – all were faced without a murmur, and in face of them all, the brave Dublin workers never lost faith in their ultimate triumph, never doubted but that their organisation would emerge victorious from the struggle. This is the great fact that many of our critics amongst the British labour leaders seem to lose sight of. The Dublin fight is more than a trade union fight; it is a great class struggle, and recognised as such by all sides. We in Ireland feel that to doubt our victory would be to lose faith in the destiny of our class. I heard of one case where a labourer was asked to sign the agreement forswearing the Irish Transport and General Workers' Union, and he told his employer, a small capitalist builder, that he refused to sign. The employer, knowing the man's circumstances, reminded him that he had a wife and six children who would be starving within a week. The reply of this humble labourer rose to the heights of sublimity.

13.5. 'It is true, sir', he said, 'they will starve; but I would rather see them go out one by one in their coffins than that I should disgrace them by signing that'.

13.6. … And then our friends write deprecatingly to the British press of the 'dislocation of trade' involved in sympathetic strikes, of the 'perpetual conflicts' in which they would involve great trade unions. To those arguments, if we can call them such, our answer is sufficient. It is this: If the capitalist class knew that any outrages upon a worker, any attack upon labour, would result in a prompt dislocation of trade, perhaps national in its extent; that the unions were prepared to spend their last copper if necessary rather than permit a brother or sister to be injured, then the knowledge would not only ensure a long cessation from industrial skirmishing such as the unions are harassed by today, it would not only ensure peace to the unions, but what is of vastly more importance, it would ensure to the individual worker a peace from slave-driving and harassing at his work such as the largest unions are apparently unable to guarantee under present methods.

13.7. ... As we believe that in the socialist society of the future the entire resources of the nation must stand behind every individual, guaranteeing him against want, so today our unions must be prepared to fight with all their resources to safeguard the rights of every individual member.

13.8. The adoption of such a principle, followed by a few years of fighting on such lines to convince the world of our earnestness, would not only transform the industrial arena, but would revolutionise politics. Each side would necessarily seek to grasp the power of the state to reinforce its position, and politics would thus become what they ought to be, a reflex of the industrial battle, and lose the power to masquerade as a neutral power detached from economic passions or motives.

II

13.9. *Introduction.* On 7 December 1913, representatives of workers, British Unions and a British MP presented proposals for ending the strike to the employers: that strikers should be treated fairly and reinstated in their jobs. These terms were rejected by the employers. Connolly condemns employers for violating the basic rules of morality that held society together, that is, that every individual be treated with respect. He claims that public opinion, popular and elite, in Ireland and abroad, agreed with him in this respect, and he calls on employers to end their lockout of ITGWU workers. SOURCE: James Connolly, 'To the working class of Dublin', *Irish Worker*, 13 December 1913.

> **13.10.** Once again the Employers of Dublin have received an offer, the acceptance of which would have enabled them to restore themselves in the estimation of the civilised world and to appear as normal human beings with human hearts and consciences. And once again they have refused to respond and to recognise the common humanity of the work people. On Sunday morning, December 7th, the representatives of Labour met in Conference with the Masters in the Shelbourne Hotel, Dublin, and after agreeing upon a proposal to set up a Conciliation Board to be established by 7th March, 1914, and to suspend all strikes and sympathetic strikes until that date, the following proposal was laid before the masters, it being explained

that its acceptance by the employers was a necessary condition of our final acceptance of the proposal just set forth: – 'The employers undertake that there will be no victimisation, and that employment will be found for all workers within a period of one month from the date of settlement'.

13.11. This Clause in the proposed settlement was drafted by Mr Arthur Henderson, MP, and agreed to by the representatives of the Joint Labour Board from Great Britain along with delegates of the local Lockout Committee, but was absolutely rejected by the employers. In its place they offered a clause in which they stated that 'they will take on as many of their former employees as they can find room for', and 'will make a bonafide effort to find employment for as many as possible'. After sending this outrageous proposal back to them twice with a declaration that we still stood by the proposal drafted by Mr Henderson, MP, the Conference finally broke up on that point.

13.12. While there may be guileless people in this world who do not know the evil meaning of the threat conveyed in the Employers' Proposal, we are certain that in the ranks of the working class there are none so simple as not to know what these gentry mean when they tell us that 'they will take on as many of their former employees as they can find room for'. They were always of that mind, and we know that since the very beginning of this fight they were willing to take on as many as they could find room for, but that they had no room for members of the Irish Transport Workers' Union. That condition remains unaltered. We had heard outside that the ban upon our Union – the Employers' Agreement – had to be withdrawn, but neither in their presence by word of mouth, nor in Conference by typewritten or other document, was any such assurance given us. As far as we have any knowledge, that document still remains.

13.13. Remember that the Employers' Agreement is denounced by every enlightened public opinion in these islands; that it is denounced by the whole trade union world; by the public of Dublin; by the Press of Great Britain; by the report of Sir George Askwith; by the verdict of the Industrial Peace Committee; and remember that the men, women, and girls locked out are idle because they nobly refused to sign this degrading document, and then ask yourselves could we consent to abandon those heroic workers to the tender mercies of the men who had planned their degradation?

13.14. Could we consent to the victimisation of workers who refused to sign a document which everybody of common sense denounces as iniquitous? We could not! There may be somewhere trade union leaders who can regard with calmness the certain victimisation of a number of their rank and file, but, thank God, we are not of their number. We regard the rank and file fighters as the real heroes of this struggle, and we will never consent to their being sacrificed, not while there is a shot in our locker or a shred of our organisation together. We have no fear or doubt of our ultimate success in this fight, but if we had we would not consent to the sacrifice of those who had trusted us and honoured us by their trust. We would rather go down nobly fighting for our noble comrades than survive ignobly by consenting to their victimisation. Brothers and sisters, the fight must go on. And be it long or short the victory will be the victory of the rank and file.

Yours,

James Connolly,

Acting general sec.,

Liberty Hall.

14. In defence of the employers

14.1. *Introduction.* Arnold Wright, travelled to Dublin in the Spring of 1914 to collect information about the Lockout. He virulently denounced the leaders of the strike as dangerous revolutionaries, represented the strikers as a misguided mob, and strongly supported the employers' stance against Larkin, the ITGWU, and the workers. He argued that Dublin's employers were not responsible for poverty or for tenement slums. If anything, employers helped the poor by providing them with jobs. The employers faced bankruptcy unless they 'grappled successfully with the labour octopus which was squeezing the life-blood out of the city's commerce'. His final assessment of the Lockout is bleak. He represents the dispute as a fight between good and evil. SOURCE: Arnold Wright, *Disturbed Dublin: the story of the great strike of 1913–14 with a description of the industries of the Irish capital* (London, 1914), p. 87.

> **14.2.** It needs, perhaps, hardly to be urged here ... that the tenement-house evil in Dublin is not to be laid at the doors of the employers ... it has, according to the best authorities, been ameliorated by the growth of Dublin industries and not heightened by them as the critics of the employers have represented. Furthermore, it is the opinion of all who have given thought to the Dublin social question that the only certain means by which this tenement-house cancer can be eliminated from the body politic is by the extension of manufacturing and trading enterprise and the consequent widening of the avenues of employment ...

> **14.3.** Employers, by the inexorable logic of events, had been driven to the conviction that they would have to make a stand if they did not wish to see their businesses ruined. Like good Irishmen they accepted without flinching the responsibility which they knew to be theirs, and went into the fight with a courageous determination not to put down their arms until they had routed the enemy and reasserted their right to manage their own affairs without constant and irritating outside interference.

> **14.4.** The organised movement of revolt against Larkinism had its inception in a meeting of certain members of the Employers' Federation which was held on August 29 ...

From the outset there was no hesitation about the proper course to be taken to rescue the community from the anarchical tyranny from which it was so sorely suffering. It was this consistency of thought, combined with promptitude of action, that ensured the remarkable triumph which was ultimately achieved over the forces of disorder.

14.5. Mr Murphy never quarrelled with Mr Larkin, nor was the latter's vilification of him … the result of an attack made on the Labour leader by one of Mr Murphy's papers. He simply declined to allow himself to be made a sacrifice on the altar of Syndicalism, and took measures accordingly, most of which, no doubt, were extremely distasteful to Mr Larkin. In that sense he quarrelled with that gentleman; but then, so also did the four hundred or more employers associated with him. The simple fact is that there has rarely been an instance in which a great principle more dominated a movement than this Dublin rising against Larkinism. Mr Murphy headed it, greatly to his honour, but probably no man ever entered a fight of the kind with less feeling of personal animosity.

14.6. Misrepresentations of his character may have been necessary in order to cover up the ugly tracks of the monster which had been gnawing at the vitals of Dublin trade until the whole community were stung to revolt. …

14.7. So far from there being any desire to crush Trade Unionism in Dublin, all the leading men in the Employers' Federation are warm supporters of it, as they realise that in these days collective bargaining is an advantage to the employers as well as to the employed, and that the best interests of Capital as well as of Labour are involved in the maintenance of a well-balanced system under responsible management. What they undoubtedly did intend to crush if they could was the anarchical system which found its embodiment in the Irish Transport and General Workers' Union. …

14.8. The incapacity revealed here for the realising true character of the forces that had been called into being in Dublin, is further strikingly shown in the unsparing condemnation of the document which the employers required their workpeople to sign as a condition of employment. 'Whatever may have been the intention of the employers', observe the Commissioners, 'this document imposes upon the signatories conditions which are contrary to individual liberty, and which no workman or body of workmen could reasonably be expected to accept'.

14.9. 'Contrary to individual liberty' is a very sweeping phrase to use in this connection. It is difficult to understand precisely what Sir George Askwith means by it. Is it his view that an employer must engage an employee without reference to his or her association with a particular organisation, however objectionable that organisation may be to him? Would it, for example, be 'contrary to individual liberty' if Mr Asquith [Liberal prime minister of Great Britain from 1908 to 1916] and the members of the Cabinet made it a condition of employment in the case of their domestic servants that they should not belong to the militant Suffragette organisations? Assuredly they would be well within their rights in enforcing a condition so necessary to the peaceful ordering of their lives, and if that is so, equally are the Dublin employers entitled to say that they will engage no one who belongs to an organisation which has shown itself capable of grievous wrongdoing. …

14.10. An exceptionally outrageous method of attack had to be met by an exceptionally direct style of defence. The conditions of the pledge exacted by the employers were not nearly so 'contrary to individual liberty' as the iniquitous system of moral intimidation and organised ruffianism that the employers were by their action seeking to break down …

14.11. The rise and decline of Larkinism in Dublin constitutes one of the most extraordinary chapters in the history of modern industrial conflict. It is a phenomenon which deserves to be studied carefully by every sociologist who wishes to take accurate note of the development of modern democratic thought.

14.12. The extraordinary personality of the leader of the movement, the amazing audacity of his plans, and the strangely powerful influence he exercised over the working population of Dublin and over many outside that class, all gave to the recent labour struggle in Dublin an interest peculiarly its own.

14.13. Though outwardly invested with the attributes of an industrial conflict, the movement stands quite outside the ordinary category of labour disturbances. It was in essence a revolutionary rising, one in which the ultimate aims of its promoters involved the destruction of Society quite as much as the betterment of the wage conditions of the workers.

14.14. Red Republicanism, Anarchism, Syndicalism, and all the extremist forms of modern revolutionary thought found expression in the literature and oratory of the movement. Even anti-clericalism of a kind was not wanting to complete the syllabus of advanced ideas to which the rising gave such blatant expression. And this in Dublin, the centre and citadel of the most disciplined force of Roman Catholicism in Europe, and the home of perhaps the sincerest conservatism – using that phrase in its broadest sense – in the Empire!

14.15. Many strange things have happened by the banks of the Liffey, but none probably stranger than that open flouting of authority – ecclesiastical quite as much as civil – which marked the progress of Larkinism.

15. Workers' defence at the Askwith Inquiry, 4 October 1913

15.1. *Introduction.* Representatives of the workers' presented their case to the Commission of Inquiry in Dublin Castle on 4 October 1913. The Inquiry was set up by the government to investigate the origins of the dispute, to resolve the grievances of workers and employers, and to end the strike. In their submission to the Commission of Inquiry, ITGWU leaders, defended their actions, and emphasised that they wanted only justice for the working classes. They did not wish to trouble the police, the courts, the employers or the general public, but simply wanted to defend the rights of the poor and improve their working and living conditions. SOURCE: Cited in Desmond Ryan (ed.), *Socialism and nationalism: a selection from the writings of James Connolly* (2 vols, Dublin, 1987), ii, pp 292–9.

15.2. … we are banded together for the purpose of elevating our class, of organising that class for the conquest of its rights.

15.3. If the public, the forces of law and order and the capitalist class are willing to co-operate with us towards that end, well and good. If, on the other hand, the social and political forces represented by these three terms unite to defeat and subdue us and to thwart our just aspirations, as we believe they have done in this case, we shall still press onward believing that eventually victory, and the verdict of history will be on our side.

15.4. This mental attitude of ours explains our position in this dispute. The learned counsel for the employers says that for the past five years there have been more strikes than there have been since Dublin was a capital. Practically every responsible man in Dublin to-day admits that the social conditions of Dublin are a disgrace to civilisation.

15.5. Have these two sets of facts no relation? We believe that they stand to one another in the relations of cause and effect, the long period of stagnation in the labour ranks of Dublin was responsible for the growth in your midst of labour and housing conditions scarcely to be equalled outside Bombay or Constantinople.

15.6. Now that the Irish Transport and General Workers' Union and its officials have set out to arouse the people; now that fierce, and it may be sometimes reckless, fighting has inspired the suffering masses with a belief in their own ability to achieve some kind of emancipation; now, in short, that the luxury, comfort, and even the security of the propertied classes are menaced, we see the quickening of a faint sense of social conscience in Dublin. But until aroused by the shock of industrial war, the propertied classes of Dublin have well deserved their unenviable notoriety, for, like the typical Irish landlords of the past, 'enforcing their rights with a rod of iron and renouncing their duties with a front of brass'.

15.7. They tell us that they recognise trade unions. For answer we say that when they did so, it was wherever the necessity of a long apprenticeship made it difficult to replace a worker if he went on strike, but whenever no such apprenticeship existed to protect the worker the Dublin employers made fierce and relentless war upon trade unions amongst the unskilled labourers.

15.8. Messrs Tedcastle and M'Cormack is an instance among shipping firms. The Tramway Company has seen at least two attempts to organise its men. It fought and crushed the attempts, and the workhouse, the insane asylum, and the emigrant ship received the ruined lives of those who made the efforts.

15.9. They complain that the Irish Transport and General Workers' Union cannot be trusted to keep its agreements. The majority of shipping firms in Dublin to-day are at present working, refusing to join in this mad enterprise engineered by Mr Murphy, and with perfect confidence in the faith of the Irish Transport and General Workers' Union. They complain of the sympathetic strike, but the members of the United Builders' Labourers' Trade Union, a union recruited from the same class of labourers as the Irish Transport and General Workers' Union, have been subjected to a sympathetic lockout because of their refusal to pledge themselves not to help the latter body if they so desired it at any time in the future. …

15.10. A more unreasonable pledge was never asked for. It is as if, instead of waiting until the contingency arose, the Transport Union were to call a strike in a shop because the employer would not sign an agreement not to lend his own money to another employer if he needed it. To such an extent has the madness of the employers led them.

15.11. We on our side say that we are proud of the spirit of solidarity exhibited in Dublin; we are proud of the manner in which organised labour in these islands has rallied to help us in defeating the attempt of the employers to dictate to the workers to what Union they should or should not belong.

16. James Connolly on the origins of the Lockout

16.1. *Introduction.* The *Daily Herald* asked Connolly to write an article to explain the causes of the Dublin Lockout. This is Connolly's version of events. He defends the ITGWU and the weapon of sympathetic strike and lists its successes. He outlines the role of William Martin Murphy as the intransigent leader of the employers. SOURCE: 'A Titanic struggle', *Daily Herald*, 6 December 1913.

16.2. In the year 1911 the National Sailors' and Firemen's Union, as a last desperate expedient to avoid extinction, resolved upon calling a general strike in all the home ports. …

16.3. The call was in danger of falling upon deaf ears, and was, in fact, but little heeded until the Irish Transport and General Workers' Union began to take a hand in the game. As ships came into the Port of Dublin, after the issue of the call, each ship was held up by the dockers under the orders of James Larkin until its crew joined the union, and signed on under union conditions and rates of pay. Naturally, this did not please the shipowners and merchants of Dublin.

16.4. But the delegates of the Irish Transport and General Workers' Union up and down the docks preached most energetically the doctrine of the sympathetic strike, and the doctrine was readily assimilated by the dockers and carters. It brought the union into a long and bitter struggle along the quays, a struggle which cost it thousands of pounds, imperilled its very existence, and earned for it the bitterest hatred of every employer and sweater in the city, every one of whom swore they would wait their chance to 'get even with Larkin and his crew'.

16.5. The sympathetic strike having worked so well for the seamen and firemen, the Irish Transport and General Workers' Union began to apply it ruthlessly in every labour dispute. A record of the victories it has won for other trade unions would surprise a good many of its critics. A few cases will indicate what, in the hands of Larkin and the Irish Transport and General Workers' Union, it has won for some of the skilled trades.

16.6. When the coachmakers went on strike the Irish Transport and General Workers' Union took over all the labourers, paid them strike pay, and kept them out until the coachmakers won. The latter body are now repaying us by doing scab work while we are out. The mill-sawyers existed for twenty years in Dublin without recognition. The sympathetic strike by our union won them recognition and an increase of pay. The stationary engine drivers, the cabinetmakers, the sheet metal workers, the carpenters, and, following them all the building trades got an increase through our control of the carting industry. As did also the girls and men employed in Jacob's biscuit factory.

16.7. In addition to this work for others we won for our own members the following increases within the last two years: cross channel dockers got, since the strike in the City of Dublin Steam Packet Company, an increase of wages of 3*s*. per week. In the case of the British and Irish Company the increase, levelling it up with the other firms meant a rise of 6*s*. per week. For men working for the Merchants' Warehousing Company 3*s*. per week, general carriers 2*s*. to 3*s*., coal fillers halfpenny per ton, grain bushellers 1*d*. per ton, men and boys in the bottle-blowing works from 2*s*. to 10*s*. per week of an increase, mineral water operatives 4*s*. to 6*s*. per week, and a long list of warehouses in which girls were exploited were compelled to give some slight modification of the inhuman conditions under which their employees were labouring. …

16.8. The labourers on the Dublin and South-Eastern Railway got increases of 6*s*. per week, and those in the Kingstown [now Dún Laoghaire] Gas Works got increases varying from 3*s*. to 10*s*. per week per man. All of these increases were the result of the sympathetic strike policy, first popularised by its success in winning the battle for the Seamen and Firemen – who are now asked to repudiate it. These things well understood explain the next act in the unfolding of the drama. Desiring to make secure what had been gained, Mr Larkin formulated a scheme for a Conciliation Board.

This was adopted by the Trades Council, at least in essence, and eventually came before the Employers' Executive, or whatever the governing committee of that body is named. After a hot discussion it was put to the vote. Eighteen employers voted to accept a Conciliation Board, three voted against.

16.9. Of that three, William Martin Murphy was one. On finding himself in the minority he rose and vowed that in spite of them he would 'smash the Conciliation Board'. Within three days he kept his word by discharging two hundred of his tramway traffic employees for being members of the Irish Transport and General Workers' Union, and thus forced on the strike of the tramway men. Immediately he appealed to all the Dublin employers who had been forced into a semblance of decency by Larkin and his colleagues, called to their memory the increases of wages they were compelled to pay, and lured them on to a desperate effort to combine and destroy the one labour force they feared.

16.10. The employers, mad with hatred of the power that had wrested from them the improved conditions, a few of which I have named, rallied round Murphy, and from being one in a minority of three he became the leader and organising spirit of a band of four hundred.

16.11. I have always told our friends in Great Britain that our fight in Ireland was neither inspired nor swayed by theories nor theorists. It grew and was hammered out of the hard necessities of our situation. Here, in this brief synopsis, you can trace its growth for yourselves.

16.12. First a fierce desire to save our brothers of the sea, a desire leading to us risking our own existence in their cause. Developing from that an extension of the principle of sympathetic action until we took the fierce beast of capital by the throat all over Dublin, and loosened its hold on the vitals of thousands of our class. Then a rally of the forces of capital to recover their hold, and eventually a titanic struggle, in which the forces of labour in Britain openly, and the forces of capital secretly, became participants.

16.13. That is where we stand to-day. The struggle forming our theories and shaping the policy, not only for us, but for our class. To those who criticise us we can only reply: we fight as conditions dictate; we meet new conditions with new policies. Those who choose may keep old policies to meet new conditions. We cannot and will not try.

17. Mr Murphy's 'New Year's Eve speech'

17.1. *Introduction.* Connolly, in this deeply ironic and amusing piece presented in the form of a 'New Year's Eve speech', mercilessly mocks William Martin Murphy. He is made out to be ruthless, heartless, greedy, with absolutely no sympathy for the hardships faced by the workers of Dublin, but now come to repent his sins against humanity and offers the hand of friendship to Larkin. SOURCE: *Irish Worker*, 3 January 1914.

17.2. We are informed that on Wednesday, December 31st (New Year's Eve), a special meeting of the Employers' Association was held in the Ancient Concert Rooms to hear an address by Mr William Martin Murphy. The meeting was called at the personal request of that gentleman, and was the most remarkable gathering that has been held since the beginning of the dispute. The great hall was taxed to its utmost, and the remarkable address was listened to in absolute silence, in fact with a feeling almost of awe-struck wonderment. We dare not speculate upon the possible results of this unique pronouncement. Mr Murphy said:

'Gentlemen, I have called you together on the eve of the New Year, 1914, because I have something to tell you that I feel can better be told upon such an occasion than upon any other. It has long been the custom amongst Christian nations to make the closing of the old year and the opening of the book of the new an occasion for the promulgation of new policies, and for the renunciation of old sins. Such of us as feel wearied and worn out with old forms of iniquity and desirous of aspiring after a newer life in which to qualify for a greater righteousness naturally choose that period in which the thoughts of men turn to change as the period best suited to mark their change of heart.

17.3. For that reason I have fixed upon this evening as the most auspicious occasion, and the one most calculated to awaken in your breasts a responsive throb for the review of the past and the announcement of the change of policy I intend to follow upon my change of heart. Yes, gentlemen, I intend to embark upon a new line of policy – a policy that I hope will reconcile me at last to the great heart of the Dublin public, of the generous Irish public from whom I have been so long estranged.

17.4. For years I have followed in Ireland a policy which set my own interests above and before everything else. I have schemed and contrived by every means to obtain control of every kind of business, even if in doing so I had to destroy the business and wreck the prospects of helpless orphans. I have never followed any policy of Christian charity, of humane pity, even of common decency, to restrain me when engaged trying to obtain possession of the business interests of those whom I considered as business rivals. I have made a fine art, or perhaps I should say a scientific business of the accumulation in my own hands of the fortunes and control of destinies of others.

17.5. My path through the business world has been marked by the ruin of others, and all over Dublin and the other scenes of my activities can be traced the sufferers – suffering in silence for the most part, as I have successfully manipulated into silence every avenue of publicity by means of which they could make themselves heard.

17.6. What I have done to the business people in this business world I have done even more ruthlessly and unscrupulously to those members of the working class who dared to cross my path. You all know the tale of the West Clare Railway. How I terrorised the whole countryside into acceptance of my terms, how I evicted poor Irish labourers for daring to ask as a weekly wage a sum not sufficient to pay for a box at the Opera for one of my guests at Dartry Hall, how I secured that this eviction should pass and win the approval of a venal Home Rule Press which had grown into popularity by the denunciation of evictions not one half as cold-blooded and merciless, and how in spite of this eviction of my poor countrymen and women I still managed to pose before the public as a pure-souled patriot and lover of my kind.

17.7. All this you know, gentlemen! You also know – for you have been participating in my crime – how I managed our latest attempt to reduce to soulless slavery the gallant workers of Dublin. You know how I managed to secure a sufficient number of slaves prepared to sell their manhood for a chance to earn a few miserable shillings; how I used those slaves, and when I was sure of their slavishness, proceeded to goad the more manly workers into revolt, and then supplanted them by the help of those Judases. How I had prepared my plans so that the Judge who tried the strikers, arrested by a police force drunken with rural hatred of the city, should feel that his own right to dividends was on trial when confronted by a working class prisoner, and should hit out vindictively with fiendish sentences accordingly.

17.8. You also know, none better, how we had our secret agents in every club, society and gathering place in the city. How we encouraged them to play upon the most sacred offices and the most hallowed institutions and to divert them to our uses. How we made priests of the Most High imagine they were obeying the call of God when in reality they were only being gulled by our carefully poisoned suggestions – made them mistake the insinuations of the devil for the inspirations of God.

17.9. How we secured that through the influence of some of our lady shareholders the uniformed ruffians of the police should be let loose to insult with foul-mouthed indecencies the brave girls who dared to strike against the unbearable conditions you imposed upon them, and when in the pride of their outraged purity they resented the insults the same police bullies beat them, arrested them, and perjured themselves to swear their liberties away. All this you know, gentlemen! You also know how we made the streets of Dublin a place of terror for every worker not prepared to sell his class; how our uniformed brutes (whom I despised even whilst using them) batoned, kicked and maimed all and sundry; how we murdered two men in Dublin and left another widow and six orphans in Kingstown [now Dún Laoghaire]; how we armed scabs to shoot at will, and how, in short, we have made of the Capital City of our country a place of slaughter, of misery, and a byword amongst the nations.

17.10. Well, gentlemen, what has it all profited us? At the end of it all we find that the workers of Dublin are still unsubdued, and I now believe are unsubduable and unconquerable. You can extract what comfort you may from that fact.

17.11. For myself now at the opening of the New Year I am determined to do what I can in the few years left me to try and make amends for all the long array of crimes against my kind of which I have been guilty. I, at least, will no longer make war upon the liberties of my poorer brothers and sisters, or use my ill-gotten wealth to exploit others. What I have done I cannot restore, but I can restore to the working class the rights of which I used my wealth to deprive them. From this night, gentlemen, I cease to hold the pistol of starvation at the heads of the poor to make them surrender their souls and liberties. I propose to go down to the Tramway Depots and hunt away the foul vermin who now pollute the cars by their presence. I propose to open the dispatch business of the *Independent* and *Herald* with Transport Union members, and if they will permit me I will grasp the hand of each and beg their pardon for my crimes against their manhood. These will be but the beginning.

17.12. From this day forward I am at the service of every honest cause, and I trust that the closing years of a life spent in unscrupulous acquisition of gold may be worthy of some honour when spent as they will be spent in trying to win instead the esteem of my fellows. Today I am sending to Jim Larkin, whom I have grown to esteem and value as a worthy citizen, an invitation to do me the honour of consenting to dine with me on New Year's Day at the Imperial Hotel. There on the spot made historic by Larkin, I propose that he and I shall make a pact of friendship, and trust that united our efforts will succeed in purging Dublin and Ireland of much of its squalor and misery, and set its feet upon the upward path that leads towards righteousness'.

(NOTE – Up to the present the invitation has not arrived, and we are wondering whether our reporter invented the speech of Mr Murphy, as Murphy's supporters have hitherto invented so many speeches attributed to Mr Larkin.)

18. After the Lockout

18.1. *Introduction.* James Connolly gave the following speech in Cork in 1915 as Acting General Secretary of the Irish Transport and General Workers' Union (ITGWU). He reminded his audience of the great difficulties that the Labour movement faced during the 1913 Lockout and how the employers persuaded the government to ban public meetings and peaceful protests in Ireland, although these rights were upheld in England. Strikers were arrested, attacked, imprisoned, even shot at, indiscriminately and unlawfully. Women, as well as men, were subjected to such treatment. Employers failed to defeat the poor workers, whose cause was a just. The strike was ultimately successful, he says, because after the Lockout, employers were generally more willing to consider workers' demands. SOURCE: 'The Dublin Lockout and its sequel', *Workers' Republic*, 29 May 1915.

18.2. You remember the great lockout in Dublin in 1913–14; you remember how the Dublin employers, smarting under the defeats inflicted upon their individual efforts to keep their workers in slavery, at last resolved to combine in one gigantic effort to restore the irresponsible reign of the slave drivers such as existed in Dublin before the advent of the Irish Transport and General Workers' Union.

18.3. You will remember how four hundred employers banded themselves together to destroy us, and pledged their sacred word of honour that they would wipe that union off the map; that when the fight was over no man or woman affiliated to us, or friendly to us, would ever be employed in Dublin.

18.4. You also remember how they did more than pledge their honour – the honour of some of them would not fetch much as a pledge – but they also deposited each a sum of money in proportion to the number of employees each normally employed, and that money deposited in the Bank in the name of their association was to be forfeited, if the depositor came to terms with the union before his fellows.

18.5. Thus strung together in bonds of gold and self-interest, you might think they were well equipped for beating a lot of poor workingmen and women with no weapons but their hands, and no resources but their willingness to suffer for the right. But they were taking no chances. They laid their plans with the wisdom of the serpent, and the unscrupulousness of the father of all evil.

18.6. Before the Lockout was declared they went to the British government in Ireland, to its heads in Dublin Castle, and they said to that government, 'Now, look here, we are going to make war upon the Irish Transport and General Workers' Union, but we believe that we cannot succeed as we should wish, while peaceful picketing is allowed. We know it is allowed in England, in Scotland, and in Wales, but we don't want it allowed in Ireland'. And the government said: 'All right, gentlemen, the law allowing peaceful picketing is only a scrap of paper; we will tear it up while the fight is on'. The employers said again: 'Good, but these Labour men and women will hold together while they are able to hold public meetings, and hear their speakers encouraging them. Could His Majesty's government not manage to suppress public meetings, whilst the fight is on?' And the government answered: 'Suppress public meetings, Why, of course: the law which permits public meetings in Ireland is just another scrap of paper, and has been torn up many a time, and oft; we will tear it up again, so as to help you in the good work of crushing the Labour movement'.

18.7. And you know, the British government kept its promise to the employers. All through that long and bitter struggle, the elementary rights won by Trade Unionists by a century of sacrifices were denied to us in Dublin, although freely exercised at the same time in England.

18.8. The locked out worker who attempted to speak to a scab in order to persuade him or her not to betray the class they belonged to, was mercilessly set upon by uniformed bullies, and hauled off to prison, until the prison was full to overflowing with helpless members of our class. Women and young girls by the score; good, virtuous, beautiful Irish girls and women were clubbed and insulted, and thrown into prison by policemen and magistrates, not one of whom were fit to clean the shoes of the least of these, our sisters.

18.9. Our right of public meeting was ruthlessly suppressed in the streets of our city, the whole press of the country was shamelessly engaged in poisoning the minds of the people against us, every scoundrel who chose was armed to shoot and murder the workers who stood by their Union.

18.10. Two men, James Nolan and John Byrne, were clubbed to death in the street; one, Byrne of Kingstown, suffered unnameable torture in the police cell, and died immediately upon release. One young girl, Alice Brady, while walking quietly homewards with her strike allowance of food, was shot by a scab with a revolver placed in his hands by an employer, and within twenty-four hours after the murder, that scab was walking the streets of Dublin a free man. Our murdered sister lies cold today in her grave in Glasnevin – as true a martyr for freedom as any who ever died in Ireland. But she did not die in vain, and none who die for freedom ever die in vain.

18.11. Well, did the unholy conspiracy against Labour achieve its object? Was the union crushed? Did our flag come down? Let me tell you our position today, and tell it by an illustration. We recently put in a demand for an increase of wages in Dublin, for all classes of labour in our union. That demand was eventually met by the employers, and at a Conference between the representatives of the Union and the Employers were prepared to settle matters through the Union, and that whatever terms were then agreed upon would determine the rates for the quays and elsewhere, wherever our men were employed. Here are a few of the advances thus agreed upon, as well as the advances arranged with other firms not represented at the Conference, but dealing directly with the Union Officials:

Stevedores' Association: one penny per ton increase on all tonnage rules. Deep Sea Boats: One shilling per day on all day wage men. Casual Cross Channel Boats: one shilling per day. Constant Cross Channel Boats: eightpence per day. Dublin and General Company's employees: four shillings. Dublin dockyard labourers: three shillings per week. Ross and Walpole: two shillings per week. General carriers' men: two shillings per week granted direct to men after receipt of letter from the Union.

18.12. These comprise the larger firms, many smaller firms also made advances as a result of action of the Union, and in every case the advance made was in proportion to the manner in which the men had stuck to their Union. The firms whose employees had fallen away gave poor increases or none at all; the firms whose members had remained loyal to the Union, paid greater increases, and so the men reaped the fruits of their loyalty, whilst those who were faint of heart were punished by the employers for lack of faith in their Union and their class. So it shall ever be.

GILLIAN M. DOHERTY AND TOMÁS O'RIORDAN

CHAPTER 10

Key concepts

1. Anglicisation and de-anglicisation

1.1. Only one aspect of the questions is treated at length here, the decline of the Irish language and the movement for its preservation and revival, an aspect of nineteenth- and twentieth-century history that goes to the heart of these problems.

1.2. Irish – the Gaelic language – declined rapidly in the second half of the nineteenth century. About half the population spoke Irish in 1841, less than a quarter (23.3 per cent) by 1851; and by 1891 only 14.4 per cent claimed to do so. Very few were literate in it. It became more and more a language of the home while English was the language of public discourse – church, law, politics, the press including the nationalist press, the national school system and the education system, and business and commerce. Literacy in English was required for all in the civil service, the army and the police force; and it was a decisive advantage for Irish emigrants who went mainly to English-speaking countries. Even Irish-speaking emigrants wrote their letters home in English because so very few were literate in Irish. There were serious gains to be made by learning English and people did so with enthusiasm.

1.3. Irish-speaking parents insisted that their children learn and speak English. The cost in cultural terms was high, as it usually is, in the case of language change in a whole community. There were the obvious losses of songs, stories, folklore, poetry and prayers. Traditional knowledge and culture was lost with the language and this resulted in great cultural impoverishment. The community lost the words, and the knowledge and ideas that accompanied them, for many kinds of natural phenomena and many aspects of nature. The education system failed to make up the deficit. The same was true in many other areas of life, particularly in work, trades, crafts, farming, boating and fishing. The terms for emotions and the whole affective area of life were also lost. In time, and with education, people acquired English-language culture but linguistic change impoverished the lives of many and for more than a generation.

1.4. While Irish people were abandoning the Irish language with alacrity, scholars were re-discovering it. German, French, and Italian scholars were busy producing editions of Irish literature that survived in the medieval manuscripts, many preserved in European libraries. Across Europe, in the nineteenth century, there was an awakening of a sense of nationality and these ideas influenced nationalists in Ireland. Some sought to curb English influence and recover as much as possible of Ireland's Gaelic past: its language, its abundant literature, its manners and customs, its games, its place names, its surnames and personal names and its history. In 1876 the Society for the Preservation of the Irish Language was formed. Some who felt that it lacked dynamism founded the Gaelic Union which published the journal, *Irisleabhar na Gaedhilge* (1882–1909). This is recognised as the starting point of the Irish language revival and the beginning of journalism in Irish. Eoin MacNeill was appointed its editor in 1894.

1.5. In November 1892 Douglas Hyde delivered a lecture to the National Literary Society, entitled 'The necessity for de-anglicising Ireland'. It was a plea to Irish people to turn aside from things English before they lost completely a sense of a separate nationality. Hyde believed that by imitating the English in their 'dress, literature, music, games and ideas only a long time after them and a vast time behind', and by abandoning the Irish language, 'we have at last broken the continuity of Irish life'. He encouraged Irish music and Gaelic games as fostered by the Gaelic Athletic Association. However, he considered virtually everything that existed in his youth as Irish even though it might well have been an earlier import from England, and he denounced virtually every development during his adult years as anglicisation.

1.6. Eoin MacNeill first proposed the establishment of the Gaelic League to preserve and to promote spoken Irish and to publish and to make available a literature in Irish. The Gaelic League, founded in 1893 by MacNeill with the help of Hyde and others, would take the language to the people and it was by far the most important of the many Irish language organisations. Hyde was its first president and remained in office until 1915. He was the League's most persuasive publicist. Father Eugene O'Growney, professor of Irish at Maynooth College, was an early supporter and his primer, *Simple lessons in Irish*, was used widely in Gaelic League language classes.

1.7. Though the objects of the Gaelic League were taken up with enthusiasm and branches were founded throughout the country, it failed to persuade the majority of the Irish people to use Irish in their everyday lives, nor did it or any other organisation have the resources to do so. However, it campaigned successfully to have the Irish language taught in schools, it encouraged the publication of a modern literature in Irish, it reinvigorated and inspired a sense of cultural nationalism, and it provided an intellectual basis for a new and urgent sense of nationality, the basis of nationalism. This sense of cultural nationalism was transmuted into political nationalism in the case of many of its members and into revolutionary nationalism in the case of some.

1.8. Unlike earlier movements concerned with antiquarian studies, medieval literature, and folklore (such as the Irish Archaeological Society and the Celtic Society patronised by the aristocracy), the Gaelic League tried to revive Irish as a spoken and literary language by organising language classes, by studying and publishing existing modern Gaelic literature (and here its achievements were remarkable) and by cultivating a contemporary Irish literature. It published a newspaper, *An Claidheamh Soluis*, and among its editors were MacNeill (1899–1901) and Patrick Pearse (1903–9). Its activities were very like those taking place elsewhere in Europe among speakers of minority languages. In the 1890s Hyde successfully campaigned to have the Post Office accept letters and parcels addressed in Irish.

1.9. Hyde insisted that the movement should be non-political and significant numbers of Protestants and Unionists became Gaelic Leaguers in the early years, a trend that never entirely disappeared. The membership of the League was particularly strong in towns and cities where it served social needs as well as those of nationality. It never had much success in the Gaeltacht (the Irish-speaking areas). There was a tendency to idealise the culture and way of life of the surviving Gaeltacht areas and it provided a stable base of identity for many in a rapidly changing world.

1.10. Public awareness of the League's work was heightened in 1899 when it opposed attempts led by John Pentland Mahaffy, provost of Trinity College, Dublin, to reduce the marks awarded for Irish in the Intermediate Examination. Mahaffy, classical scholar and wit, was contemptuous of Celtic Studies (the study of the Celtic languages, ancient and modern – Irish, Scottish Gaelic, Manx, Welsh, Breton, Cornish and Gaulish) and argued that Irish literature and language were of little value and not suitable as matriculation subjects. In answer to the question, 'In your opinion, viewing it [Irish] as a living language, has it any educational value?', Mahaffy stated:

> None. I am corroborated by the experts ... one of whom finds fault with the text books at present used, or one of them, on the grounds that it is either silly or indecent. I am told by a much better authority than any in Irish, that it is impossible to get hold of a text in Irish which is not religious, or which does not suffer from one or other of the objections referred to ... It [Irish] is often useful to a man fishing for salmon or shooting grouse in the West. I have often found a few words very serviceable.

1.11. This led to a great public controversy in which European and Irish scholars gave decisive evidence about the worth of the Irish language and its literature. Irish retained its status in the Intermediate Examination and membership of the Gaelic League increased as a result of this much-publicised victory.

1.12. By 1914 the IRB had taken control of the Gaelic League and Hyde resigned as president in 1915. William Rooney (a tireless worker for the revival of Irish, founder of the *United Irishman,* and a friend and supporter of Arthur Griffith) said that it was a mistake for an organisation 'that had charged itself with the promotion of Irish nationality' to avoid politics. Pearse described the Gaelic League as 'a school for rebellion' and advocated an Ireland that was 'not only free but Gaelic as well; not only Gaelic but free as well'. Many of the leaders of the 1916 Rising and the War of Independence came to nationalism by way of the Gaelic League. These included Pearse, Thomas MacDonagh, Éamon de Valera, and Michael Collins. Collins declared that when the history of the Gaelic League came to be written it would be found to have been the most important movement of all. It has often been said that the Gaelic League provided the officers and the GAA provided the men for the revolution. The Gaelic League itself was declared an illegal organisation in September 1919.

1.13. BIBLIOGRAPHY: Dúbhglas de hÍde, *Mise agus an Connradh (go dtí 1905)* (Dublin, 1937). Dúbhglas de hÍde, *Mo thurus go h-Americe* (Dublin, 1937). Diarmuid Coffey, *Douglas Hyde, president of Ireland* (Dublin, 1938). Myles Dillon, 'Douglas Hyde', in Conor Cruise O'Brien (ed.), *The shaping of modern Ireland* (London, 1960), pp 50–62. Brian Ó Cuív, 'The Gaelic cultural movements and the new nationalism', in K.B. Nowlan (ed.), *The making of 1916: studies in the history of the Rising* (Dublin, 1969), pp 1–27. Seán Ó Tuama, *The Gaelic League idea* (Dublin, 1972; 2nd ed. Cork, 1993). F.X. Martin & F.J. Byrne (eds), *The scholar revolutionary: Eoin MacNeill, 1867–1945, and the making of the new Ireland* (Shannon, 1973). Proinsias Mac Aonghusa (ed.), *Oireachtas na Gaeilge, 1897–1997* (Dublin, 1977). S.P. Breathnach, *Saor agus Gaelach: dearcadh an Phiarsaigh ar chultúr náisiúnta* (Dublin, 1979). Michael Tierney, *Eoin MacNeill: scholar and man of action, 1867–1945* (Oxford, 1980). Donncha Ó Súilleabháin, *An Piarsach agus Conradh na Gaeilge* (Dublin, 1981). Máire Ní Mhurchú & Diarmuid Breathnach, *Beathaisnéis, 1782–1982* (6 vols, Dublin, 1986–99). Tom Garvin, *Nationalist revolutionaries in Ireland, 1858–1928* (Oxford, 1987). Donncha Ó Súilleabháin, *Cath na Gaeilge sa chóras oideachais, 1893–1911* (Dublin, 1988). Proinsias Mac Aonghusa, *Ar son na Gaeilge: Conradh na Gaeilge, 1893–1993* (Dublin, 1993). Georg Grote, *Torn between politics and culture: the Gaelic League, 1893–1993* (Münster & New York, 1993). Seán Ó Lúing, 'Douglas Hyde and the Gaelic League', in *Celtic Studies in Europe and other essays* (Dublin, 2000), pp 77–94. Tony Crowley, *The politics of language in Ireland, 1366–1922: a source book* (London & New York, 2000). Risteárd Ó Glaisne, *De bhunadh protastúnach nó rian Chonradh na Gaeilge* (Dublin, 2000). Betsey Taylor FitzSimon & James H. Murphy (eds), *The Irish revival reappraised* (Dublin, 2004). Pádraigín Riggs (ed.), *Dineen and the Dictionary* (London & Cork, 2005).

FIDELMA MAGUIRE

2. Democracy

2.1. Democracy means government by the people, the form of government in which the people are sovereign. As an ideal and as a political programme, democracy has a long history. In modern times, democratic rule is not usually direct but is exercised by freely elected representatives of the people. It is founded on the basic belief that all individuals are equal and have an equal and inalienable right to life and liberty under the law, as freely enacted by the people. Many Western thinkers have written in some way about some form of democracy. Because the people are the source of power, democracies differ from other forms of government. This contrasts with monarchies where power resides in a sovereign or king and dictatorships where political power is held by an individual or group without involvement of the wider community.

2.2. Catholics were excluded from power for much of the eighteenth and some of the nineteenth century. By the time the franchise was extended to most males in the latter part of the nineteenth century, many Catholics had become nationalists of varying kinds. Parliamentary Reform Acts in 1832, 1850 (Ireland only), 1867–8, and 1884–5 increased the electorate as the franchise was extended. The Ballot Act, 1872 (35 & 36 Vict., c. 33) extended democracy and freedom within the United Kingdom. It required the use of the secret ballot in parliamentary and local elections. This brought to an end to the powerful pressure of employers, religious leaders and landlords on voters. The Representation of the People Act, 1884 (48 Vict., c. 3), and the Redistribution of Seats Act, 1885 (48 & 49 Vict., c. 23), reformed the system of elections and made it more democratic. The Representation of the People Act extended the franchise to male householders in counties and boroughs and to lodgers in counties. The Redistribution of Seats Act abolished separate representation for smaller boroughs (population under 15,000) and reduced from two MPs to one the representation of larger boroughs (population 15,000–50,000). These reforms changed the electoral prospects of political parties. Home Rulers were to benefit most and Liberals, whose chances of election were greatest in the boroughs, lost out. Ireland did well from these reforms and its number of MPs remained unchanged, despite Ireland's declining population and its smaller proportion of the population of the United Kingdom as a whole. Many people still did not have a vote in parliamentary elections. Males under the age of twenty-one and women (of any age) could not vote. However, after the reforms of 1884–5, there was a significant increase in the number of eligible voters. In 1861, just 13.4 per cent Irish adult males had the franchise, by 1891 this had increased to 58.3 per cent.

2.3. Michael Davitt believed that 'In Great Britain, parliamentarianism or imperialism must die. They cannot live together.' In the debates about land acts and Home Rule bills, democracy was a term used both by opponents and supporters of political and agricultural reform in Ireland. Many imperialists thought that Irish nationalists like Charles Stewart Parnell were unfit to enjoy the benefits of a domestic democratic parliament. Some liberal and conservative politicians in nineteenth-century Britain considered democracy a dangerous idea, and by giving the vote to the poorer sections of society – the unemployed and working classes – Westminster would be signing its own death warrant. They feared that these groups once enfranchised (allowed to vote) would use their new power to overthrow the governing classes. Despite these worries, both main parties at Westminster in the nineteenth century gradually extended voting rights to most of the adult male population.

2.4. If imperialists in Britain and Ireland thought democracy a dangerous idea, many prominent Irish nationalists saw it differently. Both Daniel O'Connell and Parnell, in different ways, thought that involving the masses in political life was one of the most important achievements of any nationalist leader. Their movements drew their great strength and appeal from the support of the ordinary people. Parnell is credited with the organisation of the first modern democratic party in Europe. By brilliant electioneering, powerful advocacy and skilful work in the House of Commons, Parnell held the balance of power at Westminster by 1885. His price for supporting either party was a Home Rule Bill for Ireland. Biagini argues that Home Rule was the 'single most important catalyst in the remaking of popular radicalism after 1885'. He believes that the strength of support for Home Rule from constituent groups within Liberal and radical circles from the 1890s allowed for the emergence of a Gladstonian 'popular front' that helped bring about a revival in fortunes of the Liberal party in the early twentieth century.

2.5. Conservatives chose to 'kill Home Rule with kindness' by reorganising and expanding the Irish system of local government. Between the 1890s and the early years of the new century, the government spent more money than ever on Irish local government while at the same time they widened the franchise significantly. The Local Government Act of 1898 gave county and city councils the power to direct financial and administrative matters. This effectively destroyed the power of the Ascendancy. Control over housing and public health was vested in rural and urban district councils whilst poor relief and medical charities were to be administered by boards of guardians. The earlier grand juries were replaced by elected county councils. This gave ordinary citizens a far greater say in the matters that concerned them most. John Redmond thought this Act was the most important Irish political development of his generation. It allowed nationalist politicians get experience of running cities and large bureaucracies in a way that would be helpful to them if they were ever given control over departments of state in a Home Rule Ireland. As well as leading to nationalist control of local government, property-owning women were granted limited suffrage. They could now become members of the rural district councils, though not of county councils.

2.6. In order to convince Irish nationalists that Westminster was listening to their demands for direct democratic control over the institutions that most affected their lives, the Conservative government also set up the Irish Department of Agriculture and Technical Instruction in 1899. Its first vice-president was Horace Plunkett, the famous pioneer of the co-operative movement. Despite these concessions, Irish nationalists such as Parnell and Redmond thought that the only way to establish true democracy in Ireland was by conceding Home Rule. They distrusted Westminster, arguing that it ignored the clearly expressed wishes and distinct interests of the Irish people on many occasions. If the Irish could not get democratic concessions at Westminster, some thought that the only way to resolve the problem was through the establishment of an internal assembly with its own powers. This democratic tradition would prove enduring, as Finbarr Lane noted:

many of the socio-economic prerequisites for democratisation were well entrenched by the time of independence, making Ireland a reasonably fertile ground for democracy. Crucial here were the historic interactions between Irish nationalism and the British state and the effects of British policy on Irish society, including the expansion of primary education, the timing and nature of land reforms, and the emergence of a democratic civil society during the nineteenth century.

2.7. BIBLIOGRAPHY: Seán Ó Faoláin, *King of the beggars: a life of Daniel O'Connell* (London, 1938; repr. Dublin, 1986). David E. Schmidt, 'Catholicism and democratic political development in Ireland', *Éire-Ireland*, 9:1 (1974), 59–72. F. O'Ferrall, *Catholic emancipation: Daniel O'Connell and the birth of Irish democracy, 1820–30* (Dublin, 1985). Brian Girvin, 'Nationalism, democracy, and Irish political culture', in Brian Girvin & Roland Sturm (eds), *Politics and society in contemporary Ireland* (Aldershot, 1986), pp 3–28. Donal McCartney, *The dawning of democracy: Ireland 1800–1870* (Dublin, 1987). Flann Campbell, *The dissenting voice: Protestant democracy in Ulster from plantation to partition* (Belfast, 1991). Frank McDermott, *Taking the long perspective: democracy and 'terrorism' in Ireland: the writings of W.E.H. Lecky and after* (Dublin, 1991). David George Boyce, *Ireland, 1828–1923: from ascendancy to democracy* (Oxford 1992). Ronald J. Hill & Michael Marsh (eds), *Modern Irish democracy: essays in honour of Basil Chubb* (Dublin, 1993). K. Theodore Hoppen, 'Roads to democracy: electioneering and corruption in nineteenth-century England and Ireland', *History*, 81 (1996), 553–71. Hugh Cunningham, *The challenge of democracy: Britain, 1832–1918* (London, 2001). Brian Girvin, *From union to union: nationalism, democracy and religion in Ireland-Act of Union to EU* (Dublin, 2002). Bill Kissane, *Explaining Irish democracy* (Dublin, 2002). John McGarry, '"Democracy" in Northern Ireland: experiments in self-rule from the Protestant ascendancy to the Good Friday Agreement', *Nations & Nationalism*, 8:4 (2002), 451–74. Richard Bourke, '"Imperialism" and "democracy" in modern Ireland, 1898–2002', *Boundary 2*, 31:1 (2004), 93–118. Finbarr Lane, 'Review of *Explaining Irish democracy*' by Bill Kissane, *Irish Studies Review*, 12:3 (2004), 384–385. Ronan Fanning, 'The Home Rule crisis of 1912–14 and the failure of British democracy in Ireland', in Maurice J. Bric & John Coakley (eds), *From political violence to negotiated settlement: the winding path to peace in twentieth-century Ireland* (Dublin, 2004), pp 32–48. Tom Garvin, *1922: the birth of Irish democracy* (Dublin, 2005). Ian Hughes, Paula Clancy, Clodagh Harris & David Beetham, *Power to the people: assessing democracy in Ireland* (Dublin, 2007). Eugenio F. Biagini, *British democracy and Irish nationalism, 1876–1906* (Cambridge, 2007). Peter Kellner, *Democracy: 1,000 years in pursuit of British liberty* (Edinburgh, 2009).

MARGARET FITZPATRICK AND JOHN PAUL McCARTHY

3. Feminism

3.1. Feminism is a belief in women's social, political, and economic equality with men. The Women's Movement gave political expression to feminism. The first wave of the

Women's Movement in Ireland originated in the second half of the nineteenth century and lasted until 1921. It was dominated by the question of suffrage. Throughout the ages, women were frequently characterised and treated as inferior and of secondary importance to men. Church and State institutions and practices legitimised this belief by excluding women from many of society's roles. For instance, women were barred by law from voting in elections, from serving on juries and from holding office in church. Most institutions of higher education and most professional careers were closed to women.

3.2. These social barriers prompted the growth of the feminist movement in the nineteenth and twentieth centuries. Mary Wollstonecraft (1759–97) has been called the 'first feminist' or 'mother of feminism'. Her publication, *A vindication of the rights of women*, is viewed as the starting point of modern feminism. She drew attention to the state of ignorance in which society kept women. A core objective of her critique was the call for better education of women. Similar efforts were taking place on the other side of the Atlantic. Sarah M. Grimke, an American anti-slavery leader, wrote a pamphlet entitled *Letters on the equality of the sexes and the condition of woman* in 1838. Her work focused particularly on men who used the Bible as an authoritative source for subjugating women. She provided a powerful argument that undermined the position of religious leaders.

3.3. Initially, the *Women's Movement* strove towards obtaining legal equality. The quest for the right to vote or suffrage remained primary. Success eventually arrived when New Zealand became the first country to grant women the vote in 1893. Other countries, such as the United States and Australia, soon followed. By the mid-twentieth-century, a significant proportion of the female population worldwide were actively engaged and participating in democratic elections. In Russia, women were prominent in the October Revolution that catapulted the Bolsheviks to power in 1917.

3.4. In Ireland in the nineteenth century, as in the rest of the United Kingdom, women were barred from many roles. They were not allowed stand for parliament. Only single women were permitted to hold property in their own name. Once married, anything a woman had was transferred to her husband. As with property, a woman was also obliged to hand over to her husband any wages she earned. He alone had control over their children. Irish society in the nineteenth century remained patriarchal (governed by men, husbands and fathers) and the traditional view of women as housekeeper and mother persisted. The classification of women in various censuses reflected the prevailing attitude. In the 1861 Census, women working in the family business were classified as doing the same work as their husbands. By 1881, this position had changed dramatically when all women were redefined under the heading 'indefinite and non-productive'. Thus, the state ceased to acknowledge women as workers.

3.5. The Irish philosopher and social theorist, William Thompson (1775–1833), is credited as the initiator of feminism in Ireland. The Tipperary-born feminist Anna Doyle

Wheeler (1785–1848) inspired, and co-operated in Thompson's famous feminist book, *The appeal of one half of the human race, women, against the pretentions of the other half, men* … (1825). Wheeler was a staunch advocate of political rights for women and equal opportunities in education. The *Appeal* was a response to James Mills' 'Essay on government', in which he dismissed women's rights as unnecessary, since their interests were represented or 'covered' by their husbands or fathers. The essay proposes that a social system cannot provide for the greatest happiness of the greatest number if one half that number is removed from consideration. All women it says 'and particularly women living with men in marriage … have been reduced … to a state of helplessness, slavery … and privations … are *more in need* of political rights than any other portion of human beings'. The essay as a whole is an appeal for votes for women, and is convincingly argued. In the concluding 'Address to women', Thompson and Wheeler call on women to awaken to their degraded state and to join in a principle of co-operation, intentional communities as espoused by social reformer Robert Owen's (1771–1858) followers.

3.6. Gradually, the feminist movement became more rooted in Ireland, and soon gathered pace. The fight against the Contagious Diseases Act (1864) and campaign for greater educational reform increased its membership. The Contagious Diseases Act allowed police to require female prostitutes to undergo mandatory medical examination and treatment. Women could be confined to hospitals for up to three months (later extended to one year under the 1869 Act). The justification of this by army medical officials was that it the most effective way to protect men (and their unfortunate wives) from venereal disease. Women such as Isabella Tod and Anna Haslam led the campaign for women's rights in the latter half of the nineteenth century. Based in Belfast and Dublin respectively, they led the movement in the 1860s to change the law on women's property rights. Success here came in the form of parliamentary acts in 1870, 1874 and 1882 which gradually gave married women control over their property and wages. The Contagious Diseases Acts were repealed in 1886.

3.7. Tod established the Northern Ireland Society for Women's Suffrage in 1871. She campaigned tirelessly for women's suffrage, writing pamphlets and articles, addressing meetings and sending petitions to politicians. Thomas Haslam, husband of Anna, became deeply involved in the early stages of Irish feminism. Together they established the Dublin Women's Suffrage Association (1876), renamed the Irish Women's Suffrage and Local Government Association (IWSLGA) in 1911, to demand the vote for women. As with the Haslams, many of the early pioneers of Irish feminism came from a middle class and Quaker/Protestant background. There were close ties to the British feminist movement.

3.8. Even though the IWSLGA continued to campaign for suffrage, progress was slow. Instead, it was in the field of education that feminism started to achieve success. Anne Jellicoe, a Quaker and native of Co. Laois, formed a Dublin branch of the British-based

Society for Promoting the Employment of Women. It fought for the right of working- and middle-class women to receive a decent secondary school education.

3.9. Educational reform continued to be the main focus of the feminist movement in the 1870s. Among notable successes was the inclusion of women in the government's Intermediate Education Bill (1878). This ensured that girls, as well as boys, could now sit examinations. As a result, many convents sprang up around the country with the sole purpose of educating girls. Because girls were successful, often surpassing boys, the state rewarded these newly established schools with additional funding. Further advances were made with the University Education (Ireland) Act of 1879. This gave women the opportunity (though still excluded from attending universities) to get university degrees and qualifications. Throughout the 1880s women gradually began to overcome this final educational barrier. In 1892 Alice Oldham campaigned to persuade Trinity College to open its degrees to women. She presented a memorial to the Board of Trinity College signed by 10,500 'Irish women of the educated classes'. A resolution was finally passed by the Board in 1903 that 'the time had come to admit women to teaching and degrees of Trinity College'. The college opened its doors to female students in 1904. The National University of Ireland was established in 1908, and, from its foundation its three colleges at Dublin, Cork and Galway admitted women to lectures, prizes, awards and degrees in all faculties.

3.10. Irish women also began to contribute to politics. Following Parnell and Davitt's arrests during the Land War in 1881, the Land League was largely left in the hands of women. The Ladies' Land League, now in charge, proved its effectiveness by successfully managing the day-to-day affairs of the League. This short, but significant, contribution of women to the land war cannot be underestimated. One historian claims that 'it represented an unprecedented initiative in female participation in public life'.

3.11. Since women were excluded from many nationalist organisations, Maud Gonne MacBride founded Inghinidhe na hÉireann ('Daughters of Ireland') in April 1900. She designed the movement's banner and was its first president. It aimed to promote Irish independence (though it opposed the Irish Party), women's suffrage and the Irish Ireland movement. It encouraged the buying of Irish manufactures and gave free Irish language classes. Although never radically feminist, it produced (from 1908) a magazine, *Bean na hÉireann* ('Irishwoman'), the first nationalist feminist journal in Ireland. Inghinidhe na hÉireann was absorbed into Cumann na mBan ('Women's League') in 1914. The foundation of Cumann na mBan in April 1914, in response to the formation of the Irish Volunteers, was seen by many feminists as a backward step, and some members left it when it declared support for the Irish Volunteers. Members raised funds, cooked, sewed uniforms and ran first-aid classes. In the face of criticism by suffragists, women in the organisation argued that there could be no free women in an enslaved nation. Sixty women who were members of Cumann na mBan acted as nurses, despatch carriers and in other supporting roles in the 1916 Rising.

3.12. Membership of the Irish feminist movement belonged almost exclusively to the middle and upper classes. This narrow social composition gave rise to a belief that Irish feminism was the preserve of the few and privileged. Not until James Connolly's arrival did feminism in Ireland attract women from all backgrounds. Equality and equal participation remained a central principle of Connolly's socialism. His desire that women and men involved in the socialist struggle was reflected in the Irish Citizen Army's insistence on treating men and women on an equal footing.

3.13. BIOGRAPHY, STUDIES AND WRITINGS: Rosemary Cullen Owens & Hanna Sheehy-Skeffington, *Votes for women: Irish women's struggle for the vote* (Dublin, 1975). Andro Linklater, *An unhusbanded life: Charlotte Despard, suffragette, socialist and Sinn Féiner* (London, 1980). Rosemary Cullen Owens, *Smashing times: a history of the Irish women's suffrage movement, 1889–1922* (Dublin, 1984). Rosemary Cullen Owens, *Did your granny have a hammer? A history of the Irish suffrage movement, 1876–1922* (Dublin, 1985). David Rubinstein, *Before the suffragettes: women's emancipation in the 1890s* (Brighton, 1986). Cliona Murphy, *The women's suffrage movement and Irish society in the early twentieth century* (New York, 1989). Marianne Heron, *Fighting spirit* (Dublin, 1993). Louise Ryan, *Irish feminism and the vote: an anthology of the Irish Citizen newspaper, 1912–1920* (Dublin, 1996). Margaret Ward, *Hanna Sheehy-Skeffington: a life* (Cork, 1997). Mary Cullen & Maria Luddy (eds), *Female activists: Irish women and change, 1900–1960* (Dublin, 2001). Rosemary Cullen Owens, *Louie Bennett* (Cork, 2001). Marie Mulholland, *The politics and relationships of Kathleen Lynn* (Dublin, 2002). Carmel Quinlan, *Genteel revolutionaries: Anna and Thomas Haslam, pioneers of Irish feminism* (Cork, 2002). Louise Ryan & Margaret Ward (eds), *Irish women and nationalism* (Dublin, 2004). Anne de Courcy, *Society's queen: the life of Edith, Marchioness of Londonderry* (London, 2004). Rebecca Pelan, *Two Irelands: literary feminisms, north and south* (Syracuse, NY, 2005). Linda Connolly & Tina O'Toole, *Documenting Irish feminisms: the second wave* (Dublin, 2005). Mary Pierse (ed.), *Irish feminisms, 1825–1930* (New York, 2009). Justin Quinn, *Irish writers after feminism* (New York, 2009).

EOIN HARTNETT (WITH A CONTRIBUTION BY TOMÁS O'RIORDAN)

4. Home Rule

4.1. The aim of Home Rule was the restoration of a parliament in Dublin to legislate for Irish domestic affairs. The policy was devised by Isaac Butt who said that Ireland suffered, not so much from bad government, but from hardly any. He argued that the heart of Empire beat too remotely from Irish grievances and that MPs at Westminster understood little of Irish problems and were not willing to consider them or try to solve them. It was argued that a Home Rule parliament in Dublin would understand, address and solve Irish problems. This idea was to have an enduring attraction for Irish constitutional nationalists for almost half a century, from 1870 to 1916. Revd Joseph A. Galbraith appears to have coined the term 'Home Rule'. It had an appealing brevity and ring. Its vagueness was useful politically and it enabled people of many political hues to attach their own meaning to it.

4.2. Butt envisaged a federal arrangement for Ireland, Scotland and England. The three countries would be part of a federal United Kingdom, and would share a common sovereign, executive and 'national council' at Westminster for UK and international purposes. Each would have its own parliament to legislate for domestic affairs. In Ireland's case an Irish assembly, elected on the basis of household suffrage, would decide the make-up of parliament.

4.3. Following the Disestablishment of the Church of Ireland (1869) the Home Rule League attracted significant support from disillusioned Protestant middle and upper classes who felt that their interests were not protected in Westminster. The Irish Republican Brotherhood, grateful to Butt for his work in defending Fenian prisoners, was prepared to co-operate with Home Rulers though its objective was complete independence and total separation from Britain. Fifty Home Rule MPs were elected in the 1874 general election. From this group emerged the Home Rule Party, later the Irish Parliamentary Party. Butt's policy of Home Rule caught the imagination of the people but his party's pursuit of that policy in the 1870s was not successful. His Home Rule motion was debated in the House of Commons in 1874 (30 June to 2 July) but was defeated by 458 to 61. Butt's mild-mannered style of leadership lost him much support in advanced nationalist circles. The character of the movement changed in the 1870s: landlord involvement declined and the numbers of Fenians, Catholic clergy and agrarian campaigners increased.

4.4. Butt's successor, Charles Stewart Parnell, disciplined and organised the party into an impressive political machine with widespread support and great success at the polls. He persuaded the greatest parliamentarian of the age, the Liberal leader Gladstone, of the merits of Home Rule. When Gladstone eventually committed himself to it, he used Butt's ideas and the example of Canada to construct a Bill. The first Government of Ireland (Home Rule) Bill was introduced by Gladstone in the House of Commons on 14 April 1886. The Bill was with fiercely opposed. Gladstone failed to persuade his Liberal Party MPs to support it (some 93 Liberals voted against). The radical Liberals, led by Joseph Chamberlain, and the Whigs on the right wing of the party, led by Hartington, voted with the Conservatives to defeat the measure (8 June) by 343 votes to 311.

4.5. Conservative governments from the 1880s sought to address and remedy Irish grievances, and to govern Ireland so well that there would be no demand for Home Rule. This Conservative policy, called 'killing Home Rule with kindness', brought many benefits to Ireland.

4.6. Unionists and the Orange Order (revived in 1886) feared Home Rule might mean a Dublin parliament dominated by the Catholic Church and damaging to Ireland's economic progress. The slogan of the 1880s was 'Home Rule is Rome rule'. Ulster Unionists began organising themselves. In June 1892 the Duke of Abercorn addressed the Ulster Convention of Unionist Clubs at Balmoral Show Grounds outside Belfast. Over 12,000 Unionist delegates declared 'We will not have Home Rule.'

4.7. Gladstone's second Home Rule Bill was introduced on 13 February 1893. Riots broke out in Belfast on news on the second reading of the Bill, 21–2 April. It passed its third reading in the House of Commons on 2 September 1893, but was overwhelmingly rejected by the House of Lords on 9 September by 419 to 41. The defeat of the Liberals in the 1895 election temporarily allayed Unionist fears.

4.8. By 1900 the Irish Party, which had split in 1890 over the Parnell-O'Shea affair, was reunited under John Redmond. The Liberals step-by-step approach to Home Rule became increasingly apparent in the autumn of 1904 when it was revealed that the Under-Secretary Sir Anthony MacDonnell, head of the Irish administration, was working with the Earl of Dunraven on a scheme for devolved government in Ireland through an extension of local government. While this was not Home Rule, it was certainly a step in that direction. It provoked northern Unionist hostility and failed to win unanimous nationalist approval. A conference of Ulster Unionist MPs took place in Belfast in December 1904, that resolved to form the Ulster Unionist Council (name adopted, March 1905) to co-ordinate resistance to Home Rule. The affair led to the resignation of the Chief Secretary for Ireland, George Wyndham in March 1905.

4.9. The Liberal Party enjoyed a landslide victory in the 1906 general election. The size of the government's majority gave the Irish Parliamentary Party little bargaining power. Nevertheless, in May 1907 Chief Secretary Augustine Birrell introduced the Irish Council Bill (also known as the Devolution Bill) into the House of Commons. It was intended to 'associate the people with the conduct of Irish affairs'. It was basically a reworking of MacDonnells' earlier devolution scheme. Ireland would get a 106-member chamber and receive control over 8 of 45 government departments, including education and local government. However, the scheme was a poor substitute for Home Rule and was rejected by nationalists and Unionists, albeit for different reasons. On 3 June 1907 Birrell announced that the Bill was to be dropped.

4.10. By 1909, however, the political landscape had changed. The Tory-dominated House of Lords rejected Lloyd George's radical 'people's budget' on 30 November and two General Elections followed in 1910. After the December election the Irish Party held the balance of power. H.H. Asquith declared in December 1910 that a future Liberal government would be free to consider full legislative Home Rule in return for the parliamentary support of the Redmond's Irish MPs. Andrew Bonar Law denounced the alliance as a 'corrupt parliamentary bargain' and he reminded Asquith that there was 'no length of resistance to which Ulster can go'. Asquith quickly set about introducing legislation to curb the power of the Lords. The Parliament Act was passed on 18 August 1911. It deprived the House of Lords of all power over money bills, restricted its power over other bills to a suspensive veto of 2 years, and reduced the maximum duration of parliament from 7 years to 5. The passage of the Home Rule Bill now appeared inevitable.

4.11. Sir Edward Carson was elected leader of the Irish Unionists in Commons on 21 February 1910 and he was determined to resist any new Bill. Another prominent Ulster Unionist MP, Captain James Craig stated in January 1911 that 'Germany and the German Emperor would be preferred to the rule of John Redmond, Patrick Ford [editor of the American newspaper, *Irish World*] and the Molly Maguires'. On 23 September over 50,000 Orangemen and Unionists marched from Belfast to Craigavon House to an anti-Home Rule demonstration addressed by Carson, the first of many such meetings and rallies held in Ulster. On 9 April 1912 Andrew Bonar Law, Walter Long, Edward Carson addressed a crowd of over 100,000 people at Balmoral Show Grounds.

4.12. Nonetheless, Asquith introduced the third Home Rule Bill on 11 April 1912. On 11 June T.C.R. Agar-Robartes proposed an amendment to the Bill to exclude counties Antrim, Armagh, Down and Londonderry from its provisions; declaring: 'I have never heard that orange bitters will mix with Irish whiskey.' Unionist men and women lined up in their thousands to sign. Over 471,000 signatures were eventually received from various locations inside and outside of Ulster. Carson wanted to preserve the whole of Ireland from Home Rule and he was reluctant to accept the partitionist compromise. His proposed amendment to exclude all nine Ulster counties from the Bill was defeated in early 1913. As expected, the Home Rule Bill was opposed by Unionists and Conservatives in the House of Commons and the third reading was not carried until 13 January 1913. Its defeat in the Lords on 15 July by 302 to 64 had the effect of delaying if for two years.

4.13. In March 1914 Redmond agreed to support Asquith's proposal to allow individual Ulster counties to opt out of Home Rule for a period of six years. Carson told the Commons on 9 March: 'Ulster wants this question settled now and forever. We do not want a sentence of death with a stay of execution for six years'. On 20 March General Hubert Gough, Commander of the 3rd Cavalry Brigade stationed at Curragh Camp, Co. Kildare, and 57 of his officers announced that they would prefer to be dismissed from the army to being ordered north to enforce Home Rule. The 'Curragh mutiny' revealed the limits of the government's authority. Against a rapidly deteriorating European background the Buckingham Palace Conference was convened in July 1914. Debate centred round the proposal to exclude Ulster from the Home Rule Act but the parties failed to reach a settlement. With the formation of the Ulster Volunteer Force and Irish Volunteer Force in 1913 and the arming of both sides in 1914, civil war in Ireland seemed inevitable. Ulstermen now began drilling in public. Plans for a *coup d'état* in Ulster were at an advanced stage when the First World War broke out in August. Asquith finally got the Irish parties to agree that the Home Rule Act would be suspended until the war was over. King George V signed the Government of Ireland

(Home Rule) Act, 1914, into law on 18 September but with an addendum that the Act would not come into effect until some provision had been made for Ulster.

4.14. Events in Ireland after the Easter Rising of 1916 and the general election of December 1918, made Home Rule irrelevant. Redmond's Home Rule Party was overwhelmingly defeated by Sinn Féin. Radical nationalists' demands now went much further than Home Rule. The British government attempted to settle the Irish problem with the Government of Ireland Act, 1920. It provided for two governments and two parliaments in Ireland: one for the six north-east counties; the second for the rest of the country. Ulster Unionists reluctantly accepted their Home Rule parliament and the state of Northern Ireland was established. As Craig put it: 'We believe that so long as we are without a parliament of our own constant attacks would be made upon us, and constant attempts would be made … to draw us into a Dublin parliament. We see our safety, therefore, in having a parliament of our own.' For the rest of the country the measure had come too late and partition was not acceptable. Sinn Féin refused to accept it. The result was a divided Ireland embittered by political and religious factionalism.

4.15. BIBLIOGRAPHY: Isaac Butt, *Home government for Ireland: Irish federalism!: its meaning, its objects, and its hopes* (3rd ed., Dublin, 1870; 4th ed., Dublin, 1874). Michael F.J. McDonnell, *Ireland and the Home Rule movement* (Dublin, 1908; repr. 2009). T.M. Healy, *Letters and leaders of my day* (2 vols, London, 1928). J.L. Hammond, *Gladstone and the Irish nation* (London, 1938; repr. London, 1964). Terence de Vere White, *The road to excess* (Dublin, 1946). Conor Cruise O'Brien, *Parnell and his party, 1880–90* (Oxford, 1957). F.S.L. Lyons, *The fall of Parnell, 1890–91* (London, 1960). Lawrence J. McCaffrey, *Irish federalism in the 1870: a study in conservative nationalism* (Philadelphia, 1962). L.P. Curtis, *Coercion and conciliation in Ireland, 1880–1892: a study in conservative unionism* (Princeton, NJ, 1963). David Thornley, *Isaac Butt and Home Rule* (London, 1964). F.S.L. Lyons, *Charles Stewart Parnell* (London, 1977). Edward George Power, *Gladstone and Irish Home Rule* (London, 1983). James Loughlin, *Gladstone, Home Rule, and the Ulster question, 1882–93* (Dublin, 1986). Alan O'Day, *Parnell and the first Home Rule episode, 1884–87* (Dublin, 1986). William Michael Murphy, *The Parnell myth and Irish politics, 1891–1956* (New York, 1986). Paul Bew, *Conflict and conciliation in Ireland, 1890–1910: Parnellites and radical agrarians* (Oxford, 1987). Alan O'Day, *Irish Home Rule, 1867–1921* (Manchester, 1998). D. George Boyce & Alan O'Day (eds), *Defenders of the Union: a survey of British and Irish Unionism since 1801* (London, 2001). Alvin Jackson, *Home Rule: an Irish history, 1800–2000* (New York, 2004). Stephen M. Duffy, *The integrity of Ireland: Home Rule, nationalism, and partition, 1912–1922* (Madison, NJ, 2009). Daniel Jackson, *Popular opposition to Irish Home Rule in Edwardian Britain* (Liverpool, 2009).

FIDELMA MAGUIRE AND TOMÁS O'RIORDAN

5. Irish Ireland

5.1. This is a general term for the forms of cultural nationalism that took shape during the 1890s and early 1900s. In sport, literature, language and education, there was a desire to move away from the dominant influence of England and to develop an 'Irish Ireland'. Organisations were established which did not concern themselves with political or revolutionary matters but focused on cultural nationalism that sought to develop an increased awareness of the distinctive qualities of Ireland and its people.

5.2. In September 1900, David P. Moran (1869–1936), the influential journalist and polemicist, established a weekly paper, the *Leader*, an important vehicle for disseminating his strongly expressed views on 'Irish Ireland'. In 1905 he published a collection of essays under the title *A philosophy of Irish Ireland* based on a series of articles published between 1893 and 1900. Moran said that Irish people emulated English culture while protesting against English political rule. He viewed Anglo-Irish history as the history not of Ireland but of a garrison. The Irish, Moran argued, needed to discourage Anglicisation through the revival of the Gaelic language and by opposing English economic control. In stating his concept of Irish nationalism, he pointed to what he saw as flaws in popular ideas of Irish culture, identity and independence. While he was critical of nearly every part of the national movement, he was active in the Gaelic League and in the Irish Literary Society. He organised a 'Buy Irish' campaign, and he took part in the first meeting of the steering committee to form the Irish Volunteers in November 1913. Though clearly influenced by Douglas Hyde, Moran was more overtly nationalist and has often been criticised for using chauvinistic images and crudely sectarian terminology. Although Moran is known to have employed Protestant workers and to have campaigned against anti-Catholic discrimination in the workplace, some commentators believed him to be intolerant of anything deemed non-Catholic or non-Irish. In his writing he called for cultural, political and economic nationalism whereby Ireland would be a:

> self governing land, living, moving and having its being in its own language, self-reliant, intellectually as well as politically independent, initiating its own reforms, developing its own manners and customs, creating its own literature out of its own distinctive consciousness, working to their fullest capacity the material resources of the country, inventing, criticising, attempting, doing.

5.3. More profound expressions of a broader Irish Ireland ideology are found in the Society for the Preservation of the Irish Language (1876), the Gaelic Union (1878), the Gaelic Athletic Association (1884), the Gaelic League (1893), and Cumann na nGaedheal (1893). One should also include socio-political groups such as the Land League and the Home Rule movement. Also important are the writings of Thomas Davis and the Young Irelanders of the 1840s. The motto of *The Nation* paper was suggested by Davis: 'To create and foster public opinion in Ireland, and make it racy of the soil'. He hoped it would help bring about 'a nationality of the spirit as well as the letter'. To Davis, it was not blood that made you Irish, but the willingness to be part of the Irish nation. It was he who built on idea of promoting an Irish identity. Many Irishmen (Protestant and Catholic) shared his sentiments. Most notable is Douglas Hyde. In his presidential address (25 November 1892) to the National Literary Society, Dublin 'On the necessity of de-anglicising Ireland', he argued that Ireland should follow her own traditions in language, literature and even in dress. He was to play a seminal role in the Irish Ireland movement, inspiring a new generation of young people.

5.4. Michael Cusack founded the Gaelic Athletic Association (GAA) in 1884. A teacher, and one-time enthusiast for cricket and rugby, he had become disillusioned with the social exclusiveness of existing sporting bodies and the association of sport with gambling. He convinced himself that the spread of English games was destroying national morale. By 1886, Fenians dominated the executive and Cusack himself had been ousted from the organisation. From 1901, a new generation of IRB-affiliated leaders rebuilt the GAA as an openly nationalist but not explicitly revolutionary movement that could attract broader support. The GAA was thus part of the new nationalism of the years before 1916.

5.5. Eoin MacNeill and others established the Gaelic League in 1893 to preserve and extend the use of Irish as a spoken language. It sought to revive Irish both as a spoken and literary movement. By 1906 there were over 600 branches within Ireland and several hundred more abroad. Outside of Gaeltacht areas, most of the people joining were English speakers who wished to learn Irish. Its membership was drawn mainly from the urban lower-middle classes of English-speaking Ireland. As such, it reflected the acute need for cultural roots felt by many after several decades of rapid social change. There was an inevitable tendency to idealise the culture and way of life of the surviving Gaeltacht areas. Its leadership, notably Hyde, insisted that it should be non-political and initially it attracted significant support from Protestants and Unionists. However, its members took a prominent part in the 1916 Rising and in the subsequent growth of Sinn Féin and the IRA.

5.6. Cumann na nGaedheal was founded by Arthur Griffith and the journalist William Rooney in September 1900 to diffuse knowledge of Irish economic resources, Irish history, language, music and art. At the same time, it pushed for Irish economic independence. This was to become the central aspect of Griffith's later teachings. At the Cumann na nGaedheal Convention in 1902, Griffith called for the abstention of Irish Parliamentary Party MPs from Westminster. He advocated self-government along the lines of Grattan's parliament in the organisations' paper *United Irishman*. Members of the Cumann na nGaedheal Executive formed the National Council in 1903 to protest against the proposed visit of King Edward VII to Ireland (21 July–1 August). The National Council was a means of bringing together the different types of separatist protest.

5.7. In contrast, the Irish Parliamentary Party, preoccupied as it was with the land question and the struggle for Home Rule, showed little interest in alternative bases for Irish national consciousness. It failed to associate itself in the public mind with either the Gaelic Athletic Association or the Gaelic League. D.P. Moran went so far as to describe Irish Party MPs as 'West Britons' and 'shoneens' [someone who tries to ape those they think are their betters].

5.8. At the annual convention of the National Council on 28 November 1905, Griffith proposed the policy that became known as Sinn Féin ('ourselves'), with an emphasis on Irish culutral and economic independence. By 1908 both the National Council and Cumann na nGaedheal had been amalgamated with Sinn Féin. The movement's paper of the same name was edited by Griffith until 1914. It supported Home Rule (for the whole of Ireland) and was critical of what was seen as John Redmond's pro-British stance. It called on Irish people to withdraw their co-operation from government institutions in favour of Irish ones. Other Irish-Irelanders also aimed to achieve genuine autonomy but this was not possible without self-sufficiency. However, Horace Plunkett's co-operative farming movement was important in improving the Irish agricultural economy – a plank in Griffith's platform.

5.9. The Abbey Theatre was founded in 1904. A Manchester tea merchant heiress, Miss Annie Fredericka Horniman bought the Mechanics' Institute in Dublin (1904) as a home for the Irish National Theatre Company. With £1,500 (approx. €135,000 at 2009 values) provided by Miss Horniman, the Institute was fitted out as the Abbey Theatre. It received an annual subsidy of from Miss Horniman and a patent, made out to Lady Gregory, was granted by the government. It opened on 27 December 1904 with performances of Yeats' *On Baile's strand* and Lady Gregory's *Spreading the news*. The theatre also showed plays written in Irish by Douglas Hyde. The playright, Thomas Kilroy, later wrote that the theatre had the potential to 'weld the fracture between the Anglo-Irish and Gaelic Ireland'. The Abbey made a distinguished contribution to Irish theatre and culture generally and represents another thread in the fabric of the Irish Ireland movement.

5.10. There was much disagreement among the different groups and personalities on how their aims could be achieved. In their zealousness to promote a sense of separateness, some Irish-Irelanders often developed a deep intolerance for Britain that was considered to be the source of all the negative influences helping to pervert Irish customs, values and traditions. Hyde famously revealed the contradictory behaviours of those who 'protest as a matter of sentiment' to 'hate the country which at every hand's turn they rush to imitate' – prescient words that apply as much to the whole of the twentieth century as to the day they were uttered. Hyde and other members of the Gaelic League saw the Irish language as a means of forging a deeper allegiance that might transcend politics and demonstrate a shared, traditional cultural heritage. They were to be disappointed.

5.II. BIOGRAPHY, STUDIES AND WRITINGS: D.P. Moran, *The philosophy of Irish Ireland* (Dublin, 1905; repr. & ed. Patrick Maume, Dublin, 2006). T.F. O'Sullivan, *The story of the GAA* (Dublin, 1916). Dúbhglas de híde, *Mise agus an Connradh (go dtí 1905)* (Dublin, 1937). Myles Dillon, 'Douglas Hyde', in Conor Cruise O'Brien (ed.), *The shaping of modern Ireland* (London, 1960), pp 50–62. Brian Ó Cuív, 'The Gaelic cultural movements and the new nationalism', in K.B. Nowlan (ed.), *The making of 1916: studies in the history of the Rising* (Dublin, 1969), pp 1–27. Seán Ó Tuama, *The Gaelic League idea* (Dublin, 1972; 2nd ed., Cork, 1993). F.X. Martin & F.J. Byrne (eds), *The scholar revolutionary: Eoin MacNeill, 1867–1945, and the making of the new Ireland* (Shannon, 1973). Proinsias Mac Aonghusa (ed.), *Oireachtas na Gaeilge, 1897–1997* (Dublin, 1977). Michael Tierney, *Eoin MacNeill: scholar and man of action, 1867–1945* (Oxford, 1980). Donncha Ó Súilleabháin, *An Piarsach agus Conradh na Gaeilge* (Dublin, 1981). W.F. Mandle & Pauric Travers (eds), *Irish culture and nationalism, 1750–1950* (Dublin, 1983). Máire Ní Mhurchú & Diarmuid Breathnach, *Beathaisnéis, 1782–1982* (6 vols, Dublin, 1986–99) [essential, succinct, and scholarly dictionary of biography, especially of Celtic scholars, Gaelic Leaguers and Irish authors]. Jeanne Sheehy, *The rediscovery of Ireland's past: the Celtic revival, 1830–1930* (London, 1980). Seamus Deane, *Celtic revivals: essays in modern Irish literature, 1880–1980* (London, 1985). W.F. Mandle, *The Gaelic Athletic Association and Irish nationalist politics, 1884–1924* (London & Dublin, 1987). John Hutchinson, *The dynamics of cultural nationalism: the Gaelic revival and the creation of the Irish nation state* (London, 1987). Donald Caird, 'A view of the revival of the Irish language', *Éire-Ireland*, 25:2 (1990), 96–108. T.J. Edelstein (ed.), *Imagining an Irish past: the Celtic revival, 1840–1940* (Chicago, 1992). Georg Grote, *Torn between politics and culture: the Gaelic League, 1893–1993* (Münster & New York, 1993). Patrick Maume, *'Life that is exile': Daniel Corkery and the search for Irish Ireland* (Belfast, 1993). Patrick Maume, *D.P. Moran* (Dundalk, 1995). Mike Cronin, 'Defenders of the nation? The Gaelic Athletic Association and Irish nationalist identity', *Irish Political Studies*, 11 (1996), 1–19. Patrick Maume, *The rise and fall of Irish Ireland: D.P. Moran and Daniel Corkery* (Coleraine, 1996). Patrick Maume, *The long gestation: Irish nationalist life, 1891–1918* (Dublin, 1999). Tony Crowley, *The politics of language in Ireland, 1366–1922: a source book* (London & New York, 2000). Gregory Castle, *Modernism and the Celtic revival* (Cambridge & New York, 2001). Tony Crowley, '"The struggle between the languages": the politics of English in Ireland', *Bullán: an Irish Studies Review*, 5:2 (2001), 5–21. Timothy G. McMahon, '"All creeds and all classes"? Just who made up the Gaelic League?', *Éire-Ireland*, 37:3–4 (2002), 118–68. Betsey Taylor FitzSimon & James H. Murphy (eds), *The Irish revival reappraised* (Dublin, 2004). Mike Cronin, Mark Duncan & Paul Rouse, *The GAA: a people's history* (Cork, 2009).

EOIN HARTNETT AND TOMÁS O'RIORDAN

6. Militarism/separatism

6.1. These terms refer to the pursuit of political goals, including an independent Irish republic, through the use of physical force. The most extreme and the most tenacious exponents of militant separatism were the Fenians/Irish Republican Brotherhood (IRB). The group (originally known as the Irish Revolutionary Brotherhood) was founded in Dublin on St Patrick's Day 1858 by James Stephens (1825–1901). Simulataneously, John O'Mahony (1816–77) founded the Fenian Brotherhood in New York. The movement's ultimate aim was complete independence and an Irish republic achieved by physical force. While the entire movement was popularly known as the Fenians, the IRB is often seen as the military directive of the movement (as well as the more moderate of the two groups). Until such time as a Republic was achieved the Fenians were to recognise the Supreme Council of the IRB as the Provisional Government of Ireland. Among themselves the members referred to it as 'The Society', 'The Organisation' or 'The Brotherhood'.

6.2. Stephens organised the IRB as a secret, oath-bound society that perpetuated, as he thought, the ideals of the United Irishmen and Young Ireland. Each member of the IRB had to swear an oath. One version went:

> I [*name*] in the presence of Almighty God, do solemnly swear allegiance to the Irish Republic now virtually established; and that I will do my utmost, at every risk, while life lasts, to defend its independence and integrity; and finally, that I will yield implicit obedience in all things, not contrary to the laws of God, to the commands of my superior officer. So help me God. Amen.

6.3. As a secret society the IRB quickly incurred the hostility of the Catholic Church and was denounced by the Catholic bishops in 1863. Nonetheless, it found support among the lower clergy. Its newspaper the *Irish People* first appeared on 28 November 1863 and ran for twenty-two months until it was suppressed. Three years later it was replaced by the *Flag of Ireland*, suppressed in 1874. The Archbishop of Dublin, Cardinal Paul Cullen, referring to *Irish People* in October 1865 said 'for suppressing that paper the public authorities deserve the thanks and gratitude of all those who love Ireland'. On 17 February 1867, in a sermon given in Killarney Cathedral, David Moriarty, Bishop of Kerry, declared: 'when we look down into the fathomless depths of this infamy of the heads of the fenian conspiracy we must acknowledge that eternity is not long enough nor hell hot enough to punish such miscreants'. Pope Pius IX denounced the IRB in 1869.

6.4. At the beginning of 1865 Stephens calculated that the movement was 85,000-men strong and when the American Civil War ended in April 1865 he asserted that the Fenians would act before the end of the year. However, the government kept a close eye on American soldiers moving between the two countries since the beginning of the war and was kept well informed by spies such as Pierce Nagle. The offices of the *Irish People* were raided on 15 September 1865 and Jeremiah O'Donnovan Rossa, John O'Leary, Thomas Clarke Luby and Charles Kickham were arrested on treason-felony charges. The authorities were unaware though that the secret military council of the Fenians, including Colonel Thomas J. Kelly and John Devoy, were still at large and determined to strike before the end of the year. Devoy organised the escape of James Stephens from Richmond prison on 25 November 1865 abetted by two Irish warders, Byrne and Breslin. The leadership failed to convince Stephens of the merits of a rebellion and he remained in hiding in Dublin for nearly three months before he finally decided to go to America. In December, he was denounced as a 'rogue, imposter and traitor' by American Fenians and deposed as Head Centre, being succeeded by Kelly.

6.5. In January 1867 Kelly set up his headquarters in London. The first plan was to start a guerrilla war in Ireland and the date was set for 11 February. The arms dump at Chester Castle was to be raided and the arms rushed from Holyhead to Ireland. An informer, John Corydon passed this information to the police. The raid and rising had to be called off. Although Corydon had kept the police well informed they were still poorly prepared for any rising. Outbreaks in Dublin, Tipperary, Limerick, Clare and Waterford on 5 and 6 March 1867 were easily put down. American help came after the rising. A ship called *Erin's Hope* (originally the *Jacknell Packet*) carrying 5,000 rifles, 1½ million rounds and three cannon arrived in Sligo Bay in May 1867. After an aborted landing, it proceeded to Dungarvan, Co. Waterford. The twenty-eight Fenians who put ashore near Helvick Head were quickly arrested and tried.

6.6. In September 1867 Kelly was arrested in Manchester. Thirty Fenians attacked the unescorted prison van in an attempt to rescue him. An unarmed police sergeant was killed. Kelly escaped but five men were put on trial and three, William O'Meara Allen, Michael Larkin and William O'Brien, known as the 'Manchester Martyrs', were hanged on 24 November 1867. Some 60,000 people attended the public funeral in Dublin and it won the IRB much public sympathy. In December 1867 another bungled attempt to rescue Richard O'Sullivan Burke caused an explosion at Clerkenwell House of Detention in London. Twelve people were killed and 126 injured.

6.7. The rising and its aftermath caused widespread and deep concern in England and drew Gladstone's attention to Irish affairs.

6.8. The IRB survived the failure of the rising, despite deep internal divisions. On 20 June 1867 the Irish-American republican organisation, Clan na Gael was founded in New York by Jerome J. Collins. It recognised the Supreme Council of the IRB as the government of the Irish Republic. It, too, was a secret and oath-bound organisation. It attracted many of the important IRB men who had to flee to America, including Jeremiah O'Donovan Rossa and John Devoy. Clan na Gael financed an inept bombing campaign in England in the 1880s which alienated some British support for Irish reform.

6.9. On 18 August 1869 the IRB adopted the 'constitution of Irish Republic'. The new constitution laid down that all members had to swear an oath undertaking to do their utmost to establish an independent Ireland, to be faithful to the Supreme Council, to obey their superior officers and be faithful to the constitution of the IRB. The President of the Supreme Council was also recognised as President of the Irish Republic. The IRB was now organised on a democratic basis and the partially elected Supreme Council contained representatives from around Ireland and Britain.

6.10. In 1873, the IRB gave conditional support to Butt's Home Rule programme. However, on 4 August 1876 the Supreme Council adopted a resolution withdrawing support for the Home Rule movement and requesting all members to cease such activity within 6 months. Those who remained members of the Irish Parliamentary Party would be expelled from the Supreme Council. Tensions increased within the IRB and the Fenian movement in America between those who were prepared to work with the constitutionalists and those who would not. Devoy was reluctant to abandon his arrangement with Parnell until it clearly proved fruitless while O'Donovan Rossa was wholly committed to physical force. The prospects for revolution were poor. Many Fenians were attracted to the Land League of which Parnell was president from 1879. So strong was the Parnellite movement that the revolutionary movement was largely overshadowed. Many IRB members were either expelled or chose to leave the organisation. Official sources estimated that membership had fallen from 11,000 to around 8,000. Nonetheless, this did not prevent a terrorist urban dynamite campaign in Britain, 1881–5. Financed from a fund established by O'Donovan Rossa, the campaign did not have the support of leading figures within Clan na Gael. In 1881 an attempt was made to blow up Liverpool Town Hall. In 1883 there were further explosions on the London Underground, in Government Buildings and even Scotland Yard. In December 1884, three men were killed when trying to blow up London Bridge. Four civilians were injured in January 1885 when a bomb exploded behind a gun carriage in the Tower of London.

6.11. The IRB continued to enjoy considerable influence and from 1880s on adopted the policy of infiltrating nationalist organisations. It gained more support in 1898 when it had a leading role in commemorating the centenary of the United Irish rebellion of 1798. John O'Leary was president of the IRB committee formed to commemorate the event. Other people involved in arranging the celebrations included Fred Allan, Maude Gonne, James Connolly, John MacBride and W.B. Yeats. All gathered for the centenary celebrations under the watchful eye of Dublin Castle.

6.12. By the early 1900s, the IRB had become somewhat stagnant and was losing support to open political organisations such as Bulmer Hobson's Dungannon Clubs and Arthur Griffith's Cumann na Gaedheal. The latter were soon absorbed into Griffith's other political movement, Sinn Féin. Men such as Hobson, Denis McCullough and Seán MacDiarmada helped bring about a revival in the revolutionary tradition. The Fenian Thomas Clarke returned to Ireland in 1907 after spending 15 years in English jails. His tobacconist shops in Dublin became centres of republican activity. As a member of the Supreme Council of the IRB, he called for the establishment of a Military Council to examine the feasibility of an armed insurrection in Ireland. By 1913 there were over 1,600 IRB members in Ireland and several hundred in Great Britain, still a small minority among nationalists.

6.13. In 1912 Home Rule for Ireland looked imminent. The Ulster Volunteer Force (UVF) was founded in January 1913, a momentous event that brought back the gun in Irish politics. Some Unionists had been drilling in preparation for the day they would have to defend the Union. Finance was provided by people such as Rudyard Kipling, Lord Iveagh, Lord Rothschild and the Duke of Bedford. Sir George Richardson, a retired British general, had the task of training the new army. Membership was limited to 100,000 men, between the ages of 17 and 65, who had signed the Ulster Solemn League and Covenant in September 1912. The UVF stockpiled 25,000 guns and three million rounds of ammunition after the Larne gun-running in April 1914. Carson freely admitted that 'the Volunteers are illegal, and the government knows they are illegal, and the government does not interfere with them'. With the outbreak of the First World War, the UVF was largely incorporated in the British Army as the 36th (Ulster) Division.

6.14. On 19 November 1913, a workers' militia, the Irish Citizen Army, was launched by James Connolly and James Larkin at a meeting of the Dublin Civic League in the Antient Rooms. Its origins lay in the ideas of the Protestant nationalist J.R. White. During the Lockout of 1913, he had argued that workers needed to be disciplined in preparation for the coming struggle with capitalism. It also aimed to protect workers from attacks by the Dublin Metropolitan Police and the employers' henchmen. However, by 1914 membership of the Irish Citizen Army had dropped to about two hundred. Connolly reorganised the corps and hoped that it could still play a role in the establishment of a workers' republic.

6.15. Militarism spread when the Irish Volunteers were formed in November 1913 as an answer to the UVF, ostensibly under the control of the respected academic, Eoin MacNeill. In an article in *An Claidheamh Soluis*, he urged that southern nationalists should form a volunteer movement along the lines of the UVF. He was then approached by Bulmer Hobson of the IRB who organised a public meeting at the Rotunda where the new force was established. It attracted followers of Sinn Féin, the Gaelic Athletic Association and the Gaelic League as well as members of the IRB – who had their own plan for the new force. By August 1914 membership was about 80,000 and funds were collected through John Devoy and Clan na Gael in the USA and Sir Roger Casement and Alice Stopford Green in England. Darrell Figgis and Robert Erskine Childers arranged to buy guns in Germany in July 1914. These were landed at Howth by Childers in his yacht the *Asgard*, and arrived on 26 July, 900 rifles and 29,000 rounds of ammunition.

6.16. So by the summer of 1914 there were two armed and potentially very dangerous volunteer forces in the country. In order to ensure control of the Irish Volunteers lest they should jeopardise the passage of the third Home Rule Bill, John Redmond demanded half of the seats on the Provisional Committee in June 1914. When Home

Rule was suspended with the outbreak of the First World War, membership of the Irish
Volunteers may have been as high as 180,000. Conscious of the loyalty to the Crown
being demonstrated by the UVF in the north, Redmond rallied Irish recruits to the
British war effort. At Woodenbridge in September he called on Volunteers to join the
British army and fight 'not only in Ireland itself, but wherever the firing line extends in
defence of right, of freedom and of religion in this war'. The movement split. The majority of Volunteers supported Redmond's recruitment policy and were called National
Volunteers. The other 11,000 Irish Volunteers who opposed involvement in the war were
reorganised in October 1914.

6.17. At the Annual Convention (25 October) held at the Abbey Theatre in Dublin, the
Irish Volunteers reaffirmed their allegiance to Ireland only and declared that their ulti-
mate objective was to save Home Rule and avert partition. MacNeill became Chief of
Staff and IRB members took the three key positions: Patrick Pearse was Director of
Military Organisation, Thomas MacDonagh was Director of Training, and Joseph
Plunkett was Director of Military Operations. These three together with Tom Clarke,
Seán Mac Diarmada, Eamonn Ceannt and James Connolly organised the Easter Rising
of 1916 and changed the course of Irish politics dramatically. Militant separatism and
militant Unionism were to determine Ireland's fate and bring in their train violence, factionalism and sectarianism.

6.18. BIOGRAPHY, STUDIES AND WRITINGS: Marcus Bourke, *John O'Leary: a study in
Irish separatism* (Tralee, 1967). T.W. Moody (ed.), *The Fenian movement* (Cork, 1968).
Leon Ó Broin, *Revolutionary underground: the story of the Irish Republican Brotherhood,
1858–1924* (Dublin, 1976). Thomas E. Hachey, *Britain and Irish separatism: from the
Fenians to the Free State 1867–1922* (Chicago, 1977). Colin H. Williams, *National sepa-
ratism* (Cardiff, 1982). Michael Laffan, 'Violence and terror in twentieth century Ireland:
IRB and IRA', in Wolfgang Mommsen & Gerhard Hirschfeld (eds), *Social protest, vio-
lence and terror in nineteenth- and twentieth-century Europe* (London, 1982), pp 155–174.
Beth McKillen, 'Irish feminism and nationalist separatism', *Éire-Ireland*, 17 (1982) 52–
67, 72–90. Robin Wilson, 'Imperialism in crisis: the Irish dimension', in Mary Langan
& Bill Scharz (eds), *Crises in the British state 1880–1930* (London, 1985), pp 151–78. Tom
Garvin, 'The anatomy of a nationalist Revolution: Ireland, 1858–1928', *Comparative
Studies in Society and History*, 28:3 (1986), 468–501. Tom Garvin, 'Priests and patriots:
Irish separatism and fear of the modern, 1890–1914', *Irish Historical Studies*, 25 (1986),
67–81. Seán Ó Faoláin, *Constance Markievicz* (3rd ed., London, 1987). John O'Beirne-
Ranelagh, 'The Irish Republican Brotherhood in the revolutionary period, 1879–1923',
in David George Boyce (ed.), *The revolution in Ireland, 1879–1923* (Basingstoke, 1988),
pp 137–56. E.A. Muenger, *The British military dilemma in Ireland: occupation politics,
1886–1914* (Lawrence, KS & Dublin, 1991). David Fitzpatrick, 'Militarism in Ireland,
1900–1922', in Thomas Bartlett & Keith Jeffery (eds), *A military history of Ireland*
(Cambridge, 1996), pp 379–406. Ulick O'Connor, *The troubles: Michael Collins and the*

volunteers in the struggle for Irish freedom, 1912–1922 (3rd ed., London, 1996). W.E. Vaughan, *A new history of Ireland: Ireland under the Union, II: 1870–1921* (Oxford, 1996). Vincent MacDowell, *Michael Collins and the Irish Republican Brotherhood* (Dublin, 1997). Sinéad McCoole, *Guns and chiffon: women revolutionaries and Kilmainham Gaol, 1916–1923* (Dublin, 1997). P.J. Matthews, 'Stirring up disloyalty: the Boer War, the Irish Literary Theatre and the emergence of a new separatism', *Irish University Review*, 33:1 (2003), 99–116. Peter Hart, *The IRA at war, 1916–1923* (Oxford, 2003). Owen McGee, *The IRB: from the Land League to Sinn Féin* (Dublin, 2005). M.J. Kelly, *The Fenian ideal and Irish nationalism, 1882–1916* (Rochester, NY, 2006). Paul Bew, *Ireland: the politics of enmity, 1789–2006* (Oxford & New York, 2007).

MARGARET FITZPATRICK AND EOIN HARTNETT

7. Political agitation

7.1. People get involved in politics to achieve different goals in different ways. Political agitation is the general term used to describe the various peaceable, or near peaceable, methods of politicians. The most important distinction made by historians is between those who used violence to achieve their goals and those who used only peaceful and democratic methods. It is hard to draw the line between violent and non-violent agitation: they tend to merge into each other.

7.2. Following the 1874 general election (which returned 60 Home Rulers, 33 Conservatives and 10 Liberals) the policy of 'obstruction' of parliamentary business was advocated by Joseph Biggar and later by Charles Stewart Parnell. They used the procedures of the Commons to delay legislation unconnected with Ireland and to draw attention to themselves and their objectives. They argued that since British politicians blocked Irish reforms, they were going to hold up British reforms. Biggar was infamous for making long and dreary speeches in his harsh Belfast accent. The obstructionists proposed amendments to almost every bill and made very lengthy speeches in debates in the Commons. This promoted the image of the Home Rulers as vigorous and dedicated individuals. In July 1877, Parnell and others kept the House of Commons sitting for 45 hours non-stop. These long debates often led to important amendments to individual bills before the house. Joseph Chamberlain admitted that:

> … the friends of humanity and the friends of the British Army owe a debt of gratitude to you [Parnell] for standing up alone against this system of flogging, when I myself, and other members, had not the courage of our convictions.

7.3. There was intense agitation outside parliament. Poor returns from farming, severe food shortages and widespread exploitation of tenants had given rise to the so-called 'Land War' of the 1870s and 1880s. Michael Davitt's Land League organised rural complaints and pressurised many landlords into negotiating with their tenants. The Land League did not favour violence and did its utmost to discourage it. Events of 1880 offered it a potential weapon that proved very effective. In September 1880 Parnell addressed a very large gathering at Ennis and said that any man who offended the League should be sent to a 'moral Coventry' [after Coventry in England: Royalist prisoners were sent there during the English Civil War]:

> When a man takes a farm from which another has been evicted, you must shun him on the roadside when you meet him – you must shun him in the streets of the town – you must shun in the shop – you must shun him on the fair-green and in the market place, and even in the place of worship, by leaving him alone, by putting him into a moral Coventry, by isolating him from the rest of the county, as if he were a leper of old – you must show him your detestation of the crime he has committed.

7.4. On 24 September 1880, Parnell's words were put into effect against Captain Charles Cunningham Boycott, land agent to Lord Erne, on part of his estate, Lough Mask House, Co. Mayo. Boycott had refused a demand from the Land League to reduce rents and he evicted three tenants. Local shopkeepers refused him. The staff on the estate fled in fear. English newspapers managed to raise £2,000 to help save Boycott's crops. A relief expedition of Orange labourers harvested them. Over a thousand soldiers were needed to escort the workers and the operation is said to have cost the government nearly £10,000. The Land League had a new and powerful weapon and a new word entered the English language.

7.5. The movements above are examples of different political programmes. Davitt's Land League espoused ownership of the land for men and women who tilled it. The Fenians in Ireland and America looked to Wolfe Tone's ideal of separating Ireland from the United Kingdom. Butt and Parnell fought a great parliamentary battle for a domestic Irish parliament with control over Irish social and economic resources. Cultural groups like the Gaelic League and intellectuals like Patrick Pearse and Douglas Hyde sought to give Ireland an entirely new cultural foundation. All were engaged in various forms of political agitation, that is, they demanded that their preferred political plans be implemented by the government of the day and they were willing to use a variety of means to achieve this objective.

7.6. Davitt drew on Daniel O' Connell's methods of agitation and arranged great public meetings. He used the local, national and international media to promote his cause, focusing on acts of dispossession and evictions. He encouraged confrontation between certain landlords and peasant tenants, confrontations that often became violent and sometimes resulted in physical injury or death. They were so common during the 1860s and 1870s that they attracted the continuous and keen attention of all senior British politicians. In 1878–9 the Fenian organisation (which openly supported the use of violence during political agitation) was working in harmony with Davitt's Land League and Parnell's Home Rule Party.

7.7. Parnell was one of the greatest parliamentarians in nineteenth-century Europe. By the middle of the 1880s he had transferred support from Davitt's Land League to his own parliamentary movement, the National League. His method of political agitation was to warn the British government that violence would break out in Ireland if it refused to make concessions. Parnell used parliament to promote Home Rule for Ireland. He formed the first modern political party. All his MPs signed a pledge before election that they would sit, act and vote as one in the House of Commons. Thus by the second 1885 election, he could personally count on a bloc of 85 votes in the Commons. He could make or break governments. The politics of the rest of the nineteenth century was in large measure the result of Parnell's brilliant agitation at Westminster.

7.8. Patrick Pearse and other cultural nationalists used the written word – books, periodicals, and pamphlets – in their political agitation. They sought to convince the Irish people and the British government of the merits of their cultural and educational plans. Pearse, in particular, sought to build up an international network of contacts and supporters. To this end, he undertook important lecture tours in Europe and North America. Douglas Hyde refused to be drawn into the increasingly bitter politics of pre-war Ireland, but Pearse later argued that successful political agitation required the use of force in certain circumstances. He soon joined the Irish Volunteers, became a militant nationalist, and left peaceful agitation far behind.

7.9. BIBLIOGRAPHY: J.V. O'Brien, *William O'Brien and the course of Irish politics, 1881–1918* (Berkeley, CA, 1976). Paul Bew, *Land and the national question in Ireland, 1858–82* (Dublin, 1978). M.D. Higgins & J.P. Gibbons, 'Shopkeeper-graziers and land agitation in Ireland, 1895–1900', in P.J. Drudy (ed.), *Ireland: land, politics and people* (Cambridge, 1982), pp 93–118. W.L. Feingold, 'Land League power: the Tralee poor-law election of 1881', in Samuel Clark & James S. Donnelly (eds), *Irish peasants: violence and political unrest, 1780–1914* (Manchester, 1983), pp 285–310. Emmet O'Connor, 'An age of agitation', *Saothar: Journal of the Irish Labour History Society*, 9 (1983), 64–70. J.W. Knott, 'Land, kinship and identity: the cultural roots of agrarian agitation in eighteenth and nineteenth century Ireland', *Journal of Peasant Studies*, 12:1 (1984), 93–109. Fethi Hassaine, 'Irish agitation and British parliamentary reform', *Annales du monde anglophone*, 1:2 (1995), 61–74. Frank Thompson, *The end of liberal Ulster: land agitation and land reform, 1868–1886* (Belfast, 2001). Philip Bull, 'The formation of the United Irish League, 1898–1900: the dynamics of Irish agrarian agitation', *Irish Historical Studies*, 33 (2003), 404–23. William Keaveney, *The land for the people-Robert Henry Johnstone and the United Irish League: a story of land agitation in the early twentieth century* (Dublin, 2007).

MARGARET FITZPATRICK

8. Socialism

8.1. Socialism is, in general, a doctrine and a political movement that aims at the collective organisation of society for the common good. It aims to do this by common ownership and collective control of the means of production and exchange (land, capital, industry, banks, etc.). The word first appeared in English in the early decades of the nineteenth century. In Britain, Robert Owen (1771–1858) was one of the most important early theorists and advocates of socialism.

8.2. Socialism takes many forms, and there are as many definitions of it as there are socialist groups and political parties. In Marxist theory socialism is the stage between the elimination of capitalism and the coming of communism. Worker movements, labour parties, and social democratic parties consider themselves socialist.

8.3. A significant strand in socialism, one very important in Ireland, stems from attempts to address the poor social and economic conditions of workers. With large-scale industrialisation and urbanisation at the end of the eighteenth century came severe social problems. Workers were exploited, frequently endured long hours, poor pay, inadequate housing and dangerous working conditions. Supporters of socialism quickly identified deficiencies within capitalism that needed to be addressed for the benefit of the entire community. Many condemned the competitive and selfish nature of capitalism as evil and responsible for breeding conflict between workers and the owners of the means of production. To correct this, socialists demanded a fairer distribution of a nation's wealth. Amongst the earliest supporters of socialist ideas were Robert Owen and Charles Fourier (1772–1837). Both established communities for workers, known as co-operative settlements that they hoped would embody ideal social and economic conditions.

8.4. In the middle of the nineteenth century, Karl Marx (1818–83), went even further in his definition of socialism. A German economist, Marx's basic ideas, outlined in *The Communist manifesto* (1848), stressed that all history is a series of struggles between the ruling and the working classes. He was convinced that the capitalist system would die and be replaced by a new system committed to the welfare of the nation as a whole, as opposed to individuals. Common ownership would prevail over economic privilege. To distinguish his brand of socialism from earlier ones, Marx labelled his mode of thought 'scientific socialism'. At the turn of the twentieth century many followers of Marx believed that violence, through revolution, was acceptable in efforts to replace capitalism. This right to bear arms and use violent means would later form the basis of communist doctrine.

8.5. The origins of socialism in Ireland are often traced back to the Irish Republican and Socialist Party (IRSP) founded by James Connolly in 1896. Recent studies, however, point to an earlier presence in Ireland of socialism, or at least of ideas that later formed the core principles of socialism. In 1872, branches of the International Working Men's Association (or First International) were established in Ireland. Located in Dublin, Cork, Belfast and Cootehill, these bodies identified themselves with ideas currently circulating on the continent and expressed by Marx. These early socialist forums did not last long. Strong opposition from the Catholic Church, the press, and various political groups forced them out. Socialism in Ireland was attacked for many reasons – the Church naturally rejected the socialist message because of its perceived alliance with atheism (the Catholic Archbishop of Paris had been killed during the Paris Commune of 1871). Welcoming the end of the International Men's Association, Canon Maguire of Cork, recorded with some satisfaction that 'those wretched people had been expelled from Belfast'.

8.6. Secondly, many of those active in politics in the 1870s thought socialism irrelevant to the greater objectives of Home Rule and land reform. Michael Davitt is a notable exception in this regard. However, the social composition of Ireland at this time and the predominance of peasant life was a brake on socialist development in Ireland. Farmers were far more concerned with getting ownership of land than securing better conditions for those who earned their crust in the few underdeveloped Irish industries, and they had no sympathy with farm labourers. Those in the cities were more concerned with the bread-and-butter issues of employment and housing than any type of class warfare.

8.7. The socialist movement remained on the edge of Irish politics until 1885. In January of that year, the Dublin Democratic Association came into existence in the Oddfellows Hall, 10 Upper Abbey Street. In practice this organisation developed as an offshoot of the much larger British group known as the Democratic Federation (from 1884 the Social Democratic Federation). Thus, Irish socialism throughout this period took its direction from the British socialist revival of the 1880s. In an effort to attract wider support, the association proclaimed that its objective was 'to promote and defend the rights of labour, and to restore the land to the people'. With the police authorities linking socialism and separatism in the 1880s, not surprisingly, Dublin activists tried to avoid describing their organisations as 'socialist' so as not to frighten off recruits.

8.8. The formation of the Dublin Democratic Association was important in that it provided a valuable forum for meeting and discussing issues that affected the workers of the day. In some cases hundreds attended its Saturday meetings, some which were held in conjunction with the Saturday Club at the Rotunda in Dublin. Eventually, the organisation folded because of poor finances and declining membership. One of the activists Samuel Hayes also admitted that members of the Nationalist Party 'did all they could to crush it'.

8.9. The Socialist League followed swiftly after. Once again, the Dublin branch arose out of a larger network established in Britain in December 1884 (as a breakaway from the Social Democratic Federation) Indeed, it was with the arrival of an English anarchist, Michael Gabriel, that the Dublin Socialist League began to gain ground. The League declared itself in favour of Home Rule and Gabriel set about distributing League leaflets and the group's newspaper, *The Commonweal*. It differed from previous Irish socialist groups in its radicalism. The defence and promotion of workers' rights and issues took precedence over everything else. The League explicitly denounced Parliamentary democracy as inadequate for highlighting the plight of workers. Because most MPs were drawn from the landed classes or the wealthy industrial bourgeoisie, the League viewed parliament as the defender of the status quo and thus the enemy of working class agitation. Gabriel asked:

> What would be the use of sending labour candidates to parliament? It would be no use whatever to send them to talk to capitalists and landlords whose interests were different from theirs. As working men they would never get anything by using a vote.

8.10. Most members of the Socialist League rejected the idea that change could be achieved through constitutionalism. In their own words: 'everything depended on the organisation and co-operation amongst the working class'.

8.11. Disputes and problems in dealing with fundamental political issues soon crippled the League. Its militant approach pushed it towards Marx's view of the socialist movement as international in character. Political creeds like nationalism were seen as contradictory to the goals of socialism. Nationalism and borders that separated nation states were rejected in favour of a movement to unite workers of all countries in a bid to achieve universal improvements. The Dublin Socialist League rejected the nationalist and limited Home Rule movement. Taking its cue from Marx, the Dublin League perceptively contended that Home Rule would bring 'the rule of the farmer, the publican, the clergymen and the politicians'. However, 1886 was to be dominated by the Gladstone's Home Rule Bill and the League finally collapsed in the spring of 1887.

8.12. Opposing such a popular movement as Home Rule and a leader as charismatic as Parnell earned the socialist leaders widespread contempt. Militant socialism continued throughout the later 1880s. The National Labour League in 1887 openly called for a socialist uprising in Ireland. James Bryce Killen (1845–1916), a senior Land Leaguer, approved of such militancy because the Irish worker was 'justified in using any means whatever in order to get rid of the idle class that fattened upon his misery'. He succeeded in mobilising the unemployed during 1887 and brought thousands of people onto the streets of Dublin. One manifesto issued by the League in October 1887 called on Irish workers to rise up against capitalism and asked, 'Shall you, men of Ireland, remain behind in the great struggle that labour is making for its emancipation?'

8.13. The Dublin Workingmen's Club and Dublin Socialist Club were also established in 1887 and other socialist organisations followed: the Irish Socialist Union was established in 1890, the Fabian Society in 1892 and branches of the Independent Labour Party were established in Belfast (1892), Dublin and Belfast (1894). Despite some hostile opposition, the politically diverse socialist movement stuggled on, supported by a small, but determined, group of urban activists.

8.14. Socialism had a flowering in Ireland on the arrival of James Connolly in 1896. Born in Cowgate, a slum in Edinburgh, Connolly was self-educated in politics, economics and history. He was greatly influenced by the Scottish socialist, John Leslie, who introduced him to the works of the great socialist thinkers. Attracted to Ireland by the prospect of a regular wage, Connolly immediately set about reorganising the Irish Socialist movement. The establishment of the Irish Socialist Republican Party (ISRP) followed in May 1896. It was replaced the Dublin Socialist Party in 1904. The party called for many social reforms – old-age, widows and orphans' pensions; children's allowances; free education at every level; higher wages and improved working conditions and better housing. Connolly thought (wrongly) that early medieval Ireland was a land of communal ownership and that English feudalism imposed in the twelfth century put an end to it. He declared the aim of the ISRP was 'the establishment of an Irish Socialist Republic based upon the public ownership by the Irish people of the land and instruments of production, distribution and exchange'. If separation from Britain were achieved it was essential that it be accompanied by a radical social revolution in Ireland. The party called for state control of industry, land, banks and public transport systems.

8.15. Connolly also started his own newspaper, the *Workers' Republic*, in August 1898. It took a bold stand on the rights of labour but appeared irregularly due to his precarious finances. The presses of the paper were smashed by the Dublin Metropolitan Police in late 1899 after Connolly organised a pro-Boer rally in the city. However, editions continued to appear up to 1916.

8.16. Three delegates of the IRSP attended the fifth Congress of the Second International held in Paris, September 1900. Interestingly, Connolly added a new dimension to the Irish Socialist movement. He openly championed Irish nationalism as a way to further socialism in the country. He argued that nationalists and socialists confronted a common enemy in British imperialism. Only by forming an alliance with the nationalist movement and throwing off the shackles of British imperialism could the conditions necessary for socialism occur. He blamed the British for creating the horrid slums of Dublin.

8.17. In the period 1899–1903, five members of the IRSP unsuccessfully contested Dublin municipal elections. Frustrated with the lack of progress in Ireland, Connolly left for the United States in 1903 where he was employed as an organiser for the Industrial Workers of the World (IWW). He travelled in the United States lecturing on the cause of socialism.

8.18. In 1908 James 'Big Jim' Larkin founded the Irish Transport and General Workers' Union (ITGWU). On the invitation of the Union, Connolly returned to Ireland in 1910 to work as a branch organiser. He worked first in Belfast and was particularly successful in organising women workers in the linen industry. He had much work to do in Ireland; Dublin at the turn of the twentieth century was notorious for its slums. Throughout the city, large families on tiny incomes lived in wretched conditions in one- or two-room tenement flats, racked by cholera, dysentery and typhoid.

8.19. With Larkin's help, Connolly strove to win concessions from employers. Larkin's movement has been labelled 'Syndicalist' – a term that meant many different things to different people. Larkin was a man of action and advocated direct action by workers, using their main weapon, strike. He advocated repeated strikes, sympathetic strikes, the refusal of workers to handle 'tainted goods' and general strikes. He believed in the extension of trade unions to the unorganised masses and worked towards educating them in militant class consciousness. Connolly and Larkin, vowed to end the exploitation of unskilled labourers in Dublin. To this end, Connolly persuaded the Irish Trade Union Congress (ITUC) to form the Irish Labour Party in 1912. In anticipation of Home Rule, the Irish Labour Party would give some political clout to the socialist movement in any new parliament. Larkin's continued agitation for workers started to reap rewards between 1911 and 1913. Pay increases and improved contracts of employment were achieved for farm labourers and those working in Dublin port. The ITGWU had a membership close to 10,000. Employers increasingly felt threatened by the sophistication of Dublin trade unions. Eventually, William Martin Murphy refused to allow his tramway workers to join the ITGWU. This led to the Lockout of 1913 and the defeat of the unions. To the regret of many, including Seán O'Casey, Irish socialism would never again reach the heights of 1913. Instead, nationalism and the independence movement took centre stage and pushed socialism to the side, where it has languished ever since.

8.20. WRITINGS, BIOGRAPHY AND STUDIES: All Connolly's principal writings are re-published in *James Connolly, Collected works* (2 vols, Dublin, 1987) and these are all available on the internet at http://celt.ucc.ie/englist.html (together with a fuller bibliography of Connolly). An archive of his writings is at http://www.marxists.org/archive/connolly/. James Connolly, *Socialism and the Irish rebellion: writings from James Connolly* (St Petersburg, FA, 2008). Desmond Ryan, *James Connolly: his life, work and writings* (Dublin, 1924). Cathal O'Shannon (ed.), *Fifty years of Liberty Hall* (Dublin, 1959). Desmond Ryan, 'James Connolly', in J.W. Boyle (ed.), *Leaders and workers* (Cork, 1960; repr. Cork, 1978). C. Desmond Greaves, *The life and times of James Connolly* (London, 1961). Samuel Levenson, *James Connolly: a biography* (London, 1973). Thomas Brady, *The historical basis of socialism in Ireland* (Cork, 1974). Bernard Ransom, *Connolly's Marxism* (London, 1980). Ruth Dudley Edwards, *James Connolly* (Dublin, 1981). Desmond Fennell, 'Irish socialist thought', in Richard Kearney (ed.), *The Irish mind: exploring intellectual traditions* (Dublin, 1985), pp 188–208. Emmet Larkin, 'Socialism and Catholicism in Ireland', *Studies*, 74 (1985), 66–91. Priscilla Metscher, *Republicanism and socialism in Ireland: a study of the relationship of politics and ideology from the United Irishmen to James Connolly* (Frankfurt-am-Main, 1986). Kieran Allen, *The politics of James Connolly* (London 1990). William K. Anderson, *James Connolly and the Irish left* (Dublin, 1994). Patrick Walsh, *Irish republicanism and socialism: the politics of the republican movement 1905 to 1994* (Belfast, 1994). Richard English, 'Reflections on republican socialism in Ireland: Marxian roots and Irish historical dynamics', *History of Political Thought*, 17 (1996), 555–70. Peter Berresford Ellis, *A history of the Irish working class* (London, 1996). Fintan Lane, *The ori-*

gins of modern Irish socialism, 1881–1896 (Cork, 1997). Donal Nevin (ed.), *James Larkin, lion of the fold* (Dublin, 1998). William Delany, *The Green and the Red: revolutionary republicanism and socialism in Irish history, 1848–1923* (San José, CA, 2001).

EOIN HARTNETT (WITH A CONTRIBUTION BY TOMÁS O'RIORDAN)

9. Suffragette

9.1. The term suffragette is used to describe those who campaigned for the right of women to vote in elections in the United Kingdom. It was originally used to denote a more radical faction of the suffrage movement who took part in militant protests. Suffragist is a more general term for members of the movement. The Irish suffrage movement was largely urban and middle class. The Quaker couple, Thomas and Anna Haslam, worked together for women's suffrage in Ireland. Thomas published a series of pamphlets in April, May and July 1874 aimed at promoting suffrage for women in Ireland. The journal *Women's Advocate* was the first attempt at creating a forum for debate on the subject. The Irish suffrage movement also included the Unionist Women's Suffrage Association, the Munster Women's Franchise League, the Irish Catholic Women's Suffrage Association, the Church League for Women's Suffrage (Anglican) and the Irish Women's Suffrage Federation (IWSF). In 1872 Isabella Tod established a society called the Northern Ireland Society for Women's Suffrage. The Irish Women's Suffrage Society was founded in 1873. In 1876 Anna and Thomas Haslam formed the Dublin Women's Suffrage Association (DWSA), the best known of Irish suffrage groups. As support for the movement grew, it was renamed the Irish Women's Suffrage and Local Government Association (1911) and attracted nationalists and Unionists alike. It had nearly 650 members by this time. The method of promoting suffrage was organising petitions, drawing-room meetings, and lobbying MPs.

9.2. The Registration (Ireland) Act, 1898, granted women the vote for local government elections. The Local Government (Ireland) Act, 1898, also provided for the creation of elected county councils and district councils. Women were allowed to sit on district councils and town commissions, but not on county or borough councils. Thirty-five women were elected to district councils in 1899. However, the suffrage movement did not really flourish until the beginning of the twentieth century when numerous suffrage organisations were formed throughout the country.

9.3. Militant Irish activists were imprisoned in England and Ireland and some went on hunger strike. Suffragettes carried out direct action in cities throughout the United Kingdom – chaining themselves to railings, setting fire to the contents of letterboxes, and smashing windows. In 1909 the English suffragette Emily Davison wrote her favourite quotation: 'Rebellion against tyrants is obedience to God' on pieces of paper, tied them to rocks and threw them at the carriage of the Chancellor of the Exchequer, David Lloyd George, as it drove by. She was sentenced to hard labour and was later force fed when she refused to eat. By 1911, she began to believe that the suffragette cause needed a martyr to bring it the publicity it needed. Her final act was to run on to the racetrack at the Epsom Derby, and grab the reins of the King's horse. She later died from her injuries. At the time her actions were dismissed as the act of a crazed woman but she is now seen as a martyr to the suffragette cause. The so-called 'Cat and Mouse Act' was passed by the British government in 1913. It provided for the release of sick female hunger strikers, as well as their re-imprisonment once they were healthy again. The aim was to prevent female prisoners getting any public sympathy. However, the arrest of suffragettes soon became an exercise in futility.

9.4. The more radical Irish Women's Franchise League (IWFL) was founded in 1908 with Mrs Charles Oldham as president, Hanna Sheehy-Skeffington as secretary and Margaret Cousins as treasurer. Within a year of its founding the League had a membership of over 1,000 and was also involved in Irish nationalism and the cultural revival. It strongly resisted absorption by the British-based Women's Social and Political Union on which it was modelled. It also felt that Haslam's IWSLGA was too genteel to make any significant impact on Irish society. It encouraged women to boycott the 1911 Census by absenting themselves from the home. In April 1912 women from the IWFL disrupted a meeting being held in Belfast by Winston Churchill. In the same year Hanna and Frank Sheehy-Skeffington helped establish the *Irish Citizen* paper to help spread the message of Suffrage Movement. Its motto was 'For men and women equally, the rights of citizenship; from men and women equally, the duties of citizenship message'.

9.5. Between 1912 and 1914, thirty-six women were arrested for suffrage militancy in Ireland. In June of 1912, Hanna Sheehy-Skeffington and several others broke windows in government buildings. Six were arrested and sentenced to between two and six months' imprisonment. During Prime Minister Asquith's visit to Dublin in July, suffragettes from England held a violent demonstration. One threw a hatchet in the direction of his carriage which grazed John Redmond's ear. Another attempted to burn down the theatre where Asquith was due to speak. The women were arrested and went on hunger strike. Force feeding was not used in Irish prisons. The public mood quickly turned against the more militant suffragettes and Margaret Cousins, secretary of the IWFL had to issue a public disclaimer of the attacks in Dublin. She describes the hostility of the crowd at the time:

> The only time in our suffrage decade when I had seen hat pins in women's hands as weapons was on that occasion amongst low-class women who stood in front of the lorry and shouted us down. I watched a poor-class youth with a stone in his hand. In a moment he threw it towards me as I tried to get the attention of the crowd. Then the idea got into the crowd's head that it should push the lorry out of its place. As they proceeded to do so more stones were thrown at us ...

9.6. In 1909, an Irish branch of the Conservative and Unionist Women's Suffrage Association was established in Dublin, and in the same year the Irish Women's Suffrage

Society was formed in Belfast. In 1911 was the Munster Women's Franchise League was formed in Cork city. In the same year Irish Women's Reform League was also founded in Dublin by the suffragist Louie Bennett (1870–1956). It campaigned for suffrage, technical education for girls as well as the provision of free school meals. Bennett and Helen Chenevix absorbed the IWSLGA and scattered local suffrage societies into the Irish Women's Suffrage Federation, an umbrella group for most of the non-militant suffrage societies. Some twenty-six societies with an overall membership of 300 to 400 were represented. The historian and social campaigner Mary Hayden (1862–1942) was one of the Federation's presidents, while George Russell, was one of its vice-presidents. There were some working-class women in the suffrage movement but most were female white-collar workers or professionals, or the wives of professionals.

9.7. In 1913 the Irish branch of the Church League for Women's Suffrage for Anglican women was set up. It was not, however until 1915 that the Irish Catholic Women's Suffrage Association was established, a surprisingly late start for a country where the majority were Catholic. Mary Hayden was also involved in this society along with Mrs Stephen Gwynn.

9.8. In April 1912 when Asquith introduced his third Home Rule Bill, the IWFL wasted no time in campaigning for 'Home Rule for Irish women as well as men'. The league pressurised Irish Parliamentary Party MPs to insist on the inclusion of a women's suffrage clause in the the 1912 Home Rule Bill. Both the unionist and nationalist leadership opposed the franchise for women. In 1913 Edward Carson had promised that, in the event of a Unionist provisional government being established, Ulster women would get the vote. However, Carson had to go back on his word due to opposition from other Unionists.

9.9. When it seemed that Home Rule might become a reality, the suffrage movement fractured along Unionist/Nationalist lines. Nearly 50,000 women joined the Ulster Women's Unionist Council (1911) in its first year. It supported the Ulster Unionist Party from 1912 saying 'We will stand by our husbands, our brothers, our sons, in whatever steps they may be forced to take in defending our liberties against the tyranny of Home Rule'. In September 1912, 16,000 more women than men signed the Women's declaration, the female equivalent of the Ulster Solemn League and Covenant.

9.10. The outbreak of war in August 1914 caused many women to reassess their position and their attitude to the state. Many suffragettes stopped campaigning and sought to contribute to the war effort. Women were now required to take on jobs previously done by men only. The Irish Women's Franchise League took the stance of non-involvement in the war effort. Most nationalist women saw Home Rule as the important issue and joined Cumann na mBan, which declared its support for the Irish Volunteers in November 1914.

9.11. BIOGRAPHY, STUDIES AND WRITINGS: Rosemary Cullen Owens & Hanna Sheehy-Skeffington, *Votes for women: Irish women's struggle for the vote* (Dublin, 1975).

Andro Linklater, *An unhusbanded life: Charlotte Despard, suffragette, socialist and Sinn Féiner* (London, 1980). Rosemary Cullen Owens, *Smashing times: a history of the Irish women's suffrage movement, 1889–1922* (Dublin, 1984). Rosemary Cullen Owens, *Did your granny have a hammer? A history of the Irish suffrage movement, 1876–1922* (Dublin, 1985). Cliona Murphy, *The women's suffrage movement and Irish society in the early twentieth century* (New York, 1989). Marianne Heron, *Fighting spirit* (Dublin, 1993). Emmeline Pankhurst, *The suffragettes: towards emancipation* ed. Marie Mulvey Roberts & Tamae Mizuta (London, 1993). Melanie Philips, *The ascent of woman: a history of the suffragette movement* (London, 2004). Louise Ryan, *Irish feminism and the vote: an anthology of the Irish Citizen newspaper, 1912–1920* (Dublin, 1996). Dolores Dooley & Liz Steiner-Scott (eds), *Aspects of Irish feminism* (Cork, 1997). Margaret Ward, *Hanna Sheehy-Skeffington: a life* (Cork, 1997). Mary Cullen & Maria Luddy (eds), *Female activists: Irish women and change 1900–1960* (Dublin, 2001). Rosemary Cullen Owens, *Louie Bennett* (Cork, 2001). Marie Mulholland, *The politics and relationships of Kathleen Lynn* (Dublin, 2002). Carmel Quinlan, *Genteel revolutionaries: Anna and Thomas Haslam, pioneers of Irish feminism* (Cork, 2002). Anne de Courcy, *Society's queen: the life of Edith, Marchioness of Londonderry* (London, 2004). Gender Equality Unit, Department of Education and Science, *Discovering women in Irish history* (Dublin, 2004), esp. pp 194–246.

EOIN HARTNETT

10. The Anglo-Irish

10.1. The Anglo-Irish were, for the most part, English by descent and usually loyal to the Crown. Traditionally they felt themselves no less Irish on that account. Grattan and his fellow Protestants in eighteenth-century Ireland were confident that they were the important part of the Irish nation. However, cultural nationalism of the late nineteenth century emphasised national distinctiveness and, in the minds of many, to be truly Irish was to be Gaelic and Catholic. This narrow and exclusive definition of Irishness brought the term 'Anglo-Irish' into common currency. A Protestant might still be an Irishman but the sense of difference was sharpened. The term Anglo-Irish was used to indicate that one section of the people was less truly 'Irish' than another. It was not a precise term. Many of the great 'Irish' leaders were Anglo-Irish, notably Butt and Parnell. Parnell was in no doubt that he was an Irishman and he famously stated that the only way to treat the English was to 'stand up to them'. Some historians argue that the hyphenated expression 'Anglo-Irish' widely used to distinguish this section of the Irish people reflected racism in the thinking of the time and the unhealed divisions of Ireland.

10.2. In historical terms Anglo-Irish meant the descendants and successors of the Protestant Ascendancy that had become possessed of most of the land of Ireland in the seventeenth century and ruled it in the eighteenth. They were usually members of the Church of Ireland and most traced their descent to the New English who conquered and colonised Ireland in the sixteenth and seventeenth centuries. Their Protestant faith and their politics were an important part of their identity. In time these families came to see Ireland as their home and developed a sense of being its natural leaders. Their dominant influence is reflected in the language of Ireland, in its art, literature, architecture and in many other aspects of life. W.B. Yeats famously declared that the Anglo-Irish were 'no petty people' and that their contribution to Irish life was enormous. They include such important families as the FitzGeralds, the Butlers, the Parnells, the Osbournes, the Wildes, the Manserghs and the Colthursts.

10.3. The Penal Laws discriminated against all who were not members of the Church of Ireland, the Catholic majority and the Dissenters. The Church established by law, the Church of Ireland, had status, lands, and funding and its members had access to political office and power. In the nineteenth century their claims were challenged by the rise of Catholic power that resulted from the increasing democratisation of politics. The 1870s brought important political and economic changes which eroded the privileged status of the Anglo-Irish. Landlords who could command the loyalty of their tenants in elections saw their influence vanishing fast with the introduction of the secret ballot in 1872. The increasing democratisation of the political system and the widening of the franchise in the nineteenth and twentieth centuries continued to reduce the power of the landed classes.

10.4. One of Gladstone's first acts as Prime Minister, during his first ministry from 1868 to 1874, was to disestablish the Church of Ireland – a serious blow to the Ascendancy class, and some argued (with some right) a breach of the Union. Gladstone's Land Acts of 1870 and 1881 gave the government the power to intervene in the tenant-landlord relationship in significant ways and limited the property rights of landlords. These Acts, though falling short of nationalist goals at the time, further undermined the position of many Anglo-Irish landlords.

10.5. The political power of the Anglo-Irish was further diminished by Gladstone's conversion to Home Rule – a policy that aimed to set up a parliament in Dublin and give Irishmen an important degree of political control. The Local Government Act of 1898 replaced Grand Juries with democratically elected County Councils and destroyed the power of the Ascendancy in local politics. In the nineteenth century there was a gradual but quickening decline in the political power of the Anglo-Irish community in Ireland as nationalists (often led by men who were themselves Anglo-Irish) organised political parties effectively and made many successful demands on Westminster. By the outbreak of the Great War in 1914 Home Rule was on the statute book and Anglo-Irish power seemed likely to end.

10.6. Many writers, poets and painters from the Anglo-Irish community identified strongly with Ireland. Anglo-Irish names are very prominent in the Gaelic revival movement of the late nineteenth century and in the scholarly study of Gaelic literature, history and archaeology – William Reeves, James Henthorn Todd, Samuel Ferguson, John Gwynn, Whitley Stokes, Hugh Jackson Lawlor and many others. The Anglo-Irish made a momentous contribution to the cultural life of Ireland, and particularly to Irish Studies.

10.7. Douglas Hyde, a Protestant intellectual, had the revolutionary idea of 'de-anglicising' Ireland and of reviving the Irish language, an idea that had a profound influence and far-reaching consequences. George Bernard Shaw could state 'English is the native language of Irishmen' but the Gaelic League argued that this should change and that the Gaelic language and its literature were sophisticated and important in European terms and that they should be cultivated. Hyde's contribution was recognised in a formal way when he was selected as the first President of Ireland in 1938.

10.8. Anglo-Irish literature is a term (and not a precise one) used to describe writing by Irish authors in the English language. It attempts to distinguish between that literature and English literature on the one hand and Gaelic literature on the other. It is often used to describe the work of a group of writers, including Yeats, Synge and Lady Gregory, who found inspiration in Irish history, mythology and folklore. William Butler Yeats (who won the Nobel Prize for literature in 1923) is one of Ireland's greatest poets. He claimed that the Protestants of Ireland had 'created most of the modern literature of this country'. His brother, Jack B. Yeats, also achieved great fame as a painter of unique skill and imagination, winning many awards. He was made an officer of the prestigious Legion d'honneur by the French government in 1950. In cultural and political terms, the Yeats brothers show the dual element in the Anglo-Irish world view: though Protestant in faith, and English by ancestry, both identified passionately with Ireland.

10.9. By the beginning of the First World War in 1914 it was clear that independence for Ireland, in some form, was to come and that this was only a matter of time. Many Irish Protestants feared for their future, their position, property and prospects. In July 1917 an Irish Convention representing a broad spectrum of interests met in the vain hope that Irishmen might work out a political settlement satisfactory to all. Here the Anglo-Irish were represented and participated in an attempt to decide the destiny of their country. Irish nationalists of senior standing both in the Home Rule party and later in the Sinn Féin party were keen to assure the Anglo-Irish community that its political and civil rights would be respected in an independent state.

10.10. Though, generally speaking, Irish Protestants fared fairly well in the Free State and Republic, the experience of many Anglo-Irish families during the War of Independence and Civil War of the 1920s was dreadful. Many were intimidated and murdered. Demoralised by the War of Independence and the burning of some 200 Big Houses, many fled to England. The very existence of the Anglo-Irish seemed under threat, not only from economic and political forces but also from such factors as the *Ne temere* papal decree (1908) which required, in practice, that the children of mixed marriages be raised as Catholics. This drastically reduced their numbers and Protestants as a percentage of the population dropped from 10 per cent to 6 per cent in the twenty-five years after Independence.

10.11. BIBLIOGRAPHY: Thomas MacDonagh, *Literature in Ireland: studies, Irish and Anglo-Irish* (Dublin, 1916, repr. Port Washington, NY, 1970). Terence de Vere White, *The Anglo-Irish* (London, 1972). Patrick Buckland. *The Anglo-Irish and the new Ireland, 1885–1922* (Dublin, 1972). Peter Ure, *Yeats and Anglo-Irish literature: critical essays* (Liverpool, 1974). J.C. Beckett, *The Anglo-Irish tradition* (Belfast, 1976). Mark Bence-Jones, *Burke's guide to country houses*, i: *Ireland* (London, 1978). Alan Warner, *A guide to Anglo-Irish literature* (Dublin, 1981). A. Norman Jeffares, *Anglo-Irish literature* (London, 1982). Kurt Bowen, *Protestants in a Catholic state: Ireland's privileged minority* (Dublin & Kingston, Ont., 1983). A.C. Partridge, *Language and society in Anglo-Irish literature* (Dublin, 1984). John Biggs-Davison & George Chowdharay-Best, *The cross of Saint Patrick: the Catholic Unionist tradition in Ireland* (Abbotsbrook, 1984). W.E. Vaughan, *Landlords and tenants in Ireland, 1848–1904* (Dublin, 1984). W.J. McCormack, *Ascendancy and tradition in Anglo-Irish literary history from 1789 to 1939* (Oxford, 1985). Mark Bence-Jones, *Twilight of the Ascendancy* (London, 1987). Michael Allen & Angela Wilcox, *Critical approaches to Anglo-Irish literature* (Totowa, NJ, 1989). Otto Rauchbauer, *Ancestral voices: the Big House in Anglo-Irish literature: a collection of interpretations* (Hildesheim, Dublin & New York, 1992). W.E. Vaughan, *Landlords and tenants in mid-Victorian Ireland* (Oxford, 1994). W.J. McCormack, *From Burke to Beckett: ascendancy, tradition and betrayal in literary history* (Cork, 1994). Declan Kiberd, *Inventing Ireland: the literature of the modern nation* (London, 1995). Joep Leersen et al., *Forging in the smithy: national identity and representation in Anglo-Irish literary history* (Amsterdam & Atlanta, GA, 1995). R.B. McDowell, *Crisis and decline: the fate of Southern Unionists* (Dublin, 1997). Vera Kreilkamp, *The Anglo-Irish novel and the Big House* (Syracuse, NY, 1998). Terence Dooley, *The decline of the Big House in Ireland* (Dublin, 2001). Michael McConville, *Ascendancy to oblivion: the story of the Anglo-Irish* (London, 2001). T.C. Barnard, *A new anatomy of Ireland: the Irish Protestants, 1649–1770* (London, 2003). Georg Grote, *Anglo-Irish theatre and the formation of a nationalist political culture between 1890 and 1930* (Lewiston, NY & Lampeter, 2003). David Dickson, *Old world colony: Cork and south Munster, 1630–1830* (Cork, 2005). David A. Valone & Jill Marie Bradbury (eds), *Anglo-Irish identities, 1571–1845* (Lewisburg, PA, 2008).

FIDELMA MAGUIRE

CHAPTER II

Key personalities

1. Edward Carson (1854–1935)

1.1. Lawyer and Unionist politician, he was born in Harcourt Street, Dublin, on 9 February 1854. His father was Edward Henry Carson, an architect and civil engineer. His family was of Scottish origin. His mother was Isabella Lambert, of Castle Ellen, Athenry, Co. Galway, a member of an Ascendancy landowning family. Her ancestor, General Lambert, was one Oliver Cromwell's major-generals. The young Carson was educated at Arlington House, Portarlington, and went on to study law at Trinity College, Dublin in 1871. He spent much of his time debating in the College Historical Society. He took a pass degree in 1876 and then studied at the King's Inns, Dublin. He was called to the Irish Bar in 1877.

1.2. Carson was one of the most successful lawyers of his generation. In 1886 John Gibson, Irish attorney-general, nominated him to be his Crown counsel. He is remembered for his determined prosecution against the Plan of Campaign (1886–91) and he was nicknamed 'Coercion Carson'. In 1887 he found himself heavily involved politically and under threat of assassination. He believed, as did others, that he was acting quite correctly in prosecuting tenants who refused to pay rent or who revolted against their landlords. In 1889 Carson became the youngest Queen's Counsel in Ireland. He was now a senior member of the legal profession and for the next three years worked on ordinary civil law cases. On 1 July 1892, Balfour decided to make him Solicitor-General for Ireland. He represented Dublin University as a Liberal Unionist MP between 1892 and 1918. In parliament his speech attacking the second Home Rule Bill in 1893 was highly acclaimed.

1.3. Carson transferred his legal practice to London in 1893, and swiftly built up a reputation in the courts and in the House of Commons. He was called to the English Bar in 1892 and to the Inner Bar two years later. A new and exciting period in his life began. Carson was a prominent advocate in many famous trials including *Wilde v. the Marquess of Queensberry* in 1895. Oscar Wilde ill-advisedly sued Queensberry, an eccentric and violent aristocrat, for libel. Wilde had been Carson's fellow-student in Trinity, but now he acted for Queensberry. Wilde's comment when he heard this was: 'No doubt he will perform his task with all the added bitterness of an old friend'. Carson's cross-examination was sardonic and relentless – the trial judge later wrote to him: 'I never heard a more powerful speech, or a more searching cross-examination. I congratulate you.' Wilde lost, but worse was to come. On foot of the evidence elicited by Carson in the libel case, by decision of the Director of Public Prosecutions and with the agreement of H.H. Asquith, then Home Secretary, Wilde was arrested, tried for indecency, convicted, and sentenced to the maximum of two years' imprisonment. The case destroyed Wilde's career and he died in Paris in 1900.

1.4. Carson became a member of the Irish Privy Council in 1896. His defence of Irish landlordism from the backbenches made him a critic of Lord Salisbury's Conservative government. By 1900 Carson was earning a substantial £20,000 (approx. €1.75 million at 2009 values) a year in fees. He joined the Conservative government in 1900 as Solicitor-General for England (until 1906) and received a knighthood. For the next few years he represented the Crown in many cases. He spoke on Irish affairs in parliament. He supported the demand for a Catholic University and lent his backing to the Irish Universities Act, 1908. When the National University was finally established in 1908 he hoped that it would be 'a step forward in the union of all classes and religions in Ireland for the progress of our country and its education'.

1.5. Carson helped to establish the Ulster Unionist Party in 1905. This was done in response to the grave threat to the Union posed by Home Rule. The decisive Conservative and Unionist defeat in January 1906 removed many of his ministerial rivals, leaving him free to emerge as one of the most prominent politicians in the United Kingdom. On 21 February 1910 Carson was elected leader of the Irish Unionist MPs at Westminster. In September 1911 he accepted Craig's invitation to lead the Ulster Unionists. When Arthur Balfour resigned on 8 November 1911, Carson refused to contest the leadership of the Conservative Party. The role instead went to Andrew Bonar Law who, although born in Canada to immigrant Ulster parents, possessed a strong commitment to Irish Unionism.

1.6. Carson succeeded in bringing credibility and prestige to the Unionist movement. His objective throughout was to preserve the Union between Britain and Ireland, believing it to be in the best interests of his fellow countrymen. He was an Irish patriot but not a nationalist. When the Liberals under Asquith introduced the Home Rule Bill (1912), Carson took a leading part in the formation of the Ulster Volunteers, who drilled openly to show that they were prepared to resort to arms if necessary. Ulster Unionists also planned to set up a provisional government of their own if the Bill was passed. While he accepted Agar-Robartes' proposal of June 1912 for the exclusion of four Ulster counties (Antrim, Down, Armagh and Londonderry), Carson later looked for the exclusion of the entire province. On 28 September 1912 he was the first person to sign Ulster's Solemn League and Covenant at a ceremony at City Hall, Belfast. He urged people not to be 'afraid of illegalities', and in April 1914 the Ulster Volunteers landed guns at Larne, Co. Antrim, in open defiance of the British government. However, all eyes were drawn to Europe with the outbreak of the First World War in August 1914. The Home Rule Bill became law in September 1914 but its operation was immediately suspended until after the war when the position of Ulster would be reconsidered. By this time Carson had come to realise that the rest of Ireland could not be saved from 'the most nefarious conspiracy that has ever been matched against a free people'. He did not want a divided Ireland but he accepted that Home Rule was inevitable and partition was the only solution.

1.7. When war with Germany was declared Carson immediately pledged the Ulster Volunteer Force to fight for England: 'England's difficulty is not Ulster's opportunity' he said to delegates at a meeting of the Ulster Unionist Council in Belfast. He was appointed Attorney-General on 25 May 1915 but resigned later that year in protest at the government's conduct of the war. After the Easter Rising in 1916 he was assured by Lloyd George that the six north-east counties would be excluded from the Home Rule Act (1914). He was appointed First Lord of the Admiralty in Lloyd George's coalition government on 7 December 1916, but he resigned in January 1918 after the dismissal of friend and colleague, John Rushworth Jellicoe, as First Sea Lord of the Admiralty.

1.8. When the war ended he became MP for the Duncairn division of Belfast. He published the book *Ireland and Home Rule* in 1919. With Carson's advice and with Ulster Unionist support the Government of Ireland Act was passed on 23 December 1920. Under this Act parliaments were to be established in the North and in the South. Its aim was to keep both jurisdictions under Westminster control and satisfy and reconcile legitimate Unionist and nationalist aspirations. In addition, a Council of Ireland was to be established to consider questions of common concern. Some politicians viewed the partition settlement as a temporary solution, envisaging reconciliation between north and south. Carson described the Council as 'the biggest advance towards unity in Ireland'. At Carson's request, Sir William Spender arranged that Ulster Volunteer Force members should have preference in recruitment for the new Ulster Special Constabulary which was established on 2 September 1920. In May 1921 Carson resigned the leadership of the Unionist Party to become Lord of Appeal in Ordinary in London. In 1921 he accepted a peerage as Baron Carson of Duncairn. He strongly criticised the Anglo-Irish Treaty (1921), but from a southern Irish Unionist perspective. Carson continued as a law lord, between 1921 and 1929, defending the interests of southern Unionists in the new Irish Free State. He was by now living permanently in England. He was involved in the curbing of British government policy in India in 1933.

1.9. Outside of his political roles Carson was an ardent member of the Church of Ireland. He proposed an *Alternative Prayer Book* of the Church of England (1927). He attended the opening of the new Northern Ireland parliament building at Stormont in 1932, and unveiled his own statue in front of the building in July 1933.

1.10. He died at his home at Cleve Court, Isle of Thanet, Kent on 22 October 1935 and was given a state funeral in Belfast. He was buried after much pomp in St Anne's Cathedral, Belfast. The editor of the *Belfast Newsletter* wrote shortly after:

> Of Lord Carson it may be said that he was one of those heaven-sent leaders who arise in times of crisis, to inspire a people with the will, the courage, and the faith that can

move mountains … Under Providence he was the chief instrument of the deliverance from a hateful tyranny.

The majority of Ulster Unionists shared these sentiments. Although a southerner, Carson won the hearts and minds of Ulster's men and women by the intensity of his devotion to their cause. His idealism and religious tolerance were largely uncharacteristic of the sectarianism that blighted the later history of Northern Ireland.

1.11. BIOGRAPHY AND STUDIES: St John G. Ervine, *Sir Edward Carson and the Ulster movement* (Dublin & London, 1915, reprinted, 2009). Edward Marjoribanks & Ian Duncan Colvin, *The life of Lord Carson* (3 vols, London, 1932–6). F.H. Crawford, *Guns for Ulster* (Belfast, 1947). A.T.Q. Stewart, *The Ulster crisis: resistance to Home Rule, 1912–4* (London, 1967). J.C. Beckett, 'Carson: unionist and rebel', in his *Confrontations: studies in Irish history* (London, 1972). Patrick Buckland, *Irish Unionism, 1885–1923: a documentary history* (Belfast, 1973). H. Montgomery Hyde, *Carson: the life of Sir Edward Carson, Lord Carson of Duncairn* (London, 1974). A.T.Q. Stewart, *Edward Carson* (Dublin, 1981). Richard Ellmann, *Oscar Wilde* (London, 1987). Alvin Jackson, *Sir Edward Carson* (Dundalk, 1993). John Hostettler, *Sir Edward Carson: a dream too far* (Chichester, 1997; 2nd ed., Chichester, 2000). Gillian McIntosh, 'Symbolic mirrors: commemorations of Edward Carson in the 1930s', *Irish Historical Studies*, 32 (2000), 93–112. Merlin Holland, *Irish Peacock and Scarlet Marquess: the real trial of Oscar Wilde* (London & New York, 2003) [first uncensored transcript of the trial of Oscar Wilde]. Alvin Jackson, *Home Rule: an Irish history, 1800–2000* (London, 2003). Owen Dudley Edwards, 'Carson as advocate: Marjoribanks and Wilde', in Sabine Wichert (ed.), *From the United Irishmen to twentieth-century unionism* (Dublin, 2004). Geoffrey Lewis, *Carson: the man who divided Ireland* (London, 2005).

TOMÁS O'RIORDAN

2. James Connolly (1868–1916)

2.1. Socialist, trade union leader, and writer, he was born of Irish immigrant parents in Cowgate, Edinburgh on 5 June 1868. He left school when he was eleven to work with his brother at the *Edinburgh Evening News* as a printer's 'devil', the boy who cleaned the inky rollers. He went on to work in a bakery and in a tiling factory. Social conditions in Edinburgh were dreadful. There was great poverty, overcrowding, and disease. His interest in Irish nationalism stemmed from a Fenian uncle. His socialism came from the grim experience of working-class life combined with his readings of Karl Marx and others. Raised in desperate poverty, he always carried this awareness with him and dedicated his life to defending workers' rights.

2.2. He first came to Ireland as a British soldier. At the age of fourteen he falsified his age and enlisted in the British Army to escape poverty. He joined the Royal Scots

Regiment and was posted to Ireland and served tours of duty in Cork, Dublin and later in the Curragh, Co. Kildare. Connolly read avidly during this time, developing his ideas for a better society. In Dublin he met Lillie Reynolds and they married in 1890. He deserted in 1891 when his battalion was ordered to Aldershot and returned to Scotland where he worked as a carter and became closely involved in the socialist movement under the influence of the Scottish socialist, John Leslie. In 1892, he became secretary of the Scottish Socialist Federation. He became involved with the Independent Labour Party. Unsuccessful in the Scottish elections in April 1895, he began to look for work as a political organiser outside Edinburgh. The Dublin Socialist Club invited him to become their organiser for £1 a week. In May 1896, Connolly sailed to Dublin, a city with slums worse than Edinburgh's. He founded the Irish Socialist Republican Party which aimed to secure the national and economic freedom of the Irish people. Connolly was arrested in 1897 when he protested against the visit of Queen Victoria to Dublin.

2.3. He wrote numerous articles and pamphlets on socialist issues, including *Erin's Hope*. He was a fine speaker and lectured on socialist issues in England and Scotland where he raised money to launch a weekly newspaper, the *Workers' Republic*, first published in August 1898. In 1903 he emigrated to the USA where he immersed himself in American socialism. While there he set up the Irish Socialist Federation in New York (1907). He published a monthly magazine, the *Harp*, which brought him to the notice of William O'Brien. He also published a book entitled *Labour in Irish history*, and he co-founded the 'Wobblies' or the Industrial Workers of the World.

2.4. In 1910, Connolly returned to Ireland as organiser of the new Socialist Party in Ireland. He was co-founder of the Labour Party in 1912. He was made Belfast organiser for the Irish Transport and General Workers' Union (ITGWU). The Union was to the forefront in the wave of class struggles that affected both Dublin and Belfast. Connolly and Larkin succeeded in uniting Catholic and Protestant workers against the employers. In October 1911 he led the famous Belfast Textile Workers' strike. The wave of strikes was countered by the employers in the notorious Dublin Lockout of 1913. On this occasion, Dublin employers, organised by William Martin Murphy, chairman of the Employers' Federation and owner of the *Independent* newspaper, set out to crush the workers and their organisations. The ITGWU replied by blacking Murphy's newspapers, which led to the Lockout of the workers. Connolly became the workers' leader following the arrest of James Larkin. He himself was arrested and went on hunger strike, but was released after a week. Larkin and Connolly appealed for help from abroad and in September the first food ship sailed into Dublin.

2.5. He was instrumental in establishing the Citizen Army. Its purpose was to defend workers against police attacks and to prepare for the struggle against British imperialism. In 1914 he became Acting General Secretary of Irish Transport and General Workers Union following Larkin's departure to the USA. He revived the *Workers' Republic* after the *Irish Worker* was suppressed in December 1914. He published articles attacking the

Irish Volunteers for their inactivity. Connolly warned of a 'carnival of reaction' if conscription to the British army was introduced in Ireland. He formed an Anti-War Committee and he committed the Labour movement to oppose recruitment and conscription, flying the banner, 'We serve neither King nor Kaiser, but Ireland' at Liberty Hall. The *Workers' Republic* was suppressed in 1915.

2.6. When the secret military council of the IRB decided on an armed rising in 1916, Connolly took part in the preparations with Pearse and MacDonagh. He had become convinced that a nationalist revolution was the only way to free Ireland from what he saw as imperial and capitalist oppression. Prior to 1916 he was opposed to nationalism on the grounds that it drove a wedge between the workers of the world. On Easter Monday he led his Citizen Army alongside the Volunteers under Pearse. The influence of Connolly can be seen in the Easter Proclamation of Independence, particularly in the egalitarianism of the opening address: 'Irishmen and Irishwomen …', and the striking 'We declare the right of the people of Ireland to the ownership of Ireland and to the unfettered control of Irish destinies'. Connolly served as a Commandant in the General Post Office during the Easter fighting and was badly wounded. He was sentenced to death by the Military Tribunal for his role in the Rising and was executed by a firing squad in Kilmainham Gaol at dawn on 12 May 1916. His wounds were so severe that he had to be strapped to a chair for his execution. He was first buried at the Kilmainham Gaol. His final resting place is at Arbour Hill cemetery, Dublin.

2.7. WRITINGS, BIOGRAPHY AND STUDIES: All his principal writings are re-published in James Connolly, *Collected works* (2 vols, Dublin, 1987) and these are all available on the Internet at http://celt.ucc.ie (together with a fuller bibliography of Connolly). An archive of his writings is on-line at http://www.marxists.org/archive/connolly/. Desmond Ryan, *James Connolly: his life, work and writings* (Dublin, 1924). Cathal O'Shannon (ed.), *Fifty years of Liberty Hall* (Dublin, 1959). Desmond Ryan, 'James Connolly', in J.W. Boyle (ed.), *Leaders and workers* (Cork, 1960; repr. Cork, 1978). C. Desmond Greaves, *The life and times of James Connolly* (London, 1961; repr. London, 1972). Samuel Levenson, *James Connolly: a biography* (London, 1973). Bernard Ransom, *Connolly's Marxism* (London, 1980). Ruth Dudley Edwards, *James Connolly* (Dublin, 1981). Priscilla Metscher, *Republicanism and socialism in Ireland: a study of the relationship of politics and ideology from the United Irishmen to James Connolly* (Frankfurt-am-Main, 1986). Kieran Allen, *The politics of James Connolly* (London, 1990). William K. Anderson, *James Connolly and the Irish left* (Dublin, 1994). Aindrias Ó Cathasaigh (ed.), *James Connolly: the lost writings* (London & Chicago, IL, 1997). J.L. Hyland, *James Connolly* (Dundalk, 1997). Donal Nevin, *James Connolly: a full life* (Dublin, 2005). James Connolly, *Socialism and the Irish rebellion: writings from James Connolly* (St Petersburg, FL, 2008).

EOIN HARTNETT

3. Michael Davitt (1846–1906)

3.1. Radical nationalist, revolutionary, social reformer and distinguished journalist, he was born in Straide, Co. Mayo, on 25 March 1846. His father was one of the many small-holders evicted after the Great Famine. In 1850 the family emigrated to Haslingden, a textile town in East Lancashire. He went to work at the age of eleven in a cotton mill. His right arm was mangled by machinery and was amputated. Unable to do factory work, he attended the local Methodist school and evening classes in the Mechanics' Institute. However, he was mostly self-taught and learned French, Italian and Irish. He became a skilled typesetter.

3.2. At 19 he joined the IRB. He led the local Haslingden Fenians on an unsuccessful attack on Chester Castle. In 1868 he was made organising secretary of the IRB in Scotland and England and their chief arms buyer. To cover his revolutionary activities, he became a firearms salesman. In 1870 he was arrested at Paddington Station, London, convicted of treason-felony and sentenced to fifteen years' penal servitude. He served seven years, mostly in Dartmoor, and was released on ticket of leave through the efforts of Isaac Butt, Charles Stewart Parnell and the Amnesty Association.

3.3. Davitt went to America in 1878 and met the Clan na Gael leaders including John Devoy (1842–1928). He undertook a public lecture tour and he addressed such issues as the past and present policies of nationalists and what needed to be done. He called for an end to the landlord system in Ireland and for Irish independence. Devoy, whose thinking on the land question was more advanced than his, introduced him to the ideas of James Fintan Lalor (1807–49) and his motto: 'The soil of Ireland for the people of Ireland'. Out of this came 'the New Departure', a programme with two great aims, an aggressive parliamentary campaign for Irish self-government and a vigorous demand for radical land reform, a plan slowly and reluctantly accepted in practice by the Fenians. This combination of agrarian agitation and a skilful parliamentary campaign created the politics of Parnellism.

3.4. Davitt returned to Ireland in 1878. As crops failed and farm prices fell the time was ripe for Davitt's plans. A mass protest (of about 7,000 farmers) was organised in Irishtown, Co. Mayo, on 20 April 1879. Davitt played an important part in its organisa-tion but did not attend. In the worsening agricultural crisis of 1879, he persuaded Parnell to address the second key meeting in Westport, Co. Mayo, on 8 June 1879, and to become involved in land agitation. Davitt himself addressed the Westport meeting and demanded an end to the evils of landlordism and freedom for Ireland. In August 1879, he founded the National Land League of Mayo to organise the agitation. His role was vital, his leadership dynamic. He believed that the land war could do much for Ireland and that all nationalists should support the abolition of landlordism. His slogan, 'the land of Ireland for the people of Ireland', rang as a battle-cry.

3.5. Davitt was convinced that Parnell was the only constitutional politician that could help him to achieve his aims and that he should be supported. He persuaded him to turn the Mayo Land League into a national organisation. Reluctant at first, Parnell agreed provided its programme could be advocated in parliament. Parnell issued a letter accompanied by an 'Appeal to the Irish race', written by Davitt, on 29 September 1879 and began the negotiations that led to the foundation of the Irish National Land League, in Dublin on 21 October 1879. Parnell was its first president and Davitt one of its three secretaries. But it was Davitt's plan, and the result was a movement under Parnell's leadership that had Fenian, Clan na Gael and widespread popular support. It combined, in one great agrarian movement, nationalists, moderates and constitutionalists side by side with revolutionaries, and it got strong backing and financial support from the Irish in America.

3.6. Distress in Ireland was so severe after the poor harvest of 1879 that it looked as if a catastrophe like the Great Famine was looming. For Davitt, driven by a passionate sense of social justice, the distress was the tragic result of an evil land system. He was a brilliant organiser, tirelessly active and he was imprisoned several times because of the League's vigorous prosecution of the Land War. On the eve of his arrest in 1881, Davitt, much to the annoyance of Parnell and Dillon, brought about the creation of the Ladies' Irish National Land League, one of Irishwomen's first political movements. By 1881, the government was forced by the League's actions and popular support to introduce land reforms to pacify tenants. In 1881 Gladstone's Land Act was passed. It granted the Land League's demand, that is, the three Fs – fair rent, fixity of tenure and freedom of sale – but the League fought on. Davitt could claim credit for a remarkable achievement. In the words of T.W. Moody:

> The land war of 1879–82 was decisive in several fundamental ways. The legal powers of the landlords over their lands were irremediably restricted, and without compensation, through the operation of the land act. Age-long habits of deference towards the landlords were broken by the sense of collective power that the Land League's teaching aroused in tenants. The social ascendancy of the landlords received blows from which it never recovered. And the tenants as a body became unshakeably attached to the cause of home rule, now seen to be inseparable from their cause as farmers ....

3.7. While in prison, where he was well treated, Davitt became more familiar with the ideals of the English socialist movements, and these influenced his subsequent agrarian demands. He also began an interesting memoir of prison life. He was elected MP for Meath unopposed in 22 February 1882 but was unseated because he was a convict. He was set free on 6 May 1882 as part of the terms of the Kilmainham Treaty (which Davitt, in fact, deplored as a surrender to the government). His eloquent denunciation of the Phoenix Park murders on the same day, signed also by Parnell and Dillon, marked his final disillusionment with physical force politics. Hitherto, there had always been ambiguity in his attitude to violence. Now he expressed deep revulsion against secret societies and he repudiated all connections with Fenianism, and this led quickly to an open breach with Devoy. Davitt loathed terrorism as an instrument of revolution and described O'Donovan Rossa, who espoused it, as an 'arch-scoundrel'. Of the dynamite campaign of O'Donovan Rossa and Clan na Gael, mounted against London and other British cities in 1881–7, he said:

> Principles of reform intelligently and fearlessly propagated are far more destructive to unjust and worn-out systems than dynamite bombs, which only kill individuals or knock down buildings but do no injury to oppressive institutions …

3.8. Davitt met Parnell in Avondale in September 1882 and he agreed to co-operate with him in setting up the Irish National League which put Home Rule first and land reform second. Much later, in 1903, Davitt described the founding of the National League as 'the complete eclipse, by a purely parliamentary substitute, of what had been a semi-revolutionary organisation … the overthrow of a movement and the enthronement of a man'. He held much the same view in 1882 though he did not say so. Indeed, he became a member of the organising committee of the National League, supported its programmes, and steadfastly backed Parnell's leadership until the divorce scandal broke.

3.9. He had become a keen advocate of land nationalisation, and he developed a policy based on an alliance of nationalist and British working-class interests. For him the abolition of landlordism meant ownership of the land by the state. This was utterly unacceptable in Ireland where the tenant farmers to a man wanted beyond all else to be owners of their farms. This led to an open breach with the conservative Parnell in 1884 and failed to get any support in Ireland or in Irish America. But Davitt held to his view to the end and he wrote in 1902: 'I still hold fondly and firmly to this great principle, and I believe a national ownership to be the only true meaning of the battle cry of the Land League – the Land for the People'. His plan for a 'National Land and Industrial Union of Ireland', drawn up in 1882, shows the range and originality of his social and political thinking. Its first object was 'the complete abolition of the landlord system'. Other objects were better conditions for agricultural labourers, better housing, the revival of manufacturing industries, the development of fisheries, the provision of proper scientific and technical education, and the cultivation of a national literature and of the Irish language. Its political objects were the repeal of the Union, national self-government, and improved parliamentary and local government representation and organisation.

3.10. Independent in his thinking, devoid of personal ambition or self-promotion, with a sharp and critical intelligence, Davitt had the keenest appreciation of Parnell's greatness as a leader, was constructively critical of his policies, but rightly detested the personality cult of Parnell promoted by some of his lieutenants. Anxious not to divide the national movement, he co-operated with Parnell in the Liberal alliance and in the struggle for Home Rule but he did not renounce his ideal, the complete independence of

Ireland. He strongly defended Parnell against the smears of the *Times* and his defence of the Land League before the Parnellism and Crime Commission (24–31 October 1889) was brilliant. When Parnell's leadership of the Irish Parliamentary Party was called into question as the unseemly details of the O'Shea divorce case became public, he called for his temporary retirement in an article in the *Labour World* on 20 November 1890. He was deeply troubled by the bitter divisions in the party and he did much to help in the negotiations that reunited it in 1900.

3.11. Davitt had a distinguished parliamentary career, beginning in April 1893 with the second reading of Gladstone's second Home Rule Bill. He has been described as 'virtually the parliamentary conscience of the whole British empire'. Among many other liberal causes, he championed prison reform; he denounced British war crimes in the colonies; and he resigned his seat in Westminster on 25 October 1899 as a protest against the Boer War (1899–1902) saying that 'the war would rank in history as the greatest crime of the nineteenth century'. After 1882, though he was politically influential, he was never again at the heart of Irish politics. His role was rather that of a freelance individualist, a left-wing intellectual, reformer, internationalist, unrivalled educator and champion of humanitarian causes, honoured and loved by his countrymen as the father of the Land League. He still involved himself with land problems: when William O'Brien established the United Irish Land League in 1898 to divide large estates among small farmers Davitt supported him with enthusiasm. He was bitterly critical of the Wyndham Act, 1903, seeing it as too soft on the landlords and another Tory ploy to kill Home Rule with kindness (which it was). He was a gifted and influential journalist and author. He travelled very widely – United States, Russia, Australia, New Zealand, South Africa, continental Europe, Egypt and Palestine – and wrote with sympathy and authority about the Jews in Russia, the Boers, the Maoris and other indigenous peoples. In Russia in 1903, he met the great novelist Tolstoy who admired him and congratulated him for going to prison for the sake of the Irish peasants. They met again when Davitt returned to Russia to cover the revolution of 1905.

3.12. In 1886, Davitt married an Irish-American, Mary Yore, whom he had met in Oakland, California in 1880. A lady of spirit, she brought him peace and great domestic happiness. They were given a house in Ballybrack, Co. Dublin that became known as the 'Land League Cottage', as a mark of appreciation for his life-long work for tenants' rights. For the Queen's Golden Jubilee Mary made a banner inscribed 'Evictoria' to hang over the door. From 1904 the Davitts lived in Dalkey, Co. Dublin.

3.13. Davitt was an orthodox and mostly practising Catholic. He accepted the authority of the bishops on faith and morals, but not beyond. He was always ready to reject their political opinions and their interference in politics. His Irish nation would be pluralist, internationalist, democratic and liberal. He was a supporter of non-denominational education. He wished to heal sectarian and cultural divisions. His quarrel was not with the British people but with British rule in Ireland, and he saw the labouring masses of both islands as joined by a common interest, the struggle for democracy and social justice.

What he wanted for Ireland, he wanted for all nations regardless of race or religion. Francis Sheehy-Skeffington wrote that in ways Davitt was greater than Parnell: 'Greater in his comprehensive sympathy with the oppressed all the world over … greater in the untarnished selflessness of his devotion to his country's cause; greater above all in his absolute sincerity and straightforwardness'.

3.14. Davitt died in Dublin on 31 May 1906 and, in accordance with his wishes, is buried at Straide, Co. Mayo.

3.15. WRITINGS, BIOGRAPHY AND STUDIES: D.B. Cashman, *The life of Michael Davitt* [with a history of the rise and development of the Irish National Land League] (Boston, MA, 1881; repr. with additions, London, 1882; many reprints). Davitt was a prolific writer and much of his work is reprinted in Michael Davitt, *Collected writings, 1868–1906*, ed. and intro. by Carla King (8 vols, Bristol, 2001). Important individual works are: *Leaves from a prison diary* (2 vols, London, 1884; repr. Shannon, 1972); *The Boer fight for freedom* (New York & London, 1902); *Within the pale: the true story of anti-Semitic persecution in Russia* (London, 1903); *The fall of feudalism in Ireland or the story of the Land League revolution* (London & New York, 1904; repr. Shannon, 1970). There are several biographies and many studies. Francis Sheehy-Skeffington, *Michael Davitt: revolutionary, agitator and labour leader* (London, 1908; repr. with intro. by F.S.L. Lyons, London, 1967). M.M. O'Hara, *Chief and tribune: Parnell and Davitt* (Dublin, 1919). J.E. Pomfret, *The struggle for land in Ireland, 1880–1923* (Princeton, NJ, 1930). N.D. Palmer, *The Irish Land League crisis* (New Haven, 1940). T.W. Moody, 'Michael Davitt, 1846–1906: a survey and appreciation', *Studies*, 35 (1946), 199–208, 325–34, 433–8. T.W. Moody, 'The new departure in Irish politics, 1878–9', in H.A. Cronne, T.W. Moody & D.B. Quinn (eds), *Essays in British and Irish history in honour of James Eadie Todd* (London, 1949), pp 303–33. T.W. Moody, 'Michael Davitt and the British labour movement, 1882–1906', *Transactions of the Royal Historical Society*, 5th series, 3 (1953), 53–76. T.W. Moody, 'Michael Davitt', in J.W. Boyle (ed.), *Leaders and workers* (Cork, 1965), pp 47–55. F.S.L. Lyons, *Parnell*, Irish History Series, 3 (Dundalk, 1965), esp. 6–12, 31–3. J. Cahalan, 'Michael Davitt: "the preacher of ideas", 1881–1906', *Éire-Ireland*, 11:1 (1976), 13–33. T.W. Moody, *Davitt and the Irish revolution, 1846–1882* (Oxford, 1981). Philip Bull, *Land, politics and nationalism: a study of the Irish land question* (Dublin, 1996). Carla King, *Michael Davitt* (Dundalk, 1999). Carla King, 'Michael Davitt, Irish nationalism and the British empire in the late nineteenth century', in Peter Gray (ed.), *Victoria's Ireland: Irishness and Britishness, 1837–1901* (Dublin, 2004), pp 116–30. Laurence Marley, *Michael Davitt: freelance radical and* frondeur (Dublin, 2007). John Devoy, *Michael Davitt: from the 'Gaelic American'*, ed. Carla King & W.J. McCormack (Dublin, 2008). Fintan Lane & Andrew G. Newby (eds), *Michael Davitt: new perspectives* (Dublin, 2009). Noel McLachlann, 'Michael Davitt', in James McGuire & James Quinn (eds), *Dictionary of Irish biography* (Cambridge, 2009), iii, pp 88–94.

DONNCHADH Ó CORRÁIN

4. Douglas Hyde (1860–1949)

4.1. Celtic scholar, translator, poet, cultural nationalist and president of Ireland, Douglas Hyde was born near Castlerea, Co. Roscommon, on 17 January 1860, the son of Arthur Hyde, a Church of Ireland clergyman and a descendant of the Elizabethan planter, Arthur Hyde of Denchworth, Berkshire. Hyde spent his early years in Co. Sligo (where his father was rector of Kilmactranny) and then, from 1867, at Frenchpark, Co. Roscommon. Due to a childhood illness he was educated at home. He spent most of his youth roaming the Roscommon countryside, fishing and shooting, in the company of an old Fenian, Johnny Lavin. At this time Irish was spoken by a little over a quarter of the people of Roscommon, but was in steep decline. He learned Irish from the ordinary people and studied the written language in an Irish New Testament he found in his father's house. Here in Roscommon he heard the folk tales and songs of the ordinary people that fired his imagination and here, too, he developed strong nationalist feelings.

4.2. He went to Trinity College, Dublin in 1880 where he felt alienated by its anglicised culture. He attended no lectures for the first two years and preferred to study at home. However, he was a distinguished student and he won many prizes including the gold medal for modern literature. He studied German, French, Latin, English, Celtic and history and took a BA in 1884. He had a notable talent for languages. To please his father, he read divinity and graduated with distinction but he had no taste for the clerical life. In October 1886 he came back to Trinity to study law and graduated with a doctorate in 1887. While at Trinity he joined the Contemporary Club where the questions of the day were vigorously debated, and among the participants were leading political activists (the Fenian John O'Leary; Michael Davitt, founder of the Land League; and Maud Gonne) and important writers (W.B. Yeats, T.W. Rolleston and C. Litton Falkiner). He contributed a reflective essay, 'A plea for the Irish language', to the *Dublin University Review* in August 1886, arguing that while English was necessary for all, it was essential for national honour to preserve Irish.

4.3. Hyde's life's work was to be the study and preservation of the Irish language. He was barely twenty when he joined the Society for the Preservation of the Irish Language and between 1879 and 1884 he published over a hundred pieces of Irish verse, some of them strongly nationalist. He used the pen name An Craoibhín Aoibhinn ('Delightful little branch') by which he became well known. In Dublin he associated with two different sets. The first was an Irish-language set centred about the Society for the Preservation of the Irish Language. He helped to establish the *Gaelic Journal* (*Irisleabhar na Gaedhilge*), the first important bilingual Irish periodical and he set himself to learn the older literature in Irish. The second set was a group of writers on Celtic themes but in English, among them W.B. Yeats, T.W. Rolleston and Katharine Tynan, with whom he collaborated. He contributed to W.B. Yeats' *Fairy and folk tales of the Irish peasantry* (1888).

4.4. In 1889 he published a collection of folk tales (*An leabhar sgeulaigheachta*). Here he expressed his idealist views on the value of Irish:

> Wherever Irish is the vernacular of the people there live enshrined in it memories and imaginations, deeds of daring ... an heroic cycle of legend and poem ... which contain the very best and truest thoughts ... of kings, sages, bards and shanachies of bygone ages ... if we allow one of the finest and the richest languages in Europe, which, fifty years ago, was spoken by nearly four millions of Irishmen, to die out without a struggle, it will be an everlasting disgrace, and a blighting stigma upon our nationality.

4.5. In 1890 he published *Besides the fire: a collection of Irish Gaelic folk stories*, a work that is a landmark in Irish folklore studies and in Irish literary history, because of his scholarly approach and because his translations are in the genuine English speech of the people.

4.6. With W.B. Yeats he founded the Irish Literary Society in London (1891) and the National Literary Society in Dublin (May 1892). In November 1892 Hyde delivered a manifesto to the National Literary Society under the title 'The necessity for the de-anglicising the Irish nation' in which he urged the Irish people to assert their separate cultural identity and to arrest the decay of the Irish language. He caustically attacked what he called 'West-Britonism', the copying of English manners and habits.

4.7. He spent 1891–2 in Canada as an interim professor of modern languages in the University of New Brunswick. When he returned to Ireland, he travelled the countryside collecting Irish folk tales and poetry. The result of his labour was *Abhráin grádh chúige Connacht, or, Love songs of Connacht*, first published in the newspapers and issued as a book in 1893 – the original texts in Irish with translations in verse and prose. His work had a remarkable effect. W.B. Yeats wrote: 'the prose parts of that book were to me, as they were too many others, the coming of a new power in literature'. It inspired Yeats, Synge and Lady Gregory.

4.8. Hyde married Lucy Cometina Kurtz, a wealthy Englishwoman, in Liverpool in October 1893. He signed his name in the registry book in Irish. Now he settled down in Frenchpark as a country gentleman. Here he went shooting and fishing with Lord de Freyne, the O'Conors of Cloonalis and the county gentry and socialised with them in the evenings. He was hugely popular; he mixed effortlessly with quite different people and classes; and, though firm in his convictions, he was always courteous and never quarrelled with anybody. Utterly free of religious prejudice, he was an ecumenist before his time. He did not care very much which church he attended. His *Abhráin diadha chúige Connacht, or, The religious songs of Connacht* (2 vols, 1906) is full of Catholic religious sentiment.

4.9. In July 1893 he became a joint founder, with Eoin MacNeill, of the Gaelic League (*Connradh na Gaeilge*), and remained its president until his resignation in 1915. Its purpose was to preserve Irish as a spoken language and maintain Ireland's distinctive Gaelic culture. From its establishment, the League was independent of all political parties and open to persons of any religion or none. It promoted the cause of Irish language, Irish music, Irish dancing, Irish culture, Irish games, as well as Irish industries. The League published an influential newspaper *An Claidheamh Soluis* ('the sword of light') and organised *feiseanna* and literary competitions. It successfully campaigned to have St Patrick's Day made a national holiday. *Timirí* (travelling teachers) visited all parts of the country to encourage the formation of Irish language classes. In 1905 its first college for the training of Irish teachers, Coláiste na Mumhan, was established in the Cork Gaeltacht. In 1905–6 Hyde toured the USA to raise funds for the League and collected the large sum of $64,000 (approx. €1.2 million at 2009 values). By now the League had 550 branches nationwide and had become a major cultural force.

4.10. At the Commission on Intermediate Education in 1899 there was an animated discussion on the educational value of Irish. The Trinity professors John Pentland Mahaffy, Robert Atkinson and their supporters wished to lower the status of Irish as a school subject, arguing that there was nothing in Irish fit to be studied. Hyde took them on and trounced them. He sent copies of what they had said to the leading Celtic scholars of Europe – among them Rudolf Thurneysen, Ernst Windisch and Ludwig Christian Stern in Germany; Holger Pedersen in Denmark; and Georges Dottin in France. Hyde submitted their calm scholarly replies on the outstanding quality of Irish literature to the Commission. This crushed the opposition. Irish retained its status as a school subject and the status of Irish literature and Irish scholarship was vindicated spectacularly. In 1906 he was appointed a member of the Royal Commission on University Education and, against much opposition, notably of the Catholic bishops, he was successful in making Irish a compulsory subject for matriculation into the new National University of Ireland. In this, Hyde proved an inspired campaigner and so strong was popular support that 100,000 attended a pro-Irish rally in Dublin.

4.11. In 1909 he was appointed the first Professor of Modern Irish at University College Dublin, a position that he held until 1932. He was also Dean of the Faculty of Celtic Studies. He was Chairman of the Irish Folklore Commission (1930–4) and was awarded the Gregory Medal in 1937. On his retirement, he lived at Ratra, near Frenchpark, in a house bought and given to him by the Gaelic League.

4.12. Hyde's writings are central to the Irish Revival. In 1897 Hyde, because of the insistence of W.B. Yeats, became an editor, with T.W. Rolleston and Sir Charles Gavan Duffy, of the New Irish Library, a series of books on Irish history and literature issued by the London publisher, Fisher Unwin. It published Hyde's own *Story of early Gaelic literature* in 1905. He edited *Giolla an Fhiugha* (1899) and *Gabháltais Shéarlais Mhóir: the conquests of Charlemagne* (1917), both published by the Irish Texts Society, of which he was president. His *Literary history of Ireland*, a remarkable achievement in its day and still not bettered, appeared in 1899. In 1901 he collaborated with Yeats and Lady Gregory on theatrical productions, beginning with *Casadh an tSúgáin* 'The twisting of the straw rope'. This was the first play in Irish to be performed in the Literary Theatre. This is how James Cousins describes the performance: 'A simple story; but its dressing and dialogue and the energy and delight of the actors were irresistible, and a scene of ungovernable enthusiasm followed …' Hyde later became the vice-president of the Abbey Theatre company.

4.13. The Gaelic League grew dramatically in strength. But it attracted people like Patrick Pearse and Sinn Féin activists. Now political events overshadowed Ireland. The Sinn Féin party had been founded (1905) and was working for a fully independent Ireland. Many of its members were also active members of the League. Hyde tried continuously to keep politics out of the League's affairs and, though a nationalist, never expressed any political opinion himself. But with the growing excitement following the formation of the Ulster Volunteer Force (January 1913) and the Irish Volunteers (November 1913), it became difficult to keep the League out of politics. In 1915 the Oireachtas of the League was held at Dundalk. There was a motion to add to the League's objects the further one of making Ireland 'free of foreign domination'. It passed by a large majority, but it was divisive. Besides, it was a coup: the Gaelic League was now being taken over by those identified with revolutionary politics. Hyde resigned as President, and the League's main interest became politics, not language. He was well aware of the impact on national politics of the Gaelic League. He wrote: 'The Gaelic League grew up and became the spiritual father of Sinn Féin and Sinn Féin's progeny were the Volunteers who forced the English to make the Treaty. The Dáil is the child of the Volunteers, and thus it descends directly from the Gaelic League, whose traditions it inherits'. His dream that Irish would unite all the people, regardless of politics or religion, was over.

4.14. When the office of President of Ireland was created under the Constitution of 1937, Hyde was unanimously selected by all parties and held office until his term expired in 1945. While in office, he published three volumes for private circulation: *The children of Lir* (1941), *Songs of Columcille* (1942) and *Dánta éagsamhla*. He died in Dublin, on 12 July 1949. He was given a state funeral, and a Church of Ireland service was held in St Patrick's Cathedral. The President and cabinet, Catholic politicians and people, stood outside the Cathedral in craven obedience to a canon law of the Catholic Church that forbade Catholics to attend a non-Catholic religious service. His remains were then taken across Ireland by motorcade and buried in Frenchpark churchyard, Co. Roscommon, on 14 July.

4.15. WRITINGS, BIOGRAPHY AND STUDIES: Douglas Hyde (ed. & tr.), *Beside the fire: a collection of Irish Gaelic folk stories* (London, 1890; 2nd ed. London, 1910; repr. New York, 1973; repr. Dublin, 1978). Dúbhglas de hÍde (ed. & tr.), *The love songs of Connacht* (Dublin, 1893; repr. Shannon, 1969). Douglas Hyde, *A literary history of Ireland* (London, 1899; repr. with additions by Brian Ó Cuív, London & New York, 1967, 1980). Dúbhglas de hÍde (ed.), *An sgéaluidhe Gaedhealach* (London & Dublin, 1895–1901) [with French translation by Georges Dottin]. Douglas Hyde, *The story of early Gaelic literature* (London,

1905). Dúbhglas de hÍde (ed. & tr.), *The religious songs of Connacht* (Dublin, 1906; repr. Shannon, 1969). Dúbhglas de hÍde, *Mise agus an Connradh (go dtí 1905)* (Dublin, 1937). Dúbhglas de hÍde, *Mo thurus go h-Americe* (Dublin, 1937). Diarmid Coffey, *Douglas Hyde, president of Ireland* (Dublin, 1938). Myles Dillon, 'Douglas Hyde', in Conor Cruise O'Brien (ed.), *The shaping of modern Ireland* (London, 1960), pp 50–62. Máirín Ní Mhuiríosa, *Réamhchonraitheoirí* (Dublin, 1963). Donal McCartney, 'Hyde, D.P. Moran, and Irish Ireland', in F.X. Martin (ed.), *Leaders and men of the Easter Rising* (London, 1967), pp 43–54. Brian Ó Cuív, 'The Gaelic cultural movements and the new nationalism', in K.B. Nowlan (ed.), *The making of 1916: studies in the history of the Rising* (Dublin, 1969), pp 1–27. Douglas Hyde, *Language, lore and lyrics*, ed. Breandán Ó Conaire (Dublin, 1986). Seán Ó Tuama (ed.), *The Gaelic League idea* (Cork & Dublin, 1972; 2nd ed., Cork 1993). Dominic Daly, *The young Douglas Hyde* (Dublin, 1974). Janet E. & Gareth W. Dunleavy, *Douglas Hyde: a maker of modern Ireland* (Berkeley, CA, 1991). Risteard Ó Glaisne, *Dúbhglas de h de, 1860–1949: ceannródaí cultúrtha* (Dublin, 1991). Seán Ó Lúing, 'Douglas Hyde and the Gaelic League', in his *Celtic Studies in Europe and other essays* (Dublin, 2000), pp 77–94. Gareth W. Dunleavy, *Douglas Hyde* (Lewisburg, PA, 2001). Patrick Maume, 'Hyde, Douglas', in James McGuire & James Quinn (eds), *Dictionary of Irish biography* (Cambridge, 2009), iv, pp 879–84.

DONNCHADH Ó CORRÁIN

5. James Larkin (1874–1947)

5.1. Socialist, trade union leader, and politician, Larkin was born in Liverpool, England, on 21 January 1876, the second son of impoverished Irish parents, James Larkin (1845–87) and Mary Ann McNulty (1842–1911). He spent his childhood with his grandparents in Newry, Co. Down. When Larkin was only nine years old, he returned to Liverpool to begin work at 12½*d.* per week. He was a seaman for a while and then became a foreman on the Liverpool docks. He lost his position when he sympathised with his men. Larkin believed that the working people were being unfairly treated by their employers. He was a deeply committed socialist. He joined the National Union of Dock Labourers (NUDL) in 1901. Five years later he was elected General Organiser, having successfully organised campaigns for union candidates both in local and general elections. Larkin married Elizabeth Brown on 8 September 1903 in a civil ceremony in Liverpool, and they had four sons.

5.2. During the Belfast disputes of 1907 Larkin organised sympathetic workers' strikes. He introduced the weapon of 'blacking' goods, that is, dockers refused to handle the goods of strike-breaking employers, and he even succeeded in bringing the police out on strike. He managed to unite Catholic and Protestant workers in an action against the Belfast Steamship Company in May 1907. His militant methods alarmed the NUDL, and in 1908 he was transferred to Dublin. There he reformed the Irish branch of the

Independent Labour Party. Within a year he had called three strikes, in Belfast, Cork and Dublin. He was eventually suspended by the NUDL, which refused to finance his planned industrial actions. This led to his involvement in the formation of the Irish Transport and General Workers Union (ITGWU) in 1909. This union catered for unskilled workers such as carters, dockers, labourers, and factory hands, who lived in great misery in the slums of Dublin. The ITGWU also had branches in Belfast, Derry and Drogheda. Its political programme included an eight-hour working day, provision of work for all the unemployed, and pensions for all workers at 60 years of age. In addition, it sought compulsory arbitration courts, adult suffrage, the nationalisation of the Irish transport system, and the land of Ireland for the people of Ireland. Larkin was the Union's secretary and edited its paper, the *Irish Worker and People's Advocate*.

5.3. His combination of socialism, republicanism and trade unionism became known as 'Larkinism'. His magnetic personality and gifted oratory soon attracted thousands to his union. His success caused alarm and fear among the Dublin employers who thought he was becoming too powerful and too popular with the working class of Dublin. Larkin also organised a temperance campaign and succeeded in ending the practice of paying casual labourers in public houses.

5.4. His strike tactics alienated employers and also the leaders of the Irish Trades Union Congress (TUC). He and his union were expelled from the TUC in 1909. In fact, the ITGWU was not re-affiliated until 1911 and shortly after that he became president of the TUC. In June 1910 he was sentenced to one year's imprisonment on a charge of misappropriating Cork dockers' money while working for the NUDL (at most he was guilty of sloppy accounting and not of embezzlement). He was released on 1 October 1910, following a petition from the Dublin Trades' Council to the Lord Lieutenant of Ireland, the Earl of Aberdeen. From 1911 on he attacked the Dublin employers in the *Irish Worker*. In 1912 he joined with James Connolly in forming the Irish Labour Party. Later that year he won a seat on Dublin Corporation, but he was removed after a month.

5.5. Larkin led a series of strikes involving carters, dockers, railwaymen and tram workers in the city. The employers, led by William Martin Murphy, were spurred to action. In 1913, the employers decided to destroy Larkin's ITGWU. Murphy was the owner of the *Irish Independent*, the *Irish Catholic* newspapers and Clery's department store, and he was director of the Dublin United Tramways Company. He demanded that his workers sign a pledge to remain loyal to their employers. When the workers refused, the great Lockout of 1913 followed. Other unions supported their fellow-workers and between 20,000 and 25,000 were thrown out of employment. Despite being reduced to starvation, the workers, under Larkin's leadership, kept up their struggle for eight months. Larkin was sentenced to seven months in prison for incitement but was released after protest meetings in England. Although £150,000, in money and food, came from the British labour movement, a British Trades Union Congress meeting in December 1913 overwhelmingly rejected Larkin's proposal for a general strike in Britain. By the middle of January 1914 members began returning to work. The result was in Connolly's words 'a drawn battle', but many hundreds of workers were not re-employed and had to emigrate. After 1914 Larkin's Union was low in numbers and funds.

5.6. On the outbreak of the First World War, Larkin called on Irishmen to stay out of it. In the *Irish Worker* he wrote: 'stop at home, arm for Ireland, fight for Ireland and no other land'. He also organised large anti-war demonstrations in Dublin. In October he went on a lecture tour of the USA to raise funds, leaving the management of the ITGWU to James Connolly and William O'Brien. His visit to the USA became a nine-year stay. He involved himself in the American labour movement, the International Workers of the World movement, and was a delegate to the founding convention of the American Communist Party. He lacked the money to return home and was eventually arrested and imprisoned for 'criminal syndicalism'. During his imprisonment he was annually re-elected general secretary of the ITWGU. He condemned the Anglo-Irish Treaty in 1921. From his prison cell he denounced the Anglo-Irish Treaty. Pardoned in 1923 by the governor of New York, Alfred E. Smith, Larkin was deported to Ireland.

5.7. He returned to a different Ireland but nevertheless received a hero's welcome. He failed to regain control of the ITWGU. He later argued that it was not working hard enough for worker's rights. The Union disagreed, and in 1924 they expelled Larkin. With his brother Peter, he founded the Workers' Union of Ireland. In December 1924 he visited Russia as representative of the Irish Section of the Fifth Congress of the Third International, or Comintern. In 1932, he visited Russia gain to address the Sixth Congress of the International.

5.8. Larkin returned to the Labour Party again after getting amendments to the Trade Union Act of 1941. He served on the Dublin Trades Council and became a Dublin city councillor and a deputy in Dáil Éireann from 1927 to 1932, 1937–8 and again from 1943 to 1944 (for the Labour Party). His last big success was to win a fortnight's holiday for manual workers following a fourteen-week strike. Larkin, 'friend of the workers', died in Dublin on 30 January 1947 and was buried at Glasnevin. A statue of him by the sculptor Oisín Kelly now stands in O'Connell Street, Dublin.

5.9. BIOGRAPHY AND STUDIES: Donal Nevin (ed.), *Jim Larkin and the Dublin Lockout* (Dublin, 1964). Emmet Larkin, *James Larkin: Irish labour leader, 1876–1947* (London, 1965; repr. London, 1989). C. Desmond Greaves, *The Irish Transport and General Workers' Union: the formative years, 1909–1923* (Dublin, 1982). John Gray, *City in revolt: James Larkin and the Belfast dock strike of 1907* (Belfast, 1985). Emmet O'Connor, *A Labour history of Ireland, 1824–1960* (Dublin, 1992). John Newsinger, '"The curse of Larkinism": Patrick McIntyre, *The Toiler*, and the Dublin, Lockout of 1913', *Éire-Ireland*, 30:3 (1995), 90–102. Donal Nevin (ed.), *James Larkin, lion of the fold* (Dublin, 1998). T.P. Mac Gloin, 'Hybrids: Connolly and Larkin', *Studies*, 88 (1999), 53–60. Emmet O'Connor, *James Larkin* (Cork, 2002). Pádraig Yeates, *Lockout: Dublin 1913* (Dublin, 2000). Mark Farmer,

'James Larkin and the Workers' Union of Ireland', *Études Irlandaises*, 26:1 (2001), 101–15. John Newsinger, *Rebel city: Larkin, Connolly and the Dublin labour movement* (London, 2003). Joseph Deasy, *Fiery cross: the story of Jim Larkin*; with new introduction by Francis Devine & Niamh Puirséil (2nd ed., Dublin, 2004).

MARGARET FITZPATRICK

6. Charles Stewart Parnell (1846–91)

6.1. Landlord and politician, Charles Stewart Parnell was born into a Protestant aristocratic and land-owning family at Avondale, Co. Wicklow on 27 June 1846, the seventh child of John Henry Parnell and Delia Tudor Stewart (the daughter of an American naval hero, Commodore Charles Stewart). His early schooling was in England where he attended a girls' school in Yeovil, Somerset. He contracted typhoid and was brought home for private tuition. He later went to a school in Kirk Langley, Derbyshire, from which he was expelled, and then to Great Ealing School. When his father died in 1859 the young Parnell inherited the Avondale estate. The family lived in a succession of homes in the Dublin area during the 1860s. Parnell also attended Revd Whishaw's Academy in Chipping Norton. He went on to Magdalene College, Cambridge, but did not graduate.

6.2. In 1874, at the age of twenty-seven, Parnell abruptly resolved to enter Home Rule politics and in the following year he was elected to represent Co. Meath in the House of Commons and joined the Home Rule party led by Isaac Butt. In the beginning he was a reluctant speaker and contributed little to debates during his first year in the Commons. He soon gained a mastery of parliamentary procedure and his powers of leadership became evident. He established himself as an advanced nationalist when he joined in obstructionist tactics in parliament with Joseph Biggar, a determined and rugged Belfast-born nationalist and member of the Supreme Council of the IRB. Parnell seems to have relied heavily on the support of Fenian sympathisers. One of his earliest remarks in parliament was in support of the 'Manchester Martyrs'. These were three Irishmen hanged in Manchester in November 1867 for killing a policeman during a botched Fenian escape. Parnell worked hard to secure amnesty for the remaining prisoners (including Michael Davitt) who had been imprisoned for gun running in 1870.

6.3. In 1877 Parnell became President of the Fenian-controlled Home Rule Confederation of Great Britain, against the wishes of the party leader, Isaac Butt. By this time Parnell had won the support of the leading Irish-American republican organisation, Clan na Gael. The Catholic bishops were highly suspicious of him, partly because of his politics, partly because he was Protestant. They were very unhappy about his parliamentary obstructionism and his connections with the Fenians. For his part, Parnell tried to win them over by supporting their demand for state aid for Catholic schools and for a Catholic University.

6.4. He identified and highlighted most forcibly the tenant farmers' grievances about the system of land-holding at the Westport land meeting in June 1879. Here he gave his most famous speech: 'You must show the landlords that you intend to keep a firm grip on your homesteads and lands. You must not allow yourselves to be dispossessed as you were dispossessed in 1847'.

6.5. The National Land League was founded in October 1879, on Michael Davitt's initiative. The League aimed to improve conditions for tenant farmers, demanding, in the short term, the 'three Fs – fair rent, fixity of tenure and freedom of sale'. In the long term the League hoped to abolish the landlord system altogether and make the tenants the owners of their farms through state-aided land purchase. Parnell was elected the first President of the Land League at a meeting in the Imperial Hotel, Dublin, on 21 October 1879. Davitt's passion for social justice inspired him to found the Land League and he remained its national driving force and organiser. This together with Parnell's parliamentary skill in Westminster made the Land League a powerful and revolutionary force in Irish politics.

6.6. Shortly after the Land League was founded, Parnell went to the United States to raise money. He travelled 16,000 miles in the United States and Canada, spoke in more than 60 cities and raised about £60,000 (approx. €5.75 million at 2009 values) for famine relief and £12,000 (approx. €1.15 million) for the League. In early 1880 the Conservative Prime Minister, Disraeli, called a general election. The election was a triumph for Parnell who was elected for three constituencies, Meath, Mayo and Cork city. He opted to represent Cork, which he did for the rest of his life. He was proposed as leader of the Irish Parliamentary Party and despite the opposition of moderate Home Rulers, Fenians and the Catholic Church he won. Parnell's supporters were united, his opponents were not.

6.7. In April 1881, Gladstone introduced a Land Bill which gave tenants the three Fs. This Act brought improvements for tenants and it was welcomed by the better-off tenants who would benefit from it but it excluded almost 280,000 tenants who were either leaseholders or were in arrears. Parnell knew that his followers were divided over the Act and in an effort to prevent his movement from breaking up he matched his speeches to his audiences. He advised the better-off tenants 'to test the Act' and he pointed out its weaknesses to those who did not benefit from it. The Act contained land purchase clauses and 731 tenants bought land under its provisions.

6.8 On 13 October 1881, Parnell was arrested under the Coercion Acts. He wrote to Katharine O'Shea when he was taken: 'Politically it is a fortunate thing for me that I have been arrested, as the movement is breaking fast and all will be quiet in a few months, when I shall be released'.

6.9. He knew that he could not be blamed for the break up of the Land League that he expected to result from the divisions among tenants over the Land Act. Instead he and other Land League leaders were lodged in Kilmainham Gaol – agrarian martyrs. From there they issued the 'No rent manifesto', calling on the tenants to pay no rent and to boycott the Land Courts until the 'suspects' were released. It was said that Parnell, at the time of his arrest, remarked that 'Captain Moonlight' would take his place, and so it proved. By the start of 1882, Irish agrarian unrest escalated to unprecedented levels (3,433 episodes of agrarian violence were recorded) and it was clear to both Gladstone and Parnell that it was time to reach a compromise.

6.10. The Kilmainham Treaty was agreed. The agreement was that Gladstone would amend the Land Act of 1881 to include tenants in arrears and leaseholders; drop coercion; and release 'suspects' in police custody. In return, Parnell would help to pacify the people of Ireland and cooperate with the Liberal Party in forwarding Liberal principles and measures of general reform. Parnell was released on 2 May 1882 and crossed directly to England where he made a dramatic appearance in the House of Commons.

6.11. On 6 May 1882, Lord Frederick Cavendish, the Chief Secretary, and his Permanent Under-Secretary, Thomas Burke, were stabbed to death in the Phoenix Park, Dublin, by the Invincibles, a group of extreme nationalist assassins. Parnell was deeply shaken by the assassinations, even to the extent of writing to Gladstone offering to resign as an MP, an offer rejected by Gladstone.

6.12. Parnell now resolved on a different course. In October 1882 he effectively replaced the semi-revolutionary National Land League movement with the disciplined pledge-bound Irish National League that was centralised under his own control and that of his faithful followers. It superseded both the Land League and the Home Rule League and, by 1886, it had over 1,200 branches. The National League was to serve the parliamentary party well and to act as an efficient party machine dedicated to choosing candidates for election, raising funds for the party, and getting the voters out on election day. It turned the Home Rule movement into a modern united political party that was organised at local, county, national, and parliamentary party level. It controlled political expression and national sentiment to a large extent and was politically effective. It paid its MPs who needed the money and that, no doubt, helped to secure their loyalty. By the next general election, in 1885, Parnell and his supporters controlled the National League to such an extent that only candidates approved by them could be elected as Home Rulers. Gladstone himself was impressed by the regular attendance and the disciplined voting of Parnell's post–1885 party.

6.13. Parnell's first objective was Home Rule; land law reform was a poor second. As early as October 1880, in a speech in Galway, he had said of his role in the land war: 'I would not have taken off my coat and gone to this work if I had not known that we were laying the foundation in this movement for the regeneration of our legislative independence'. He now, in 1882, focused on constitutional politics and turned away from revolutionary groups. He devoted himself to his main political ambition, that of winning Home Rule by negotiation with the political parties in Westminster. The land question became less pressing. Parnell was alarmed by the militancy of the women of the Ladies' Land League that had taken over the work of the imprisoned leaders, and on his release from prison, in May 1882, he set about dissolving the organisation (August 1882). This was done in a humiliating way, by cutting off its funds, which caused bitterness and resentment among the women and it is said that his sister Anna, a founder of the Ladies' Land League, never spoke to him again.

6.14. The 1885 general election was a triumph for Parnell and for the National League. Parnell, with a party of 86 Home Rule MPs, held the balance of power at Westminster. When it became clear that Gladstone favoured Home Rule for Ireland the Home Rule party switched its support and put the Liberals into power, in January 1886. Gladstone had not yet persuaded enough members of his party of the merits of Home Rule but nevertheless he introduced a Home Rule Bill in May 1886. It was opposed by Unionists in Ireland, Conservatives in Britain, and by the right-wing Whigs and the left-wing radicals (led by Joseph Chamberlain) of Gladstone's own Liberal party. The Bill was defeated, in June 1886. In the ensuing election of 1886 the Liberals fell from power.

6.15. Parnell and the Home Rule party remained strong. Gladstone's support for Home Rule was regarded in Ireland as a triumph and indeed Parnell's success in persuading Gladstone, one of the greatest leaders and parliamentarians of the age, of the merits of Home Rule, was a great achievement. He had 'set the Home Rule argument on its legs', as Gladstone said much later. Parnell's success in 1885 and 1886 and the danger represented by his 86 MPs encouraged the Tories to adopt a policy of 'killing Home Rule with kindness', another great achievement, in its own way, that would bring many benefits to Ireland.

6.16. In 1887 the *Times* published a series of articles under the title 'Parnellism and crime', in which the Home Rule leaders were accused of complicity in crimes and outrages during the Land War. Parnell was accused of supporting the assassination of the Chief Secretary of Ireland in the Phoenix Park. The evidence against him turned out to be letters forged by the journalist Richard Piggott who did it for money. Piggott later shot himself in Spain after being confronted by British police in the spring of 1888. Parnell's innocence served to unite all shades of nationalist opinion around him and enhanced his standing with a British public that had been very hostile towards him. He was now at the pinnacle of his career, the 'uncrowned king of Ireland'.

6.17. In 1890, Captain William O'Shea, a former member of Parnell's party, got a divorce from his wife, Katharine, with whom Parnell had been living (and who bore him two daughters, Claire and Katharine). Captain O'Shea, in an effort to benefit from the will of Katharine's wealthy aunt, made the case public. This was a serious blow to Parnell's political ambitions and to his career. Most of his party deserted him and he rapidly lost public support. Many took the view that he was no longer a fit person to lead the Irish

Parliamentary Party. Michael Davitt's call for Parnell's temporary retirement in *Labour World*, 20 November 1890, was supported by many. Gladstone informed the party chairman that there could be no alliance with the Liberals while Parnell remained leader. Parnell, a proud and passionate man beneath his aloof exterior, refused to stand down. This produced a bitter split in the parliamentary party on 6 December 1890 when Justin McCarthy led 44 members out, leaving Parnell with 27. Parnell went on to suffer several by-election defeats. He continued to fight for the leadership and he made many ambiguous speeches that seemed to appeal to the Fenian tradition. Davitt called this period 'the crowning disgrace of his career'. The Catholic hierarchy issued their condemnation in June 1891. They stated that Parnell, 'by his public misconduct, has utterly disqualified himself to be ... leader'.

6.18. Parnell's health deteriorated in 1891. Despite illness, and a warning from his doctor not to do so, he kept an engagement to speak at Creggs, Co. Galway, 27 September 1891. He did so in torrential rain, returned to Dublin, and then to Brighton. He fell ill and died suddenly at Brighton on 6 October 1891, at the age of forty-five, just five months after he had married Katharine O'Shea. James Joyce was to describe him as 'strong to the point of weakness'. His funeral to Glasnevin Cemetery, Dublin, 11 October, was attended by nearly 250,000 people. In December 1895 Gladstone said of Parnell: 'I cannot tell you how much I think of him, and what an interest I take in everything concerning him. A marvellous man, a terrible fall.'

6.19. BIOGRAPHY AND STUDIES: T.P. O'Connor, *The Parnell movement: with a sketch of Irish parties from 1843* (London, 1886). T.P. O'Connor, *Charles Stewart Parnell: a memory* (London, 1891). Frank Hugh O'Donnell, *A history of the Irish Parliamentary Party* (2 vols, London, 1910). R. Barry O'Brien, *The life of Charles Stewart Parnell*, with a preface by John E. Redmond (London, 1910). Katharine O'Shea, *Charles Stewart Parnell: his love story and political life* (2 vols, London, 1914; repr. 1 vol. London, 1973). John Howard Parnell, *Charles Stewart Parnell: a memoir* (London, 1921). Conor Cruise O'Brien, *Parnell and his party, 1880–90* (Oxford, 1957). F.S.L. Lyons, 'The economic ideas of Parnell', in Michael Roberts (ed.), *Historical Studies*, II (London, 1959), pp 60–78. F.S.L. Lyons, *The fall of Parnell, 1890–91* (London, 1960). Michael Hurst, *Parnell and Irish nationalism* (London, 1968). F.S.L. Lyons, 'The political ideas of Parnell', *Historical Journal*, 16 (1973), 749–75. F.S.L. Lyons, *Charles Stewart Parnell* (London, 1977; new edition, 2005). R.F. Foster, *Charles Stewart Parnell: the man and his family* (Hassocks, 1979). Emmet Larkin, *The Roman Catholic Church in Ireland and the fall of Parnell, 1888–1891* (Chapel Hill, NC, 1979). Alan O'Day, *Parnell and the first Home Rule episode, 1884–87* (Dublin, 1986). William Michael Murphy, *The Parnell myth and Irish politics, 1891–1956* (New York, 1986). Paul Bew, *Conflict and conciliation in Ireland, 1890–1910: Parnellites and radical agrarians* (Oxford, 1987). Emmet Larkin, 'The fall of Parnell: personal tragedy, national triumph', *Studies; an Irish Quarterly Review*, 80 (1991), 358–65. D.G. Boyce & Alan O'Day (eds), *Parnell in perspective* (London, 1991). Donal McCartney (ed.), *Parnell: the politics of power* (Dublin, 1991). Frank Callanan, *The Parnell split, 1890–91* (Cork, 1992). Frank Callanan, *T.M. Healy* (Cork, 1997). Robert Kee, *The laurel and the ivy: the story of Charles Stewart Parnell and Irish nationalism* (London, 1993). Tim Hodge, *Parnell and the Irish question* (Harlow, 1998). Alan O'Day, *Charles Stewart Parnell* (Dublin, 1998). Alan O'Day, *Irish Home Rule, 1867–1921* (Manchester, 1998). Sean McMahon, *Charles Stewart Parnell* (Cork, 2000). Donal McCartney & Pauric Travers (eds), *The ivy leaf: the Parnells remembered: commemorative essays* (Dublin, 2006). Paul Bew, *Ireland: the politics of enmity, 1789–2006* (Oxford & New York, 2007).

MARGARET FITZPATRICK (WITH CONTRIBUTIONS BY FIDELMA MAGUIRE)

7. John Redmond (1856–1918)

7.1. Politician and party leader, John Edward Redmond was born at Ballytrent House, Kilrane, Co. Wexford on 1 September 1856, the eldest son of William Archer Redmond, nationalist MP for Wexford. The Redmonds were a well-established Catholic gentry family. His mother, Mary, was the daughter of Major Hoey of Hoeyfield, Co. Wicklow. He was educated at Clongowes Wood College and later at Trinity College, Dublin. After graduating he became a clerk in the House of Commons. Redmond was to devote his entire life to politics. He was elected MP for New Ross in 1881. A very able speaker, he quickly established himself within the Irish Parliamentary Party and the National League. In the early 1880s he toured Australia and America with his brother William, and raised nearly £30,000 (approx. €2.8 million at 2009 values) for the Irish Party's funds. He read law at Gray's Inn, London; he was called to the English Bar in 1885, and to the Irish Bar two years later, but he never practised. He sat as MP for North Wexford from 1885 until 1891 and for Waterford City 1891–1918. Although not an agrarian radical, he took part in the Land War (1879–82) and Plan of Campaign (1886–91) and was briefly imprisoned in 1888 for incitement.

7.2. Redmond was deeply opposed to the use of physical force. He was committed to political change by constitutional means. He was a zealous admirer of the British House of Commons. He sought only limited Irish self-government, considering it undesirable that Britain and Ireland should be wholly separated, and he had no wish to see the dismemberment of the British Empire. Redmond was leader of the minority that supported Parnell during the split of 1890, following the O'Shea divorce case. He led the Parnellite remnant of the party – just nine members in January 1892. He sat on the Recess Committee (established 1895) that sought to consider the means by which Irish farmers could best be served and the way suitable legislation could help them. Its meetings were held during the parliamentary recess. Its recommendations led to the establishment of the Department of Agriculture and Technical Instruction (1899). Redmond welcomed the Local Government Act, 1898 that provided for the creation of elected county and district councils. He saw it as an important step towards Irish self-government. He also retained his contact with influential Irish-Americans, and he travelled to the USA in 1895 and 1899.

7.3. On 30 January 1900 nationalist MPs agreed to a reunification of the Irish Parliamentary Party and Redmond was elected leader on 5 February. His leadership had been contested by old anti-Parnellites, most notably by William O'Brien and Tim Healy. He was an important member of the Land Conference of 1902, from which came the Land Act of 1903. This Act gave a dramatic impetus to tenant land-purchase. He was also involved in the negotiations that resulted in the foundation of the National University in 1908. The year 1910 marked a high point in Redmond's political career. The two general elections of that year left the Tories and Liberals deadlocked. The Irish Party now held the balance of power at Westminster. Redmond used this leverage to persuade the Liberal government of H.H. Asquith to introduce the third Home Rule Bill, in April 1912. Not since the days of Parnell had a nationalist leader wielded such influence over government policy.

7.4. By 1913, Ulster Unionists led by Sir Edward Carson were implacably opposed to Home Rule, and they posed a serious threat to Redmond's Irish Party. There was increasing militancy and the growing threat of civil war in Ireland. The Liberal MPs privately admitted that special treatment might be required for Ulster. Asquith reported to the King that there would be 'careful and confidential inquiry … as to the extent and character of the Ulster resistance'. In January 1913 the Ulster Volunteer Force (UVF) was set up and pledged to 'use all means that may be necessary to defeat the present conspiracy to set up a Home Rule parliament in Ireland'. In response, the Irish Volunteers were established in November 1913 under the leadership of the nationalist, Eoin MacNeill, with ideals unshakeably opposed to those of the UVF. In July 1914, Redmond and John Dillon, represented the Irish Party at the Buckingham Palace Conference. It was summoned by King George V to break the deadlock over the third Home Rule Bill. Carson and James Craig represented Unionist interests. Carson was prepared to settle for Irish Home Rule only if the six north-eastern counties were permanently excluded. Redmond would only agree to a temporary exclusion. He was opposed to partition saying 'the two nation theory is an abomination and a blasphemy'. With very little compromise from either side, the Conference broke up without agreement.

7.5. When the war broke out in August 1914, Redmond proposed in the House of Commons that Ireland should be guarded by the Volunteers, north and south, and that British troops should be withdrawn from Ireland. The government thwarted his efforts. He had hoped that the common cause in the war would unite all Irish people. Nevertheless, the Government of Ireland Bill was passed on 18 September together with another bill (September 15) postponing the implementation of Home Rule until the end of the War. The position of Ulster remained unresolved and the government reserved the right to make legislative arrangements for the province.

7.6. Having apparently secured Home Rule, an invigorated Redmond encouraged members of the Irish Volunteers to join the British army and in a speech at Woodenbridge, Co. Wicklow, 20 September 1914, he pledged his support to the Allied cause. The words he addressed to the Irish Volunteers were:

> The interests of Ireland – of the whole of Ireland – are at stake in this war. This war is undertaken in the defence of the highest principles of religion and morality and right, and it would be a disgrace for ever to our country and a reproach to her manhood and a denial of the lessons of her history if young Ireland confined their efforts to remaining at home to defend the shores of Ireland from an unlikely invasion, and to shrinking from the duty of proving on the field of battle that gallantry and courage which has distinguished our race all through its history. I say to you, therefore, your duty is twofold. I am glad to see such magnificent material for soldiers around me, and I say to you: 'Go on drilling and make yourself efficient for the Work, and then account yourselves as men, not only for Ireland itself, but wherever the fighting line extends, in defence of right, of freedom, and religion in this war'.

7.7. Militant nationalists reacted angrily but the great majority of the Volunteers supported Redmond and became known as the National Volunteers. In May 1915 Redmond declined Asquith's offer of a seat in the War Cabinet saying that 'the principles and history of the party I represent make the acceptance of your offer impossible'. Despite rebuffs he continued to encourage Irishmen to join the British forces. Over 120,000 Irishmen fought in the First World War. His brother William was killed at the front in 1917. The minority of Volunteers who disregarded Redmond's plea were dominated by the IRB and retained the title Irish Volunteers.

7.8. The 1916 Easter Rising was a shattering blow to his life-long policy of constitutional action. He described the Rising as a 'German intrigue' and he failed to grasp the changing mood of Irish public opinion. While he did not agree with their methods, his pleas, and John Dillon's, that the rank and file of the rebels be treated leniently were ignored. In the House of Commons on 8 May 1916, Redmond warned the government that the executions were alienating many 'who have not the slightest sympathy with the insurrection'. Sinn Féin re-organised in 1917 and became Redmond's strongest opposition.

7.9. On Redmond's suggestion, the new Prime Minister, David Lloyd George established an Irish Convention in 1917 in an attempt to find a settlement of the demands for Irish Home Rule. The first meeting took place on 25 July in Trinity College, Dublin. Sir Horace Plunkett was elected Chairman. Unionists and nationalists sent representatives but Sinn Féin boycotted the Convention. Redmond angered some of his party members, when in an attempt to form an alliance with southern Unionists, he said any Dublin parliament should waive its right to collect customs duties. The Convention made little headway and it ended on 5 April 1918 having failed to reconcile conflicting nationalist and unionist demands. Comprehensive defeats in the 1917 by-elections showed just how far the party had fallen. Redmond felt betrayed when he was informed of the government's proposals for conscription in Ireland in 1918. Increasingly disillusioned, he died suddenly on 6 March 1918. Later that year, in the general election of December, his party's representation at Westminster completely collapsed, and Sinn Féin triumphed.

7.10. SPEECHES, BIOGRAPHY AND STUDIES: John Redmond, *Home Rule speeches*, ed. with intro. by R. Barry O'Brien (London, 1910). L.G. Redmond-Howard, *John Redmond, the man and the demand: a biographical study in Irish politics* (London, 1910). Warre B. Wells, *John Redmond: a biography* (London, 1919; repr. 2009). Stephen Lucius Gwynn, *John Redmond's last years* (London, 1919; repr. 2006). Denis Gwynn, *The life of John Redmond* (London, 1932). P.N.S. Mansergh, 'John Redmond', in C.C. O'Brien (ed.), *The shaping of modern Ireland* (Dublin, 1960), pp 38–49. F.S.L. Lyons, 'Dillon, Redmond, and the Irish home rulers', in F.X. Martin (ed.), *Leaders and men of the Easter rising* (London, 1967), pp 29–41. John M. McEwen, 'The Liberal party and the Irish question during the First World War', *Journal of British Studies*, 12:1 (1972), 109–31. Paul Bew, *John Redmond* (Dundalk, 1996). Joseph Finnan, '"Let Irishmen come together in the trenches": John Redmond and Irish party policy in the Great War, 1914–1918', *Irish Sword*, 22 (2000), 174–92. Michael Wheatley, 'John Redmond and federalism in 1910', *Irish Historical Studies*, 32 (2001), 343–64. Joseph Finnan, 'Punch's portrayal of Redmond, Carson and the Irish question, 1910–18', *Irish Historical Studies*, 33 (2003), 424–51. Joseph P. Finnan, *John Redmond and Irish unity, 1912–1918* (Syracuse, NY, 2004). James McConnel, 'Recruiting sergeants for John Bull? Irish Nationalist MPs and enlistment during the early months of the Great War', *War in History*, 14:4 (2007), 408–28.

TOMÁS O'RIORDAN

8. Hanna Sheehy-Skeffington (1877–1946)

8.1. Feminist, journalist, socialist and nationalist, Hanna Sheehy-Skeffington was born on 27 May 1877 in Kanturk, Co. Cork. She belonged to a prosperous farming and milling family. Her father, David Sheehy (1844–1932), was a member of the IRB and later an MP, and had been imprisoned no less than six times for revolutionary activities. Her uncle was the renowned Land League priest, Fr Eugene Sheehy. When the family moved to Dublin in 1887, Hanna attended the Dominican Convent in Eccles Street. She was one of the first of a new generation of women to graduate from an Irish university, being conferred with a BA in languages from the Catholic St Mary's University College for Women in 1899. She went on to study for a period in France and Germany and took an MA in modern languages in Dublin in 1902. She taught for a period in the Rathmines School of Commerce. In June 1903 she married Francis Skeffington (1878–1916), a university registrar who was prominent as a controversial journalist with socialist and pacifist sympathies. He was a vegetarian and a teetotaller. He proved a beloved companion who was both kind and humorous.

8.2. Hanna Sheehy-Skeffington was a very talented orator. She was well versed in international as well as Irish national affairs and was influential in literary, political, pacifist and feminist movements. Her independence of thought and her wit brought acclaim from all. She co-founded the Women Graduates' and Candidate Graduates' Association (1901). She and her husband Francis were deeply involved in the suffragette movement and, with Margaret Cousins, they founded the militant Irish Women's Franchise League in 1908. She was much condemned in 1909 for refusing to allow her newborn son, Owen Lancelot, to be baptised.

8.3. She contributed articles on education and feminist issues to the *Nation* newspaper and the *Bean na hÉireann* journal. In 1912 she and her husband founded the influential paper the *Irish Citizen*, aiming to promote the rights and responsibilities of citizenship for both sexes. She contributed many articles in support of Irish women's right to vote. In 1911 she was the founding member of the Irish Women's Workers' Union. She was imprisoned for five days in 1912 for breaking several window panes of the War Office in protest at the exclusion of women from the franchise in the third Home Rule Bill. She was a close associate of the labour leader James Connolly. During the Dublin 1913 Lockout, she worked in the soup kitchen set up in Liberty Hall, the Dublin headquarters of the Irish Transport and General Workers Union. She was jailed again, this time for assaulting a policeman, while attempting to leaflet the Conservative leader, Bonar Law, in Dublin. She went on hunger strike and was released after five days.

8.4. A pacifist like her husband, she supported him in his campaign against conscription at the beginning of the First World War, an activity for which he got gaol. During the Easter Rising of 1916 she carried messages to the GPO where her uncle, Fr Eugene Sheehy, gave spiritual aid to the rebels. Her husband, though an Irish nationalist, opposed attempts by the Irish Volunteers and the Citizen Army to overthrow British rule by force. He was arrested on 25 April while trying to prevent looting in Dublin. He was detained that night and the next morning, was taken from his cell by Captain J.C. Bowen-Colthurst of the Royal Irish Rifles. With two other prisoners, Sheehy-Skeffington was brought into the barracks yard and shot without trial. Hanna immediately began to campaign for justice, forcing the Royal Commission to hold an inquiry, which led to the court-martial of her husband's killer. She refused compensation of £10,000 from the British army following his execution. On 8 May 1916 Francis Sheehy-Skeffington's body, which had been buried at Portobello Barracks, was exhumed and reburied in Glasnevin Cemetery in Dublin.

8.5. In December 1916, Hanna undertook a lecture tour of the United States. She spent the next few years speaking in support of Sinn Féin and of Irish independence. She spoke at over 250 meetings and succeeded in raising significant funds for Michael Collins. She published a pamphlet called *British militarism as I have known it*, which was banned in Ireland and England until after the First World War. In July 1917 she returned secretly to Ireland. In January 1918, on behalf of Cumann na mBan, she personally presented Ireland's claim for self-determination to President Wilson. Upon her return to Ireland she was arrested and imprisoned together with Countess Markievicz, Kathleen Clarke and Maud Gonne-MacBride in Holloway Gaol, London. They were released after they went on hunger strike.

8.6. In 1917 she was appointed to the executive of Sinn Féin. In 1919 she published *Sinn Féin in America*. During 1920 she acted as judge in the Republican courts in south Dublin. In the same year she was elected Sinn Féin councillor on Dublin Corporation. She was also an executive member of the White Cross Fund set up to aid needy families of Volunteers involved in the War of Independence. With many other suffragettes, she rejected the Anglo-Irish Treaty. She took the anti-Treaty side in the Civil War. She was appointed to the first executive of Fianna Fáil in 1926 but resigned the following year in protest against de Valera who agreed to take the oath in order to enter the Dáil.

8.7. In 1930 she went on a six-week tour of Russia. A year later, she took over as editor of the *Republican File*, a republican-socialist journal, after the jailing of its editor Frank Ryan. Subsequently she became assistant editor of *An Phoblacht*, the organ of the Irish Republican Army. She was jailed yet again for a month for demanding the release of republican prisoners and protesting against partition at a public meeting in Newry, Co. Down.

8.8. In 1935, as a speaker for the Women's Graduates Association, she opposed the Conditions of Employment Bill which feminists considered a draconian measure against women workers. She objected to the place of women in de Valera's Constitution of 1937. She was a founder of the Women's Social and Progressive League, a party that came into being after a mass protest of women at the Mansion House, Dublin. It failed to win significant support although it campaigned strongly in the 1938 general election. In 1943, at the age of sixty-six, she stood as an independent candidate in the general elections, demanding equality for women. None of the four feminist candidates received any support from the electorate.

8.9. Hanna Sheehy-Skeffington spent the remainder of her life fighting for the rights of the individual, for workers, for the republic and most consistently, for the feminist cause. She died in Dublin in April 1946 and was buried in Glasnevin. Her sisters, Mary and Kathleen, were married to Thomas Kettle and Francis Cruise O'Brien respectively.

8.10. WRITINGS, BIOGRAPHY AND STUDIES: Hanna Sheehy-Skeffington, *Reminiscences of an Irish suffragette* (Dublin, 1975). R.M. Fox, *Rebel Irishwomen* (Dublin & Cork, 1935; repr. Dublin, 1967). Margaret Ward, *Unmanageable revolutionaries: women and Irish nationalism* (London, 1983). Rosemary Cullen Owens, *Smashing times: a history of Irish women's suffrage movement, 1889–1922* (Dublin, 1984). Leah Levenson & Jerry H. Natterstad, *Hanna Sheehy-Skeffington: Irish feminist* (Syracuse, NY, 1986). Andrée Sheehy-Skeffington, 'A coterie of lively suffragists', in Alf MacLochlainn & Andrée Sheehy-Skeffington, *Writers, raconteurs and notable feminists: two monographs* (Dublin,

1993), pp 34–52. Margaret Ward, *Hanna Sheehy-Skeffington: a life* (Cork, 1987). Maria Luddy, *Hanna Sheehy-Skeffington* (Dublin, 1995). Margaret Ward, *Hanna Sheehy-Skeffington: suffragist and Sinn Feiner* (Dublin, 1996). Margaret Ward, 'Hanna Sheehy-Skeffington', in Mary Cullen & Maria Luddy (eds), *Female activists: Irish women and change 1900–1960* (Dublin, 2001), pp 89–112.

MARGARET FITZPATRICK AND EOIN HARTNETT

9. Isabella Tod (1836–96)

9.1. Feminist, philanthropist and social reformer, Isabella Maria Susan Tod was born on 18 May 1836, in Edinburgh, Scotland. Her father, James, was a Scottish merchant, and her mother, Maria Isabella (née Waddell), was from Co. Monaghan. The family came to live in Belfast in the 1860s. Tod was proud of her Scottish background, and often referred to the fact that one of her ancestors signed the Solemn League and Covenant at Hollywood, Co. Down, in 1646. Another proud recollection was that her great-grand-father was a colonel in the Volunteers of 1782. One of her ancestors was Revd Charles Masterton, a leading Presbyterian minister of Belfast in the seventeenth century. Her attachment to the Presbyterian faith was strong and her religious beliefs were to influence her political life.

9.2. Tod was largely self-educated: she had no formal education. It is clear that her mother was a major influence on her life and Tod looked after her until her death in 1877. Her interest in the affairs of women was apparently fostered by her mother whose encouragement led her to engage in private study. Her initial means of raising the status of women (and making herself an income) was through writing, and in the 1860s and the 1870s she contributed pieces anonymously to the *Dublin University Magazine*, the *Banner of Ulster* and the *Northern Whig*. The National Association for the Promotion of Scoial Science held its first annual meeting of 1867 in Belfast. Tod closely identified with its aim of alleviating social problems of the day. She wrote that the Association gave her her first experience 'of direct political effort for social purpose, and [I] was also first led by it to speak in public'. Women like Tod now had a public platform from which to debate important issues relating to women's status in society.

9.3. Tod was a pioneer in lobbying for dramatic changes in girls' education at the second and third levels, which would qualify them for proper employment. She successfuly petitioned Queen's University in Belfast to allow women to sit university examinations. However, women were awarded certificates in place of degrees. The Belfast Ladies' Institute, of which Tod was Secretary, also played an important role in winning the rights of girls to take academic tests. The Ladies' Collegiate School, Belfast (1859), the Queen's Institute, Dublin (1861), Alexandra College, Dublin (1866), and the Belfast Ladies' Institute (1867) owe their existence to her campaigns. In 1878 she organised a delegation to London to put pressure on the government to include girls in the Intermediate

Education Act. This allowed girls to sit public examinations on the same terms as boys. In 1874, Tod published a paper entitled *On advanced education for girls in the upper and middle classes*. It had been presented in 1867 at a meeting of the National Association for the Promotion of Social Science. She called for practical education along the lines of the Belfast Ladies' Institute. The Institute organised lectures on modern languages, astronomy, history and other topics. Tod also acted as Secretary of the Institute that further campaigned to allow women access to University education in Ireland. This was secured under the University Education Act (1879), which established the Royal University of Ireland as an examing body. By 1889 more than 700 women had passed examinations in arts subjects. Tod was also the main influence behind the establishment of the Ulster Head Schoolmistresses' Association, formed in 1880. This association worked closely with the Central Association of Irish Schoolmistresses and other Ladies interested in Irish Education (AISLIE), established in Dublin in 1882.

9.4. Tod was involved in the important campaign to amend the laws governing married women's property. As an active member of the Presbyterian Church, she was a regular visitor to the deprived parts of Belfast, and was well aware of the economic exploitation of women. She was the only woman called to give evidence to the 1868 Select Committee Inquiry on the Married Women's Property. She advocated that any reforms must cover both working- and middle-class women. She was determined that the changes should go beyond protecting women's right to their wages and include their rights to possess property of their own. She also served on the executive of the Married Women's Property Committee, which was based in London. Through her activities on this Committee, Tod came to know reformers such as Caroline Norton, Frances Power Cobbe, Lydia Becker, Elizabeth Wolstenholme and Josephine Butler. Under, the Married Women's Property Act of 1870, wages and property that a wife earned through her own work would be regarded as her own property.

9.5. She had a lifelong interest in temperance. In 1874 she and Margaret Byers formed the Belfast Women's Temperance Association (BWTA). Tod was a committee member, and she undertook speaking engagements to further the cause. By 1875 the BWTA had opened three temperance food houses in the city, one of which offered 'nutritious dinners to girls engaged in factories'. The Belfast Ladies' Temperance Association expanded from supporting temperance to starting schemes for social reform. The Association established a Prison Gate Mission and a home for alcoholic women. It began classes in cookery and hygiene, and attempted to raise the moral and social standards of the homes of the poor. In 1882 the BWTA opened a house for destitute girls. By 1889 it claimed to have forty branches around the country. In 1894 all these branches merged to form a single organisation, the Irish Women's Temperance Union. In addition to her temperance activities in Ireland, Tod also acted as vice-president of the British Women's Temperance Association, from 1877 to 1892. In 1893 she became vice-president of the Irish Women's Total Abstinence Union, a position she held until her death in 1896.

9.6. Tod also called for the repeal of the Contagious Diseases Acts (1864, 1866, 1869). Under these Acts, prostitutes were forced to undergo medical examination for venereal disease and she considered this an infringement of women's civil liberties. The National Association for the Repeal of the Contagious Diseases Acts (NARCDA) and the Ladies' National Association (LNA), both formed in England in 1869, had branches in Ireland. Tod and Anna Haslam were involved in the campaign right from the beginning. Tod served on the executive committee of the London-based LNA and the general council of the NARCDA. By 1871 three branches of the LNA had been established in Belfast, Dublin and Cork. Tod was elected secretary of the Belfast branch. In Ireland, the LNA was a small and local affair and it served to support the aims of the parent body in London. In practice, this meant fundraising, organising petitions to parliament against the Acts, promoting higher standards of morality and trying to change public opinion by distributing pamphlets and papers and by holding meetings.

9.7. She used the work of the women in LNA to support women's claim to the vote. She established the Northern Ireland Society for Women's Suffrage (NISWS) in 1871, which was linked to the London Women's Suffrage Society. She remained secretary of the NISWS until the 1890s. She travelled the country tirelessly speaking at public meetings on the suffrage issue. She lobbied for formal political rights for women and played a key role in three areas: first, the fight for parliamentary suffrage; second, the issue of municipal voting for women; and third, the attempts to have women elected as Poor Law Guardians. The first area was not resolved in her lifetime, but the success of women in the other two owed much to her efforts. The women of Belfast were granted the municipal franchise in 1887; the women of the rest of Ireland in 1898. Tod hoped that enfranchised women would 'care less for party politics than men do, and more for the great social and moral questions which ought to be the end for which party politics are only the means'. Through her tireless efforts, she was to become a friend of many leading English suffragists – Lydia Becker, Helen Blackburn, and Josephine Butler.

9.8. Tod was vehemently opposed to the Irish Home Rule Bills and this lost her some friends in the suffrage movement. She organised a Women's Liberal Unionist Association in Belfast and spoke on platforms in Devon, Cornwall, and London. She argued that: 'Home Rule would destroy Ireland's economic base, not only would there be a withdrawal of capital … many skilled artisans would come over to England which would not tend to raise wages'. She hoped for a 'separate jurisdiction' for Ulster so that 'we can continue to do some good for the rest of Ireland. But no conceivable good for any created could come from being crushed under such a parliament.' She worked tirelessly as a publicist and was the only woman member of the executive committee of the Ulster Women's Liberal Unionist Association in 1888. While she campaigned in England, her organisation in Ireland raised a petition, signed by 30,000 women, which was presented to Queen Victoria asking her not to give her royal assent to the Bill, should it be passed.

9.9. The last years of Tod's life were dogged by bad health. Her tireless work was much appreciated by many individuals in both England and Ireland. In 1884 she was presented with a testimonial of £1,000 contributed mainly by her 'English fellow workers in various philanthropies'. In November 1886 she was presented with a full-length portrait as a token of appreciation for her work in Ireland. Another testimonial, some years later, consisted of an album, which contained 120 signatories, many from the front rank of the Unionist Party. Her last public appearance, just before her death, was at a meeting about distressed Armenians. She died at her home in Belfast on 8 December 1896. She is regarded as one of the most prominent feminists of the nineteenth century.

9.10. WRITINGS AND STUDIES: Isabella M.S. Tod, *On the education of girls of the middle classes* (London, 1874); repr. in Dale Spender (ed.), *The education papers: women's quest for equality in Britain, 1850–1912* (New York, 1987). Maria Luddy, 'Isabella M.S. Tod', in Mary Cullen & Maria Luddy (eds), *Women, power and consciousness in nineteenth-century Ireland: eight biographical studies* (Dublin, 1995), pp 197–230. Heloise Brown, 'An alternative imperialism: Isabella Tod, internationalist and "good Liberal Unionist"', *Gender & History*, 10 (1998), 358–80. Diane Urquhart, 'An articulate and definite cry for political freedom: the Ulster suffrage movement', *Women's History Review*, 11:2 (2002), 272–92. Noel Armour, 'Isabella Tod and liberal unionism in Ulster 1886–96', in Alan Hayes & Diane Urquhart (eds), *Irish women's history* (Dublin, 2004), pp 72–87. Georgina Clinton & Linde Lunney, 'Tod, Isabella Maria Susan', in James McGuire & James Quinn (eds), *Dictionary of Irish biography* (Cambridge, 2009), ix, pp 388–90.

TOMÁS O'RIORDAN

10. William Butler Yeats (1865–1939)

10.1. Writer, dramatist, founder of the Abbey Theatre, and the greatest modern poet writing in English, William Butler Yeats was born on 13 June 1865 at Sandymount Avenue, Dublin. He was the son of John Butler Yeats, a barrister who became a fine (though financially unsuccessful) portrait painter and Susan Pollexfen, the daughter of a wealthy Sligo merchant family. Shortly after his birth the family moved to London, where his father thought he might have more success. Yeats went to the Godolphin School, Hammersmith, but spent delightful holidays in Sligo with his grandparents. When the family returned to Dublin in 1880 he attended Erasmus Smith High School, in Harcourt Street, Dublin. His father wished him to go to Trinity College, following the family tradition, but he refused: he feared that would not meet the entrance requirements. Instead he studied at the Metropolitan School of Art, Dublin, in 1884–5, and then in 1886 at the Royal Hibernian Academy.

10.2. At the Metropolitan he became friendly with the mystic and poet George Russell (known as Æ) and a group of others interested in the occult. At the Contemporary Club, where there was a ferment of ideas and lively debate, he met Douglas Hyde, Stephen

Gwynn, John O'Leary, Michael Davitt and other important figures. From an early age he had been writing poetry and plays in imitation of Shelley and Spenser, and about 1886 he decided to abandon art and devote himself to writing.

10.3. Yeats published his first lyrics in the *Dublin University Review* in 1885. He worked for some time as literary correspondent for American newspapers, including the *Boston Pilot*. His interest in Irish myth and his commitment to the cause of Irish national identity stemmed mainly from living in the West of Ireland and from his contact with the Fenian, John O'Leary. He joined the Blavatsky London Lodge of the Theosophical Society (1887) and the Hermetic Order of the Golden Dawn (1890). Yeats' experiments with the occult were as much a matter of the poetic imagination as a pursuit of the supernatural. He met most of the poets of his generation at the Rhymers' Club, which he helped found. In 1891 he helped establish the Irish Literary Society of London. The following year, in Dublin, he joined with John O'Leary in founding the National Literary Society to publicise the literature, folklore, and legends of Ireland. In 1888 he had published *Fairy and folk tales of the Irish peasantry* and his *Irish fairy tales* appeared in 1892.

10.4. In 1889 he published *The wanderings of Oisin*, a long, highly imaginative poem based on Irish mythology, and in 1892 *The Countess Cathleen*, his first poetic play. His volume of folk stories, *The Celtic twilight*, appeared in 1893. In 1895 he edited *A book of Irish verse*. In his volumes *Poems* (1895) and *The wind among the reeds* (1899) he appears as a symbolist who sees the poet as a diviner of deeper truths. Three collections of poems appeared in 1897: *The secret rose, The tables of the law* and *The Adoration of the Magi*.

10.5. Yeats first met the love of his life, Maud Gonne, in 1889. For him she symbolised the spirit of tragic beauty and Irish nationalism. He proposed marriage to her in 1891 but was rejected. He was impressed by her revolutionary activities and she was the subject of many of his love poems. His long-sustained passion for her had enormous consequences for his politics and his poetry. When he later wrote of nationalist politics in his *Autobiographies* as 'the fixed ideas of some hysterical woman, a part of the mind turned into stone', he had her in mind. He became active in advanced nationalist politics after the Parnellite split (1890) and tried to mobilise nationalist literary groups as a basis for an Irish artistic revival. He joined the IRB and played a prominent part in organising the celebrations of the centenary of the 1798 Rising.

10.6. In 1894 he met Lady Augusta Gregory, a talented, generous and capable woman whose house and gardens at Coole Park, Co. Galway, offered a warm welcome to writers and artists. She encouraged him and helped him establish the Irish Literary Theatre. George Moore and Edward Martyn (who had introduced Yeats to Lady Gregory) joined Yeats as the directors of the Irish Literary Theatre Society. It had its first performance, Yeats' *The Countess Cathleen*, in 1899 and there was a great lot of controversy over it, including its condemnation by Cardinal Logue of Armagh. In 1902 Maud Gonne played the title role in *Cathleen Ni Houlihan,* a nationalist play co-authored by Yeats and Lady Gregory, and it was a dramatic triumph. He was still deeply in love with her, but she rejected him again and to his horror married Major John McBride in 1903.

10.7. Collaboration with Frank and William Fay led to the founding of the Irish National Theatre, Yeats and Lady Gregory being co-directors. After the turn of the century he abandoned active politics and devoted himself to writing. Annie Horniman, a wealthy Englishwoman from Manchester, bought the Mechanics' Institute in Abbey St, Dublin, for the Irish Theatre in 1904 and gave it a subsidy for some years. On the opening night, 27 December 1904, the Abbey Players presented a treble bill, *On Baile's Strand* and *Cathleen Ni Houlihan* and *Spreading the news* by Lady Gregory. It produced a new Yeats play nearly every year. In 1906, under a new constitution, Yeats, Lady Gregory and J.M. Synge were appointed directors. Yeats remained a director until his death. The founding of the Abbey, which was in his own words 'a small dingy and impecunious theatre', marked the launching of a dramatic movement that made Dublin an important literary capital in the first quarter of the century. Yeats took a firm stand against Catholic clerics and advanced nationalists who quarrelled over the political and moral role of the theatre.

10.8. Yeats was, above all, famous as a great poet. An American lecture tour (1903–4), organised by his American patron, John Quinn, helped establish his reputation. In 1913 he received a Civil List pension of £150 a year, but he refused a knighthood in 1915. A year later he proposed again to Maud Gonne, now a widow since the execution of her husband John MacBride, for his part in the Rising. She refused yet again.

10.9. His greatest achievement in poetry came with the publication of four volumes between 1919 and 1933. *The wild swans at Coole* (1919), *Michael Robartes and the Dancer* (1921), *The tower* (1928), and the *Winding stair* (1933). Several of his poems were written in honour of the executed leaders of the 1916 Rising, some of whom had been fellow-workers in the literary movement.

10.10. In 1917 Yeats married Georgie Hyde Lees (1892–1968); she was 26 and he was 52. Marriage changed his life and Georgie influenced his poetry. In *A vision* (1925), a piece full of symbolism, he set out his ideas on mankind and art, and this was the framework of later poems. Two children were born, Anne in 1919, and Michael in 1921. He bought Thoor Ballylee, a small derelict tower-house in Co. Galway (close to Lady Gregory's home) in 1917 and 82 Merrion Square, a fine Georgian house in Dublin, in 1922.

10.11. Together with other distinguished Irishmen, he was made a Senator of the Irish Free State by President Cosgrave and he played an active role in the Senate, especially on social and cultural policy. He chaired the committee on the design of the new Irish coinage. Later he made a remarkable contribution to the debate on divorce, including a noble defence of the Irish Protestant tradition with which he strongly identified:

We are one of the great stocks of Europe. We are the people of Burke; we are the people of Grattan; we are the people of Swift and Parnell. We have created the most of the modern literature of this county.

10.12. He received honorary degrees from the Queen's University of Belfast and University College Dublin. In 1923 he was awarded the Nobel Prize for Literature, and in 1932 he co-founded with George Bernard Shaw the Irish Academy of Letters, for the promotion of creative writing in Ireland.

10.13. In the mid-twenties, his health began to fail. From 1927 on, on medical advice he spent many winters in Italy and France. One of his last major literary undertakings was his editorship of the controversial *Oxford book of modern verse, 1892–1935* (1936). Despite age and ill-health, his output was remarkable, especially his powerful *New poems* (1938) and *Last poems* (1938–9). Late in the winter of 1938 he left Ireland for the Riviera in failing health. He died at Roquebrune, Cap Martin, in the south of France on 28 January 1939. His remains were brought back to Ireland in 1948 and re-interred in the churchyard of his great grandfather's parish at Drumcliff, Co. Sligo. His headstone bears his own cryptic epitaph:

> Cast a cold eye
> On life, on death.
> Horseman, pass by!

10.14. WRITINGS, BIOGRAPHY, AND STUDIES: *Collected poems of W.B. Yeats* (London, 1949). *Collected plays* (London, 1952). A. Norman Jeffares (ed.), *Yeats' poems* (Dublin, 1989) [many times reprinted]. John Kelly (ed.), *The collected letters of W.B. Yeats* (3 vols, Oxford, 1986–97) [in progress]. Autobiographies: *Reveries over childhood and youth* (1915), *The trembling of the veil* (1922), and *Dramatis personae* (1936). Joseph Hone, *W.B. Yeats, 1865–1939* (London, 1942). Richard Ellmann, *Yeats: the man and the masks* (London, 1948). Richard Ellmann, *The identity of Yeats* (London, 1954). Conor Cruise O'Brien, 'Passion and cunning: an essay on the politics of W.B. Yeats', in A. Norman Jeffares & K.W.G. Cross (eds), *Excited reverie: a centenary tribute to William Butler Yeats* (London, 1965). A. Norman Jeffares, *W.B. Yeats* (London, 1971). Denis Donoghue, *Yeats* (London, 1971). Frank Tuohy, *Yeats* (London, 1976). Elizabeth Cullingford, *Yeats, Ireland and fascism* (London, 1981). Grattan Freyer, *W.B. Yeats and the anti-democratic tradition* (Dublin, 1981). A. Norman Jeffares, *A new commentary on the poems of W.B. Yeats* (London, 1984). Mary Lou Kohfeldt, *Lady Gregory: the woman behind the Irish renaissance* (London, 1985). A. Norman Jeffares, *W.B. Yeats: a new biography* (London, 1988). Terence Brown, *The life of W.B. Yeats: a critical biography* (Oxford, 1999). R.F. Foster, *W.B. Yeats: a life* (2 vols, Oxford, 1997–2003). W.J. McCormack, *Blood kindred: W.B. Yeats: the life, the death, the politics* (London, 2005). Terence Brown, 'Yeats, William Butler', in James McGuire & James Quinn (eds), *Dictionary of Irish biography* (Cambridge, 2009), pp ix, 1087–93.

DONNCHADH Ó CORRÁIN

Index

References are to chapter and main section numbers except where specified (i.e. table and figure numbers).

1905 Russian Revolution, 11.3
1913 Lockout, 2.16, 8.1–15, 9.1–15, 10.8, 11.2
1916 Easter Rising, 1.14, 8.12, 10.1, 10.3–4, 11.1–2, 11.7–8, 11.10
Abbey Theatre, Dublin, 3.11, 9.7, 10.5, 11.10
Aberdeen, Ishbel Maria Gordon, Lady, 3.12, 8.15
Aberdeen, John Hamilton-Gordon, 1st Marquess, 9.5, 9.9, 11.5
The Adoration of the Magi (1897), 11.10
Agar-Robartes, T.C., 10.4, 11.1
agriculture, 1.8, 2.4, 2.7, 2.9
Ahmad, Muhammad ('The Mahdi'), 4.7
Alexandra College, Dublin, 1.12, 2.10, 11.9
Alexandra Dock, Belfast, 4.14, 5.18
Amateur Athletic Association of England (AAA), 7.2
America, United States of: 1.14, 2.4, 2.6, 4.8, 8.1, 8.5, 11.3, 11.7, 11.10
Anglican, *see* Church of Ireland
Anglo-Irish Treaty (1921), 11.1, 11.8
Antrim, county, 1.8, 1.11, 2.12, 3.2, 3.9, 4.12, 11.1
Armagh, county, 1.8, 5.10, 11.1
Arrears of Rent (Ireland) Act, 1882, 2.7
Arts & Crafts Society of Ireland (1894), 3.12
Asgard, the yacht, 1.14, 10.6
Ashbourne, Edward Gibson, 1st Baron, 2.7, 4.8
Askwith, Sir George, 8.8, 9.11–14
Askwith Commission of Inquiry (1913), 8.8, 9.10, 9.15
Asquith, Herbert Henry, 1.8, 1.12, 9.14, 10.4, 10.9, 11.1, 11.7
Australia, 2.4, 10.3, 11.7
Austro-Hungarian Empire, 1.13, 5.3
Avondale, Co. Wicklow, 6.6, 11.3, 11.6

Balfour, Arthur James, 1st Earl, 1.6, 2.7–8, 4.10, 4.15, 11.1
Ballot Act, 1872, 4.8, 10.2, 10.10
Battle of the Boyne (1690), 4.11

Bean na hÉireann, 10.3, 11.8
Belfast, city, 1.11, 2.1–2, 2.11–15, 3.7–8, 4.11–12, 4.14, 5.6, 5.17–18, 6.2, 7.14, 8.4–5, 9.12, 10.3, 10.7–8, 11.1, 11.5, 11.9
Belfast Ladies' Institute, 11.9
Belfast Newsletter, 4.10–11
Belfast Women's Temperance Association, 11.9
Bennett, E.M., 6.13, 7.13
Bennett, Louise [Louie], 1.12, 10.9
Beresford, Charles William de la Poer, 1st Baron, 7.1
Beresford Place, Dublin. 8.5, 9.5, 9.8
Biggar, Joseph Gillis, 1.4, 2.6, 5.10, 10.7, 11.6
Birmingham, England, 8.8, 8.13
Birrell, Augustine, 1.8, 10.4
Blackrock College, Co. Dublin, 7.1
Blennerhassett, Sir Roland Ponsonby, 4th Baronet, 1.2, 2.10
Boer War, Anglo– (1899–1902), 10.8, 11.3
Boycott, Charles Cunningham, 2.7, 4.11, 10.7
Boyne (1690), Battle of the, 4.11
Bright, John, 2.3, 5.9
British Trade Union Congress (TUC), 8.5, 8.7, 8.11, 11.5
British Women's Temperance Association, 11.9
SS Britannic, passenger liner, 2.12
Buckingham Palace conference (1914), 1.8, 10.4, 11.7
Builders' Labourers' Union (BLU), 8.11
Burke, Thomas Henry, 1.5, 11.6
Butler, Mary Lambert [Máire de Buitléir], 1.13
Butt Bridge, Dublin, 9.8
Butt, Isaac, 1.2–3, 1.5, 4.2, 4.6, 10.4, 10.6, 10.10, 11.3, 11.6
Byrne, John, 9.7, 9.18

Cadogan, Mary Sarah, Lady, 3.12
Cameron, Sir Charles A., 8.3, 9.3, 9.10
Cambridge University, 1.5, 9.1, 11.6
Canada, 4.8, 4.15, 5.3, 5.16, 10.4, 11.4
Carnarvon, Henry Howard Molyneux Herbert, 4th Earl, 4.8–9, 5.5

Carson, Edward Henry, 1.8–9, 1.13, 7.1, 8.10, 9.5, 9.9, 10.4, 10.9, 11.1, 11.7

Casement, Roger David, 1.14, 10.6

Cashel, Co. Tipperary, 7.4, 7.14

Cathleen Ni Houlihan (1902), 3.11, 11.10

Catholic Church, 1.3, 1.5, 1.7, 2.10, 3.2–4, 3.6, 4.12, 5.10, 5.14, 7.15–16

Catholic Emancipation (1829), *see* Catholic relief

Catholic relief, 1.1, 3.6

Catholic Truth Society (1899), 9.3

Cavendish, Frederick Charles, Lord, 1.5, 2.7, 4.10, 11.6

The Celtic Times, 6.6, 6.13, 7.12

The Celtic Twilight (1893), 11.10

Census of Ireland: 1861, 10.3; 1881, 10.3; 1901, 9.3; 1911, 8.2–3, 9.1, 9.3

Central Board scheme, 4.6, 4.9

Chamberlain, Joseph, 2.7, 4.6, 4.9–10, 4.11–13, 5.5–6, 5.10, 10.4, 10.7, 11.6

Chart, David Alfred, 8.2–3, 9.2

Chenevix, Helen, 1.12, 10.9

Childers, Robert Erskine, 1.14, 10.6

The children of Lir (1941), 11.4

Christian, J.A., 6.3, 7.9

Church League for Women's Suffrage, 10.9

Church of Ireland (Anglican), 2.10, 3.2–3, 3.6, 3.8, 10.10

Church Street, Dublin, 8.2, 9.2–3

Churchill, Lord Randolph, 4.9, 4.11, 5.10

Churchill, Winston Leonard Spencer, 10.4, 10.9

Citizen, see Dublin Monthly Magazine

Claidheamh Soluis (1899), 1.14, 3.10, 10.1, 11.4

Clan na Gael (1867), 1.14, 2.5–6, 10.6, 11.3, 11.6

Clare, county, 2.9, 5.10, 10.6

Clery's Department Store, Dublin, 8.6, 11.5

Clongowes Wood College, Co. Kildare, 7.1, 11.7

Cloyne, Co. Cork, 1.2, 7.4

Coláiste na Mumhan, Ballingeary, Co. Cork, 3.10

Collins, Michael, 10.1, 11.8

Coercion Acts, 1.4, 2.7, 4.5, 4.7, 4.10, 4.11–13, 4.15

The Communist Manifesto (1848), 10.8

Congested Districts Board, 2.7–8, 2.10

Connacht, province of, 1.4, 5.14

Connacht Telegraph, 2.5

Connolly, James, 8.2, 8.5, 8.7, 8.10–15, 9.6, 9.13, 9.17, 10.3, 10.6, 11.5, 11.8

Connradh na Gaeilge, *see* Gaelic League

Conservative & Unionist Women's Franchise Association, 10.9

Contagious Diseases Act, 1864, 10.3

Co-operative Movement, 2.9, 10.2, 10.4

Cork, city, 1.5, 2.8, 2.12, 5.1, 7.8, 7.14, 7.16, 8.5–6, 10.3, 10.8, 11.2, 11.6

Cork Examiner, 5.1, 6.2, 6.5, 7.3

Cosgrave, William Thomas, 1.13

The Countess Cathleen (1892), 3.11, 11.10

Cousins, Margaret, 10.9, 11.8

Craig, James, 1.9

Cranwell, Mia, 3.12

Croke, Thomas William (Archbishop of Cashel), 1.5, 1.7, 3.4, 6.2, 6.4–5, 6.10–11, 6.13–14, 7.3–4, 7.7–8, 7.13–15

Cromwell, Oliver, 2.7, 4.15, 11.1

Crooksling Sanatorium, Co. Wicklow, 2.13

Cullen, Paul (Archbishop of Armagh), 1.1, 5.7, 10.7

Cumann na mBan (1914), 1.12, 10.3, 10.9, 11.8

Cumann na nGaedheal (1900), 1.13, 10.5–6

Curtis, Lewis Perry, 4.15

Cusack, Michael, 6.1–3, 6.5–6, 6.10, 7.1–4, 7.7–9, 7.11, 10.5

Daily Citizen, 9.12

Daily Express, 6.5

Daily Herald, 8.11, 9.16,

Daily Telegraph, 6.2, 7.3

Dalkey, Co. Dublin, 7.11, 11.3

Dalmeny House, Edinburgh, Scotland, 4.9

Daly, James, 2.5–6

Dargan's Island, *see* Queen's Island

Dartry Hall, Dublin, 9.17

Davin, Maurice, 6.1–2, 6.5, 6.8–9, 6.11–14, 7.2–3, 7.13

Davis, Thomas Osborne, 1.10, 3.10, 6.8, 10.5

Davitt, Michael, 1.5, 2.5–8, 6.2, 6.5, 6.10–11, 6.13, 7.3, 7.8–11, 7.13, 10.2–3, 10.7–8, 11.4, 11.6, 11.10

de Valera, Éamon, 10.1, 11.8

Derry, *see* Londonderry

Devon Commission (1843–5), 5.13

Devoy, John, 1.14, 2.5–6, 10.6, 11.3

Dicey, Albert Venn, 5.8

Dillon, John, 1.8, 1.12, 2.6–7, 4.15, 5.10, 6.8, 7.17, 8.10, 10.9, 11.3, 11.7

Disraeli, Benjamin, 1.3, 4.15, 11.6

Distestablishment of Church of Ireland (1869), 1.1, 3.3, 3.6, 4.1, 4.12, 10.4

Dominican College, Sion Hill, Dublin, 2.10,

Dominican Convent, Eccles Street, Dublin, 11.8

Doneraile Agricultural Bank, 2.9

Down, county, 1.8, 1.11, 2.12, 3.2, 3.9, 4.12, 11.1

Drama in muslin (1886), 3.7

Dublin, city, 1.2–14, 2.4, 2.6–7, 2.9, 2.12–16, 3.11, 4.2–3, 4.8, 4.10–12, 4.14–15, 5.1, 5.5–6, 5.10, 6.1, 6.6, 6.11–12, 7.3, 7.8–9, 7.12, 7.14–15, 7.17, 8.1–15, 9.1–18, 10.3–4, 10.6, 10.8, 11.2, 11.5

Dublin Castle, 2.11, 4.12, 5.5, 6.2, 6.9, 10.6

Dublin Chamber of Commerce, 8.1, 8.6

Dublin Civic Exhibition (1914), 8.15

Dublin Employers' Federation, 2.16, 8.5–6, 8.11, 9.14, 9.16–17

Dublin Metropolitan Hurling Club, 6.1, 7.1, 7.2

Dublin Metropolitan Police (DMP), 4.12, 8.3, 8.8, 9.8, 10.8

Dublin Metropolitan School of Art, 11.10

Dublin Royal Hibernian Academy, 11.10

Dublin Socialist Party, 10.8

Dublin United Arts Club, 3.11

Dublin United Tramways Company, 2.16, 8.6–7, 9.7, 9.12, 9.15, 11.5

Dublin University Magazine, 11.9

Dublin University Review, 11.4, 11.10

Dublin Women's Suffrage Association (1876), 1.12, 10.3, 10.9

Dudley, Georgiana Elizabeth Moncreiffe, Lady, 3.12

Dun Emer Guild, 3.12

Dún Laoghaire, Co. Dublin, 8.7, 9.12, 9.16–17

Dungannon Clubs, 1.13, 10.6

Dungarvan, Co. Waterford, 4.4, 6.5

École des Hautes Études, Paris, 3.10

Eden Quay, Dublin, 8.5, 8.7, 9.8

education, 2.10, 4.8

Educational Endowments (Ireland) Act, 1885, 4.8

Edinburgh, Scotland, 2.12, 4.12, 5.14, 8.5, 10.8, 11.2, 11.9

Edinburgh Evening News, 11.2

Edward VII, King of the United Kingdom of Great Britain & Ireland, & Emperor of India, 1.13

Ellis, Sir Thomas Ratcliffe, 8.8

Emmet, Robert, 7.16

England's case against Home Rule (1886), 5.8

Ennis, Co. Clare, 2.7, 6.13

Erin's Hope, ship, 10.6, 11.2

Erasmus Smith High School, Dublin, 11.10

Fairy and folk tales of the Irish peasantry (1888), 11.4, 11.10

famine, 1.1, 2.4; the Great Famine, 2.1, 2.3, 6.1, 11.3

Fenians, *see* Irish Republican Brotherhood (IRB)

Ferguson, Samuel, 1.2

Feuchtwanger, Edgar J., 4.10

Figgis, Edward Darrell, 1.14, 10.6

First World War (1914–18), 1.8–9, 1.12, 2.9, 2.16, 3.2, 4.15, 8.14–15, 10.4, 10.6, 10.10, 11.5, 11.8

Fitzgerald, Lord Edward, 7.16

Fitzgerald, P.N., 6.11–13

Forster, William Edward, 2.7, 5.5

Fourier, Charles, 10.8

Freeman's Journal, 1.4, 5.3, 5.10, 6.1, 6.5, 6.8, 6.11, 6.13, 7.2–4, 7.7, 7.9–10, 7.15, 9.8

Frenchpark, Co. Roscommon, 11.4

From a Hermitage (1915), 8.13

Gaelic Athletic Association (1884), 1.5, 1.10, 3.10, 7.1–17, 10.1, 10.5–6

Gaelic Journal (*Irisleabhar na Gaedhilge*), 10.1, 11.4

Gaelic League (1893), 1.10, 1.12, 1.14, 3.10, 7.4, 8.13, 10.1, 10.5–7, 10.10, 11.4

Gaelic Union, 10.1, 10.5

Gaiety Theatre, Dublin, 3.7

Galway, county: 1.2, 1.11, 2.8, 5.10, 6.14, 7.17, 8.5, 10.3, 11.1, 11.6, 11.10

Geddes, Wilhelmina, 3.12

General Post Office (GPO), Dublin, 8.13, 9.8, 11.2, 11.8

George V, King of the United Kingdom of Great Britain & Ireland, & Emperor of India, 1.8, 1.9, 9.5, 10.4, 10.9, 11.7

George, David Lloyd, 1.8, 10.9, 11.1, 11.7

Gladstone, Herbert John, 4.10, 5.2

Gladstone, William Ewart, 1.2–3, 1.5, 1.8, 2.7, 3.3, 3.6, 4.1, 4.6–15, 5.1–18, 10.4, 10.10, 11.6

Glasnevin Cemetery, Dublin, 6.14, 7.17, 9.18, 11.5–6, 11.8

Gonne [MacBride], Maud, 1.12, 1.13, 10.3, 10.6, 11.4, 11.8, 11.10

Gordon, Charles George, 4.7

Goschen, George Joachim, 4.12, 5.14

Government of Ireland Act (1920), 10.4

Grammatica Celtica (1853), 3.10

'Grattan's parliament', 1.13, 4.4, 4.12, 4.15, 5.1, 5.14

Gray, Edmund Dwyer, 5.10, 6.5

Green, Alicia Sophia Amelia Stopford, 1.14, 10.6

Gregory, Lady Augusta, 1.11, 2.7, 3.11, 10.5, 10.10, 11.4, 11.10

Griffith, Arthur, 1.13, 8.3, 8.10, 8.15, 10.1, 10.5–6

Guild of Irish Art Workers (1910), 3.12

Guinness, Edward Cecil, 1st Earl of Iveagh, 10.6

Guinness' Brewery, 2.11, 2.12, 2.15

Gwynn, Stephen, 8.10, 10.9, 11.10

Habeas corpus, 4.5

Hall, Anna Maria, 7.1

Hall, Samuel Carter, 7.1

Harcourt Street, Dublin, 8.3, 11.1

Harland & Wolff shipyard, 2.11, 4.11, 5.18

Harrington, Timothy Charles, 2.7, 6.9, 7.3

Harris, Matthew, 2.6, 5.10

Hartington, Spencer Compton Cavendish, Marquess, 4.10, 4.12, 5.2, 10.4

Haslam, Anna Maria, 1.12, 10.3, 10.9

Haslam, Thomas Joseph, 1.12, 10.3, 10.9

Hatherley, William Page Wood, 1st Baron, 5.4

Hawarden Castle, Flintshire, Wales, 4.10

'Hawarden kite', 4.10, 5.2

Hayden, Mary Teresa, 1.12, 10.9

Hayes' Hotel, Thurles, Co. Tipperary, 6.2, 6.5, 6.12, 7.3, 7.8

Healy, Timothy Michael, 1.8, 4.4, 4.12, 5.10, 6.2, 7.17, 8.8, 11.7

Heatherside Sanatorium, Co. Cork, 2.13

Hennessy, William Maunsell, 3.10

Hobson, John Bulmer, 1.13, 1.14, 10.6

Hoctor, P.T., 6.6, 6.11–12, 7.13

Holloway Gaol, London, 11.8

Hollywood, Co. Down, 11.9

Home Government Association, 1.2, 4.2

Home Rule, 1886: 1.1–8, 2.12, 3.6, 4.1–1, 5.1–18, 7.3, 10.2, 10.4–5, 10.8, 11.3, 11.6; 11.9; 1893: 1.8, 10.4, 11.9; 1912: 1.9, 1.12–14, 9.5, 9.9, 10.4, 10.6, 10.9–10, 11.1, 11.7–9

Home Rule Confederation of Great Britain, 1.5, 4.2, 11.6

Home Rule League, 1.2, 4.2, 10.4

Home Rule Party, *see* Irish Parliamentary Party

Hone, Eva Sydney [Evie], 3.12

Horniman, Annie Fredericka, 10.5

housing conditions, 2.14, 8.1–3, 9.1–3, 9.14

Housing of the Working Class (Ireland) Act, 1908, 2.14, 9.3

Howth Harbour, Co. Dublin, 1.14, 10.6

Hugh Lane Gallery, Dublin, 3.11

Hyde, Douglas, 3.10, 10.1, 10.5, 10.7, 10.10, 11.4, 11.10

Illustrated Sporting & Dramatic News, 7.1

Imperial Hotel, Dublin, 8.6–7, 9.6, 9.8, 9.17, 11.6

India, 3.5, 4.10–11, 5.16

Industrial Schools (Ireland) Act, 1868, 2.10

Inghinidhe na hÉireann (1900), 1.12–13, 10.3

In the shadow of the glen, 1.11

Intermediate Education (Ireland) Act, 1878, 1.12, 2.10, 11.9

Intermediate Education Inquiry Commission (1898–9), 11.4

Industrial Workers of the World (IWW), 10.8, 11.2

International Working Men's Association, 10.8

Intoxicating Liquors (Ireland) Act, 1902, 3.7

Irish Agricultural Organisation Society (1894), 2.9

Irish Agricultural Wholesale Society (1897), 2.9

Irish Amateur Athletics Association (IAAA), 6.3–6, 7.7, 7.11

Irish Catholic Women's Suffrage Association 10.9

Irish Citizen, 10.9, 11.8

Irish Citizen Army, 1.12, 8.12, 10.3, 11.2, 11.8

Irish Council Bill (1907), 1.8, 10.4

Irish Education Act, 1892, 2.10
Irish Folklore Commission, 11.4
Irish Freedom (1910), 1.13
Irish Homestead (1895), 2.9, 9.11
Irish Independent, 8.6–7, 9.17, 11.2, 11.5
'Irish Ireland', 3.10–11, 10.3, 10.5
Irish Labour Party, 10.8, 11.5
Irish language, 1.12, 3.10, 3.11, 6.2, 10.1
Irish Literary Society (1891), 3.11, 10.5, 11.4, 11.10
Irish Literary Theatre (1898), 3.11, 11.10
Irish Loyal & Patriotic Union (1885), 4.10, 5.6–7, 5.14
Irish National Land League, 1.5, 1.12, 2.6–7, 4.2, 4.4, 4.8, 4.10–11, 5.5, 6.2, 6.13, 7.4, 7.8, 10.3, 10.5–7, 11.3–4, 11.6–8.
Irish National Theatre Society (1903), 3.11, 10.5
Irish Parliamentary Party, 1.6–7, 3.4, 4.2, 4.4, 5.3, 5.10, 6.2, 6.8–9, 6.11, 6.13–14, 7.3, 7.6, 7.13, 7.17, 8.10, 10.3–5, 10.7, 11.6–7
Irish Republican Army (IRA), 10.5, 10.6
Irish Republican Brotherhood (IRB), 1.1, 1.2, 1.4–5, 1.11, 1.13–14, 3.3, 4.1–2, 5.7–8, 5.18, 6.2, 6.6, 6.8–9, 6.11–12, 6.14, 7.13, 7.16–17, 8.12, 10.1, 10.5–7, 11.2–4, 11.6, 11.10
Irish Republican & Socialist Party (IRSP), 10.8, 11.2
Irish Socialist Federation (1905), 11.2
Irish Sportsman, 6.1, 6.3, 6.4, 7.2, 7.3
Irishtown, Co. Mayo, 2.5
Irish Times, 1.2, 8.2, 8.11, 9.10–12
Irish Trade Union Congress, 10.8, 11.5
Irish Transport & General Workers' Union (ITGWU), 1.12, 2.16, 8.5–8, 8.10–12, 8.15, 9.5–7, 9.9, 9.12–17, 10.8, 11.2, 11.4, 11.8
Irish Unionist Alliance (1891), 5.6
Irish Universities Act, 1908, 1.8, 2.10, 11.1
Irish Volunteer Force (1913), 1.12–14, 10.4, 10.6–7, 11.4, 11.7, 11.8
Irish Women's Franchise League (1908), 1.12, 10.9, 11.8
Irish Women's Suffrage Federation (1911), 10.9
Irish Women's Suffrage & Local Government Association (1901), 1.12, 10.3, 10.9
Irish Women's Suffrage Society, 10.9
Irish Women's Temperance Union, 11.9
Irish Women Workers' Union, 8.5, 11.8
Irish Worker & People's Advocate, 8.3, 8.5, 9.4, 9.6, 9.13, 9.17, 11.2, 11.5

Jacob's biscuit factory, 2.12, 8.5, 8.11, 9.16
Jellicoe, Anne William, 1.12, 10.3
Joyce, James Augustine Aloysius, 1.7, 11.6

Kavanagh, Patrick, 8.14
Keane, Dr William (bishop of Cloyne), 1.2
Kerry, county, 1.2, 2.8, 5.14, 7.1
Kettle, Thomas, 8.7–8, 11.8
Kickham, Charles Joseph, 6.6, 10.6
Kildare, county, 5.6, 11.2
Kilkenny, county, 1.7, 7.1
Kilmainham Gaol, Dublin, 1.5, 2.7, 11.2, 11.6
Kilmainham Treaty (1882), 11.3, 11.6
King's Inns, Dublin, 11.1
Kingsbridge [now Heuston] Railway Station, Dublin, 6.4
Kingstown *see* Dún Laoghaire
Kipling, (Joseph) Rudyard, 10.6
Kurtz, Lucy Cometina, 11.4

Labour World, 11.3, 11.6
Labourers' (Ireland) Act, 1883, 2.7
Ladies' Collegiate School, Belfast, 11.7
Ladies' Land League (1880), 1.12, 2.7, 10.3, 11.3, 11.6
Ladies' National Association, 11.9
The lake (1905), 3.7
Lalor, James Fintan, 11.3
Lambert, Isabella, 11.1
land acts, *see* land tenure
Land League, *see* Irish National Land League
land tenure: Landlord & Tenant (Ireland) Act 1870, 2.3, 4.1, 10.10; Land Law (Ireland) Act, 1881, 1.5, 2.7, 4.12, 10.10, 11.3, 11.6; Purchase of Land (Ireland) Act ('Ashbourne Act'), 1885, 2.7, 4.8; Land Law (Ireland) Act, 1887, 2.7; Purchase of Land (Ireland) Act ('Balfour Act'), 1891, 2.7, 2.8; Irish Land Act ('Wyndham Act'), 1903, 1.8, 11.3, 11.7; Irish Land Act ('Birrell Act'), 1909, 1.8
Land War, 1.5, 2.5, 10.3, 10.7, 11.3, 11.6–7
Laois, county, 1.12, 10.3
Larkin, Delia, 1.12, 9.12
Larkin, James, 2.16, 8.3–15, 9.5–6, 9.8–10, 9.12, 9.14, 9.16–17
Larne, Co. Antrim, 4.11, 10.6, 11.1
Law, Andrew Bonar, 1.14, 11.8
Leeds Mercury, 4.10, 5.2

Leinster, provincee of: 4.10, 5.14
Leitrim, county, 1.8, 1.13, 2.8
Leo XIII (Count Vincenzo Gioacchino
  Raffaele Luigi Pecci), Pope, 9.3
Liberal Women's Unionist Association, 11.9
Liberty Hall, Dublin, 8.5, 8.8, 9.7, 9.12–13, 11.8
Limerick, county, 7.14, 10.6
List, Georg Friedrich, 1.13
Liverpool, England, 8.1, 8.8, 10.6, 11.4, 11.5
Local Government (Ireland) Act, 1898, 1.12,
  10.2, 10.9–10
Logue, Michael (Archbishop of Armagh), 7.15
Londonderry, county, 1.8, 2.12, 5.18, 11.1, 11.5
Londonderry, Edith Vane-Tempest-Stewart,
  Lady, 3.12
Longford, William Pakenham, 4th Earl, 5.6
Louis XIV, King of France & Navarre, 5.16
Lynch, Sister Concepta, 3.12

McBride, Major John, 11.10
McCabe, Edward Cardinal (Archbishop of
  Dublin), 1.12
McCarthy, Justin, 1.7, 7.3, 11.6
MacDiarmada, Seán [John MacDermott],
  1.13, 10.6
MacDonagh, Thomas Stanislaus, 1.14, 10.1,
  10.6, 11.2
MacHale, John (Archbishop of Tuam), 1.4, 2.5
McKay, John, 6.2, 7.3
MacNeill, Eoin [John], 1.14, 3.10, 10.1, 10.5–6,
  11.4, 11.7
Magdalen asylums, 8.3
Mahaffy, John Pentland, 10.1, 11.4
The man from Aranmore (1905), 3.12
Manchester, England, 1.5, 8.4, 8.7–9, 10.5, 10.6
Manchester Guardian, 9.9
'Manchester Martyrs', 1.5, 7.16, 10.6, 11.6
Mandle, W.F., 6.6, 6.13
Manning, Henry Edward, Cardinal
  (Archbishop of Westminster), 4.6
Mansion House Committee (1881), 2.4
Markievicz, Constance Georgine, Countess,
  1.13, 11.8
Married Women's Property Committee, 11.9
Martyn, Edward, 3.11, 11.10
Marx, Karl, 10.8, 11.2
Maynooth College, Co. Kildare, 3.4, 3.6, 10.1
Mayo, county, 1.11, 2.5, 2.6, 2.8, 10.7, 11.3

Mechanics' Institute, Dublin, 10.5, 11.3,
  11.10
Medical Poor Relief (Ireland) Act, 1851, 2.13
Meath, county, 1.4, 4.8, 11.3, 11.6
Methodism, 3.2, 3.6
Methodist College, Belfast, 2.10
Meyer, Kuno, 3.10
Michael Robartes & the Dancer (1921), 11.10
Midleton, William St John Fremantle
  Brodrick, 1st Earl, 1.9
Midlothian, Scotland, 4.9, 5.17
Monaghan, county, 3.2, 4.2, 5.18, 11.9
Moody, Dwight Lyman, 3.6
Moore, George Augustus, 3.7, 11.10
Moran, David P., 10.5
Morley, John, Viscount, 4.10, 5.2
Mountjoy Jail, Dublin, 8.8
Munster, province of, 1.4, 4.10, 5.14
Munster Women's Franchise League, 10.9
Murphy, William Martin, 2.16, 8.5–7, 8.10–11,
  8.14–15, 9.5–6, 9.9–10, 9.14, 9.16, 10.8, 11.2,
  11.5
music, popular, 3.13

National Association for the Promotion of
  Social Science, 11.9
National Council (1903), 1.13
National Labour League, 10.8
National Literary Society (1892), 3.11, 10.1,
  11.4, 11.10
National Teachers' Residences (Ireland) Act,
  1875, 2.10
National Union of Dock Labourers (NUDL),
  8.5, 11.5
National Union of Railwaymen (NUR), 8.7, 8.11
National University of Ireland (1908), 1.8, 1.12,
  2.10, 3.7, 3.10, 10.3, 11.1, 11.4, 11.7
Ne Temere decree (1907), 3.3, 10.10
Nenagh, Co. Tipperary, 6.12
New Ross, Co. Wexford, 11.7
New York, 1.12, 8.15, 11.5
Newry, Co. Down, 11.5, 11.8
New Zealand, 2.4, 10.3
Nolan, James, 8.7–8, 9.7–8, 9.18
'No rent manifesto' (1882), 2.7, 11.6
Northern Ireland Society for Women's
  Suffrage (1871), 10.3, 10.9, 11.9
Northern Whig, 11.9

O'Brien, Conor Cruise, 6.14
O'Brien, Francis Cruise, 11.8
O'Brien, William, 1.2, 1.8, 2.7–8, 4.15, 5.10, 6.2, 6.13, 7.3, 7.8, 7.13, 7.17, 8.12, 11.2–3, 11.5, 11.7
O'Casey, Seán, 10.8
O'Connell, Daniel, 1.1, 10.2, 10.7
O'Connell Street, Dublin, 8.3, 8.8, 8.13, 9.5–6, 9.8, 11.5
O'Connor, Thomas Power, 5.5, 5.10
O'Curry, Eugene, 3.10
O'Donnell, Frank Hugh, 2.8, 2.10
O'Donovan, John, 3.10
O'Donovan Rossa, Jeremiah, 10.6, 11.3
O'Grady, Standish Hayes, 3.10
O'Growney, Revd Eugene, 3.10, 10.1
O'Kelly, Seán Thomas [Seán Tomás Ó Ceallaigh], 1.13
O'Leary, John, 6.6, 6.8, 6.10, 6.13, 10.6, 11.4, 11.10
O'Mahony, John, 10.5
O'Shea, Katharine (*other married name* Parnell), 1.7, 2.7, 3.4, 5.4, 5.10, 7.17, 11.6
O'Shea, William Henry, 1.7, 2.7, 5.10, 11.6
obstructionism, 1.4, 10.7
Orange Order, 2.7, 3.8–9, 4.11, 5.18, 10.4
Our Lady of Mercy College, Blackrock, Co. Dublin, 2.10

Pall Mall Gazette, 4.12
Paris, France, 3.10, 5.7, 7.4
Parliament Act, 1911, 1.8, 1.13, 10.4
Parnell, Anna Mercer, 1.12, 2.7
Parnell, Charles Stewart, 1.4–5, 1.7–8, 1.12, 2.4–7, 3.4, 4.2–3, 4.8–15, 5.1–18, 6.2, 6.6, 6.8, 6.10–11, 6.14, 7.3, 7.6, 7.8–9, 7.16–17, 10.2, 10.4, 10.6–8, 10.10, 11.3, 11.5, 11.7
Parnell Commission (1889), 11.3
Parnell, Fanny Isabel, 1.12
Parnell, John Henry, 11.6
Parnell, Katharine, *see* O'Shea, Katharine
Partridge, William P., 8.5, 8.7
Pearse, Patrick Henry, 1.14, 8.13, 9.11, 10.1, 10.6–7, 11.2, 11.4
Pedersen, Holger, 3.10, 11.4
Peel, Sir Robert, 4.9
Perpetual Crimes Act (or Coercion Act), 1887, 2.7

Petrie, George, 3.10
Philosophy of Irish Ireland (1905), 10.5
Phoenix Park, Dublin, 1.5, 1.7, 2.7, 4.10, 7.11, 11.3, 11.6
Pirrie, William James, 4.11
Pius IX (Giovanni Maria Mastai-Ferretti) Pope, 10.7
Pius X (Giuseppe Melchiorre Sarto) Pope, 9.12
Plan of Campaign, 2.7, 3.4, 6.9, 6.13, 11.1, 11.7
The playboy of the western world (1907), 1.11, 3.11
Plunkett, Horace Curzon, Sir, 1.8, 2.7, 2.9, 10.2, 10.5
Poland, 2.2, 4.12, 5.5
Power, Jane [Jennie] Wyse, 1.12
Power, John Wyse, 6.2, 6.9, 6.13, 7.3
Presbyterian Church, 3.2–3, 3.5, 3.6, 3.9
Prevention of Crime (Ireland) Act, 1882, 4.5
Prisoners (Temporary Discharge for Ill Health) Act 1913 – also known as the 'Cat and mouse Act', 10.9
Protection of Person & Property Act (1881), 2.7, 4.5
Public Libraries (Ireland) Act, 1894, 3.7
Purser, Sarah H., 3.11, 3.12

Quakers, *see* Religious Society of Friends
Queen's Colleges (Belfast, Cork & Galway), 1.5, 2.9, 6.6
Queen's Institute, Belfast, 11.9
Queen's Island, Belfast, 4.14, 5.19
Queen's University of Belfast, 1.12, 2.10, 3.7

railways, 2.1, 2.14
Ralahine Agricultural & Manufacturing Co-operative Association, 2.9
Rathmines School of Commerce, Dublin, 11.8
reading, popular, 3.13
rebellion, Fenian (1867), 10.5–6
rebellion of United Irishmen (1798), 1.11, 10.6, 11.10
Recess Committee (1895–6), 1.8, 11.7
Redistribution of Seats Act, 1885, 4.3, 10.2
Redmond, John Edward, 1.8, 1.12–14, 8.8, 10.2, 10.4, 10.6, 10.9, 11.7
Redmond, William Archer, 1.8, 11.7
Reeves, William (Bishop of Down, Connor & Dromore), 3.10, 10.10